VIKING

MASALAMANDI

Sadaf Hussain is an author, chef, food writer, two-time TedX speaker and co-host of an award-winning food podcast, *Naan Curry*. One of the finalists on *MasterChef India* in 2016, Sadaf consults restaurants and assists them in developing new menus and establishing themselves in the market. He was also a researcher and contributor to *Forgotten Food of Rampur,* a project commissioned by the University of Sheffield in 2023. Sadaf writes for online and offline journals, exploring not only food but also the stories behind it. Fascinated with food lore, he is a chronicler of the customs, traditions and rituals surrounding food.

For him, food is just a conversation starter, and definitely not the end in itself.

Sadaf Hussain

ADVANCE PRAISE FOR THE BOOK

'The magic of Indian cuisine lies in the way we use spices. Few people understand the secrets of spicing as well as Sadaf, with his encyclopaedic knowledge of our food and its history'—**Vir Sanghvi, veteran journalist and food writer**

'Spices and spice mixes have been the cornerstone of Indian cuisine, rooted in our traditions, folklore and home kitchens. The uniqueness of every household's cooking lies in its distinct use and blend of spices. Add to this the magic, the art and science of spice blending, and you have a truly intoxicating and heady mix.

'As a chef, I am thrilled for Sadaf's book, which delves deeply into the understanding of spices, spice blends and their application. I often say that if anything shaped the map of the world, it was spices. Sadaf, through this book, is redefining the culinary map of India, viewing it once again through the lens of its spices.

'This is an excellent book that explores spice blends through the lenses of culture, history, art and a touch of science, and keeps the romance of food alive'—**Ranveer Brar, celebrity chef,** *Masterchef India* **judge and author**

'With *Masalamandi*, Sadaf Hussain invites us to savour the rich Indian cuisine. Every masala used in the dishes, with its multiple versions, tells a story and ignites our palate to embark on an unforgettable culinary journey!'—**Rana Safvi, writer, scholar and translator**

'The Indian culinary universe is built on sophisticated pairing of multiple spice flavour molecules, and every part of India has worked out combinations that define their regional cuisine. I cannot think of anyone more qualified than Sadaf to explore this delicious diversity. *Masalamandi* takes the reader on a remarkable journey, one where the reader discovers how the exact same set of main ingredients can taste so remarkably different just by combining slightly different spices'—**Krish Ashok, author of** *Masala Lab: The Science of Indian Cooking*

'Sadaf's tryst with spices began when he was very young. Very early in life, he figured out that spices, when blended into our cooking, carry unique aromas and flavours, and even cultural histories, that can add layers of complexity to food. And in a country as vast as ours, these spice blends are not only about flavour but are deeply intertwined with India's cultural heritage. And who better than a passionate pupil, nay, scholar of cuisines and spices, than Sadaf Hussain to take you through our country's culinary history, diversity and traditions?'—**Kunal Vijayakar, food writer, author, actor and television personality**

'Sadaf Hussain spins a yummy food romance and layers it with the aromas of spices; blending culinary history, social anecdotes and delicious recipes with age-old *nuskhas* [remedies]. His documentation is not merely a record but a journey to understand and taste how a bunch of the same whole spices in varying ratios can give birth to delectably different recipes. In restaurants or home kitchens, wherever cooks are searching for a signature spice of a particular city or region, this book will become their go-to guide—a treasure trove of gourmet discounts for those craving regionality. I am a fan and cannot wait to put this exciting cookbook to work in my kitchens'—**Suvir Saran, celebrity chef, cookbook author and educator**

'Sadaf's story of Indian spices is equal parts sweet and spicy. His extensive travel experiences through the length and breadth of the country come alive as he takes us on this journey with him'—**Sonal Ved, journalist and author of** *Whose Samosa Is It Anyway?: The Story of Where 'Indian' Food Really Came From*

'As they say, spice is life! Adding a sprinkle of masala to your daily life will perk you up and make it a whole lot flavourful—and that's exactly what Sadaf aims to do with this book'—**Anahita N. Dhondy, chef, author and TV presenter**

MASALA MANDI

A GUIDE TO THE WORLD OF
INDIAN SPICE BLENDS

Sadaf Hussain

PENGUIN

VIKING

An imprint of Penguin Random House

VIKING

Viking is an imprint of the Penguin Random House group of companies
whose addresses can be found at global.penguinrandomhouse.com

Published by Penguin Random House India Pvt. Ltd
4th Floor, Capital Tower 1, MG Road,
Gurugram 122 002, Haryana, India

Penguin
Random House
India

First published in Viking by Penguin Random House India 2024

ISBN 9780143466550

Typeset in Bembo Std by Manipal Technologies Limited, Manipal
Printed at Replika Press Pvt. Ltd, India

www.penguin.co.in

This is a legitimate digitally printed version of the book and therefore might not
have certain extra finishing on the cover.

To Anjum, Bilqis and the family sil batta

Nazir' yaar ki hum ne jo kal ziyafat ki
Pakaya qarz manga kar pulav aur quliya

I arranged a banquet for my beloved, Nazir
And took a loan to cook a pulao and quliya

—Nazir Akbarabadi

CONTENTS

FOREWORD

THE STORY OF SPICES IS ENTWINED WITH THE HISTORY OF India. The subcontinent became famous in the millennia before the birth of Christ as the land of exotic and aromatic spices. It became the entrepôt where traders from ancient Rome, Arabia and China rubbed shoulders in bustling marts. The maritime spice route played a crucial role in the rise and fall of empires beyond Indian shores. Not surprisingly, spices became the stuff of legend and lore. These memories are stirred as one turns the pages of *Masalamandi*.

If one examines Indian cuisines in the mirror of Indian music, individual spices appear like musical notes and spice blends like ragas or melodies that create magic in harmony with the changing cycle of the season. However, there is more to spice mixtures than aesthetic pleasure. Their therapeutic dimension is no less significant. Ayurveda as well as Unani Tibb have built an impressive edifice on the time-tested knowledge about the medicinal properties of spices and spice blends. One more aspect of spice mixtures/blends is that some are based on regional variations—garam masala, sambar masala and achar masala used in different parts of India testify to this. These define the unique identity of local food and are inseparable from the popular imagination with the 'personality' of a people.

Sadaf Hussain has taken a deep dive into the fathomless sea and come up with more than a handful of shining pearls. He wears many hats—celebrity chef, columnist, meticulous researcher and author of books for children and adults. Unlike many of his peers, he doesn't shy away from painstaking research in libraries or fieldwork across the length and breadth of our vast and varied land. Ever since I met him half a decade ago, my appreciation for his work has only grown. Bubbling with infectious enthusiasm, he generates an impressive momentum for all his forays.

The superb collection of spice blends that Sadaf has curated here, one hopes, will wean us all—those addicted to pre-processed, packaged spice blends loaded with fillers, artificial flavours and fragrances, preservatives, etc.—away. Nothing can please the palate more than freshly ground or pounded 'prepared for the occasion' spices. I can do no better than to wish more power to Sadaf's mortar–pestle and pen.

New Delhi   Pushpesh Pant
November 2024   Indian food critic and historian

INTRODUCTION

WHY I AM TALKING ABOUT SPICES

S PICES HAVE ALWAYS ADDED MAGIC TO A RECIPE. I CALL THEM the 'rooh' (soul) of a dish.

Each spice box houses a world of stories. You could consider them a part of one's generational wealth; they speak of the origin of countless traditional family recipes—from family favourites to family secrets. After all, it is the spice box that I use that makes my biryani different from yours or your dum aloo different from mine.

However, for me, spices have always been about more than just seasoning. Their story is as much about the sociology of food as it is about flavour. India is now known for a cuisine that uses a range of spices but the story of how they all ended up in one basket is very distinct. In many cases, these spices are used not just to carry the flavour, but also for their medicinal properties. They are an expression of philosophy and science—backed by the weather, environment, economics, and philosophical interplay, reflecting the very essence of human interaction. Consider the chilli pepper, which started its journey from the Americas and revolutionized cuisines from India to Indonesia. Or black pepper, often referred to as 'black gold', which was once traded as currency. These spices did not just add flavour but were pivotal in the creation of a global economic network that reshaped the world.

My interest in spices grew when I noticed my mother and my aunts making a simple spice blend at home—just a simple paste of onion, ginger, garlic, black pepper, turmeric and other spices. Much before families started using readymade spice blends, I recall us making the paste that would last for two or three days on a *sil batta*.* Before we romanticize this, let me clarify—we used sil batta simply because there was no electricity or the luxury of owning a futuristic inverter fridge or mixer grinder. Hence, the paste was either to be made fresh every day or for 2–3 days at a time. The process of grinding the paste was always fascinating to me. I would sit next to the ladies who were making the paste and watch this entire soap opera unfold in front of me, all the while asking questions to salvage my curiosity.

My parents tell me that they always knew I would go on to do something in the world of food because I loved eating and cooking. Interestingly, they also rightly predicted that I would one day write a book on spices and give them the respect they deserve. And here we are.

Unboxing Spice Blends

Technological advancements have made our lives easy and simple, and ensured we can get boxed spices and spice blends that can be stored for long. During a conversation, Salma Husain, food historian and author, told me that when she was a kid, she had never seen a box packed with spices in her Mumbai house. There would always be huge boxes of whole spices, which a specialist would then use to create a spice blend for the specific dish being cooked on that particular day. Someone from her family would pick out the different kinds of whole spices, lay them on the plate and hand them over to the lady who would then make either a paste or a powder using a sil batta or *imam/hamam dasta*.†

---

* Grindstone.
† Mortar and pestle.

Back when I was a child, one afternoon, I also tried creating a similar spice blend of my own. When my mom was busy cooking in the kitchen, I decided it was the perfect time to play 'master chef'. My mission? To create the ultimate spice blend that would put all other spice blends to shame.

I tiptoed into the kitchen, eyes glinting with mischief, and reached for the spice rack. There it was—a lineup of jars filled with mysterious powders and seeds. I grabbed a handful of everything—cumin seeds, turmeric, chilli powder, cinnamon, even cloves, nutmeg and so on. With a triumphant grin, I dumped them all into a bowl, gave it a good stir and blended them into a smooth powder in my white mixer grinder (which made enough noise to tell everyone in the neighbourhood that I was up to something).

Feeling like a true culinary genius, I decided to take a whiff of my masterpiece. *Big mistake.* The moment my nose got near the bowl, a cloud of spice dust exploded in my face. I gasped, inhaling a lungful of chilli powder and turmeric. My eyes watered, my nose burned and I sneezed so hard I nearly toppled over.

My mom rushed in, alarmed by the sound of my sneezes echoing through the house, which was louder than the sound of the mixer grinder. She found me in the kitchen, eyes red and streaming, face covered in yellow and red dust, looking like I had just fought a battle with the curry monster—and lost. She couldn't help but laugh at the sight, which only made me sneeze more.

From that day on, my mom made sure to keep me away from the spice rack. But I learned a valuable lesson—culinary mastery takes more than just mixing everything. And always, always approach spice blends with caution—or risk turning into a sneezing, spice-covered mess. Sometimes, if you add too much of one ingredient, it can turn into a disaster, from chilli to salt, nutmeg, fenugreek seeds or mustard. The beauty of our spice blends is that, in most dishes in Indian cuisine, a single whole spice is never the star—it is the combination that shines. This combination could be based on flavour, aroma, texture, medicinal properties, availability, season, and many other factors.

In my kitchen today, spices are sacred ingredients that link me to the rhythms of the seasons and the flavours of my heritage. They are both a bridge to the past and a gateway to new culinary adventures. Whether it was while researching this book or creating menus or when I experiment with foods from the past, I'm always transported to another time. I wonder why we don't use food or the food alleys (especially the older towns) around the world as living museums.

Spice Up My Plate

Let's focus on the magic that happens on the plate for a minute. In culinary terms, the transformative power of spices is unparalleled. They elevate the mundane to the sublime, turning simple meals into celebrations.

Each spice houses a unique profile of phytochemicals, essential oils and aromatic compounds that, when understood and harnessed, can elevate cooking from routine to art. Embarking on the journey of spices therefore is not merely about rediscovering the flavours that have adorned our dishes; it is a profound exploration of how these humble yet potent elements shape our shared human experience. With each sprinkle and dash, spices do more than enhance our meals—they deepen our connection to the world, enriching our understanding of life itself.

The Chemistry of Flavour

The magic begins with flavour compounds. For instance, the pungency of black pepper comes from piperine, while the warm, woody notes of cinnamon are a courtesy of cinnamaldehyde. These compounds interact with our sensory receptors—those gatekeepers of taste and smell—to deliver the distinct sensations we associate with each spice.

Scientific explorations, like those noted in Stuart Farrimond's *The Science of Spice*, suggest that understanding the properties of these compounds not only enhances our culinary skills but also our appreciation of food. By recognizing which chemicals cause which sensations, we can create more harmonious blends and predict how a spice will behave under different cooking conditions.[1]

Heat and Spice: More Than Just a Dance of Tongues

Capsaicin, the fiery compound in chilli peppers, is a perfect example of how spices interact with our physiology. It binds us to pain receptors on our tongues, the same receptors that react to physical heat, tricking our brains into feeling that spicy burn. Interestingly, this reaction also triggers endorphins, the body's natural painkillers, providing a natural high—explaining perhaps why some of us are drawn irresistibly to spicy foods.

Turmeric: The Golden Spice

No discussion of spice science would be complete without turmeric, celebrated not only for its bold colour and earthy flavour but also for its medicinal properties. Cumin seeds, the active compound in turmeric, has been extensively studied for its anti-inflammatory and antioxidant properties. It exemplifies how traditional uses of spices in medicine are supported by contemporary science, bridging the gap between old wives' tales and pharmacological research.

Synergy in Spices

The concept of synergy, where the combined effect of spices is greater than the sum of their parts, is vital in understanding their full potential. The traditional garam masala, a staple in Indian cuisine, combines several spices, each with its own set of flavour compounds. When these are blended, they interact not just with the individual ingredients of a dish but also with each other, creating a complex flavour profile that is impossible to achieve with any single spice.

Preservation and Protection

Historically, many spices were valued for their preservative qualities before the advent of modern refrigeration. The antimicrobial properties of spices like clove and cinnamon are now understood in terms of the active chemicals they contain, which can inhibit the growth of bacteria and fungi. This not only helps in preserving food but also in protecting the human body from various infections.

Colour and Appeal

The vibrant colours in spices also play a significant role in their appeal. The deep reds of paprika, the bright yellows of turmeric and the lush greens of herbs are all derived from natural pigments that are potent antioxidants. These colours not only make our dishes visually appealing but also contribute to our health, fighting free radicals and reducing oxidative stress.

Reshii beautifully encapsulates the sentiment in her book where she states, 'India has taken all of these (spices) and a host of others and incorporated them in supremely sophisticated ways into its regional cuisines, even going on to become the largest producer and consumer of spices in the world.'[2] This highlights not only India's significant role in the global spice trade but also its ability to adapt and integrate these spices into its diverse culinary traditions.

Elevating Spices with Precision

Grinding spices is an essential skill, which might explain why we have specialists dedicated to it, especially in Indian cuisine where spices are pivotal. Modern methods of blending spices vary from cold grinding to hot, each playing a unique role. Sometimes, you might hear advice to toast the spices before blending, while in other instances, you may be instructed to add them directly without dry roasting.

Transforming whole spices into finer particles not only intensifies their flavour but also unveils a complexity that pre-ground spices simply cannot match. Mastering the art of grinding spices allows for a personalized touch to the texture and intensity of your spice blends, elevating your dishes to new heights.

I remember watching my family grinding spices on the sil batta with some salt when I was a kid. At that time, I didn't know the reason, and interestingly, neither did my family. I was always told this is how it is. When I grew older and started digging for more information, I realized that on a sil batta or hamam dasta, the salt helps create friction, thereby ensuring a smoother grind.

There are several methods to grind spices, each with its own unique advantages. One of the most time-honoured and fulfilling techniques is the use of a mortar and pestle or hamam dasta. Though this technique is true in our Indian subcontinent text, it can be applied the world over as well. This ancient tool enables you to manually crush and grind spices, drawing out their essential oils and aromas through controlled pressure and motion. For those who prefer a quicker, more efficient method and practical machine, electric spice grinders can easily be used.

But more than the technique and mindless making powder of spices, it is important for you to understand the texture you aim to achieve and the specific characteristics of the spices you are working with. You would not make a fine powder while making a kosha mangsho but for butter chicken, you might. To evoke my inner Kafka, I would say grinding spices is not merely a mechanical act; it is a transformative ritual that transcends the mundane, infusing each dish with profound depth, richness and soul. In this seemingly simple process lies the essence of culinary experimentation, where the coarse and raw are meticulously metamorphosed into the fine and intricate. This art, much like the subtle complexities of life itself, reveals hidden layers and nuances that pre-ground packet spices, devoid of personal touch, can never replicate. To master the grinding of spices is to engage in a dance with the elements.

If you ask me, Indian cuisine is like a classic Madan Mohan composition—rich, complex and layered. Think of the song 'Ae Dil Mujhe Bata De' from the movie *Bhai Bhai* (1959), where every element plays a specific role, from Geeta Dutt's melodious voice to each instrument creating a charming and unforgettable melody. The spice blends in food from the Indian subcontinent are just the same—each spice is there to play its part and not because you found the shape of a spice 'interesting'. I would categorize them into three groups, each contributing to the harmony of flavours that fill Indian kitchens. You may define them differently, but based on my understanding, this is how I see them.

1. The Basic Spices

The essence of Indian cuisine lies in its foundational spices— cumin seeds, coriander, mustard, turmeric and chilli powder. These basic spices are like the first notes of a melody, setting the stage for all that follows. Cumin seeds (jeera) brings a warm, earthy depth, while coriander (dhania) adds a fresh and slightly citrusy flavour. Black mustard seeds (rayi) add a sharp, pungent flavour, often used in tempering to release their aroma. Turmeric (haldi), with its vibrant golden hue, not only enhances flavour but also brings a touch of ancient medicinal wisdom to the dish. Then there is chilli powder (lal mirch), giving dishes their characteristic heat and spice, and asafoetida (hing), adding a unique savoury touch and aiding digestion.

Together, these spices form the backbone of Indian cooking—a foundation that lets other ingredients shine.

2. Complementary Spices

Complementary spices are like harmonies that enrich the main tune. Spices like fennel seeds (saunf), known for its digestive properties, and fenugreek (methi), celebrated for its health benefits, work alongside the basic spices to create depth. Carom seeds (ajwain) add their unique sharpness, enhancing the flavours of vegetables and pulses, making each dish come alive with character.

3. Aromatics or Secondary Spices

The third group, aromatic spices, brings a subtle yet profound impact. Aromatic or secondary spices are the subtle yet defining brushstrokes that elevate Indian cuisine into something extraordinary. These spices add depth, elegance and complexity to every dish. Green cardamom (elaichi), with its sweet and floral aroma, is used to flavour desserts, curries, and the ever-famous masala chai. Black cardamom (kali/badi elaichi) offers a contrasting smoky note, perfect for meat and rice dishes, adding a bold depth that lingers. Cinnamon (dalchini) brings a gentle warmth, enriching both curries and rice dishes like pulao. Cloves (laung) are small but potent, lending a sharp intensity to marinades, pickles, and garam masala blends. Nutmeg (jaiphal) and mace (jaivitri) each contribute a slightly sweet, aromatic complexity, often used in small amounts to enhance both savoury and sweet preparations. Saffron (kesar), the most luxurious of all, is used sparingly, bringing a golden colour and a delicate, floral warmth to special dishes and desserts. Finally, bay leaf (tej patta) imparts a subtle bitterness, adding depth to stews, curries, and rice.

These aromatic spices are like the finishing notes of Madan Mohan's melody—transforming a dish from something good into something unforgettable.

In Indian cooking, where the harmony of spices can define a meal, mastering the skill of grinding spices can significantly enhance the flavour and aroma of your food. Whether you are making a robust garam masala, a fragrant curry powder or a simple chai spice blend, the process of grinding spices brings you closer to the essence of Indian cuisine, connecting tradition with the modern culinary landscape.

The most important question to ask after 'To be or not to be' is 'to toast or not' and if the answer is yes, then how much? Is it that simple?

Toasting spices is an ancient culinary practice that significantly enhances their flavour and aroma, transforming even the simplest ingredients into extraordinary culinary experiences. This is where you apply heat to whole or ground spices, which activates their essential oils, intensifying their taste and adding a layer of complexity to dishes.

In the culinary traditions of the Indian subcontinent, the use of whole and powdered spices is often employed in two distinct stages. Take, for example, the preparation of a delectable mutton korma. The cooking process begins by heating oil and tossing in whole spices such as bay leaves, black cardamom, cinnamon sticks and chillies. These whole spices infuse the oil, creating a rich base flavour.

As you continue cooking, you add onions and other ingredients, followed by a powdered spice blend. This blend typically includes ground versions of the whole spices already used. Over the phone one day, Krish Ashok explains this technique, noting that whole spices form the foundational flavour profile, while the powdered spices are added later to introduce top notes of fragrance and enhance the overall flavour complexity. This layered approach ensures that each dish has a depth of flavour and a well-rounded aroma. As a chef, I can tell you that the whole spices added directly to the oil are typically raw and not toasted, whereas the powdered spice blends are almost always toasted before being used. This method ensures that the whole spices infuse their robust, unadulterated flavours into the oil, while the toasted powdered spices add more nuanced flavour and aroma to the dish.

The key to successful toasting lies in careful attention to the process. Over-toasting or burning spices can result in bitter, unpleasant flavours. The aim is to gently coax out the essential oils and natural sugars within the spices, resulting in a harmonious blend of taste and aroma. Toasting also releases volatile compounds that add depth and nuance to the spice mix, making it more multi-dimensional.

Toasting can be achieved using various methods, each offering unique advantages. My favourite, however, is a dry cast iron skillet because of its direct heat contact and ease of monitoring. Simply heat the skillet over medium to low heat, add the spices and stir frequently until they become fragrant. It's crucial to keep a vigilant eye, as spices can quickly transition from perfectly toasted to burnt. If you do enjoy creating your spice blends and by the end of this book, feel motivated, then I would suggest toasting every spice individually or based on their size and weight.

I believe that just as new chefs in restaurants are first taught to master the basics of chopping and peeling, they should also be trained in the art of toasting spices and creating spice blends tailored to their dishes. However, many restaurants typically rely on pre-packaged spice blends, from kitchen king to biryani masala. Even when they create their own blends, it's often a mix of various powdered spices, resulting in what they call the 'secret blend'.

Finally, how do you store your spices?

When it comes to storing your spices, it's time to get practical. Sure, a masala dabba sounds like a romantic addition to your kitchen—it's aesthetically pleasing and adds a touch of tradition. But let's be real—it doesn't always do the job. While it looks pretty on your shelf, keeping all your spices in one of these dabbas means you'll lose their essence and intensity pretty quickly.

Those masala dabbas are often not airtight. If you decide to go for the most beautiful and expensive spice box, remember to use it wisely. Store small batches of spices in the dabba for everyday use, but keep the rest in airtight containers. This way, you maintain the freshness and potency of your spices, ensuring they continue to bring robust flavours to your dishes.

Effective storage is key to maintaining the freshness and quality of spices, ground and whole. Elements such as light, moisture, heat and air can degrade the quality of spices over time. Light makes their colour fade, heat makes essential oils dissipate, and moisture can lead to caking and mould growth.

To protect your spice blends, retain their colours and flavours, and prevent oxidation, store them in airtight containers, keeping them away from direct sunlight and heat sources. Using opaque containers or jars can further shield the spices from light exposure, which can diminish their flavour and aroma. Refrigeration also helps preserve volatile oils, flavour and aroma and slows microbial growth.

Here's something wonderful to know—while dried spices lose their aroma, flavour and colour over time, they aren't deemed completely spoiled. Whole spices last longer than ground ones—while the former goes on for typically 1–3 years, the latter lasts 6 months–1 year. Spice blends and seasonings have a shelf life of about 1 year. You will, of course, find many materials which will tell you that you can store them for longer. To that, I would say, 'Sure, you can.' But remember that while they will be edible, they will not have the same intensity and flavour.

If you really want the best flavours, create fresh spice blends each time (as recommended by cooking experts in my family and Krish Ashok). Freshly ground spices deliver the most evolved and superior flavour. Think about why we grind coffee beans fresh—it's to get the freshest and most flavourful cup of coffee. The same goes for tea; you brew it fresh at home for the best taste. You wouldn't prepare it in advance and store it in the fridge to reuse and reheat. My advice—keep your spices fresh for the best results.

To awaken fully to the world, one must savour the freshness of every moment. As Auguste Escoffier, the great chef and the man who is considered the father of modern cuisine, once famously said, 'La bonne cuisine est la base du véritable bonheur,' which translates to 'good food is the foundation of genuine happiness.'[3] And, good food comes from great spice blends, the freshest ingredients and balance.

Beyond the Plate

The historical impact of spices extends beyond their culinary uses. In ancient times, spices were so highly valued that they were often used as gifts for kings and deities. They played a pivotal role in rituals and ceremonies as their aromas were believed to be pleasing to the gods. This divine association elevated spices to a status that was intertwined with both spirituality and power.

The economic implications were equally profound. The spice trade was not merely a commercial activity; it was a catalyst for some of the most significant historical developments, including the rise and fall of empires, the discovery of new continents and the unfolding of international trade laws that still impact global commerce today.

Today, the cultural implications of spices are evident in the way they have infiltrated local traditions and practices around the world. From the use of saffron in Indian and Persian cuisines to the integration of cinnamon in Mexican and Middle Eastern dishes, spices have helped shape the culinary landscapes of various cultures, making them an intrinsic part of our global heritage.

As spices traversed the globe, they did more than flavour food—they became a medium through which cultures could interact, blend and evolve. They influenced trade policies, international relations, and even the personal fortunes of those who grew, sold and consumed them. Their influence is embedded in the pages of history books and the recipes passed down through generations, telling a story that is as much about human endeavour as it is about culinary delight.

As we dig deeper into the narratives etched by spices across the globe, we encounter the profound roles spices have played in medicinal traditions. For centuries, spices like ginger, turmeric and clove have been cornerstones in the traditional medicine chests of cultures from Asia to the Americas and praised for their anti-inflammatory and healing properties. The interplay between spices and health offers a compelling chapter in our tale, illustrating how these botanicals soothe, heal and fortify human life.

That's not all. Spices, even the ones that are not native to India, also have a unique role to play in our lifestyle, culture, language and daily lives.

In my conversation with Krish Ashok, the author of *Masala Lab: The Science of Indian Cooking,* on the use of spices in our daily cooking, he mentioned how the use of spices not only varies from region to region but also changes with one's social status; the pungency and strength depend on your or your family's wealth. If you are rich, you will probably use saffron in your cooking and other such good-quality spices. If you are not wealthy, you will have to make do with lower standards of spices.

Perhaps, because of its affluence, Lucknow uses spices differently—people in the city use saffron and potli masala simply to add flavour. I say that that is a level of affluence and opulence, unlike what you might find in the food in Delhi or Bihar, where spices are either used fully or sparingly.

Spices have also found a way to become a part of how we communicate. There are so many regional language idioms that use spices and lend beautiful meaning to conversations. There is one phrase in Punjab that is also common in many north Indian states: *masaledaar gapp*, which means spicy or exaggerated gossip. Another is *mirchi lagna*, which means to get offended or be incensed. In Marathi, *saakhaarecha tondaacha mithacha* implies someone sweet in front and salty behind. Another favourite of mine from Punjab is *namak swaad, mirchi tez*, meaning salt for taste and chilli for heat, symbolizing a balance of flavours (and personalities). The iconic song 'Main Toh Raste Se Jaa Raha Tha, Main Toh Bhel Puri Khaa Raha Tha' from *Coolie No. 1* (1995) or 'Mohabbat Hai Mirchi' from *Chura Liya Hai Tumne* (2003) talks about the effect of chillies. Or, as Marryam H. Reshii writes in her book, *The Flavour of Spice: Journeys, Recipes, Stories*, so 'integral is chilli to our cuisine that the most damning indictment of a meal in India is the sentence: *Namak mirchi kam hai* [There's not much salt or chillies in this dish].'[4]

I met a pandit (who was also a singer) in Benaras when he was tying a mirchi–nimbu garland outside the shop where I was sitting and enjoying my tea. If you grew up in India or have travelled here, it is rather impossible not to see this unique 'garland' outside shops or on the streets, especially on Saturdays. When I asked him about it, he narrated a story:

Once upon a time in a small Indian village, there were two friends: Mirchi and Nimbu. They were known for their unique potential and vibrant behaviour. Mirchi was fiery and bold while Nimbu was tangy and refreshing.

One hot summer day, the villagers were preparing for a grand festival. The village chief approached the two friends and said, 'We need something special to protect our homes from evil spirits during the festival. Can you help us?'

Mirchi, always eager to showcase her strength, said, 'I can scare away any evil spirit with my fiery heat!' Nimbu, cheerful and energetic, chimed in, 'And I can cleanse and purify with my sour tanginess.'

The village chief was impressed and decided to use their combined powers. He instructed the villagers to make a garland using red chillies and fresh lemons. The garland was hung on the doorway of every house in the village.

As the festival began, the vibrant garlands swayed in the breeze, emitting a blend of spicy, fiery and tangy aromas. The villagers felt safe and protected, and the evil spirits were nowhere to be seen.

Throughout the festival, the villagers celebrated with joy, knowing that Mirchi and Nimbu were watching over them. The friends were proud of their contribution and realized that their unique qualities were even more powerful when combined. From that day on, it became a tradition in the village to hang a garland of mirchi and nimbu on doors during festivals and special occasions. And eventually, this became a regular affair.

At the end of the story, he laughed, finished the tea which he had picked up while narrating the story, kept the glass down and walked away from the shop singing a new song in a new raag. When I saw everyone around me smiling and giggling, I knew that this was nothing but a folktale shared for my enjoyment.

This wasn't the first tale spiced with a little tadka that I had heard in my life though. The appeal of spices has inspired countless literary and artistic expressions, especially in the subcontinent. From the spicy metaphors in the poetry of Rumi, who used saffron and cinnamon as symbols of passion and sacrifice, to the vibrant depictions of spice markets in the paintings of Paul Klee, spices have enriched the human imagination in myriad ways. Various spices have also played significant roles in literature, movies and songs, depicting fear or romance. They are muses that have sparked creativity across different media, echoing their versatility and profound impact. For example, Chitra Divakaruni's *The Mistress of Spices* uses Indian spices as metaphors to weave myths and historical tales. Divakaruni presents her novel as magic, mystery and love—a tribute to India's deep relationship with spices. Inspired by Bengali folktales and epics her grandmother once told, Divakaruni brings these stories to life through personification and magical realism. She uses characters like Tilo, Lalita and Geeta to explore themes of alienation, identity, and the struggle against patriarchy, illustrating how these strong women break barriers and find self-realization.[5]

Then there are also the emotions and memories that spices tend to evoke in us, ones that are from our own lives. For instance, the scent of cardamom and cinnamon instantly transports me to my mother's kitchen, where she cooked sevai for Eid or made a good korma masala. Such is the power of spices—they are time capsules that preserve moments of our lives.

* * *

In this book, I aim to show you my love for spices and peel back the layers of time to reveal how spices have been more than just background artists in the theatre of human history. As we delve into the intricate dance of flavours that spices bring to our palates, we will also uncover the silent yet profound influence they exert on our social and cultural fabric. This narrative is not just about what spices do to our food but also what they do to us—how they shape our identity, our traditions, and our connections to the past and each other.

As we engage with these kinds of flavours in this book, we also engage with a universal history of migration, trade and cultural exchange. This narrative, enriched by the spices that have flavoured our past, invites us to re-examine not just the foods we eat but also the stories we tell about where we come from and how we've come together. It challenges us to think about how the humblest of seeds can change the world, influencing what we eat, how we trade and the way we live.

As you flip through the pages of this book, you'll notice an interesting pattern. For some dishes, like a biryani of a particular origin, you'll find the complete recipe—a simple, approachable version to serve as a basic template. For others, you'll only find the recipe, nuskha or tareeka (way) of the spice blend. And this choice is intentional.

My purpose with this book is clear—I want to encourage you to step away from those boxed, ready-made spices at the grocery store and try your hand at making your own blends at home. It's an invitation to rediscover the art and science of spice mixing that defines our culinary heritage.

In that way, this book isn't *mukkamal* (complete); it's *adhoora* (half). The idea is to leave room for your creativity and experimentation—to let you bring your own flair and flavour to the table.

This ongoing journey through the world of spices is more than a culinary adventure; it's a continuous discovery of our collective human heritage, flavoured by the very spices that have made our meals—and our histories—richer and more interconnected.

Let's begin.

* * *

ESSENTIAL SPICES FOR EVERY KITCHEN

Carom Seeds (Ajwain)

Carom, sometimes mistakenly called a lovage seed, packs a flavourful punch! This tiny gem shouldn't be confused with nigella or celery seeds, which share similar names in India. A key ingredient in many Indian dishes, carom plays an integral part in legumes or pakodas because it helps in digestion and bloating. Oma water, an infusion of carom seeds, has a long history as a natural remedy for stomach aches, diarrhoea, indigestion and various other ailments.

Embraced by North Indians, Pakistanis, North Africans and Iranians, carom has a particular affinity for starchy companions like legumes, root vegetables, breads and green beans. It helps break down these starchy foods and meats, making them easier to digest. Flavour-wise, it also beautifully complements other common spices.

Aniseed (Patli Saunf)

Aniseed, with its distinctive licorice flavour, has captivated taste buds for centuries. The Portuguese call it 'erva doce', meaning 'sweet herb,' highlighting its pleasantness. Even the Arabs have a term, 'kamun halu', which literally means 'sweet cumin seeds'.

While sometimes mistaken for fennel seeds in Asian cultures due to their similar flavours and names (Indian 'saunf' for both), aniseed has its own unique identity. To differentiate, Indians have a clever term, 'patli saunf', meaning 'thin fennel seeds'.

Aniseed's flavour profile goes beyond just licorice. It boasts a sweetness that dances with warm, fruity undertones, all balanced by a subtle hint of camphor. This complexity makes it distinct from its close relatives, fennel seeds and star anise, offering a more delicate and camphor-forward experience.

Asafoetida (Hing)

Asafoetida's name is a fascinating paradox—a clash between the heavenly and the earthly. In Sanskrit, it was called *hingu*, which evolved into 'hing' in Hindi, 'imgu' in Kannada, 'inguva' in Telugu, and 'him' in Bengali, among other Indian languages. Across the world, it had diverse names—the Persians called it 'anghuzeh', the Greeks, 'aza', and the Arabs, 'haltit' or 'tyib'. In Swahili, it was known as 'mvuje'. Europeans, however, were less kind, referring to it as 'devil's dung' or 'stinking gum'. But for the English world, it was derived from the Persian word for 'resin' (aza) and the Latin for 'fetid' (foetida), which translates literally to 'godly stink'. This aptly captures the essence of this unique spice.

To the ancient Persians, asafoetida wasn't just a pungent condiment; it was 'the food of the Gods'. The Romans, too, revered it as 'Persian silphium', a prized ingredient for their sauces and wines.[1] Across the millennia, asafoetida's journey has taken it from the divine realm to the hearths of ancient India and Iran, where it served a dual purpose—a flavour enhancer and a medicinal remedy.

Today, asafoetida reigns supreme in the vegetarian kitchens of India. Imagine a pale brown resin, darkening with age, possessing an acrid bite and an unmistakable garlicky aroma—not exactly love at first whiff. But this is where asafoetida's magic lies. Used with a light touch and tempered in hot oil, it undergoes a remarkable transformation. The harshness fades, revealing a symphony of shallot and garlic notes that elevate vegetarian dishes to new heights.

Indian Bay Leaf (Tej Patta)

Unlike its European cousin, the bay leaf, this variety belongs to the cinnamon family. It is known as 'tamala pattra' (Sanskrit for 'dark leaf') or 'tejpat' (Hindi for 'pungent leaf'). The Romans themselves were enthralled by its aroma, incorporating it into perfumes and brewing concoctions. In this book, when you see bay leaves, consider them to be tej patta.

In Indian kitchens, the Indian bay leaf performs a vital role. It takes centre stage during the pre-'tadka'. Here, it releases very few notes. While it may not be the flashiest spice, its muted tones are what make it a master conductor, harmonizing the bold flavours of meat curries and vibrant vegetable creations.

Think of it this way—the Indian bay leaf isn't a flamboyant soloist; it's the dependable bassist, providing a deep, grounding presence that elevates the entire culinary experience. And while its cinnamon-like origins might hint at a muted sweetness, its true magic lies in its ability to subtly enhance the other spices, bringing out their full potential.

I personally don't find this to be the most inspiring spice in the world. The flavours are muted and similar to cinnamon because of its origin. You can easily ignore this for your dish or use just these leaves while making pulao or tea.

Caraway Seeds (Shahi Jeera)

Caraway seeds is often mistaken for cumin seeds's close relative. In India, it's known as 'vilayati jeera', which literally translates to 'foreign cumin seeds'. But caraway seeds is more than just a lookalike. It's the dried, ripe fruit of a plant, used whole or ground. While the seeds take centre stage, the feathery leaves add a touch of elegance as a garnish, and the root boasts a surprising resemblance to parsnips, with a delightfully crisp texture.

Roman soldiers enjoyed bread flavoured with its unique notes, and as their empire expanded, so did caraway seeds's popularity. The spice even found a place in the afterlife—the Ancient Egyptians placed caraway seeds in tombs to ward off evil spirits. But its influence wasn't limited to the physical world. Once considered a key ingredient in love potions, it was believed to prevent fickleness and ensure a steady heart. By the 16th century, caraway seeds had firmly established itself in British kitchens, gracing loaves of bread, pastries and cakes with its complex flavour profile.[2]

The taste itself is sweet, warm and reminiscent of dill and anise. But caraway seeds isn't a one-note wonder—its slightly sharp, bitter and even soapy aftertaste adds a touch of complexity. However, overcooking can make it bitter.

Green Cardamom (Choti Elaichi)

The green cardamom or choti elaichi, crowned the 'queen of spices', holds court as the world's third most expensive treasure, following only saffron and vanilla. Its reign stretches back over 2000 years, captivating the senses of Indians, Greeks, Romans and civilizations as far-flung as China. The word 'cardamom' itself whispers of its Persian origins, echoing through Greek and finding its way into countless languages.[3]

This fragrant queen hails from the lush greenery of South India. While Vikings, traversing the spice routes via Constantinople, introduced it to Scandinavia, cardamom's allure had already captivated the ancient world.[4] It decorated dishes, beverages, medicines and even perfumes.

Cardamom often is the basis of Indian, Iranian and Arabian cuisine. Arab and Turkish coffees wouldn't be the same without its presence. The Bedouin Arabs, with their ingenious touch, infuse coffee pots with cardamom pods, ensuring each cup is kissed by its unique aroma.

From savoury to sweet, cardamom conquers all. In India, it's the irreplaceable heart of curries, pulaos, garam masala blends and countless other spice mixtures. And when it comes to Indian desserts, its presence is equally essential.

Cardamom has a warm note with a hint of citrus and camphor. Home remedies will tell you that chewing on a seed will give you fresh breath and is a perfect antidote to a garlicky indulgence or a lingering alcoholic warmth or smoke.

Cardamom's reputation extends beyond its culinary prowess. It's believed to be a stimulant, offering a cooling effect on the body. Perhaps this is why, in India, a cup of tea in the summer sun might be graced with cardamom, while its winter counterpart wouldn't.

Black Cardamom (Badi Elaichi)

Black cardamom, or badi elaichi, stands out as a bold and distinctive spice in the spice world. With its smoky, heady aroma and sharp, citrusy undertones, it belongs to the 'warm' spice family, alongside black pepper, cloves and chillies.

Scientifically known as Amomum subulatum, black cardamom is part of the Zingiberaceae family, including ginger. Its pods are tough, wrinkled and about an inch long, casing tiny, dark seeds with concentrated flavours. These pods are the heart of the spice, lending their smoky essence to dishes across South Asia and beyond.

There are two notable species of black cardamom: Amomum subulatum and Amomum tsao-ko. The former, smaller and bolder, is the star of Indian kitchens, while the latter is used in Chinese cooking, where its larger pods impart a subtler smokiness.

It's essential to recognize that black and green cardamom are worlds apart. Green cardamom whispers subtle sweetness into a dish, while black cardamom roars with robust, earthy tones. Their flavours are not interchangeable—each tells a unique story.

Chillies

Chillies are undoubtedly the fierce chieftains of the spice world! They completely change the flavour game wherever they go. From smoky Latin American dishes to fiery African curries, chillies are a key ingredient in many cuisines around the globe, including Asia, the Caribbean and even some parts of Eastern Europe.[5]

Originally from Mexico, chillies have been around since at least 7000 BCE! Christopher Columbus was actually looking for black pepper when he stumbled upon chillies in the Americas. He thought they were even hotter, so he brought them back to Europe. From there, chillies hitched a ride on ships and spread to Africa, India and Asia, becoming a beloved part of each region's food.

One big advantage of chillies? Their seeds can last for years, which turned out to be a lifesaver during long journeys by sea. They also come in all shapes, sizes and colours! They can be fiery hot, sweet and fruity, or even have earthy, smoky or floral notes. The heat level can vary a lot too.

Cinnamon and Cassia (Dalcheeni)

Cinnamon and cassia, chilli's close cousins, have been around for ages. They've even played a role in ancient ceremonies! The Egyptians used cinnamon and cassia as embalming spices during mummification rituals. These spices were not native to

Egypt and were highly prized due to their scarcity and cost. Pharaoh Hatshepsut even sent expeditions around 1500 BCE to the land of Punt to procure aromatics, including cinnamon-wood and myrrh.[6]

According to an ancient inscription, the 'royal linen'—alongside precious stones and cinnamon—was listed among the yearly tributes sent from Punt to Pharaoh Rameses III in the 12th century B.C.[7] These items, highly valued in that era, may have originated from India, where they were readily available at the time. However, Hornell suggests that cinnamon, in particular, might have been sourced from Sri Lanka during this period.[8]

The origins of cinnamon remained a closely guarded secret of Arab merchants until the 10th century. To maintain their monopoly and justify high prices, they wove elaborate, often false, tales about its source. Scholars now suggest that cinnamon during this period likely came from Sri Lanka, a theory warranting further investigation.[9] Cassia and cinnamon held profound cultural significance in ancient civilizations. Egyptians used them in embalming rituals, while Hebrews incorporated them into sacred anointing oils. Native to Sri Lanka, Malabar and China, these spices did not grow in the Middle East, making them highly prized imports through guarded trade routes.[10]

There are a few types of cinnamon, but cassia and Ceylon cinnamon (also called canela) are the most common. Cassia, nicknamed 'Chinese wood', is popular in East and Southeast Asia, and even the US (sometimes mixed with Ceylon). Ceylon cinnamon is a favourite in Mexico, Europe, South Asia and England.

Cassia has a thicker, rougher bark than Ceylon cinnamon. It also has a stronger smell and taste, which is kind of sweet and spicy with a bitter bite. Ceylon cinnamon is known for its warm, sweet flavour with hints of clove and citrus. It's more delicate than cassia.

Clove (Laung)

Cloves look exactly like tiny nails, which is why the French named them 'clou' (pronounced kloo). In fact, in the Spice Islands of Indonesia, people would plant a clove tree for every child born. A healthy tree meant good luck for the child, who would even wear a clove necklace as protection![11]

Cloves are an ancient spice used for more than just flavouring meat curries. As early as 200 BCE, the Chinese used them as breath fresheners for the emperor. Arab traders brought cloves to the Romans and Greeks, who even used them in love potions. Later, Europeans went to war over cloves, all because they were so valuable.[12]

Ancient texts from distant lands shed light on the significance of cloves and their uses. The Indian *Carakasamhita* advises, 'One who desires clean, fresh, fragrant breath should keep nutmeg and cloves in the mouth,' a sentiment echoed by a Chinese text from the second century. Another Indian source highlights the medicinal value of cloves (*lavanga*), recommending their inclusion in remedies for coughs, hiccups, vomiting, and mouth and throat inflammations.[13]

Cloves are dried flower buds. They start out pink and turn a deep reddish brown when dried. They have a strong, spicy smell with hints of wood and sweetness. Their taste is sharp and bitter, with a numbing feeling on your tongue – definitely a bold spice!

Coriander (Dhania)

Coriander is a spice with a long history. People have been using it for both flavour and medicine for thousands of years. In fact, coriander seeds were even found in the tombs of the Pharaohs dating back over 3000 years! The Romans weren't just known for their impressive empire; they were also big fans of coriander, using it to flavour their bread as they conquered Europe.[14]

The name 'coriander' actually comes from the Greek word for 'bed bug' because some people think the leaves smell a bit like those pesky insects (don't worry, most people don't agree!). Coriander is mentioned in ancient texts from both India and Greece, and even the famous Greek doctor, Hippocrates, recommended it for its medicinal properties.[15]

This versatile plant offers more than just seeds. In the culinary world, chefs use coriander seeds, leaves, stems and even the root! Each part has its own unique flavour profile.

Coriander seeds are small and round, and their flavour changes as they ripen. Green coriander seeds have a strong, almost grassy smell, while ripe seeds have a sweet, spicy and nutty taste with a hint of citrus. They can also have subtle hints of cedar and floral notes.

Cumin Seeds (Jeera)

In India, cumin seeds has been a flavour favourite since ancient times, even earning the name 'sughandan', which means 'good smelling' in Sanskrit.

Cumin seeds's history dates back over 5000 years, with seeds excavated in Syria from 2000 BCE. Evidence of its use in Egypt during the New Kingdom (16th–11th century BCE) and mentions in the Bible (Isaiah 28:27) highlight its early significance. Originating in Egypt, cumin seeds spread across the Middle East, where it remains a staple seasoning. From there, it travelled to Iran, India and the Far East, while Spanish explorers introduced it to the Americas, influenced by the Moors.

India stands out as the largest producer and exporter of cumin seeds, making it an integral part of its cuisine and culture.[16]

It has a strong, spicy, earthy and sweet aroma with a slightly bitter and pungent taste. This bitterness is more noticeable in ground cumin seeds, but fear not, coriander often comes to the rescue, balancing things out. If you want to tame the bitterness even further, try dry roasting your cumin seeds before grinding. This releases a toasty, nutty flavour that makes the spice less harsh.

But cumin seeds isn't the only player in the game. Black cumin seeds (shahi jeera/caraway) seeds are smaller, darker and boast a sweeter taste with hints of lemon and caraway seeds. Toasting cumin seeds, either in oil or dry roasted, unlocks a nutty depth, making its flavour richer and more mellow.

Fennel Seeds (Saunf)

Fennel seeds hold a delightful licorice aroma and mildly sweet flavour that have been captivating taste buds for centuries. These little seeds are best bought whole and can be ground or dry-roasted to release their full potential. The flavour is so similar to anise, cumin seeds and caraway seeds that many cultures use them interchangeably.

Legend has it that Prometheus used the stem of the fennel seeds plant, a fast-burning herb, as a tool to steal fire from the gods. Defying divine authority, he descended to earth with the stolen fire, sharing this closely guarded secret with humanity. Fire, considered a sacred mystery that the gods deemed unfit for mankind, was now in human hands. By uncovering and teaching this divine secret, Prometheus overstepped his bounds and disrupted the natural order. As a result, Zeus, enraged by his defiance and the dissemination of such knowledge, punished Prometheus severely for his transgression.

Roman warriors believed that consuming fennel seeds enhanced their strength and endurance in battle while maintaining their lean physique. This belief aligns with the Greek word for fennel seeds, *marathon*, meaning 'grow thin'. Following their triumph at the Battle of Marathon, also known as the 'place of fennel seeds', the Greeks celebrated their victory with woven fennel seeds as a symbol.

The Ayurvedic Pharmacopoeia of India advocates using dried fennel seeds or fennel seeds extracts to address various ailments, including anorexia and colic in children. This traditional practice finds support in ancient Chinese pharmacopoeia, which similarly acknowledges fennel seeds's medicinal benefits.[17]

In fact, in Lucknow and Kashmir, the top flavour of often a few dishes would be fennel seeds.

Fenugreek Seeds (Kasuri Methi)

Methika (Sanskrit), fenugreek was cultivated in Egypt as early as 1000 BCE. Fenugreek seeds were prized throughout the Middle East and India for their flavour, medicinal properties and even as a fumigant (a fancy word for something burned to create a pleasant smell). Europe, however, mainly used fenugreek for its medicinal benefits.

Egyptians and Indians shared a clever trick—they'd soak the seeds in water until they swelled up, then use them to bring down fevers and aid digestion. By the year 1050 CE, fenugreek's fame had spread all the way to China! Despite its name ('foenum graecum' translating to 'Greek hay' in Latin), fenugreek wasn't actually used as a spice in Greek cooking. The name likely comes from the dried leaves' hay-like aroma.[18]

Fenugreek seeds themselves are quite aromatic, with a scent reminiscent of curry powder. On their own, the seeds have a bitter taste. Roasting them mellows the bitterness and unlocks a surprising sweetness, with an aroma like burnt sugar and a taste that can be compared to maple syrup.

Garlic

Garlic is one ingredient that's loved (and sometimes loathed) around the world. This pungent powerhouse adds its magic touch to dishes everywhere, from the creamy French aioli to the robust Vietnamese pho. Believe it or not, the name 'garlic' isn't as exciting as its flavour. It comes from the Anglo-Saxon word 'garleac', which simply means spear plant.

For thousands of years, people haven't just enjoyed garlic's taste—they've also used it for medicinal purposes. As early as 3700 BCE, Egyptians were using garlic to stay healthy and strong. It was a loyal companion for travellers on long journeys. While the Romans believed it boosted strength and courage, the Greeks even used garlic to fight off colds and coughs.[19]

Garlic's popularity as both a flavour and a fighter against illness has made it a staple ingredient in countless dishes across the globe. Along with its partners-in-crime, ginger and onion, it forms a flavour 'trinity' that's essential in many Asian cuisines.

The intensity of a garlic punch depends on the variety. Freshly cut garlic can range from mild and sweet to super strong. Some varieties mellow out during cooking, while others leave a lingering kick that garlic lovers adore (and others might avoid).

Ginger

Ginger isn't just a delicious spice—it's a revered remedy with a long and fascinating history! A treasured ingredient for over 5000 years in Asia, it is used by both Indians and Chinese for its flavour and medicinal properties. The Sanskrit word for ginger is 'shringavera', which means 'shaped like a deer's antlers'.

In Ayurveda and traditional Chinese medicine, it's a popular natural remedy for calming the stomach, easing nausea and even curing motion sickness. From curries and stir-fries to marinades and soups, ginger's unique spicy-sweet flavour adds a delightful depth.

Ginger's journey to the West involved Arab traders, who brought it to the Mediterranean region before the 1st century CE. The Greeks even used ginger to create gingerbread, which later evolved into the gingersnaps, cakes and biscuits we know and love today. Spanish explorers then got in on the action, cultivating ginger in Jamaica and exporting it to Europe in the 16th century.[20]

Fresh ginger has a juicy, spicy aroma with a hint of refreshing sweetness and a citrusy lemon note.

Curry Leaf

The quintessential ingredient for poha, Maharashtrian vada pav or Jackie Shroff's anda curry patta, the unassuming kari leaf (also called curry leaf) is a powerhouse of flavour. For centuries, these little leaves have been gracing dishes throughout India and Sri Lanka, adding a depth of aroma and taste that's truly irreplaceable.

Known as 'kariveppilai' in Tamil, these aren't just any leaves. When rubbed or bruised, they emit a strong, warm and a distinct 'curry' aroma. This unique fragrance translates into an amazing flavour that elevates curries, chutneys, vegetables and even beverages!

Nutmeg and Mace (Jaiphal and Jaivitri)

Nutmeg and mace—two spices, one fruit! Legend has it that Emperor Henry VI himself ordered the streets of Rome to be fumigated with nutmegs before his coronation (talk about a grand entrance!).

For a long time, the source of nutmeg and mace was a closely guarded secret. The Portuguese managed to keep it under wraps for a whole century—from the early 1600s—until they were ousted from the Spice Islands by the Dutch. The Dutch then became the new guardians of this spicy treasure and were determined to hold onto their monopoly. They even tried to restrict the nutmeg tree to just two islands. But they underestimated the power of nature (and pigeons!). These feathered friends were responsible for spreading nutmeg seeds to nearby islands, proving the Dutch efforts to be futile. Arab traders introduced mace in the European spice market in the 11th century as a popular beer flavouring. Its popularity soared again in the 17th century, thanks in part to the Dutch nutmeg monopoly.[21]

Both nutmeg and mace have a gloriously warm, sweet and aromatic scent. Their tastes are similar, with nutmeg being slightly sweeter and mace offering a more intense aroma but with some bitter notes.

Mustard

In ancient India, mustard seeds were a symbol of fertility and abundant life. Their use as a spice stretched across the globe, with the Greeks, Chinese, Indians and Africans incorporating them into their cuisines for centuries.

The Romans played a key role in spreading mustard love. They introduced mustard paste to central and northern Europe, and even invented the first table mustard. This 'burning must', called 'mustum ardens' in Latin, was made by grinding mustard seeds (sinapis) with grape must.[22]

Pythagoras, the famed Greek thinker, suggested using mustard paste to treat scorpion stings. Hippocrates, the father of medicine, also valued mustard for its medicinal properties, recommending it for both internal and external applications. These tiny seeds were even used to send a spicy message in ancient times. Legend has it that Darius III of Persia sent Alexander the Great a bag of sesame seeds, likely to represent the vast size of his army. Alexander, not one to be intimidated, countered with mustard seeds, symbolizing not just numbers but also strength.[23]

In religious text, The Bible compares the kingdom of heaven to a tiny mustard seed that flourishes into a large plant.

There's a whole world of mustards out there! Yellow or white mustard originates from southern Europe and western Asia. Brown mustard is native to northern India, China, and parts of Africa and Iran. Black mustard comes from the south Mediterranean region. The cultivation of these mustard varieties has spread to places like Nepal, Russia, Canada, and even Central and South America.[24]

Finally, toasting whole mustard seeds in hot oil unlocks a delightful secret—a nutty, sweetish and aromatic flavour that takes it to a whole new level.

Onions

Onions are a culinary companion with a long history tracing back to Asia. They've been a valued ingredient for centuries, with the Latin word 'cep' even referring specifically to them. While Grecian cultures appreciated them for their medicinal properties, Egyptians enjoyed the raw vegetables.

Today, onions remain an essential part of many cuisines around the world. Whether they're sautéed, roasted or pickled, they add layers of flavour and complexity to dishes. In India, they are not just prized for their taste but also for the texture and body they bring to curries.

The onion family offers a delightful variety of flavours. Some varieties are known for their pungent kick, while others are mild and sweet. Interestingly, onions don't release their flavour magic until they're cut or bruised. This sets off an enzymatic reaction, creating a mixture of sulphur compounds that tantalize our senses.

Regular white or yellow onions are the powerhouses of the onion world. They have a strong, sharp odour when raw, which mellows into a sweet flavour when cooked. Red onions are on the gentler side, offering a pleasant and sweet experience even when raw. Pearl onions are known for their lack of strong aroma but transform into a delightful sweetness when cooked. Shallots add a touch of sophistication to dishes with their slightly pungent and sweet flavour. Scallions are the mildest of the bunch, offering a subtle sweetness that makes them perfect to be used raw.

Black Pepper (Kali Mirch)

Black pepper, the undisputed 'king of spices', boasts a rich history that stretches across continents. The word 'pepper' itself has Indian origins, derived from the Sanskrit 'pippali', which refers to the Indian long pepper, a close relative of the black pepper. Native to the Malabar Coast of southwest India, the black pepper's journey to the world stage began with Arab traders who introduced it to Egypt and Europe.

Not just a seasoning in ancient times, the black pepper was a precious commodity. Measured and valued like gold, it played a crucial role in trade, accepted as payment for taxes, rents, dowries and even ransoms. The Romans, known for their lavish feasts, used black pepper liberally to enhance their food. In Europe, it became a symbol of status, associated with fine cuisine. This high regard for black pepper fuelled European exploration, with nations vying to discover the fastest routes to secure this coveted spice.[25]

But black pepper isn't the only member of the pepper family with a fascinating history. Long pepper, also known as pippali, has roots in India and Indonesia. Highly sought after in ancient Greece and Rome, it later gained popularity across Europe. It was commonly used in cooking and preparing hippocras, a spiced medicinal wine, until the 1500s. However, its cultivation challenges outside its native regions and higher costs led to its decline in favour of black pepper. With Columbus's introduction of allspice powder (kababchini) and chilli peppers from the Americas, long pepper eventually faded from European culinary traditions.[26]

Black pepper offers a unique earthy and rich aroma, followed by a powerful, pungent taste that reflects its earthy fragrance, whereas, white peppers lack the earthiness of black pepper, offering a cleaner, less complex flavour with a milder pungency.

Green peppers are lighter in flavour than black pepper—while they still pack a punch, they lack the complexity of their black counterparts. Long pepper/pippali are tiny berries that merge into a single rod-like structure, and offer a taste similar to black pepper with a subtle sweetness and a slightly more intense kick.

Saffron (Kesar)

The name 'saffron' originates from the Arabic word 'za'faran', meaning yellow, hinting at the vibrant colour that has captivated cultures for millennia. Sanskrit offers another name, 'kumkum', further solidifying its significance.

The story of saffron stretches back to 2300 BCE when the Sumerians used it as a dye. Its yellowish-orange hue has held auspicious meaning across various cultures. In Hindu temples, saffron paste (known as *kungumam*) adorns religious ceremonies. Buddhist monks don saffron-coloured robes, and even Irish kings wore cloaks of this prized colour.

The origins of saffron cultivation are believed to be around ancient Greece and Turkey. Arab traders then carried this precious spice to Spain, Iran and Kashmir (India), where it became a popular colouring and flavouring agent.[27]

Part of what makes saffron so expensive is its labour-intensive harvesting and processing. Each delicate flower is hand-picked, and the precious saffron threads are meticulously separated from the rest of the bloom before drying. This meticulous process also contributes to its reputation as one of the oldest and most expensive spices in the world.

The aroma of saffron is truly distinctive—a warm, lingering fragrance that adds a sharp metallic and floral note to the dish.

Star Anise

This star-shaped wonder comes from the Illicium verum tree, native to the lush landscapes of southern China and northern Vietnam. For centuries, star anise has been a staple in both cuisines, gracing dishes as well as traditional medicine practices. Its journey to European kitchens began in the 17th century, courtesy of explorers and traders who were enthralled by its unique shape and potent flavour. It then quickly became a sought-after commodity, finding its way into both culinary creations and medicinal remedies.[28]

Legends tell a tale of a divine gift bestowed upon humanity by the gods. In traditional Chinese culture, the star anise is a symbol of protection and good fortune. It is sometimes incorporated into religious ceremonies and offerings, representing the blessings of the deities.[29]

Star anise has a strong, sweet and licorice-like taste, similar to aniseed but with an extra kick. This intensity comes from a high concentration of anethole, a key aromatic compound. Its powerful flavour makes it a key ingredient in Chinese five-spice powder and the soul-warming Vietnamese soup, pho.[30] Its versatility extends beyond savoury dishes, as star anise can also enhance the flavours of sweet treats. It is my absolute favourite spice.

Tamarind (Imli)

Tamarind literally means 'Tamr-e-Hind' (date of India). Despite the name, it isn't actually related to dates! While its origins are believed to be in East Africa, tamarind has become a beloved ingredient throughout India, Southeast Asia and the West Indies, where its unique sour flavour adds a delightful twist to various cuisines.[31]

The key element of this fruit is a dark brown, dry pod containing a fleshy pulp inside. Imagine a cinnamon-coloured pod with a dark brown, almost black, fleshy centre surrounding small black seeds. This pulp is where the magic happens!

The flavour profile of tamarind is unlike any other— between sweet, sour and fruity notes, it has a sharp and fruity taste with a molasses-like sweetness. To top it all off, there's a hint of acidity that adds a touch of complexity.

Turmeric (Haldi)

Nicknamed the 'Indian saffron' for its golden hue, turmeric boasts a flavour profile that's as captivating as its history. The name itself is believed to have originated from the Latin 'terra merita', meaning 'merit of the earth', hinting at the value this spice has held for centuries.

Marco Polo, the famous explorer, was intrigued by turmeric during his travels to Southern China. He described it as a vegetable with the 'properties of true saffron, as well the smell and the colour', while acknowledging that it wasn't actually saffron.[32]

The use of turmeric stretches back far in time, with its mentions dating back to 1500 BCE in the Vedas, the sacred Hindu scriptures.[33] Here, it was referred to as 'haridra'. An essential ingredient in Indian cuisine, it adds both colour and flavour to curries, stews and sauces. Its influence extends beyond India, finding a prominent place in Southeast Asian cooking as well.

In the Indian subcontinent, turmeric holds a special place, revered for its symbolic association with fertility. Wedding ceremonies often incorporate a haldi ceremony, where both bride and groom are adorned with turmeric paste.

But turmeric isn't just about aesthetics. Fresh turmeric boasts a vibrant orange flesh and an intriguing aroma that combines musky and earthy notes with hints of ginger, black pepper and a touch of bitterness. This unique fragrance can fade over time and with exposure to light, so it's best to store turmeric carefully to preserve its flavour potential.

BIRYANI

෨

BIRYANI IS AN EMOTION FOR MANY I KNOW ACROSS the world. It, for sure, is poetry in my family. If biryani was jazz music, my mother was the maestro and spices were the artists playing various chords. She made the best biryani in the world, and I would like to believe I come second. For those who are ignorant or live far off in the world outside the Indian subcontinent, it is my duty to describe biryani. A popular and flavourful South Asian dish, it is made with aromatic spices, rice and meat or vegetables and known for its rich and complex flavours. The exact ingredients and preparation methods can vary widely depending on the region and personal preferences, leading to numerous regional variations of biryani. And this is exactly what this entire book is all about. There are so many different ways to cook biryani—you can change the rice, mix up a few spices and meat, and get a completely new version of the dish.

In Bihari weddings, biryani was never considered the go-to dish—if you had to serve good food, it had to be pulao, mutton qaliya or korma. Biryani was always looked down upon in many traditional families. The main dish with an intricate nature was Murgh Musallam—a whole bird stuffed with fried onion, poppy seeds and dry fruits, and grilled to perfection. This requires tricks and techniques and hence, to impress the *baraat*,* one would always serve this. I would always put

---

* The groom's procession.

Ammi's biryani, unique to our home, at the pinnacle. The one that she made or the one that I cook at home is inspired from many places but it is our *ghar ki biryani*. Though it has potatoes, it is not like the Kolkata biryani (we like it a little spicy); you can call it a Hyderabadi version, but frankly, it is just a homely biryani.

In my first book, I stayed away from biryani because I wanted to focus on other dishes, their history and anecdotal stories. But as destiny had it, biryani became the basis on which I reached out to the publishers to secure the contract. After all, biryani is love. When asked what the two dishes I love to serve my friends and guests are, I say 'biryani,' and, the second dish is in the 11th chapter. Hint: it sounds similar to *aadaab*. After all, every food has its own *aadaab-e-mu'aasharat*.*

If you are from northern India, there is a high likelihood that you prefer a long-grain rice biryani. If you are from Lucknow, you would consider your version of biryani to be the best, with its delicate flavour, aroma and tender meat rendering more flavour to the entire eating experience, and can write a 10-volume book on biryani. Nawab Mirza Jafar Hussain writes in his book, *Lucknow Ka Dastarkhwan*,'. . . *Biryani Dilli se yahan aayi aur shiddat ke saath napasand hui. Isko behtar banane ki mutadad kosha shaheen shahi daur mein ki gayi thi aur uss jawab mein uss se behtar pulao tayyar hue the.*' (People really didn't like the biryani that came from Delhi. A lot of work went into making it better during the time of the royal Mughals and, as a result, even better pulaos were made.)[1]

Lucknow is also a city renowned for its culinary creativity, as evidenced by two unique biryani variants that grace its tables. One such variant is imbued with the sweet aroma of jasmine, a subtle yet distinct fragrance achieved through the addition of a few carefully measured drops of jasmine essence, resulting in the exquisite 'motiya ki biryani'. The

---

* Etiquettes and mannerisms.

other biryani which I found interesting at a friend's house in Lucknow (and later saw in a book by Pratibha Karan) was ananas or pineapple biryani, a blend of tradition and tropical zest.[2] Tender pieces of mutton are lovingly marinated in a mixture that sings of the subcontinent's flavours—a paste made from fresh ginger, garlic and fiery chillies, combined with the freshness of coriander and mint leaves, the crunch of thinly sliced onions, and the tang of whisked curd, all brought together with the sweet, juicy chunks of pineapple. This medley is left to intermingle for a brief interlude, allowing each flavour to be fully embraced by the meat. This biryani has a mildly sweet flavour to it, but imagine it as a surprise pack that you would get when you dive into the biryani. This flavour reminds me of the biryani I make—I usually add dried apricot, which my family loves because it gives a kick of sweetness while they are chewing on the spicy biryani and lifts the flavour.

But if you are from Hyderabad, as the stereotype goes, you might be waking up with a biryani plate on your side and sleeping with another biryani next to you. The sun and moon may be witnesses to your love for biryani.

It is easy to find the origin story of biryani but people still get confused and assume that the Mughals introduced it to India—which is true and false at the same. It is true because it was during the Mughal realm but false if you assume this dish to have come during Abu'l-Fath Jalal-ud-din Muhammad Akbar or simply Emperor Akbar's time.

The common history of biryani points us to Mehr-un-Nissa, popularly known as Noorjahan, wife of Khurram, popularly known as Shah Jahan. One day, she was roaming in her barracks in Agra. When she noticed that her army was very skinny, she doubted if they could actually fight. She then ordered her chief cook to create a dish that would be easy for soldiers to carry and also had all the necessary elements to bulk up and fight the war. Lo and behold, we had biryani! One perspective suggests that the term 'biryani' stems from 'birinj', the Persian term for rice. Another viewpoint proposes that it evolved from 'biryan' or 'beriyan', Persian for 'to fry' or 'to roast'. This is fitting, considering biryani's preparation often involves roasting rice with fried onions and meat seasoned with subtle spices. An alternate association links it to 'bereshtan', a Persian word meaning 'to roast [onions]', aligning with the dish's typical cooking process.

However, even though this story has more masala and layers (pun intended), it is not necessarily true. In a conversation with me, Neha Vermani, a historian of early modern South Asia, particularly the Mughal Empire and regional kingdoms, shared that a dish similar to Zer biryani existed before the Mughal rule started in the Indian subcontinent. She went on to say, 'in the Safavid cookbook, this dish exists so there is a high likelihood that it travelled to India, but pulao was always put as a superior dish and could be the reason why biryani was not necessarily popular in that era.'[3] Many food and cultural historians also point out that references to biryani only appear around the 18th century. Salma Husain, a food historian and author, translated *Nuskha-e-Shahjahani*, which mentions a few biryani recipes including Zer biryani noormahali (vegetarian paneer biryani).[4] This also puts a stop to the age-old argument that vegetarian biryani is not biryani.

Vermani points out that the version of biryani that exists in Iran uses herbs like dill, coriander and other fresh grass to add flavour, while the Indian version relies more on spices like cinnamon, cardamom, etc. But it is very different from the one we have now. Perhaps, back then, it was only 6–7 types but now it could go all the way to 25–30 as well.

If we go back in time, author Nilanjan Hajra documents a story from 200 CE in the region now known as Tamil Nadu, where there is mention of a dish resembling today's recipe.[5] The 5 great epics of Tamil literature, penned between 100–1000 CE, talk about 'Oon Soru'. Modern food lovers will note its striking resemblance to the contemporary Dindigul Thalakapatti biryani. This culinary delight has journeyed from the north to the south with key ingredients like fine rice, mutton, ghee, ginger, cinnamon, coriander and coconut milk.

In an online lecture, Salma Husain says that during the 16th and 17th centuries, biryani was a signature dish of Isfahan, the Persian capital.[6] The classic version was made with fire-roasted lamb, cut into small chunks, seasoned with herbs and cooked over an open flame. This roasted meat was then tucked into layers of delicate bread and presented for consumption. I recall a similar dish I had at SodaBottleOpenerWala, a Parsi restaurant in Delhi's Khan Market, with a triangular paratha and juicy, shredded meat on top with caramelized onion, chutney and other condiments. They also called it Irani biryani.

In modern times, biryani has taken on many forms throughout India, becoming a national favourite with over 100 variations. From Hyderabad's buzzing lanes to the regal kitchens of Awadh, and down to Kerala and Kolkata, everyone continues to search for the perfect biryani recipe.

In Kerala, you might taste the Malabar version, which often uses fish or prawns instead of meat, with bold spices. West Bengal offers the Dhakai biryani, possibly influenced by the sea traders. The Bohri biryani on the West Coast is known for its gentler flavour that appeals to many. In Delhi, the Moradabadi biryani has made a comeback, while in Rajasthan, a special biryani is prepared for pilgrims at the Ajmer Sharif shrine, similar to the Matka Peer biryani in Delhi. Each region adds its own twist.

Even though Vermani says that she can't conclude what rice was used during Shah Jahan's time, in modern times, we see long-grain basmati rice listed almost everywhere. In her book, *Sehat Bakhsh Dastarkhwan* (1996),[7] Parveen Naaz suggests aged thin-grain rice, which you can think of as basmati rice, considering it is a long, aged and fine rice variety. Another tip she gives is how the biryani rice should be. She writes, '*Chawal chhidke hue rehna chahiye aur salone ho.*' (The rice grains should

5

be separate and white). I recall a similar nugget I received at Lucknow's famous Idrees biryani shop. I was told that when the rice is thrown on the floor, each grain should be separate. If they stick together, it is not good biryani.

Even though the biryani in south India is made with short-grain rice, I have noticed a change there as well. Many of the food joints are now moving to long-grain versions because that is what they are seeing online. Why should only the royals and politicians be allowed to make changes to our diet? These small restaurants can also do it.

In modern times, my favourite spice brand is Shan Masala (which is originally from Pakistan—India gets its share from Dubai). They have figured out a way to create spice mixes that are different from every other blend they have, whereas most Indian brand spices are either an upgraded version of garam masala or do not have the perfection that can add flavour to a cauldron of biryani.

If you follow the recipes below, you might be able to see the differences over time within the spices that were used from old books to different regions, houses and times.

Ammi's Biryani

Ingredients

Chicken: ½ kg
Basmati rice (soaked and boiled with the following spices): ½ kg
Black cardamom (badi elaichi): 2
Bay leaves (tej patta): 2
Star anise: 2
1-inch cinnamon stick
Cloves (laung): 6
Curd: ¾ cup
Potatoes, sliced, boiled and fried: 3
Ghee to cook: ¼ cup and an additional 3 tbsp
Onions, medium, sliced: 5
Ginger garlic paste: 1 tbsp

For the Spice Blend:
Bay leaf: 1
Black pepper (sabut kali mirch): 8–9
Star anise: 1
2-inch cinnamon sticks
Cloves: 4–5
Black cardamom: 1
Green cardamom (choti elaichi): 4
Red chilli powder: 1½ tsp
Turmeric (haldi) powder: ½ tsp
Cumin (jeera) powder: 1 tsp
Coriander (dhania) powder: 1 tsp
Garam masala powder: 1 tsp
Salt to taste

ADDITIONS

Green chillies: 4–5
Dried plums: 6
Mint leaves (pudina): 50 gm
Saffron (kesar): A pinch dissolved in 50 ml water
Biryani attar: 4–6 drops
Garam masala: 2 tsp

STEPS

1. Dry roast all the spices in the spice blend section, leaving garam masala and salt aside.
2. Let it rest and grind all the spices together, leaving the green cardamom and cinnamon sticks aside.
3. Mix the whole and the powdered spices with the dried plums, and your biryani masala is ready.
4. In a pot, add oil and the onions and fry until golden brown. Take out half the fried onions and set aside.
5. To the remaining fried onions, add ginger garlic paste and mix well.
6. Add and fry the chicken until it changes colour.
7. Add the biryani masala and whisked curd, and cook on a medium flame for 6–8 minutes.
8. Add slit green chillies and salt to taste.
9. Cover and cook for 8–10 minutes.
10. Take out half of the cooked chicken and set it aside.
11. Layer the chicken with rice on top, fried onions, chopped mint and coriander leaves, boiled potatoes, 1½ tbsp melted ghee and 1 tbsp garam masala. Repeat the process for the second layer.
12. Drizzle saffron-infused milk on top and the remaining gravy, if any.
13. Seal the lid with whole wheat flour dough or with aluminium foil and put the lid on. Put some heavy weight on top to keep the air sealed in the pot. Puncture five holes for the biryani to breathe in the pot.

14. Keep the dum on a low flame for 15 minutes.*
15. Take it off the flame and let it rest for 15 more minutes.
16. Serve hot.

Please note:

1. The grains of the biryani rice should not stick to each other.
2. Boil the rice only 70–80 per cent; don't cook it fully; and completely strain the water.
3. If you don't like whole spices, take them out of the rice pot after the rice is boiled.
4. Make a thick gravy; less gravy is better. More gravy will make the biryani rice lumpy and sticky.
5. Control the use of biryani (meetha) attar; it can make the biryani bitter. You can also use kewra or rose water.
6. A heavy-bottomed pan is advisable for making a delicious biryani—it will retain the flavour and the chicken in the bottom won't get burned or stuck to the bottom of the vessel. Alternatively, you can put the pot on the *tawa* or small skillet on a medium flame. The tawa will regulate the heat and cook or dum slowly.
7. Curd raita goes best with biryani, along with freshly cut onion and cucumber slices.
8. In general, the qorma for biryani is made with only curd, but many recipes also ask for tomatoes.
9. The above recipe is a template; you can use the same process to switch the meat of your choice or vegetables.
10. Mentioned below are the spice blends from different locations that can be tried while still sticking to the template given above.

---

* Dum cooking is a method where food is sealed in a pot and simmered slowly over a low flame, allowing the flavours to meld beautifully over time. The word 'dum' literally means 'to steam' or 'breathe', reflecting the gentle cooking process. While it's a staple in Mughlai cuisine, its roots go back to Persian and Central Asian kitchens.

Purani Dilli's Deghi Biryani

Ingredients

Bay leaves: 2
Cinnamon sticks: 2
Black cardamom: 1
Green cardamom: 4
Star anise: 1
Cloves: 4
Black pepper: 6–8
Salt to taste

Additions

Green chilli pickle: 2 tbsp
Rose water: 1 tsp
Kewra water
Yellow or orange food colour

Steps

1. Gather all the whole spices and make sure they are clean and dry.
2. If desired, lightly roast the whole spices (except salt) on a low flame for about 2–3 minutes until fragrant.
3. Allow the spices to cool, then grind them in a spice grinder or mortar and pestle until fine.
4. Add salt to the ground spice mixture and stir well to ensure even blending.
5. Store the blend in an airtight container in a cool, dark place. The blend can be kept for up to 6 months for the best flavour.

Note: No tomatoes are to be used in the gravy.

Awadhi Biryani

Ingredients

Cardamom: 8
Cloves: 4
1-inch cinnamon stick
Nutmeg (jaiphal): ¼ tsp
Chilli powder: 3 tsp
Mace powder (javitri): ¼ tsp
Garam masala: 2 tbsp
Salt to taste

Additions

Saffron: A pinch dissolved in 50 ml water
Biryani attar: 4–6 drops

Steps

1. Gather all the ingredients, ensuring they are clean and dry.
2. Dry roast the whole spices (cardamom, cloves, cinnamon) on a low flame for about 2–3 minutes, if desired, to enhance the aroma.
3. Once the roasted spices have cooled, grind them into a fine powder using a spice grinder or mortar and pestle.
4. Mix the pre-ground spices (nutmeg, chilli powder, mace powder, garam masala, and salt) until evenly combined.
5. Store in an airtight container in a cool, dark place for up to 6 months to retain freshness.

Note: No tomatoes are to be used in the gravy.

Bohri Biryani

Ingredients

Black cardamom: 2
Green cardamom: 3
Cloves: 6
Black pepper: 6–8
1-inch cinnamon stick
Nutmeg: ¼ tsp
Mace powder: ¼ tsp
Nigella seeds (shahi jeera): 2 tsp
Salt to taste
Turmeric powder: ½ tsp
Red chilli powder: 1 tbsp
Garam masala powder: 2 tbsp

Additions

Saffron: A pinch, dissolved in 50 ml water
Kewra water: 1 tsp
Mint leaves: 50 gm
Coriander leaves: 50 gm

Steps

1. Collect all the spices and ensure they are clean and dry.
2. Dry roast the whole spices (cardamom, cloves, black pepper, cinnamon, caraway seeds) for 2–3 minutes on low heat until aromatic.
3. Allow the spices to cool, then grind them to a fine powder.
4. Add the remaining powdered spices (nutmeg, mace, turmeric, chilli powder, garam masala and salt) and mix well.

5. Store the blend in an airtight container in a cool, dark spot. The blend stays fresh for up to 6 months.

Note: No tomatoes are to be used in the gravy.

Chettinad Biryani I

Ingredients

Green cardamom: 6
Cloves: 8
Black pepper: 6
1-inch cinnamon stick
Nutmeg: ¼ tsp
Bay leaves: 2
Salt to taste
Red chilli powder: 1½ tbsp

Additions

Green chillies, chopped: 6–8

Steps

1. Gather the whole spices and ensure they are clean and dry.
2. Optionally, dry roast the whole spices (cardamom, cloves, black pepper, cinnamon, bay leaves) on low heat for 2–3 minutes until aromatic.
3. Let the spices cool and grind them to a fine powder.
4. Mix the nutmeg, salt, and red chilli powder to ensure everything is evenly incorporated.
5. Store the spice blend in an airtight jar in a cool, dark place for up to 6 months.

Note: Cook this Chettinad biryani with 8 tomatoes and 2 cups of coconut milk

Coimbatore Biryani

Ingredients

Cloves: 8
Green cardamom: 6
2-inch cinnamon stick
Green chillies: 5
Turmeric powder: 1 tsp
Salt to taste

Additions

Lemon juice: 2 tbsp
Mint leaves: 30–50 gm
Coriander leaves: 30–50 gm

Steps

1. Collect all the ingredients and ensure they are clean and dry.
2. Dry roast the cloves, cardamom, and cinnamon for about 2–3 minutes on low heat if desired.
3. Let the spices cool, then grind them to a fine powder.
4. Add the turmeric powder and salt, and mix well until everything is evenly combined.
5. Store the blend in an airtight container away from direct sunlight for up to 6 months.

Note: Cook this Coimbatore biryani with 3 tomatoes and 2 cups of milk.

Katchi Memoni Biryani

Ingredients

Green cardamom: 6
Cloves: 6
Black pepper: 6
½-inch cinnamon sticks: 6
Red chilli powder: 3 tsp
Turmeric powder: ½ tsp
Green chillies, slit: 6
Salt to taste

Additions

Lemons, juiced: 2
Saffron: A pinch dissolved in 50 ml water
Mint leaves: ½ cup
Coriander leaves: 1 cup
Fresh coconut, ground to paste: ½ cup

Steps

1. Gather all the whole spices and ensure they are clean and dry.
2. Optionally, dry roast the whole spices (cardamom, cloves, pepper, cinnamon) on low heat for 2–3 minutes until fragrant.
3. Once cool, grind the whole spices to a fine powder.
4. Mix the chilli powder, turmeric, and salt to ensure everything is evenly incorporated.
5. Store in an airtight container in a cool, dark area for up to 6 months.

Hyderabadi Biryani

Ingredients

Bay leaf: 1
Red chilli powder: 1 tsp
Nigella seeds: ½ tsp
Black pepper: ½ tsp
Green cardamom: 5
Cloves: 6
2-inch cinnamon sticks
Mace blades: 3
Green chillies: 8
Salt to taste

Additions

Lemons, juiced: 2
Saffron: A pinch dissolved in 50 ml water
Coriander leaves: ⅓ cup
Mint leaves: ¼ cup
4 tbsp of cashew nut, musk and melon seeds and dry coconut paste can be used in the gravy.
If preparing *kacchi* gosht biryani, marinate meat in 2 tbsp of raw papaya paste for 24 hours.

Steps

1. Gather all the ingredients, ensuring they are clean and dry.
2. Dry roast the whole spices (bay leaf, caraway seeds, pepper, cardamom, cloves, cinnamon, mace blades) on low heat for 2–3 minutes if desired.
3. Let the spices cool completely, then grind them to a fine powder.

4. Mix the red chilli powder and salt, and stir well to ensure everything is evenly blended.
5. Store the blend in an airtight container in a cool, dark spot for up to 6 months.

Salem Biryani

Ingredients

Turmeric: 3 tsp
Bay leaves: 2
Cloves: 6–8
Green cardamom: 5
Star anise: 1
Poppy seeds (khus khus): 1 tbsp
Green chillies: 4
Garam masala: 1½ tbsp
Coriander powder: 1½ tbsp
1-inch cinnamon sticks
Red chilli powder: 1 tsp
Salt to taste

Additions

Lemons, juiced: 2
Mint leaves: ¼ cup
To be cooked with 2 tomatoes

Steps

1. Collect all the ingredients and make sure they are clean and dry.
2. Optionally, dry roast the whole spices (bay leaves, cloves, cardamom, star anise, cinnamon stick, poppy seeds) on low heat for 2–3 minutes until aromatic.

3. Let the spices cool, then grind them to a fine powder.
4. Add the remaining powdered spices (turmeric, garam masala, coriander powder, chilli powder, and salt), and mix well.
5. Store in an airtight container in a cool, dry place for up to 6 months.

Ambur Biryani

Ingredients

Bay leaf: 2
Cloves: 6–8
Green cardamom: 5
Coriander powder: 1½ tbsp
Red chilli powder: 2 tsp
Salt to taste

Additions

Mint leaves: ¼ cup
To be cooked with 2 tomatoes

Steps

1. Gather all the ingredients, ensuring they are clean and dry.
2. If desired, dry roast the bay leaves, cloves, and cardamom on low heat for 2–3 minutes until fragrant.
3. Allow the roasted spices to cool, then grind them to a fine powder.
4. Mix in the coriander powder, red chilli powder, and salt, and stir until evenly combined.
5. Store the blend in an airtight container in a cool, dark place for up to 6 months.

Calcutta Biryani

Ingredients

Bay leaf: 1
Cloves: 6
Black pepper: 1 tsp
1-inch cinnamon stick
Yellow chilli powder: 3 tsp
Nigella seeds: ½ tsp
Calcutta garam masala: 1½ tbsp
Salt to taste

Additions

Cooked with medium-sized sliced, boiled and fried potatoes.
Dried plums should be used for a tangy flavour.
Saffron: A pinch dissolved in 50 ml water
Mint leaves: ¼ cup

Steps

1. Gather all the ingredients and ensure they are clean and dry.
2. Optionally, dry roast the whole spices (bay leaf, cloves, black pepper, cinnamon stick, caraway seeds) on low heat for 2–3 minutes to bring out their aroma.
3. Let the spices cool, then grind them into a fine powder.
4. Add the yellow chilli powder, garam masala and salt, and mix well.
5. Store the blend in an airtight container in a cool, dark spot for up to 6 months.

Bihar Biryani (Eastern)

Ingredients

Poppy seed paste: 1 cup
Green chilli paste: ⅓ cup
Black pepper powder: 1 tsp
Bay leaf: 1
Cloves: 6
2-inch cinnamon stick
Cumin seeds (jeera): 1 tsp
Green cardamom: 4
Salt to taste

Steps

1. Collect all the ingredients and make sure they are clean and dry.
2. Dry roast the whole spices (bay leaf, cloves, cinnamon stick, cumin seeds, cardamom) on low heat for 2–3 minutes until aromatic.
3. Allow the spices to cool, then grind them into a fine powder.
4. Mix in the poppy seed paste, green chilli paste, black pepper powder, and salt, ensuring everything is well incorporated.
5. Store the blend in an airtight container in the refrigerator for up to 1 month due to the wet ingredients.

Aloo Bukhara Biryani

Ingredients

Chilli powder, roughly ground: 1 tsp
Kabab chini: 12
Bay leaf: 2

Cloves: 6
2-inch cinnamon stick
Green cardamom: 4
Salt to taste

ADDITIONS

Cooked with medium-sized, sliced, boiled and fried potatoes.
Dried plums should be used for a tangy flavour.
Mint leaves: ¼ cup

STEPS

1. Gather all the ingredients and ensure they are clean and dry.
2. Dry roast the whole spices (kabab chini, bay leaf, cloves, cinnamon stick, cardamom) on low heat for 2–3 minutes.
3. Allow the roasted spices to cool completely before grinding them to a fine powder.
4. Add the chilli powder and salt, and mix well to create a uniform blend.
5. Store the blend in an airtight container in a cool, dark place for up to 6 months.

SINDHI BIRYANI

INGREDIENTS

Coriander seeds: 1 tbsp
Bay leaf: 1
Black cardamom: 1
Black pepper powder: 1 tbsp
Fennel seeds (saunf): 1 tsp
Dried red chillies: 2
2-inch cinnamon stick

Garam masala: ½ tsp
Salt to taste

ADDITIONS

Dried plums should be used for a tangy flavour.
Mint and coriander leaves: ¼ cup
To be cooked with 2 tomatoes.

STEPS

1. Gather all the whole spices and ensure they are clean and dry.
2. Dry roast the coriander seeds, bay leaf, black cardamom, fennel seeds, dried red chillies, and cinnamon stick on low heat for 2–3 minutes until fragrant.
3. Let the spices cool, then grind them to a fine powder.
4. Add the black pepper powder, garam masala, and salt, and mix well until evenly combined.
5. Store the blend in an airtight container in a cool, dry place for up to 6 months.

KHOJA BIRYANI

INGREDIENTS

Red chilli paste: 80–100 gm
Cumin seeds: 2 tsp
1-inch cinnamon stick
Green cardamom: 8
Black cardamom: 2
Cloves: 3
Turmeric powder: ½ tsp
Coriander powder: ½ tsp
Salt to taste

Adjust the chilli paste as per your taste.
Rose water: 2 tsp

STEPS

1. Gather all the ingredients, ensuring they are clean and dry.
2. Dry roast the whole spices (cumin seeds, cinnamon stick, green cardamom, black cardamom, cloves) on low heat for about 2–3 minutes until aromatic.
3. Allow the spices to cool, then grind them into a fine powder.
4. Add the red chilli paste, turmeric powder, coriander powder, and salt, and mix well until all ingredients are evenly combined.
5. Store the blend in an airtight container in the refrigerator for up to 1 month due to the wet chilli paste.

BOMBAY BIRYANI

INGREDIENTS

Bay leaf: 1
Turmeric powder: 1 tsp
Red chilli powder: 1 tbsp
Turmeric powder: 1 tbsp
Coriander powder: 1 tbsp
Cloves: 6–8
Green cardamom: 6–8
Carom seeds (ajwain): 1 tsp
Fenugreek leaves (kasuri methi): 2 tbsp
Dried mango powder (aamchur): 1 tbsp
Black pepper powder: 1 tbsp
Salt to taste

ADDITIONS

Dried plums should be used for a tangy flavour.
Potatoes, boiled and peeled
Mint and coriander leaves: ¼ cup
To be cooked with 2 tomatoes.

STEPS

1. Gather all the ingredients and make sure they are clean and dry.
2. Dry roast the whole spices (bay leaf, cloves, cardamom, carom seeds) on low heat for 2–3 minutes if desired.
3. Allow the roasted spices to cool, then grind them to a fine powder.
4. Add the turmeric powder, red chilli powder, coriander powder, fenugreek leaves, dried mango powder, black pepper powder, and salt, and mix well until everything is combined.
5. Store the blend in an airtight container in a cool, dark place for up to 6 months.

LUCKNOWI PINEAPPLE BIRYANI

INGREDIENTS

Pineapple (ananas), cut in ½ inches: ⅔ cup
Poppy seeds paste: 50 gm
Bay leaf: 1
Green cardamom: 2
2-inch cinnamon stick
Cloves: 4
Nutmeg, crushed/powdered: ⅛ tsp
Mace blades: 3
Nigella seeds: ½ tsp

Steps

1. Gather all the ingredients, ensuring they are clean and dry.
2. Dry roast the whole spices (bay leaf, cardamom, cinnamon stick, cloves, mace blades, caraway seeds) on low heat for 2–3 minutes if desired to enhance the flavour.
3. Allow the roasted spices to cool, then grind them to a fine powder.
4. Add the nutmeg and mix well to ensure everything is evenly incorporated.
5. Store the blend in an airtight container in a cool, dark spot for up to 6 months.

Motiyon ki Biryani

Ingredients

Fresh bay leaves: 2
Cloves: 4–5
Green cardamom: 4
2-inch cinnamon stick
Yellow chilli powder: 1½ tsp
Nutmeg, crushed/powdered: ¼ tsp
Mace blades: 3

Additions

Use green chillies for extra flavour.
Adding half a cup of fresh cream while cooking the meat will enrich the flavour and give it a creamy texture.
Mint and coriander leaves: ¼ cup
Saffron, soaked in warm milk: 1 tsp
Jasmine essence: 2 drops

1. Collect all the ingredients and ensure they are clean and dry.
2. Dry roast the whole spices (bay leaves, cloves, cardamom, cinnamon stick, mace blades) on low heat for 2–3 minutes if desired.
3. Allow the spices to cool, then grind them into a fine powder.
4. Mix in the yellow chilli powder,
5. Nutmeg, and saffron (soaked in milk), ensuring all ingredients are evenly combined.
6. Store the blend in an airtight container in a cool, dark place for up to 6 months.

Dum Biryani

Ingredients

Red chilli powder: 2 tsp
Turmeric powder: 1 tsp
Garam masala: 1½ tsp
Raw papaya paste: 1 tbsp
Muskmelon and poppy seed paste: 5 tbsp
Cloves: 4–5
Nutmeg, crushed/powdered: ¼ tsp
Mace blades, crushed: ½ tsp
Star anise: 2
Saffron, soaked in warm milk: 1 tsp
Kewra water: 2 tbsp

Additions

This version of biryani in Lucknow is cooked in tomato paste and not necessarily in curd (but I cook it in curd).

An extra sprinkle of Lazzat-e-taam (refer to p. 321) spice mix will add more flavour to the dish.

STEPS

1. Gather all the ingredients and ensure they are clean and dry.
2. Dry roast the whole spices (cloves, star anise) on low heat for 2–3 minutes if desired.
3. Let the roasted spices cool, then grind them to a fine powder.
4. Mix in the chilli powder, turmeric powder, garam masala, nutmeg, crushed mace blades, raw papaya paste, muskmelon and poppy seed paste, saffron, and screw pine water, ensuring an even blend.
5. Store the blend in an airtight container in the refrigerator for up to 1 month due to the wet ingredients.

DILLI MATKA PEER KI BIRYANI

INGREDIENTS

Green cardamom: 10
Cloves: 10
Bay leaves: 4
2-inch cinnamon sticks
Black pepper: 1 tsp
Dried red chillies, whole: 8
Kashmiri chilli powder: 1½ tsp

ADDITIONS

This version of biryani uses long-grain *sella** rice.

---

* A type of parboiled rice (which means it has been partially boiled in its husk).

Instead of saffron, it asks for a yellow food colour.
Add green chillies for extra flavour.

1. Gather all the ingredients and ensure they are clean and dry.
2. Optionally, dry roast the whole spices (green cardamom, cloves, bay leaves, cinnamon stick, black pepper, and dried red chillies) on low heat for 2–3 minutes until aromatic.
3. Let the spices cool completely, then grind them into a fine powder using a spice grinder or mortar and pestle.
4. Mix in the Kashmiri chilli powder, ensuring the blend is even and well combined.
5. Store the blend in an airtight container in a cool, dark place for up to 6 months to maintain freshness.

HOME-MADE BIRYANI

INGREDIENTS

Bay leaves: 5
Kashmiri red chillies*: 4
Mace: 3 blades
Green cardamom: 10
Black cardamom: 3
Star anise: 3
Coriander seeds: 2 tbsp
2-inch cinnamon stick
Nutmeg, whole: 1
Cumin seeds: 1 tbsp
Cloves: 2 tsp
Black pepper: 1 tbsp

---

* Kashmiri is for colour mostly, while red chilli is usually for the heat.

Mint leaves, dried: ¼ cup
Fennel seeds: 1 tsp
Turmeric: ½ tsp
Saffron: 1 pinch

STEPS

1. Dry roast Kashmiri red chillies, bay leaves, coriander seeds, cumin seeds, mace, cinnamon stick, nutmeg, cloves, black cardamom, star anise, green cardamom, black pepper and fennel seeds on the pan. It should take about 3–5 minutes.
2. Remove the roasted spices from the pan and let them cool completely. Once cooled, transfer them to a spice grinder.
3. Add dried mint leaves, turmeric and saffron to the grinder. Grind all the ingredients together to a fine powder.
4. Store the biryani masala in an airtight container to maintain its freshness.
5. Use this freshly prepared biryani masala in your favourite biryani recipes to add a rich and aromatic flavour. Follow the specific biryani recipe instructions for the best results.

CHETTINAD BIRYANI 2

INGREDIENTS

1-inch cinnamon sticks: 6
Bay leaves: 10
Cloves: 1 tbsp
Green cardamom: 1 tbsp
Turmeric powder: 1 tbsp
Garam masala powder: 1 tbsp

Saffron strands: 1 tsp
Guntur chillies: 6–8

1. Dry roast the whole spices (cinnamon sticks, bay leaves, cloves, chillies and green cardamom) until fragrant.
2. Allow the spices to cool, then grind them into a fine powder.
3. Add the turmeric powder, garam masala powder and saffron strands to the ground mixture. Mix thoroughly and store the blend in an airtight container.
4. Use this adjusted blend in your biryani recipe, following the cooking steps provided earlier. This spice blend will add a rich and aromatic flavour to your biryani.

CHETTINAD BIRYANI 3

INGREDIENTS

1-inch cinnamon sticks: 3
Cloves: 1 tbsp
Black pepper: 1 tbsp
Star anise: 3
Black cardamom: 3
Bay leaves: 4
Garam masala powder: 2 tbsp

STEPS

1. Dry roast cinnamon sticks, cloves, black pepper, star anise, black cardamom and bay leaves until fragrant. Let the spices cool, then grind them into a fine powder.
2. Add garam masala powder to the ground mixture and mix thoroughly.

3. Store the blend in an airtight container.
4. This biryani masala is suitable for 1 kg of meat. Use 4–6 tbsp of this blend along with the tomatoes and coconut milk mentioned in the gravy ingredients to add a rich and aromatic flavour to your biryani. Follow the rest of the cooking steps from your biryani recipe.

TEEVANJI'S BIRYANI

INGREDIENTS

Mixed kidneys and liver: 250 gm
Salt: 2 tsp (or to taste)
Mutton with bones: 250 gm
Long-grained rice: 2 cups
Ghee or oil: 1 cup
Green cardamom: 4
Cloves: 4
Bay leaves: 4
Red chilli powder: 1 tbsp
Brandy (optional): ¼ cup
Coriander–cumin powder: 1 tbsp
Garam masala powder: 1 tsp
Orange, red and green food colour (optional): A few drops
Saffron strands soaked in 2 tbsp hot milk: ½ tsp

For the Paste:
Onions, large, minced: 2
Ginger paste: 1 tbsp
Garlic paste: 1 tbsp
Green chillies, roughly chopped: 4
Coriander leaves, chopped: ½ cup
Mint leaves, chopped: ¼ cup

For the Marinade:
Curd, whisked: 1 cup
Medium tomatoes, chopped: 4
Salt: ½ tsp (or to taste)

For Garnish:
Almonds (badam), blanched, peeled and sliced: 4 tbsp
Pistachio nuts, blanched, peeled and sliced: 4 tbsp
Rose petals, dried

STEPS

1. Thoroughly rinse the kidneys and liver under running water. Place them in a pan with 1 tsp salt and enough water to cover. Soak for 15 minutes. Drain and remove membranes, threads and fat. Rinse again, drain and pat dry. Cut into 1-inch cubes. Wash the mutton, drain, pat dry and cut into serving pieces.
2. In a bowl, mix the ground paste with the marinade. Add the kidneys, liver and mutton. Mix well, ensuring all pieces are coated. Marinate for about 5 hours.
3. Wash the rice thoroughly and soak it in water for 30 minutes.
4. Heat ghee or oil in a large pan over medium heat. Add whole spices (cinnamon, cloves, cardamom and bay leaves) and sauté until fragrant.
5. Add the marinated kidneys, liver and mutton, along with their marinade, to the pan. Add red chilli powder and brandy (if using). Cover and cook on low heat for 35–40 minutes, stirring occasionally, until the meat is tender and the gravy thickens.
6. In a separate pan, bring 4 cups of water and 1 tsp salt to a boil. Drain the soaked rice and add it to the boiling water. Cook until the rice is almost done and the water is absorbed.

7. Divide the cooked rice into four portions. If using food colours, mix each colour with about ¼ tsp water. Sprinkle the colours onto three portions of the rice and mix gently.

8. Grease a large pan. Layer the rice and meat mixture alternately, starting and ending with rice. Cover tightly with a lid. Cook on very low heat until the rice is fully cooked and dry. If the lid is not tight enough, cover the pan with aluminium foil before placing the lid. For even heating, place the pan on a tawa over low heat.

9. Transfer the biryani to a serving platter. Drizzle the soaked saffron and its liquid on top. Garnish with blanched almonds, pistachio nuts and rose petals. Serve hot with naan.

Kerala-Style Dum Biryani

Ingredients

1-inch cinnamon stick: 3
Green cardamom pods: 10
Cloves, whole: 8
Black pepper: 1 tsp
Bay leaves: 3

Steps

1. In a spice grinder or clean coffee grinder, combine the cinnamon stick, green cardamom pods, whole cloves, black pepper and dried bay leaves.

2. Grind these whole spices into a fine powder. Set the prepared spice blend aside.

3. In a large bowl, combine the chicken pieces, curd, 1 tsp of salt, red chilli powder, turmeric, about one-fourth of the fried onions and the prepared spice blend.

4. Stir well to coat the chicken evenly. Cover and refrigerate for 3–5 hours.

5. Use the marinated chicken and follow the rest of the biryani recipe steps to prepare the dish.

6. This spice blend will infuse your biryani with rich and aromatic flavours.

7. This spice blend is perfect for 1 kg (approximately 2 pounds) of chicken. Use 4–6 tbsp of this blend to obtain the best flavour.

Abdul Mastan's Biryani

Ingredients

Red chilli, whole: 50 gm
Coriander seeds: 2 tbsp
Cumin seeds: 1 tsp
Cloves: 4
Nutmeg, small, grated: ¼
Fennel seeds: ½ tsp
Black pepper (do not grind): ½ tsp
Green cardamom (do not grind): 3
Bay leaves (do not grind): 1½
Kewra (do not grind): ½ tsp
1-inch cinnamon sticks (do not grind): 2
Aloo bukhara (do not grind): 3

Steps

1. Heat a pan on high heat. Once it's moderately hot, reduce the flame to low. Add whole red chillies, cumin seeds, coriander seeds, cloves, nutmeg and fennel seeds. Dry roast on low heat for about 1–2 minutes until aromatic.

2. Transfer the roasted spices to a bowl and let them cool down completely. Grind the mixture to a fine powder.

3. Add black pepper, green cardamom, bay leaves, kewra, cinnamon sticks and aloo bukhara to the ground spice mix. Mix well to combine.

4. Store the spice blend in an airtight container. Use this blend as required in your recipes. For 1 kg of mutton, use 6–8 tbsp of this spice blend. Follow the cooking steps mentioned in the original recipe to prepare your dish.

BHATKAL BIRYANI

INGREDIENTS

Ginger powder (sonth): 2 tbsp
Garlic powder: 1 tbsp
Red chilli powder: 2 tbsp
Garam masala powder: 1 tsp
Turmeric powder: 1 tsp
Salt: 1½ tsp (or to taste)

STEPS

1. Dry roast cinnamon, cloves, bay leaves, black pepper, star anise seeds and black cardamom until fragrant. Grind the roasted spices into a fine powder.

2. Add the red chilli powder, garam masala, turmeric powder and salt to the ground spices. Mix well.

3. For this biryani, use the spices along with tomatoes and onions to cook the meat gravy and add chopped coriander leaves. You can also use fresh ginger garlic paste.

4. Further, use the cooked meat and follow the rest of the biryani recipe steps to prepare the dish.

Chef Kunal Kapur's Moradabadi Chicken Biryani[*]

Ingredients

Chicken, with bone: 1 kg
Salt to taste
Lemon juice: 3-4 tbsp
Green chilli paste: 2 tbsp
Ginger garlic paste: 2 tbsp
Fennel powder: 1 tbsp
Coriander powder: 2 tbsp
Javitri: 2–3 blades
Cinnamon sticks: 2
Bay leaves: 2
Black pepper: 10–12
Cardamom pods: 5
Cloves: 5
Nutmeg, small: ¼
Curd: 1 cup

For cooking:
Ghee/oil: 1 cup
Onions, sliced: 1½ cup
Water: 2½–3 cups (approx.)
Green chillies, slit: 5–6
Basmati rice: 2 cups
Salt to taste
Saffron: A pinch, dissolved (preferably in milk)

---

[*] Chef Kunal Kapur is an Indian chef and restaurateur known for hosting and judging *MasterChef India*.

Steps

1. Mix the chicken with salt, lemon juice, ginger garlic paste, curd, green chilli paste, javitri, star anise, bay leaf, nutmeg, black pepper, cloves, cardamom, cinnamon, coriander powder and fennel powder. Set aside for 30 minutes.
2. Heat oil in a *handi* (large pot) and add sliced onions. Fry until brown and then remove some for garnishing. Add slit green chillies to the remaining onions, followed by the marinated chicken. Cook on high heat for 2 minutes, then reduce the heat, cover and cook until the chicken is 80 per cent done. Do not add water.
3. Once the chicken releases oil, add water. Bring to a boil, adjust the salt and add the soaked rice. Cook on a high flame until it boils again, then reduce the heat, cover and cook until the rice absorbs all the water.
4. Garnish the rice with fried onions, ghee, kewra water and dissolved saffron. Serve hot with biryani raita.

Moradabadi Biryani 2

Ingredients

Ghee: 2 tbsp
Lime juice: 1 tbsp
Curd: ½ cup
Green chillies: 8–9
Garlic paste: 1 tbsp
Ginger paste: 1 tbsp
Black cumin seeds: ½ tsp
Bay leaves: 2
Cinnamon sticks: 2
Star anise: 1
Mace: 1 blade
Black cardamom: 2

Cardamom: 6
Black pepper: 1 tsp
Cloves: 12
Nutmeg, grated: ¼ tsp
Fennel powder: 1½ tsp
Coriander: 1 tsp
Salt: 1¼ tsp (or to taste)

STEPS

1. Dry roast black cumin seeds, bay leaf, cinnamon sticks, star anise, mace blade, black cardamom, cardamom, black pepper, cloves, nutmeg, fennel powder and coriander in a pan until fragrant.
2. Let the spices cool, then grind them into a fine powder.
3. Mix the ground spice blend with ghee, lime juice, curd, green chillies, garlic paste, ginger paste and salt. Add the chicken pieces and coat them well with the marinade.
4. Cover and refrigerate for at least 30 minutes, preferably overnight, for best results. For the detailed recipe, follow the steps mentioned above.

DHAKAIYA BIRYANI

INGREDIENTS

Nutmeg: 1
Mace: 2
Cloves: 6
White pepper: 1 tsp
1-inch cinnamon stick: 2
Green cardamom: 8
Black cardamom: 2
Bay leaves: 3

Cumin powder, roasted: 1 tbsp
Salt: 1 tsp (or to taste)

1. Take a heavy-bottomed pan and heat it on a low–medium heat.
2. Roast nutmeg, mace, cloves, white pepper, cinnamon sticks, green cardamom, black cardamom, bay leaves and roasted cumin powder until fragrant. Grind all the roasted spices into a fine powder.
3. Store the spice blend in an airtight container.
4. This spice blend is for 1 kg of mutton. Use 4–6 tbsp of this spice blend in the recipe. Follow the cooking steps from the recipe above, adjusting for mutton. Or, you can follow your own steps as well.

DINDIGUL MUTTON BIRYANI

INGREDIENTS

Coriander seeds: 2 tbsp
Cashew nut: 15
Cumin seeds: 1 tbsp
Stone flowers (kalpasi): 1½ tbsp
Cardamom: 8
Black pepper: 1 tbsp
Bay leaves: 4
Star anise: 3
1-inch cinnamon sticks: 2
Mace, whole: 1
Cloves: 10
Nutmeg, grated: 1
Fennel seeds: 1 tbsp

STEPS

1. Combine coriander seeds, cashew nuts, cumin seeds, stone flowers, cardamom, black pepper, bay leaves, star anise, cinnamon, mace, clove, nutmeg and fennel seeds. Grind into a fine powder.
2. Store the spice blend in an airtight container.
3. This spice blend is for 1 kg of mutton. Use 4–6 tbsp (or adjust based on your palette) of this spice blend in the recipe. Follow the cooking steps from the recipe above. Unique ingredients in this biryani include the use of stone flowers, cashew nuts and the final touch of banana leaf during cooking. This version is also cooked with Seeraga Samba rice.

DONNE BIRYANI

INGREDIENTS

Cinnamon sticks: 4–5
Cloves: 10–12
Cardamom: 5–6
Black pepper: ½ tbsp
Green chillies: 3–4
Onions, large, sliced: 2
Mint leaves: ½ handful
Coriander leaves: 1 large bunch
Fenugreek leaves: 1 small bunch
Red chilli powder: 2 tbsp
Turmeric powder: 1 tsp
Ginger garlic paste: 2 tbsp

STEPS

1. **Grind spices (1):** Heat oil in a pan and add cinnamon, cloves, cardamom, black pepper, green chillies and sliced onions. Fry till the onions are light brown, then grind to a smooth paste with water.

2. **Grind spices (2):** In the same pan, add oil, mint leaves, coriander leaves and fenugreek leaves. Fry lightly, then grind to a smooth paste with water.

3. Mix the chicken with chilli powder, turmeric, ginger garlic paste, curd and salt. Marinate for 30 minutes or overnight.

4. Heat oil, add the whole spices (from the 'to grind' list) and then add sliced onions. When the onions turn translucent, add ginger garlic paste, turmeric and the marinated chicken. Cook for 5–7 minutes on a medium flame.

5. Add the onion paste, mix well and then add the green paste. Cover and cook for 10 minutes on a medium flame. Add lemon juice and water, and bring to a boil.

6. Add soaked *jeerakasala* rice* to the boiling mixture. Cover tightly and cook on a low flame for 20 minutes until the rice is done.

7. Fluff with a fork, add ghee and let it sit for 5 minutes. Serve with boiled eggs and raita.

Notes: Fresh fenugreek leaves add a unique flavour and green colour. Adjust water based on the gravy's consistency. Use a neutral oil for cooking and add ghee for flavour at the end.

---

* Jeerakasala is a short-grain rice from southern India that's got a really distinct taste and smell. When cooked, it has a slightly sticky texture.

Padmaja Prashanthi's
Nagpur Biryani

Ingredients

Coriander seeds: 4 tbsp
Cumin seeds: 1 tbsp
Nigella seeds: 1 tbsp
Green cardamom: 4 tbsp
Black cardamom: 10–12
1-inch cinnamon stick: 6
Black pepper: 2 tbsp
Cloves: 2 tbsp
Dried fenugreek leaves: 2 tbsp
Turmeric: ½ tbsp
Mace: 5–6 blades
Nutmeg, small: ½
Byadgi dry chillies: 15
Bay leaves: 10
Salt: 2–3 pinches (or to taste)

Steps

1. Heat a pan on high heat. Once it's moderately hot, reduce the flame to low. Add coriander seeds, cumin seeds, caraway seeds, green cardamom, black cardamom, cinnamon, black pepper, cloves, dry fenugreek leaves, mace, byadgi dry chillies and bay leaves. Dry roast on low heat for about 1–2 minutes until aromatic.
2. Transfer the roasted spices to a bowl and let them cool down completely.
3. Once cooled, transfer the spices to a grinding jar. Add salt and turmeric. Grind the mixture coarsely.

4. Store the aromatic biryani masala in an airtight glass container. This masala can be used for various types of biryani such as chicken, mutton, egg or vegetable biryani, and it will stay fresh for 5–6 months.

Easy Calcutta Biryani

Ingredients

Yellow chilli powder: 2 tsp
Turmeric: 1 tsp
Red chilli powder: 4 tsp
Dried red chillies, broken: 10
Calcutta garam masala: 2 tsp
Nigella seeds: 2 tsp
Salt: 1 tsp (or to taste)

Steps

1. Heat a pan on high heat. Once it's moderately hot, reduce the flame to low. Add black and red chilli along with caraway seeds. Dry roast on low heat for about 1–2 minutes until aromatic.
2. Transfer the roasted spices to a bowl and let them cool down completely. Once cooled, transfer the spices to a grinding jar. Grind the mixture with all the powder spices to a fine powder.
3. Use this blend as required in your recipes. This is sufficient for 1 kg of meat. Follow the cooking steps mentioned in the original recipe to prepare your dish.

CHACHI'S BIHARI BIRYANI

INGREDIENTS

Chicken/mutton: 1 kg
Curd, whisked: 1 cup
Ginger paste: 2 tsp
Garlic paste: 2 tsp
Green chilli paste: ½ cup
Poppy seeds, toasted and paste: ½ cup
Black pepper powder: 1 tsp

For the rice:
Long-grain rice: 1 kg
Green cardamom: 6
1-inch cinnamon sticks: 2
Cloves: 6
Bay leaves: 4
Cumin seeds: 1½ tsp
Ghee: 3 tbsp
Oil: 4 tbsp
Salt: 1½ tsp (or to taste)

STEPS

1. Marinate the chicken with ginger paste, garlic paste, green chilli paste, poppy seeds, curd, pepper powder and salt. Set aside for 1 hour. Wash and soak the rice in water for about 20 minutes. Drain and set aside.

2. Heat oil in a heavy-bottomed pan. Add cardamom, cinnamon, cloves, bay leaves, cumin seeds and salt. After a few seconds, add the marinated chicken and stir until it boils. Cook until the oil separates and the chicken turns golden brown.

3. Add soaked rice to the chicken and fry for 2–3 minutes. Add water until it is about 1 inch above the rice and chicken. Add ghee.
4. Once it starts to boil, lower the heat, cover and cook for 15–20 minutes until the chicken and rice are fully cooked.
5. Serve hot with garlic and boondi raita.

Assamese Kampuri Biryani

Ingredients

Basmati rice: 2 cups
Bay leaves: 3
Green cardamom: 4
Black cardamom: 2
1-inch cinnamon stick
Cloves: 6
Salt to taste

For the Chicken:
Chicken, cut into medium pieces: 500 gm
Curd: 1 cup
Ginger paste: 2 tsp
Garlic paste: 2 tsp
Red chilli powder: 2 tsp
Turmeric powder: 1 tsp
Garam masala powder: 2 tsp
Salt: 1 tsp (or to taste)
Mustard oil: 4 tbsp

Other:
Potatoes, cut into halves: 2
Peas, frozen: 1 cup
Saffron: A few strands

Onions, finely sliced: 2
Oil for frying
Ghee: 2 tbsp
Coriander leaves: A handful

Steps

1. Combine the chicken with curd, ginger paste, garlic paste, red chilli powder, turmeric powder, garam masala powder, salt and mustard oil. Marinate for 2 hours.
2. Boil the basmati rice with bay leaves, green cardamom, black cardamom, cinnamon sticks, cloves and salt. Drain the rice and set aside.
3. Heat oil in a pan and fry the sliced onions until golden brown. Set aside. In the same oil, fry the marinated chicken for 5–7 minutes.
4. In a deep pan, layer fried chicken, cooked rice, fried onions, potatoes and peas.
5. Soak saffron strands in warm milk and pour over the rice. Pour the melted ghee on top of the rice, cover the pan tightly and cook on a low flame for 20 minutes.
6. Garnish with fresh coriander leaves and fried onions. Serve hot.

Ayemen Fatima's Hyderabadi Kacche Gosht ki Biryani

Ingredients

For the Masala 1:
Green cardamom: 2 tsp
Black pepper: 1½ tbsp
1-inch cinnamon stick: 4
Clove: 1½ tsp

Nigella seeds: 2½ tbsp
Dried red chillies: 2 tsp
Turmeric: ½ tsp
Red chilli powder: 1 tbsp

For the Masala 2:
Salt: 2 tsp (or to taste)
Turmeric: 1 tsp
Red chilli powder: 3

STEPS

1. Put all the spices from (1) in a grinder and make a fine powder of it. There is no need to pan-roast them before.
2. Use this mixture in 2 kg of meat.
3. When making the biryani, use 400–500 gm of whisked curd to marinate your meat with the spice blend (2) along with 1 tbsp ginger garlic paste, 1 tbsp green chilli paste and the juice of 2 lemons.

CHAI

~

WHILE MY PERSONAL PENCHANT IS FOR COFFEE, I must concede that the process of tea brewing and the conversations that spin around these hot, caffeinated beverages are captivating in a way that surpasses their counterparts. From the ancient alleyways to the chic new-age cafes, tea is a ubiquitous offering; in India, even a coffee shop would not find a request for masala chai out of place.

Globally, teas from the Indian subcontinent are lauded for their excellence; a label from India, Pakistan or Sri Lanka is a hallmark of quality, even in a distant European city. Yet, traditionally in India, children, myself included, were discouraged from consuming tea due to a prevalent belief that it darkens the skin—a notion rooted in the cultural preoccupation with fair complexion, linked to the idea that fairer skin confers advantages in life akin to the early bird securing the worm.

It wasn't until my mid-twenties that I experienced authentic chai in a roadside shop in Bhopal. It was a moment of sheer revelation—the rich, creamy taste enveloping my senses converted me into a chai aficionado. This new-found appreciation didn't eclipse my existing affection for coffee, affirming that one can indeed have dual allegiances.

In India, chai transcends mere refreshment; it is the essence of hospitality and a catalyst for connection, binding people together in every setting imaginable. The phrase '*Chalo chai ho jaye*' (Let's have tea) is not just an offer but an expression of communal spirit and inclusivity. It is a drink for no reason and every season. It is served in homes, board meetings, college canteens, cafes, weddings and *walimas.**

The Western introduction to tea may be traced back to the 17th century, with the Dutch East India Company's imports into Europe, and it was not until the 18th century that the English East India Company began significant imports from China. With the threat of losing their Chinese trade monopoly, the British endeavoured to cultivate tea within India.

In 1776, the famous botanist Sir Joseph Banks was asked to write up some notes on the same, and he said that India should start growing tea. A few years later in 1780, Robert Kyd (who later founded the botanical garden in Calcutta in 1787) tried growing tea in India using seeds from China. A little while after that, Robert Bruce (Scottish arms trader and mercenary soldier on the north–east frontier of India) found wild tea plants in the Brahmaputra Valley. Finally, 12 chests of Indian tea from Assam were shipped to England for sale in 1838.[1]

The cultivation initiatives gained traction following the end of the Chinese monopoly in 1833, culminating in the formation of the Assam Tea Company in 1839, which commenced marketing in Europe.

The British endeavoured to position tea as an aspirational commodity, a symbol of affluence or the aspiration towards it. In 1901, the viceroy of India, Lord Curzon, initiated a trial to popularize tea among Indians in specific regions. Despite achieving some level of success, this initiative was discontinued by 1904. The Indian Tea Association, established in 1881, reported in its yearly summary that the 3-year campaign had failed to produce satisfactory outcomes that would suggest a burgeoning market for tea in India. The entrenched cultural

---

* Wedding receptions in the Islamic tradition.

fondness for traditional drinks such as sharbats led to a reluctance among the populace to embrace tea.

It was the Anglophile 'bhadralok'—a new class of Bengali gentlefolk during British rule—who first adopted tea drinking in the latter half of the 19th century, a testament to the influence of British ideology on Indian society. Yet, through clever marketing tactics aimed at broadening its appeal, chai has transcended its origins as an imported custom to become a symbol of unity that bridges diverse cultural identities, shedding its image as a foreign imposition linked to colonial rule.[2]

Advertising strategies evolved, eventually framing chai as an indigenous product and countering its association with colonial enterprises. Philip Lutgendorf discusses in his essay, 'Making Tea in India: Chai, Capitalism, and Culture', how advertising initially targeted British residents and the aspiring Anglophone elite, portraying tea as the civilized product of a colonized land.[3] Despite these efforts, the domestic market remained small until the Great Depression, which shifted the focus towards the Indian consumer.

Philip Lutgendorf, in his essay for the academic journal *Thesis Eleven: Critical Theory and Historical Sociology,* mentions,

Advertising during the first three decades of the twentieth century [...] was largely aimed at resident Britishers and the Anglophone elite who aspired to their lifestyle. It celebrated tea as a natural product of a colonised and 'tamed' jungle, raised in geometrically arrayed and manicured 'gardens' and picked by dark-skinned, subaltern women, who offered it at a gleaming white table to equally white consumers. As long as the financial returns from the exports were profitable, there was little inducement to pursue a domestic market that would inevitably yield a lower return.

Promotional campaigns became more aggressive, with enamel signs and demonstrations at public gatherings illustrating the

British method of tea preparation. In scattered efforts, the Tea Cess Committee ventured to sow the taste for tea in public spaces, with Indian Railways at the heart of their campaign. Howrah's station, in the bustle of Calcutta, became a stage where complimentary cups of tea greeted hands while modest paper packets sold for a piece whispered of warm comforts unknown to the gavel's strike. There, amidst the steam and clatter, the British art of tea—a pour, a steep, a strain, softened by milk's sweetness and sugar's kiss—unfolded before travellers' eyes. Yet, as the 1930s dawned, tea's embrace had warmed but only a few, as India's harvest still sailed across seas, with nine-tenths bound for distant lands. The railway stations, markets and even mobile kettles in Bengal played pivotal roles in advertising tea. The adaptation of tea into Indian culture transformed it from a colonial import to a staple of domestic life, with local methods of preparation diverging significantly from the British approach, creating a new, distinctly Indian tradition of tea consumption. The British were horrified because they had failed to teach the Indians how to make the beverage the 'correct way'. However, in the end, that did not matter because now, when you look around, you don't just have one version of tea. Every state, city and house has its own version.

In fact, English Babus and brown sahibs were made to take mandatory tea breaks by the British to promote tea. A nation that was never addicted to tea but was more of a sharbat and kadha fan gave in and started enjoying this caffeinated brew. I would go as far as to say that we have more tea in our veins than blood, such is the fan base.

In a popular Hindi cult classic, *Andaz Apna Apna* (1994), Aamir Khan and Salman Khan share a cup of tea and say, '*Do dost ek pyaale mein chai piyenge, isse dosti badhti hai.*' (When friends drink tea in one cup, the friendship between them strengthens.) One could imagine the fandom for tea—from a nation that was far away from tea as a preferred choice of beverage to a nation that shares a relationship over a cup of tea.

Chai in India is not merely a beverage but a phenomenon that resonates through every aspect of society, from boardrooms to weddings, symbolizing unity and the overcoming of its colonial past to becoming an integral part of India's cultural fabric. The subcontinent chai connoisseurs would say it is not merely consumed but experienced, as each sip whispers the story of India, a tale as old as time, served in a vessel as humble as the earth from which it came.

Most Indian teas are made with spices—from ginger, cardamom, cinnamon to a range of spice blends—depending on geographical location, season and, of course, likeness. Many would just enjoy a strong milk tea with fresh ginger in it, while others, say in Gujarat, would like something else. I don't think one can point to a particular spice blend as the best one, and that is how it should be. While researching for this book, I travelled to many small and bigger towns, and picked up their spice blends. I picked one tea blend from Mahabaleshwar, another from Ahmedabad and one from Mumbai. I also picked up chai masala from INA Market and Khari Baoli in Delhi. One each from Kolkata, Kashmir and Kerala were also a must.

I think there is beauty in making fresh chai masala—even though you can surely make a powder of these spices, you may want to use it fresh when you are making your tea. Whether you want to add chai masala before you boil the tea or afterwards is a personal preference.

Winter Chai

Ingredients

Nutmeg, grated: 1 tbsp
Green cardamom: 2 tbsp
Cloves: 1 tsp
Tulsi Seeds: 5–6
Licorice root (mulethi): ½ tsp
Ginger powder: 2 tbsp
Cinnamon sticks, crushed: 2 tbsp
Black pepper: 1 tbsp

Steps

1. Transfer all the ingredients to a spice grinder or mortar and pestle. Grind to a fine powder.
2. In a large bowl, combine all the ground spices. Mix thoroughly to ensure even distribution.
3. Store the winter chai masala in an airtight container in a cool, dry place. Proper storage will maintain its freshness and potency for several months.

Special Winter Chai

Ingredients

Saffron: A pinch
Nutmeg, grated: 1 tbsp
Green cardamom: 3 tbsp
Cloves: 2 tsp
Tulsi leaves: 5–6
Licorice root (mulethi): ½ tsp
Ginger powder: 3 tbsp

Dried mint leaves: 3 tbsp
Fennel seeds: 3 tbsp
Black cardamom, crushed: 1
2-inch cinnamon sticks, crushed
Black pepper: 1 tbsp
Rose petals, dried: 2 tsp

STEPS

1. Transfer all the ingredients to a spice grinder or mortar and pestle. Grind to a fine powder.
2. In a large bowl, combine all the ground spices. Mix thoroughly to ensure even distribution.
3. Store the special winter chai masala in an airtight container in a cool, dry place. Proper storage will maintain its freshness and potency for several months.

SUMMER CHAI

INGREDIENTS

Green cardamom, with the shell on: ¼ cup
Fennel seeds: 2 tbsp
Cloves, whole: 2 tsp
Carom seeds (ajwain): 1 tsp
Ginger powder: 2 tsp
Cinnamon powder: ½ tsp
Black pepper: ½ tsp

STEPS

1. Transfer all the ingredients to a spice grinder or mortar and pestle. Grind to a fine powder.
2. In a large bowl, combine all the ground spices. Mix thoroughly to ensure even distribution.

3. Store the summer chai masala in an airtight container in a cool, dry place. Proper storage will maintain its freshness and potency for several months.

Special Summer Chai

Ingredients

Green cardamom, with the shell on: ¼ cup
Fennel seeds: 2 tbsp
Cloves, whole: 2 tsp
Carom seeds: 1 tsp
Dried ginger powder: 2 tsp
1-inch cinnamon stick
Black pepper, whole: ½ tsp
1-inch fresh lemongrass: 2

Steps

1. Transfer all the ingredients, apart from the lemongrass, to a spice grinder or mortar and pestle. Grind to a fine powder.
2. In a large bowl, combine all the ground spices. Mix thoroughly to ensure even distribution.
3. Store the special summer chai masala in an airtight container in a cool, dry place. Proper storage will maintain its freshness and potency for several months.

Note: Add fresh lemongrass directly to the chai.

Basic Summer Chai

Ingredients

Green cardamom, with the shell on: ¼ cup
Fennel seeds: 2 tbsp

Cloves, whole: 2 tsp
Carom seeds: 1 tsp

STEPS

1. Transfer all the ingredients to a spice grinder or mortar and pestle. Grind to a fine powder.
2. In a large bowl, combine all the ground spices. Mix thoroughly to ensure even distribution.
3. Store the basic summer chai masala in an airtight container in a cool, dry place. Proper storage will maintain its freshness and potency for several months.

Basic Gujarati Chai

INGREDIENTS

Dried ginger: 80 gm
Cinnamon: 10 gm
Cloves: 5 gm
Black pepper, whole: 5–7 gm
Green cardamom: 10 gm

STEPS

1. Transfer all the ingredients to a spice grinder or mortar and pestle. Grind to a fine powder.
2. In a large bowl, combine all the ground spices. Mix thoroughly to ensure even distribution.
3. Store the basic Gujarati chai masala in an airtight container in a cool, dry place. Proper storage will maintain its freshness and potency for several months.

SPECIAL GUJARATI CHAI

INGREDIENTS

Green cardamom: ¼ cup
Dried ginger powder: ¼ cup
1-inch cinnamon sticks: 3
Pepper powder or black pepper: ⅛ cup
Clove powder: 1 tbsp
Fennel seeds: 1 tbsp
Nutmeg powder: 1 tsp

STEPS

1. Transfer all the ingredients to a spice grinder or mortar and pestle. Grind to a fine powder.
2. In a large bowl, combine all the ground spices. Mix thoroughly to ensure even distribution.
3. Store the special Gujarati chai masala in an airtight container in a cool, dry place. Proper storage will maintain its freshness and potency for several months.

STREET-STYLE CHAI/CUTTING CHAI

INGREDIENTS

Cardamom, crushed: 3
1-inch ginger, grated: 1
Fennel seeds: 1 tsp

STEPS

1. Use this spice blend fresh in your tea while boiling.

Surati Chai

Ingredients

Black pepper: 4 tbsp
White pepper: 2 tbsp
Cardamom: 2 tbsp
Dried ginger powder: 2 tbsp
1-inch cinnamon stick
Ganthoda powder (pipramul): ½ tbsp
Cloves: 4–6
Nutmeg, grated: ¼ tsp

Steps

1. Crush the cinnamon stick and grate the nutmeg, if necessary, to facilitate grinding.
2. If desired, lightly dry roast the black pepper, white pepper, cardamom, cinnamon stick and cloves separately on a medium to low flame until aromatic. Allow to cool completely.
3. Transfer all the ingredients to a spice grinder or mortar and pestle. Grind to a fine powder.
4. Store the spice mix in an airtight container in a cool, dry place. Proper storage will maintain its freshness and potency for several months.

Nooh Chai

Ingredients

Green cardamom: 30
Fennel seeds: 2 tbsp
Dried ginger powder: 2 tbsp

1-inch cinnamon: 2
Black pepper: 2 tsp
Saffron: 10–12 strands
Cloves: 6–8 tbsp
Salt: ½ tsp (or to taste)

STEPS

1. Transfer all the ingredients to a spice grinder or mortar and pestle. Grind to a fine powder.
2. Mix thoroughly to ensure even distribution.
3. Store the nooh chai masala in an airtight container in a cool, dry place. Proper storage will maintain its freshness and potency for several months.

PUDINA CHAI

INGREDIENTS

1-inch ginger, grated: 1
Cloves: 4
Mint leaves: 10
Cardamom powder: ¼ tsp
Cinnamon powder: ¼ tsp
Nutmeg powder: ¼ tsp

STEPS

1. Add all the ingredients to 2 cups of boiling water and let the natural oil release.
2. Mix your 2½ tsp tea leaves and brew for 3 minutes.
3. Add 2 cups of full-fat milk.
4. Boil till the desired consistency and strength of the tea is reached.

5. Serve hot.
6. Note: This would taste great if made fresh.

Sulaimani Chai

Ingredients

Ginger powder: 10 tbsp
Cloves: 1 tbsp
Cinnamon sticks: 5 tbsp
Cardamom: 2 tbsp

Steps

1. Transfer all the ingredients to a spice grinder or mortar and pestle. Grind to a coarse powder.
2. Mix thoroughly to ensure even distribution.
3. Store this blend in a cool, dry place. Proper storage will maintain its freshness and potency for several months.

CHAAT MASALA

∾

THE INDIAN SUBCONTINENT FOOD IS SO INTRICATE AND varied that it could take more than one lifetime to truly understand its depths. Delving into this culinary expanse is akin to the experience of enjoying Mohiniyattam while nestled in a cosy wooden house in Kerala. This dance form, seemingly simple at first glance, reveals its intricate layers upon closer examination, much like the various spice blends that are the heart and soul of Indian cuisine. One such blend, chaat masala, embodies a concept that is quintessentially Indian—'chatpata.' This term, often translated into English as tangy or spicy, fails to capture its full essence. It's more than a taste—it's a sensation, an experience similar to the complex flavour profile of umami. Chatpata is a versatile descriptor, applicable to everything from food and people to unpredictable weather, seamlessly fitting into numerous contexts and scenarios.

The greatest culinary conundrum, however, is whether to categorize this blend as a mere seasoning or to elevate it to the status of main spice blends like those found in biryani or kababs. While traditionally used as a finishing touch—a sprinkle on top of dishes ranging from chaats and fruits to kababs and the refreshing jaljeera water—its role is pivotal. Despite some considering jaljeera and chaat masala as distinct entities, a logical analysis reveals their similar purposes—enhancing the flavours of otherwise bland foods. Rich in vitamin C due to the presence of mango powder, these blends are not only flavourful but also beneficial, especially when feeling nauseated. What unites them under the chatpata umbrella is their shared taste profile—a burst of tangy, spicy goodness that adds an extra layer of complexity to any dish.

The smell of these chatpata masalas is often off-putting to many because it has a rotten egg smell that comes from the use of black salt, but sprinkle just a pinch on your favourite food and see the magic happening in front of you. In February 2023, I was in Agra, exploring flavours and folktales, and in this exploration, I went to grab tea early in the morning at a shop in Old Agra. He was also serving toast with butter, with the option of sugar or savoury. I have tried sugar-spread butter toast in many places, so I thought of trying the savoury option. I got a thick layer of butter spread on crispy semolina rusk toast with an Agra version of chaat masala, along with a piping hot cup of tea with a thick layer of clotted cream. Tea made with full-fat milk and the flavour of crushed ginger was great to wake up even the dead souls—a kind of tea that you would get in every other shop around the country—but it was the toast that did the magic for me. Usually, people who bake like to stuff their faces with a mixture of whisked sugar and butter, and I was also used to it, but this was different. A blend of spices that had more of an earthy tone to it, along with a hint of black pepper and chillies and a sharp flavour of mango powder. The ones we usually get in Delhi have a range of various spices and you can count them when you put a pinch on your tongue, but the simplicity of this spice blend was unique to me. Even if you can ignore the thick layer of butter on the toast, you won't be able to forget the lingering spices in your blend. This curiosity brought me to the house of Tahir Ahmed Qureshi, founder of Agra Heritage Walk and a 7th-generation Agra*wala*. He and his mother served the best meal I could have ever asked for in Agra, which followed a similar 'Mughlai' template and yet had its own distinctive flavour, the local Agra flavour. I was talking to him about the chaat masala, and he handed me a small jar of the same spice blend, which reeked 'home-made'. He informed me that it was made by a lady in his community who also sells it, and I was happily buying it to add to my collection of knowledge. It had the same spiciness that I had tasted in the morning. The first thing I do is always smell my spices. If I call spice the soul, then it must reach my soul and senses, and not just sit on my palate. One whiff of this home-made goodness and I felt Agra's street flavours in me. I took a pinch and the flavours were on point, with a balance of cumin seeds, coriander, black pepper, mango powder, table salt, black salt and carom seed. One thing it was missing, which was there at the shop, was red chilli, but surprisingly, it was not being missed in the blend. It was great to see a home-made version with a balance of salt in it.

Usually, many of the street food vendors would sprinkle a blend that they would call their 'secret spice' and 'our own'. Both of these terms are right, and I am not the one to dismiss them. However, during the research of this book, Akhtar Jawed, who has a kabab shop in Old Delhi, exposed many of the other street vendors. He said, 'We usually bring chaat masala from the market and mix in lots of yellow and red chillies along with salt. When you eat fresh and hot kababs or pakodas sprinkled with this blend, you will love it because it is hot and smeared with extra salt; this is usually the secret.' He gave me the recipe, but not the exact proportion—that was for me to figure out. Despite my inquiries, Jawed refused to divulge his precise recipe, offering only a knowing smile and a look that seemed to say, 'You wish to uncover all the secrets.' This trend of closely guarding spice blends is common among shop owners, who often keep the exact ratios and ingredients from even their cooks, be it out of caution or tradition. This secrecy extends to renowned establishments like Aslam Butter Chicken, Karim's and Ghalib Kabab Corner in Nizamuddin, where inquiries about their spice blends are met with a simple invitation to enjoy the flavour, attributing their culinary success to divine blessings rather than revealing their trade secrets. This is a great way to say we don't want to tell.

Bilal Syed, a 65-year-old elderly caterer in Jamia, tells me a story that takes place in the bylanes of New and Old Delhi about the origin of this spice blend. He says that it was during Badshah Shah Jahan's reign when we got this magical blend that is making food popular and delicious even now. One day, when the Badshah was not well, he was advised to eat only bland food like khichdi. When he got bored of having the same tasteless food, his *khansamas*[*] created this blend that was not just good for gut health and nausea but equally tasty. When I returned home and started finding out more about the origin, I found many similar stories, but they were mentioned as 'legends'. So if we believe it, we have to think of these as folklore or myths about the food during the Mughal era.

In *Chai, Chaat & Chutney*, Chetna Makan explores various chaats of the country. She describes, 'As far as I'm concerned, this is one spice blend that should be in the cupboard at all times! Sour, refreshing, and with a very tangy kick, it's the masala that makes chaat so special, but it's also great added to curries, salads, chutneys, and even fresh fruits.' She describes Kolkata as her favourite street food place with so much 'chatpata' flavour, but I would argue further—I feel 'chatpata' or Indian umami flavour is intrinsic to the Indian palate.[1] Pick any city, and you will have their version of chaat masala. However, let's be honest. Not many bother whipping up this spice blend at home—it's probably because grabbing a masala mix off the shelf requires far fewer brain cells than measuring out a dozen spices yourself! Why sweat it when you can just twist a cap or rip up a box and sprinkle away, right?

In Delhi's market, I came across three packaged and branded chaat masalas amidst the rack full of so many global brands: Noorie, Allah Bande and Bhai Jumma. Noticeably, almost

---

[*] Cooks.

everyone loves Bhai Jumma and its iconic green packet with details written in Urdu, Hindi and English. Unlike many other chaat boxes, this one has no fruits or spices for representation purposes. My father is perhaps the biggest fan; he does not like any brand other than Jumma Chaat. He says, 'It is different.' Nobody knows what that really means!

One thing spice lovers must know is that, usually, there are three colours of chaat masala—it could be brown, yellow or black. The black version is a lot more popular in the streets of Old Delhi, where you would find every other chaat-papdi shop sprinkling it on top of the dishes they create.

In Old Delhi, the Ramazan taste is heightened by the refreshing drink Rooh Afza and Bhai Jumma chaat masala— both of these being the talk of the town among food lovers and those who observe fasts.

Simple Chaat Masala

Ingredients

Black salt: ½ cup
Dried kachari: 30 gm
Dried red chillies: 9
Dried yellow chillies: 9
Coriander seeds: 4 tbsp
Dried mint leaves: 3 tbsp
Cumin seeds: 2 tbsp
Carom seeds: 1 tbsp
Salt: 2½ tbsp (or to taste)
Black pepper: 1 tbsp

Steps

1. Dry roast all the whole spices on a low to medium flame for 3–4 minutes.
2. Let the mixture cool down and bring it to room temperature.
3. Mix all the dried and roasted whole spices, and blend to a fine powder.
4. Transfer it to an airtight container.

Khala ka Chaat Masala

Ingredients

Black salt: ½ cup
Salt: ⅓ cup (or to taste)
Coriander seeds: ½ cup
Cumin seeds: ½ cup
Black pepper: ¼ cup

Dried mango powder: 25 gm/ ¼ cup
Dried red chillies: 12
Asafoetida (hing): ¼ tsp

STEPS

1. Roast the whole spices first, and then finely grind all the spices together.
2. Dry roast all the whole spices on a medium flame.
3. Stir continuously to ensure your spices don't burn.
4. Roast for 3–4 minutes and take them out of the pan.
5. Mix all the dried and roasted whole spices, and blend to a fine powder.
6. Transfer it to an airtight container.

BLACK CHAAT MASALA

INGREDIENTS

Cumin seeds: 1 cup
Coriander seeds: ⅔ cup
Dried mango powder: ½ cup
Black salt: ¼ cup
Black pepper: ¼
Dried red chillies: 7–8
Carom seeds: 2 tbsp
Salt: ¼ cup (or to taste)
Long pepper (pipali): 2
Dried mint leaves: ½ cup

STEPS

1. Roast the whole spices first, and then finely grind all the spices together.

2. Dry roast all the whole spices on a medium flame.
3. Stir continuously to ensure your spices don't burn.
4. Roast for 3–4 minutes and take them out of the pan.
5. Mix all the dried and roasted whole spices, and blend to a fine powder.
6. Transfer it to an airtight container.

Royal Cafe's Lucknowi Chaat Masala

Ingredients

Cumin powder, roasted: 1 cup
Coriander powder: ½ cup
Salt, roasted: ⅓ cup
Black salt: ⅓ cup
Dried mango powder: 10 tbsp
Yellow chilli powder: 5 tbsp
Fennel powder: 4 tbsp

Steps

1. Mix all the spices together till they are nicely homogenized.
2. Transfer it to an airtight container.

Chef Ranveer Brar's Lucknowi Chaat Masala[2]

Ingredients

Cumin seeds: 1½ tbsp
Fennel seeds: 1 tbsp
Coriander seeds: 1 tbsp
Black pepper: 10–15
Salt: 1 tsp (or to taste)
Black cardamom: 1

Dried Kashmiri red chillies: 4–5
Dried mango powder: 1 tsp
Asafoetida: A pinch

STEPS

1. Roast the whole spices first, and then finely grind all the spices together.
2. Dry roast all the whole spices on a medium flame.
3. Stir continuously to ensure your spices don't burn.
4. Roast for 3–4 minutes and take them out of the pan.
5. Mix all the dried and roasted whole spices, and blend to a fine powder.
6. Transfer it to an airtight container.

BIHARI CHAAT MASALA

INGREDIENTS

Cumin seeds: 100 gm
Black pepper: 50 gm
Kashmiri red chilli: 100 gm
Black salt: 150 gm

STEPS

1. Roast the whole spices first, and then finely grind all the spices together.
2. Dry roast all the whole spices on a medium flame.
3. Stir continuously to ensure your spices don't burn.
4. Roast for 3–4 minutes and take them out of the pan.
5. Mix all the dried and roasted whole spices, and blend to a fine powder.
6. Transfer it to an airtight container.

Bihari Chaat Masala 2

Ingredients

Coriander seeds: 100 gm
Kashmiri red chilli powder: 60 gm
Cumin seeds: 50 gm
Clove: 6 gm
Green cardamom: 6 gm
Black pepper: 2 tbsp
Cinnamon: 8 gm
Salt: 12 tbsp (or to taste)
Black salt: 6 tbsp
Dried mango powder: 3 ½ tbsp
Citric acid powder/crystal: 2½ tsp
Asafoetida: ½ tsp
Dried ginger powder: 1 tbsp

Steps

1. Roast the whole spices first, and then finely grind all the spices together.
2. Dry roast all the whole spices on a medium flame.
3. Stir continuously to ensure your spices don't burn.
4. Roast for 3–4 minutes and take them out of the pan.
5. Mix all the dried and roasted whole spices, and blend to a fine powder.
6. Transfer it to an airtight container.

Ramzan Special Fruit Chaat Masala

Ingredients

Dried mint leaves: ½ cup
Red chilli powder: 10 tbsp
Cumin seeds: 8 tbsp

Carom seeds: 2 tsp
Nigella seeds: 4 tsp
Coriander seeds: 4 tbsp
Dried ginger: 40 gm
Black pepper: 4 tsp
Nutmeg: 30 gm
Citric acid: 8 tsp
Dried mango powder: 4 tbsp
Black salt: 5 tbsp
Salt: 5 tbsp (or to taste)
Dried pomegranate seeds (anardana): 1 tbsp

STEPS

1. Roast the whole spices first, and then finely grind all the spices together.
2. Dry roast all the whole spices on a medium flame.
3. Stir continuously to ensure your spices don't burn.
4. Roast for 3–4 minutes and take them out of the pan.
5. Mix all the dried and roasted whole spices, and blend to a fine powder.
6. Transfer it to an airtight container.

KARACHI SPECIAL SPICY CHAAT MASALA

INGREDIENTS

Coriander seeds: 100 gm
Brown onion, fried: 100 gm
Kashmiri red chilli powder: 50 gm
Cumin seeds: 4 tbsp
Black salt: 50 gm
Carom seeds: 4 tbsp
Citric acid: 2½ tbsp
Garlic powder: 5 tbsp

1. Roast the whole spices first, and then finely grind all the spices together.
2. Dry roast all the whole spices on a medium flame.
3. Stir continuously to ensure your spices don't burn.
4. Roast for 3–4 minutes and take them out of the pan.
5. Mix all the dried and roasted whole spices, and blend to a fine powder.
6. Transfer it to an airtight container.

DAHI BADE SPECIAL CHAAT MASALA

INGREDIENTS

Guntur chilli: 150 gm
Cumin seeds: 60 gm
Coriander seeds: 60 gm
Mango powder: 3 tbsp
Citric acid: 2½ tsp
Black pepper: 3 tsp
Carom seeds: 2 tsp
Cloves: 1 tsp
Salt: 5 tbsp (or to taste)
Black salt: 3 tsp

STEPS

1. Roast the whole spices first, and then finely grind all the spices together.
2. Dry roast all the whole spices on a medium flame.
3. Stir continuously to ensure your spices don't burn.
4. Roast for 3–4 minutes and take them out of the pan.

5. Mix all the dried and roasted whole spices, and blend to a fine powder.
6. Transfer it to an airtight container.

Peeli Mirch Chaat Masala

Ingredients

Black salt: 100 gm
Salt: 50 gm (or to taste)
Dried yellow chillies: 40 gm
Dried Kashmiri yellow chillies: 20 gm
Cumin seeds: 70 gm
Coriander seeds: 60 gm
Mango powder: 3 tbsp
Citric acid: 2½ tsp
Black pepper: 3 tsp
Carom seeds: 3 tsp

Steps

1. Roast the whole spices first, and then finely grind all the spices together.
2. Dry roast all the whole spices on a medium flame.
3. Stir continuously to ensure your spices don't burn.
4. Roast for 3–4 minutes and take them out of the pan.
5. Mix all the dried and roasted whole spices, and blend to a fine powder.
6. Transfer it to an airtight container.

Punjabi Chaat Masala

Ingredients

Cumin seeds: 1 tsp
Black pepper: 1 tbsp
Salt: 1 tsp (or to taste)
Dried mint leaves: 2 tbsp
Asafoetida: ½ tsp
Dried mango powder: 2 tbsp
Black salt: 2 tsp
Ginger powder: 3 tbsp
Red chilli powder: 2 tbsp
Tartaric acid: 1 tsp
Yellow chilli powder: 1½ tbsp

Steps

1. Start by dry roasting the cumin seeds until they give off a pleasant aroma. This should take just a couple of minutes over medium heat.
2. In a spice grinder, combine the dry roasted cumin seeds with black pepper and dried mint leaves. Grind to a fine powder.
3. Combine all the ingredients. Transfer the ground spices to a mixing bowl. Add salt, asafoetida, dried mango powder, black salt, ginger powder, chilli powder, tartaric acid and yellow chilli powder. Stir well to ensure even mixing.
4. Store the chaat masala in an airtight container to preserve its flavours.

CHOLE AND RAJMA

ॐ

SEVERAL YEARS AGO, THERE WAS A DEBATE ABOUT WHETHER
khichdi should be declared India's national dish. Fortunately,
that idea was not adopted. Yet there's widespread consensus
on one thing—if any single ingredient epitomizes the culinary
unity of India, it's the versatile chickpea, also known as
garbanzo, chana dal or Bengal gram. Legend has it that when
Aurangzeb imprisoned Shah Jahan in the Agra Fort, he was
allowed to choose just one ingredient to sustain him, and he
chose Bengal gram. This decision underscores the ingenuity
of both the emperor and his chefs, as Bengal gram can be
transformed into a myriad dishes—from halwa and puri to sabzi
and main courses—simply by altering its form, whether raw,
boiled, cooked or powdered.

Even though Delhi is a melting pot of world cuisines, it is
perhaps best represented by its beloved dish, chole bhature.
The flavours of chole are distinctively sharp, spicy and tangy,
with a slightly mushy texture that demands to be savoured hot.
The bhature complement it perfectly—crispy on the outside
and soft like a pillow on the inside. Unlike the quick snack
that is vada pav, chole bhature is a dish to be enjoyed leisurely.
While encouraging you to sit down, relax and immerse yourself
in the rich flavours, this dish epitomizes the spirit of Delhi—
simultaneously sweet and sharp, seemingly brusque at first, but
ultimately welcoming and comforting.

In Delhi, the pace is laid-back; everything unfolds in its own time. You can swap out the bhatura for rice, puri, kulcha or pav, and Delhiites will happily adapt. In many homes, chole is a Sunday staple. My brother often ventures out to enjoy his favourite chole bhature from places like Nagpal or Sitaram Diwan Chand, where patrons show remarkable loyalty to this beloved fiery dish. Mister Tikku, a Delhi-based food content creator, passionately describes the dish as an emotion and also, his first love.

While ingredients like avocado or olives might be considered luxury items, seldom experienced by many due to their high cost, chickpeas bridge the gap between the affluent and the impoverished, finding a place in the pantries of all socio-economic classes. Historically, the Romans recognized chickpeas as a staple food for the lower classes. The term 'buyer of roasted chickpeas' was commonly used in ancient Rome to denote someone of modest means, illustrating the deep-rooted association of chickpeas with economic accessibility.

Chickpeas come in two primary varieties—kabuli and desi. The kabuli type features large, light-coloured seeds, and is native to the Mediterranean Basin and Western Asia. In contrast, the desi variety has small, dark seeds, and is native to India and Eastern Asia. Despite the name, chickpeas are not peas; although they share a round shape, they are more closely related to beans than to peas. Around the world, chickpeas are known by many names: 'hamaz' in Arabic, 'shimbra' in Ethiopian, 'nohut' or 'leblebi' in Turkish, 'chana' in India, and 'garbanzo' in Latin America, which is the origin of the term 'garbanzo bean'.

Long ago, I heard a joke so bad that it should come with a warning label—'Proceed at your own risk.' 'What's the difference between Black Eyed Peas and chickpeas? Well, the Black Eyed Peas can still drop a beat, but chickpeas? They can only hummus one.'

Bengal gram, a staple pulse crop in India for centuries, makes up nearly 40 per cent of the country's total pulse production, and its derivatives are used almost everywhere. According to common legends, it is so auspicious that many households ban the use of it during a mourning period.

In his book, *A Historical Dictionary of Indian Food*, K.T. Achaya explains that the pulse got its English name because the British first came across it in Bengal. In Sanskrit, it is called chanaka, in Hindi, chana, in Tamil, kadalai, in English, chickpea, and its botanical name is Cicer arietinum.[1]

Chickpeas have been valued not just as food but also for their medicinal properties. As far back as the 9th century BCE, the Greek poet Homer mentioned chickpeas as both sustenance and a form of treatment. In ancient Rome and India, chickpeas served similar dual purposes. The ancients often consumed it after dinner as a snack, typically accompanied by a beverage. This culinary practice was even noted by the Greek philosopher Plato in *The Republic*, where he mentions chickpeas as a snack, underscoring their long-standing role in diet and health.[2]

Alan Davidson, in *The Oxford Companion to Food*, notes that chickpeas were first cultivated in the Levant and ancient Egypt, but are now widely used across regions, from India to North Africa, as well as in areas influenced by Arab traders, such as Sicily and Spain. He explains that the botanical name 'arietinum' comes from the resemblance of the seed, curled at the sides, to a ram's skull (hence the connection to Aries, the ram). The generic name Cicer is linked to the famous Roman orator Cicero, whose family supposedly had an ancestor with a chickpea-shaped wart on his face![3]

Colleen Taylor Sen writes in her book, *Feast And Fasts: A History Of Food In India*, that chickpeas came from Western Asia to the Indus Valley in the 4th millennium BCE, and considering they are part of winter crops, they probably got adopted in North India easily.[4]

But the chapter says 'chole and rajma', so we must focus on these red beans, which are popular not just in Delhi, but Punjab, Jammu, Nagaland and Guwahati, to name a few other states. It is not just about Delhi, after all.

Vir Sanghvi, in one of his articles about beans, writes,

> Rajmah is a name we give the kidney bean in North India. All kidney beans come from Mexico, where they have been extensively cultivated for 2000 years. They belong to the breed Phaseolus Vulgaris, which is capable of many variations: haricot beans, pinto beans and the rest are all part of the same breed. The kidney bean came to India relatively recently—late 19th century perhaps—and was first grown by the French, and then by the British, who passed it on to Punjabis. There is a great rajmah tradition in Jammu and in Uttarakhand but it is not at all ancient: it probably evolved not much further back than the 20th Century.[5]

He further explains that the reason it is called rajma is because of its resemblance to lobia, which we Indians were familiar with already and popularized as rajmasha for centuries. It is also called rajmah because of the already popular masha ki dal; hence masha first became maa and then rajma. Although, masha ki dal is now called maa ki dal.

Sohel Sarkar writes in his story for *Whetstone* that Achaya attributes the introduction of the bean to India to the French colonizers. While the French first arrived in India in the 1680s, the bean likely made its way to the subcontinent after the second French intervention in Mexico in the 1860s. Initially, it didn't settle in northern India, but rather in the French colonies of Pondicherry, Karaikal and Mahé in the south.

According to Sarkar, Achaya notes that 'the English in India found them to be a pleasant foodgrain,' and beans were initially grown as garden crops until the 19th century, only later becoming commercial crops. This commercial cultivation eventually enabled the beans to spread northward over time.[6]

In contemporary cuisine, chickpeas have gained immense popularity due to the rise of plant-based diets. They are featured in innovative dishes, including chickpea pasta, snacks and even desserts, reflecting their adaptability and nutritional benefits.

However, even Indian-origin chefs and food personalities have also promoted rajma chawal as their favourite comfort food. Chefs such as Hemant Oberoi and Vikas Khanna called this dish 'your quarantine comfort food' while chef–restaurateur Nikhil Merchant made it for a Covid-relief fundraiser cookalong during India's harrowing second wave.

But in my opinion (as a north Indian boy), a traditional chole with puri/bhatura or even chole gosht tastes the best.

AMRITSARI CHOLE

INGREDIENTS

Dried chickpeas (chole), soaked overnight: 1 cup
Oil or ghee: 2 tbsp
Onion, large, finely chopped: 1
Tomato, large, finely chopped: 2
Green chillies, slit: 2–3
Ginger garlic paste: 1 tbsp
Bay leaves: 2–3
Black cardamom: 1
Green cardamom: 2–3
Cloves: 4–5
1-inch cinnamon stick
Cumin seeds: 1 tsp
Coriander powder: 1 tsp
Cumin powder: 1 tsp
Turmeric powder: 1 tsp
Red chilli powder: 1 tsp
Garam masala: 1 tsp
Dried pomegranate seeds: 1 tbsp
Dried mango powder: 1 tsp
Salt to taste
Fresh coriander leaves, chopped for garnish
Lemon wedges, for serving

STEPS

1. Drain the soaked chickpeas and rinse them well.
2. In a pressure cooker, add the chickpeas along with 3–4 cups of water and a pinch of salt.
3. Cook for 6–7 whistles or until the chickpeas are soft and cooked through. If using a pot, simmer for about 60–90 minutes until tender.

4. Drain and set aside, reserving the stock.
5. Heat oil or ghee in a large pan over medium heat.
6. Add the bay leaves, black cardamom, green cardamom, cloves, cinnamon sticks and cumin seeds. Sauté for a few seconds until fragrant.
7. Add the chopped onions and green chillies. Sauté until the onions turn golden brown.
8. Add the ginger garlic paste and cook for 2–3 minutes until the raw smell disappears.
9. Add the chopped tomatoes and cook until they become soft and the oil starts to separate.
10. Add coriander powder, cumin powder, turmeric powder, red chilli powder and salt. Mix well and cook for another 2–3 minutes.
11. Add the cooked chickpeas to the pan and mix well with the masala.
12. Add the dried pomegranate seeds or dried mango powder and chole masala (if using).
13. Pour 1–2 cups of the reserved stock to achieve the desired consistency.
14. Cover the pan and let the chole simmer on low heat for 15–20 minutes, allowing the flavours to meld together.
15. Stir occasionally and adjust the consistency with more stock if needed.
16. Add garam masala and mix well. Cook for an additional 2 minutes.
17. Garnish with fresh coriander leaves.
18. Serve hot with puri, bhature, naan or steamed rice.

Lucknowi Lapetu Chole

Ingredients

Coriander seeds: 50 gm
Cumin seeds: 25 gm
Black cardamom: 1
1-inch cinnamon stick
Cloves: 3–4
Bay leaves: 2–4
Fennel seeds: 1 tbsp
Black pepper: 1 tbsp
Cardamom: 1 tsp
Mace: 1 tsp
Nutmeg: ¾ tsp

Steps

1. Lightly toast the dry spices in a dry pan until they release their aromatic oils. Be careful not to burn them.
2. Allow the toasted spices to cool, and then grind them to a fine powder.
3. Mix all ground spices thoroughly to ensure a homogenous blend.
4. Store the blend in an airtight container in a cool, dark place for up to 6 months to retain its freshness and aroma.

Malvani Chana

Ingredients

Dried Kashmiri red chillies: 15 gm
Coriander seeds: 2 tsp
Cumin seeds: ½ tsp
Cloves: 4–6
Nigella seeds: ½ tsp

Cardamom: 2
Black cardamom: 1
Poppy seeds: 1 tsp
Star anise: 1
1-inch cinnamon stick
Dried coconut (khopra), grated: 1 tbsp

STEPS

1. Lightly toast the dry spices in a dry pan until they release their aromatic oils. Be careful not to burn them.
2. Allow the toasted spices to cool and then grind them to a fine powder.
3. Mix all ground spices thoroughly to ensure a homogenous blend.
4. Store the blend in an airtight container in a cool, dark place for up to 6 months to retain its freshness and aroma.

KALA CHANA AMTI

INGREDIENTS

Mustard seeds: 1 tsp
Fresh coconut, grated: 2½ tbsp
Dried curry leaves: 8–10
Maharashtrian goda masala: 1½ tbsp
Red chilli powder: 2 tsp
Turmeric powder: 1 tsp
Salt to taste

STEPS

1. If cooking fresh, use fresh coconut and curry leaves.
2. Mustard seeds should be put in the hot oil in the beginning.
3. Mix goda masala with chilli powder and turmeric powder.

4. Mix all ground spices thoroughly to ensure a homogenous blend.
5. Store the blend in an airtight container in a cool, dark place for up to 6 months to retain its freshness and aroma.

JAISALMER CHOLE

INGREDIENTS

Turmeric powder: ¼ tsp
Salt: 1 tsp (or to taste)
Red chilli powder: 1½ tsp
Coriander powder: 3½ tsp
Garam masala powder: 1½ tsp
Asafoetida: A pinch
Cumin seeds: 1½ tsp
Gram flour (besan): 4 tsp

STEPS

1. Mix all ground spices thoroughly to ensure a homogenous blend.
2. Store the blend in an airtight container in a cool, dark place for up to 6 months to retain its freshness and aroma.
3. Jaisalmer chole is usually cooked like kadhi, hence, whisk the gram flour and curd together while making this dish.

DELHI CHOLE MASALE

INGREDIENTS

Red chillies, whole: 4–5
Coriander seeds: 3 tsp
Cumin seeds: 2 tsp
Black pepper: 8–10

1-inch cinnamon stick
Cloves: 6–7
Black cardamom: 2
Green cardamom: 4–5
Fennel seeds: 1 tsp
Bay leaves: 3
Dried pomegranate seeds: 1 tbsp
Dried fenugreek leaves: 1 tbsp

STEPS

1. Dry roast the whole spices and let them come down to room temperature.
2. In a blender mix the spices, dried pomegranate seeds and dried fenugreek leaves. Blend them to fine powder.
3. Keep the masala in an airtight container.

CHEF AJAY SIOTRA'S DOGRI CHOLE[*]

INGREDIENTS

1-inch cinnamon stick
Cumin seeds: 2 tbsp
Black cardamom: 1 tbsp
Ginger powder: 2 tbsp
Turmeric powder: 2 tbsp
Salt: 2 tbsp (or to taste)
Dried red chillies: 2 tbsp
Dried pomegranate seeds: 1½ tbsp
Fennel powder: 2 tbsp

---

[*] Chef Ajay Siotra, hailing from Jammu, is renowned for his mastery of Indian haute cuisine. A talented culinary artist, he showcased his skills as a participant on *MasterChef India Season 5*.

STEPS

1. Gather all the whole spices and ensure they are clean and dry.
2. Lightly toast the whole spices (cinnamon stick, cumin seeds, black cardamom and dried red chillies) in a dry pan over medium heat until they release their aromatic oils, about 3–4 minutes. Be careful not to burn the spices.
3. Allow the toasted spices to cool completely, then grind them into a fine powder using a spice grinder or mortar and pestle.
4. Add the ground spices (ginger powder, turmeric powder, salt, dried pomegranate seeds and fennel powder) to the mixture and stir thoroughly to ensure an even blend.
5. Store the spice blend in an airtight container in a cool, dark place. This blend can be stored for up to 6 months for optimal flavour.

CHEF JATIN KHURANA'S LUDHIANA CHOLE[*]

INGREDIENTS

Bay leaves: 2–3
Black cardamom: 1
1-inch cinnamon stick
Coriander powder: 3 tbsp
Cumin powder: 2 tbsp
Turmeric powder: 1 tsp
Red chilli powder: 2 tsp
Dried pomegranate seeds: 1 tbsp
Stone flower (pathar ke phool): 2 tbsp

---

[*] Chef Jatin Khurana is a Ludhiana-based chef. He is a managing partner at Bing Hospitality, and owner and founder at The Urban Bhukkad. He was also a participant in *MasterChef India season 5*.

Long pepper: 2
Salt: 1 tbsp (or to taste)
Dried ginger powder: 1 tsp
Dried mango powder: 1 tbsp

STEPS

1. Dry roast the whole spices and thoroughly mix with all the ground spices to ensure an even distribution.
2. Blend all of them to get a fine, smooth powder.
3. Store the spice blend in an airtight container in a cool, dry place to preserve its freshness and potency.

BIHARI CHOLE

INGREDIENTS

Turmeric powder: 2 tsp
Kashmiri chilli powder: 3 tbsp
Bay leaf: 2–3
Cumin seeds: 2 tsp
Ginger powder: 1½ tbsp
Black pepper: 2 tsp
Cloves: 4
1-inch cinnamon stick: 2
Salt: 3 tsp (or to taste)

STEPS

1. Dry roast the whole spices and mix with all the ground spices thoroughly to ensure an even distribution.
2. Blend all of them to get a fine, smooth powder.
3. Store the spice blend in an airtight container in a cool, dry place to preserve its freshness and potency.

BENGALI CHOLE

INGREDIENTS

Coriander seeds: 6 tbsp
Cumin seeds: 4 tbsp
Bay leaves: 5
Cloves: 10
Green cardamom: 10
1-inch cinnamon stick: 2
Dried red chillies: 10

STEPS

1. Lightly roast the coriander, cumin seeds, cloves, cardamom, cinnamon sticks and dry red chillies until they release their aromatic oils but are not burnt.
2. Allow the spices to cool after roasting, then grind them finely. For a more textured blend, you can coarsely grind the spices.
3. Combine all ground spices thoroughly to ensure a homogenous mixture.
4. Store the spice blend in an airtight container in a cool, dry place. This blend should maintain its potency for several months.

SHADIWALE AMRITSARI CHOLE

INGREDIENTS

Dried red chillies: 4–6
Bay leaf: 2–3
Coriander seeds: 4 tbsp
Cumin seeds: 2 tbsp
Black pepper: 10–12

Cloves: 6
Cardamom: 6
Mace: 1
1-inch cinnamon
Nutmeg: ¼ tsp
Black cardamom: 3
Ajwain: 2 tsp
Dried fenugreek leaves: 2 tbsp
Dried pomegranate seeds: 2 tbsp
Dried mango powder: 2 tbsp

STEPS

1. Dry roast all the whole spices and let it cool.
2. Blend them and make a fine powder.
3. Store the spice blend in an airtight container in a cool, dry place to preserve freshness and potency.

DELHI RAJMA

INGREDIENTS

Red kidney beans, soaked overnight: 2 cups
Water: 4 cups (or as needed)
Salt: 1½ tsp (or to taste)
Cooking oil: 2–3 tbsp
Butter: 2 tbsp
Onion, medium, chopped: 3
Tomato, medium, chopped: 3
Ginger garlic paste: ½ tbsp
Red chilli powder: 1½ tsp (or to taste)
Cumin powder: 1½ tsp
Turmeric powder: 1 tsp
Kashmiri red chilli powder: 1 tsp
Coriander seeds, roasted and crushed: ½ tbsp

Garam masala powder: ½ tsp
Water: 1 cup (or as needed)
Fresh coriander, chopped: A handful
Additional fresh coriander, chopped for garnish
Butter for garnish
Onion rings for garnish
Lemon wedge for garnish

STEPS

1. In a pot, combine the red kidney beans, water and salt. Mix well, bring to a boil, remove any scum that forms, cover and cook over medium heat until the beans are tender (for about 45–50 minutes). Increase the heat and continue cooking until approximately ½ cup of water remains. Set aside.
2. In a wok, heat the cooking oil and butter until the butter melts.
3. Add onions and fry until light golden.
4. Add tomatoes and ginger garlic paste; mix well and cook for a minute.
5. Stir in salt, red chilli powder, cumin powder, turmeric powder, Kashmiri red chilli powder, crushed coriander seeds and garam masala powder. Cook for 1–2 minutes.
6. Add water, bring to a boil, then cover and simmer on low heat for 7–8 minutes. Increase the heat and cook for about 3–4 minutes until the oil begins to separate.
7. Add the boiled kidney beans along with their cooking water; mix well.
8. Add chopped fresh coriander, cover and simmer on low heat for another 8–10 minutes.
9. Garnish with more fresh coriander, butter, onion rings and a lemon wedge. Serve with boiled rice.

Kashmiri Rajma

Ingredients

Coriander seeds: 3 tbsp
Nigella seeds: 2 tsp
Salt: 2 tbsp (or to taste)
Kashmiri chilli powder: 3 tbsp
Turmeric powder: 2 tsp
Fennel seeds: 3 tsp
Dried ginger powder: 3 tsp

Steps

1. Dry roast all the whole spices and let it cool.
2. Blend them with the powdered spices and make a fine powder.
3. Store the spice blend in an airtight container in a cool, dry place to preserve freshness and potency.

Chef Ajay Siotra's Jammu Rajma

Ingredients

Black cardamom: 4–6
1-inch cinnamon sticks: 2
Green cardamom: 8–10
Cloves: 15–20
Black pepper: 20–25
Bay leaf: 4–6
Salt: 2 tbsp (or to taste)
Red chilli powder: 2 tbsp
Cumin seeds: 1 tbsp
Asafoetida: 2 tsp

1. Dry roast all the whole spices and let it cool.
2. Blend them with the powdered spices and make a fine powder.
3. Store the spice blend in an airtight container in a cool, dry place to preserve freshness and potency.

HOME-STYLE RAJMA

INGREDIENTS

Cumin seeds: 2 tbsp
Salt: 2 tbsp (or to taste)
Turmeric powder: 2 tbsp
Red chilli powder: 2 tbsp
Coriander powder: 2 tbsp
Garam masala: 1 tbsp

STEPS

1. Dry roast the cumin seeds and let it cool.
2. Mix the powdered spices and roasted cumin seeds.
3. Store the spice blend in an airtight container in a cool, dry place to preserve freshness and potency.

GUJARATI RAJMA

INGREDIENTS

1-inch cinnamon sticks: 3
Bay leaves: 5–8
Black cardamom: 5
Cloves: 15
Black pepper: 30

Cumin seeds: 2 tsp
Asafoetida: ½ tsp
Kashmiri red chilli powder: 2 tbsp
Coriander powder: 3 tsp

STEPS

1. Dry roast all the whole spices and let it cool.
2. Blend them with the powdered spices and make a fine powder.
3. Store the spice blend in an airtight container in a cool, dry place to preserve freshness and potency.

CURRY

∾

I MAGINE YOURSELF IN A LIVELY PAN–INDIAN RESTAURANT in Connaught Place, Delhi. The restaurant full of chaotic but soothing sounds—glasses clinking, cutlery scraping, the clamour of overlapping voices rising over the music. The smoky scent of tandoori meats and yellow or red gravies fills the air. This scenario, familiar to many, perfectly encapsulates the rich diversity of Indian curry dishes. However, defining what a curry is can be as complex as the countless spices that compose it. The term 'curry', used broadly, encompasses a range of gravy-based dishes, each distinct in flavour and origin.

It first appeared in Western literature in Jan Huygen van Linschoten's *Discours of Voyages into ye Easte & West Indies* (1598), translated by William Phillip. Linschoten describes a dish of fish and rice served in a somewhat sour broth, calling it 'Carriil' [Dutch *carrijl*].[1]

It wasn't until 1747 that curry and its recipe made its first appearance in a cookbook. In *The Art of Cookery Made Plain and Easy*, published in 1747, Hannah Glasse included a recipe titled 'to make a currey the Indian way', using fowl or rabbit meat. This was a pivotal moment in culinary history, presenting curry in a form familiar to the Western palate for the first time.[2]

Colleen Taylor Sen, in her book *Curry: A Global History*, aptly notes that if any dish deserves global recognition, it's curry. From the streets of Beijing to the homes in Warsaw, curry enjoys worldwide popularity. Sen's definition of curry as a spiced stew paired with a starch resonates with the global palate. However, tracing the term's origins reveals a more localized beginning.[3] The Tamil word *kari*, meaning a dish cooked with pepper, is the root of the English word curry. This term has evolved, now often encompassing any home-made Indian dish with gravy, especially when explaining Indian cuisine to foreigners.

Madhur Jaffrey, an Indian cookbook author, initially critiqued the term 'curry' for its oversimplification of India's culinary diversity. She titled her book *The Ultimate Curry Bible*, reflecting the term's widespread acceptance and usage. This evolution underscores how curry has transcended its simplistic connotations and become a global culinary staple. In 1974, she also published *An Invitation to Indian Cooking*. In the introduction, she writes:

> To me the word 'curry' is as degrading to India's great cuisine as the term 'chop suey' was to China's . . . 'Curry' is just a vague, inaccurate word which the world has picked up from the British, who, in turn, got it mistakenly from us . . . If 'curry' is an oversimplified name for an ancient cuisine, then 'curry powder' attempts to oversimplify (and destroy) the cuisine itself.[4]

Lizzie Collingham, in *Curry: A Tale of Cooks and Conquerors*, suggests that Europeans, particularly the British, broadly categorized diverse Indian dishes like rogan josh, dopiaza, and qorma under the term 'curry'. This generalization perhaps overlooks the distinctiveness of each regional dish.[5]

The classic Anglo-Indian curry, a legacy of British India, is often considered the archetypal 'curry'. As described by Colonel Kenney–Herbert (Wyvern), this involves sautéing onions, adding meat or fish, and simmering in a liquid base like water, stock, tomatoes or coconut milk, with spices added during the cooking process.[6] While purists might argue for this specific definition, the term 'curry' has undoubtedly expanded to embrace a broader range of dishes, reflecting the diversity and adaptability of Indian cuisine.

If you delve into the market's array of 'curry powders', you'll notice each brand offers a unique blend of herbs and spices. Common ingredients like turmeric, ginger, cinnamon, cloves and cumin seeds are often present, but the proportions vary significantly. This diversity mirrors the vast culinary landscape of India, where regional preferences dictate the contents of each masala dabba (spice box).

In the book, *Curry*, Sen suggests that through the 1800s, curry emerged as a familiar dish in the United States, with curry powder becoming a staple flavour.[7] Mary Randolph's *The Virginia Housewife*, one of the earliest American cookbooks, features at least six recipes calling for curry powder, including instructions for making the powder itself.[8] Eliza Leslie's popular *Directions for Cookery, in Its Various Branches* offers a 'genuine East India receipt for [chicken] curry', complete with mulligatawny soup and freshly ground curry powder recipes.[9] *Mrs. Hill's New Cook-Book*, tailored to the Southern States, includes curried meat stews and roasts, a 'rice chicken pie' in curry powder gravy, various preparations for a calf's head, and Mrs Hill's recipe for curry powder—a blend of coriander seed, turmeric, ginger, black pepper, mustard, allspice powder, cumin seeds and cardamom.[10] The high cost of transporting spices to the colonies and Britain likely spurred the popularity of pre-blended, ready-made curry powder.

She further quotes Madhur Jaffrey who remarkably says, 'What you don't need is curry powder.'[11] For me, this explains the subcontinent dishes in a more subtle manner. Much like Jaffrey, other chefs, my grandmother and I would agree that curry powder just simplifies all our food and renders the same flavour in everything. Imagine using madras curry powder in nihari, biryani, qorma and aloo bhujiya. They all would taste and smell the same with just a difference in the ingredients.

Interestingly, curry or curry powder has transcended its culinary use, sometimes serving as a racial epithet. In 2012, at a conference in Orange County, I was playfully dubbed 'curry boy' by a Canadian girl. While not intended maliciously, this nickname made me reflect on how people outside the subcontinent perceive our cuisine. Yet, we too harbour stereotypes—whether it's the north–south divide in India, the belief that Europeans only eat pizza and pasta or negative assumptions about African food. Such realizations prevent me from taking a moral high ground on the matter.

Even before the globalization hit in the truest sense, the flavours of the curry took over the kitchens globally. It happened because of the French, British, Portuguese and everyone who came to the 'curry' nations and took the recipe with them only to modify it based on their needs and palate.

The beauty of such dishes is that one can have them with rice, roti or by themselves—you are not limited in your approach. You can eat it with a side of dried fish and pickle or simply salads and chutneys. My grandmother used to have it with rice, some gravy-based meat dish and mango (when in season)—a combination I could never understand.

In movies like *The Lunchbox* (2013), *Cheeni Kum* (2007) and *Piku* (2015), as well as older classics like *Chitchor* (1976), *Gol Maal* (1979) and *Bawarchi* (1972), curries aren't just there in the background—they almost play a role of their own. It's like they're more than just food—they represent family, culture and comfort.

In my family, curry-based dishes held a prominent position, surpassing even biryani in popularity. Among these, pulao and gosht were iconic. Gosht was often prepared with potatoes, gourd or other seasonal vegetables, and occasionally served on its own. In *The Classic Cuisine of Lucknow*, Mirza Jafar Hussain, a descendant of the nawabi aristocrats of Lucknow, provides a culinary memoir that elaborates on numerous varieties of qorma (or korma) and qalya (or qaliya)—essentially curries for both meat and vegetable enthusiasts.[12]

Similarly, Delhi's lanes are known for their rich variety of gravy-based dishes. Surprisingly, however, korma, despite being favoured by both royalty and commoners, is absent from *Nuskha-e-Shahjahani*, translated from Persian by Salma Yusuf Husain.[13] In my conversation with Husain, she indicated that, based on documentary evidence, korma may not have been a commonly preferred dish during the reign of Emperor Shah Jahan. By contrast, Emperor Bahadur Shah Zafar's table featured several varieties of korma, including preparations involving various fowls, fish and meats.

On one hand, qorma or korma was considered a rich people's food and many houses made (and still make) qalya (or qaliya), which is a thinner gravy-based dish. In *Shahjahanabad: The Living City of Old Delhi*, Rana Safvi elaborates on the culinary traditions surrounding korma and qalya, emphasizing that korma was considered a special dish, typically prepared for significant occasions due to the intensive roasting of meat and spices involved. In contrast, qalya was part of everyday meals, characterized by the use of turmeric and raw onion paste. The key distinction lay in the ingredients and preparation techniques—korma utilized fried onion paste and curd, avoiding turmeric entirely, whereas qalya incorporated turmeric as a defining element.[14]

In the 'Spread of Bounties: Culinary Manuals and Knowledge in Mughal South Asia', Neha Vermani emphasizes the prominence of sweet-sour and mildly sweet flavour profiles in various Mughal dishes, particularly in qalya preparations. These dishes were crafted using ingredients such as lemon, sugar syrup (chāshnī), saccharine fruits and unripe or tart produce, which contributed to their distinct taste. Different variations of qalya were made with meats, vegetables or even fruits, such as qalya shakarqand (sweet tuber), qalya māhī (fish) and qalya anba (mango). This focus on sweet and tart flavours, combined with rich spices, reflects an ideal of culinary refinement in Mughal cuisine, showcasing their sophisticated approach to balancing flavours.[15]

Even though curries of all kinds, from the humble to the elaborate, have graced our tables in the past and present, we must acknowledge that convenience has now replaced creativity for many. As people find themselves with less time, creativity has, quite literally, jumped out the window, making way for ready-made spice blends that have taken over the aroma of our kitchens. Where once no standard recipe existed, curry powder—despite its lack of standardization in the past, but now standard—serves as a staple flavour in many dishes, especially in dhabas (roadside eateries) and street-side shops. These places often rely on generic spice mixes like "kitchen king" for vegetarian fare and "meat masala" for non-vegetarian dishes, resulting in a predictable sameness in flavour across their offerings.

A notable mention in the history of curry powder is the 'Madras curry powder', popularized globally by P. Vencatachellum Pillai and his son, P.V. Subramania Pillai. Established in 1860, P. Vencatachellum Condiments became known for its high-quality ingredients and proprietary recipes. The Madras curry powder, a blend featuring red chillies, turmeric, coriander, black pepper, curry leaves and several other ingredients, did not just become popular in the UK amongst the commoners but was also a preferred choice at Buckingham Palace.

Addressing the topic of curry and curry powders in India is indeed challenging, given the endless variety of curries and gravy-based dishes across the subcontinent. Numerous cookbooks have been dedicated to exploring these diverse recipes, each representing different states and regions. This section is a modest attempt to highlight some of the well-known curry powders that have gained popularity in their respective areas, acknowledging the complexity and richness of India's culinary heritage.

In recent times, I stumbled upon Vadouvan French masala, which is a popular masala blend in Pondicherry, especially in the homes of Indo-French families. Unlike the other kinds of spice blends across India, this blend can be used in making vegetarian or meat and fish dishes. The use reminds me of Kashmiri ver masala. Azmat Ali Mir, owner of Sarposh, Bangalore, helped me understand that ver masala can be used in any dish, from kababs to gravies. I told her I used ver masala in my omelette and she approved of it, which essentially means you can use it in anything. This is one masala which can be used as a flavour enhancer to the main spice blend. I have seen many using this blend in gravies and hence, I am putting it here in this section.

When you look online and ask people what the most famous curry in India is, you will surely get the answer—but is that the right answer? Can you actually put a stamp on the most famous curry in India? No, you cannot, and you should not.

This section will have varieties and versions of spice blends of various dishes from various states, so a chicken curry or a simple vegetable stew will have regional flavours and options.

Harjeet Kohli's Butter Chicken

Ingredients

For the Marinade:
Chicken Thighs, skinless and boneless, cut into 1½-inch pieces: 500g
Oil: ½ tbsp
Hung curd: ¼ cup
Kashmiri chilli powder: ½ tbsp
Coriander powder: ½ tbsp
Turmeric powder: ¼ tsp
Ginger garlic paste: ¾ tbsp
Garam masala powder: ½ tsp
Salt: ½ tsp (or to taste)

For the Gravy:
Ghee: 2 tbsp
Butter: 2 tbsp
½-inch cinnamon stick
Green cardamom: 3
Cloves: 3
Dried Kashmiri red chillies: 2–3
Garlic: 3 cloves
Onion, roughly chopped: ½ cup
Cashew nuts: ¼ cup
Tomatoes, roughly chopped: 3–4 (approx 250 gm) or Canned diced tomatoes: ½
Kashmiri red chilli powder: ½ tsp
Ketchup: 1 tbsp
Dried fenugreek leaves: ½ tbsp
Salt: ½ tsp (or to taste)
Fresh cream: 2 tbsp

Prepare the Marinade:

1. Mix all the ingredients listed under the marinade. Add the chicken pieces to the mixture while ensuring they are well coated. Cover and let it marinate for 15–30 minutes.

Prepare the Gravy:

1. Heat ½ tbsp oil and ½ tbsp butter in a skillet or pan. Add cinnamon, cardamom, cloves, red chillies and garlic. Sauté for a minute or until fragrant.
2. Add the onions and sauté on high heat for 2–3 minutes until they turn pink and translucent.
3. Add tomatoes and cashew nuts. Stir, then reduce the heat to a simmer. Cover and cook for 10–15 minutes until the tomatoes break down and become pulpy.
4. After cooling completely, transfer the mixture to a blender and blend until smooth.
5. In a separate pan, heat ½ tbsp of oil. Add the marinated chicken pieces and sear each side for 2–3 minutes on high heat until a char forms. Remove and set aside.

Finalize the Gravy:

1. Pour the puree back into the pan. Add chilli powder, ketchup, salt and ⅛ cup water. Bring to a boil, then reduce the heat to low. Cover and cook for 15–20 minutes until the gravy changes to a deep orange colour.
2. Add the seared chicken pieces to the gravy and simmer for 10 minutes. Stir in the dried fenugreek leaves and fresh cream.

Smoke the Chicken (optional):

1. Place a small steel bowl in the middle of the pan with the butter chicken. Heat a piece of charcoal or lump coal until red hot and place it in the bowl.

2. Pour 1 tsp of oil or ghee over the hot coal. As soon as it starts smoking, cover the pan with a lid and smoke for 3–4 minutes. Remove the bowl before serving.

Moti Mahal-Style Butter Chicken

Ingredients

For the Marinade:
Chicken, boneless, skinless: 1 kg
Fresh lime juice: 1½ tbsp
Red chilli powder: 1½ tsp
Garam masala: 3 tsp
Salt to taste
Curd: ⅜ cup (or 6 tbsp)
Garlic, minced: 1½ tbsp
Fresh ginger, finely minced: 1½ tbsp

For the Sauce:
Oil: 3 tbsp
Onions, finely chopped: 1½
Tomatoes, medium, chopped: 6
Garlic, minced: 1½ tsp
Fresh ginger, minced: 3 tsp
Kashmiri chilli powder: 1½ tbsp
Garam masala: 1½ tbsp
Cumin powder: 1½ tsp
Salted butter: 3 tbsp
Heavy cream: ½ cup

Note: The method to be followed for this blend as well as the others is the same as for the recipe above.

Steps

For Marinating the Chicken:

1. In a mixing bowl, combine fresh lime juice, red chilli powder, garam masala and salt.
2. Add yogurt, minced garlic and minced ginger root to the mixture, and stir well to create a smooth marinade.
3. Add the boneless chicken chunks to the marinade, ensuring they are thoroughly coated.
4. Cover the bowl and refrigerate for at least 1–2 hours, allowing the flavours to infuse into the chicken.

For Making the Sauce:

1. Heat the oil in a heavy-bottomed pan over medium heat.
2. Add the finely chopped onions and sauté for about 6–8 minutes until they become golden brown.
3. Add the minced garlic and ginger, and sauté for another 1–2 minutes until fragrant.
4. Add the chopped tomatoes and cook until they soften, about 8–10 minutes.
5. Add Kashmiri chilli powder, garam masala, cumin powder and salt, and stir well to combine.
6. Let the mixture simmer on low heat until it thickens, and then blend the sauce to a smooth consistency using a hand blender or a regular blender.
7. Return the blended sauce to the pan, add the salted butter, and cook on low heat until the butter is fully incorporated.
8. Stir in the thick cream and mix well to achieve a velvety texture. Cook for another 2–3 minutes on low heat.

Final Preparation:

1. Preheat your oven or grill to 200°C (400°F).
2. Place the marinated chicken pieces on skewers or spread them on a baking tray. Grill or bake the chicken for 15–20 minutes, turning halfway through until the chicken is fully cooked and slightly charred.

3. Add the cooked chicken pieces to the prepared sauce and let it simmer for another 5–7 minutes until the chicken absorbs the flavours.

4. Serve hot with naan, roti or steamed basmati rice.

HOME-STYLE BUTTER CHICKEN

INGREDIENTS

Chicken, with bone: 1 kg
Refined oil: 2 tbsp
Kashmiri red chilli powder: 2 tsp
Tomato puree: 1 cup
Coriander seeds: 1½ tsp
Cinnamon, crushed: 1½
Cloves: 4
Butter: 350 gm
Red chillies (phaphda or bhaonagri), whole: 3
Coriander powder: 1 tsp
Fenugreek powder: 1 tsp
Bay leaves: 2
Salt: 1½ tsp (or to taste)
Onion, medium, sliced: 2
Dried fenugreek leaves, crushed: 4 tbsp

For the Marinade:
Onion paste: 2 tsp
Garlic paste: 1 tsp
Curd: ½ cup
Green cardamom: 2–3
Ginger paste: 1 tsp
Mace powder: 1 tsp
Black cardamom: 2
Sugar: ½ tsp

1. Follow the same steps mentioned above in the recipe for marinating the chicken, preparing the sauce and combining everything. Adjust the cooking time as necessary to accommodate the use of bone-in chicken.

SARANSH GOILA-STYLE BUTTER CHICKEN[*16]

INGREDIENTS

½-inch cinnamon stick
Bay leaves: 2
Cumin seeds: 2 tbsp
Coriander seeds: 1½ tsp
Green cardamom: 1 tbsp
Black pepper, whole: 1 tbsp
Cloves: 2 tsp
Dried red chillies: 2
Nutmeg, grated: ⅛ –¼ tsp
Mace powder: ½ tsp
Fenugreek leaves: 2 tsp
Salt to taste

For the Tandoori Chicken:
Chicken thighs and drumsticks: 4
Hung curd: 50 gm
Mustard oil: 1½ tsp
Ginger garlic paste: 4 tsp
Kashmiri red chilli paste: 1 tbsp
Cardamom powder: ⅛–¼ tsp

---

[*] Saransh Goila is an Indian chef and a winner of the *Food Food Maha Challenge*. He founded a Mumbai-based restaurant 'Goila Butter Chicken' and is the author of the food travelogue *India on my Platter*.

Garam masala: ½ tsp
Salt: ½ tsp (or to taste)

For the Butter Chicken Sauce Base:
1-inch cinnamon stick
Bay leaf: 1
Cloves, whole: 4
Mace blade: 1
Black cardamom: 1
Green cardamom: 4
Roma tomatoes, roughly chopped: 1 kg
Onion, peeled, roughly chopped: 250 gm
Garlic, peeled, roughly chopped: 50 gm
Cashew nuts: 60 gm
Honey: 1 tsp
Water: 150 ml
Milk: 150 ml
Coriander powder: 3 tsp
Kashmiri chilli powder: 1½ tsp
Fenugreek leaves: 2 tbsp
Salt to taste
Butter: 70 gm
Thickened cream: 2 tbsp

STEPS

1. For preparing the Goila-style butter chicken, follow the same steps as mentioned in the above recipe for making the marinade, sauce and combining all elements.

Note: In this version, the sauce base uses additional ingredients like cashew nuts and honey for added richness and sweetness. Also, adjust the grilling or cooking time accordingly for bone-in chicken pieces.

Dhaba-Style Butter Chicken

Ingredients

Cardamom: 5
2½-inch cinnamon stick
Black pepper: 5–8
Ginger garlic paste: 2½ tsp
Tomato puree: 1½ cups
Red chilli powder: 2 tsp
Salt to taste
Sugar: 2½ tbsp
Garam masala powder: 2 tsp
Fenugreek leaves: 5 tbsp
Curd: 2 cups
Chicken tikka pieces: 1 kg

Steps

1. To prepare the dhaba-style butter chicken, follow the same steps outlined in the above butter chicken recipe for creating the marinade, sauce, and combining all the elements.

Note: This recipe uses chicken tikka pieces, adding a smoky, tandoori flavour to the final dish. The sauce is also slightly sweeter, with the addition of more sugar for that classic dhaba-style richness.

Lucknow Home-Style Butter Chicken

Ingredients

For the Gravy:
Chicken: 1 kg
Tomatoes, large, cut into half: 8
Onions, large, sliced: 4–6
Garlic: 6–8
2-inch ginger, sliced
Degi mirch: 2 tbsp
Cloves: 10–12
2-inch cinnamon stick
Bay leaves: 6
Black pepper: 10–12
Green cardamom: 4
Butter: 4 tbsp
Salt to taste
Fresh cream: 6 tbsp
Honey: 2 tsp
Kewra water: 2–4 drops
Dried fenugreek leaves, toasted and crushed: 2 tbsp

For the Tadka:
Butter: 4 tbsp
Red chilli powder: 2 tbsp
Coriander powder: 2 tsp

Steps

1. Follow the same steps for marination, sauce preparation, and combining the elements as mentioned in the above butter chicken recipe.
2. In this version, additional flavours such as kewra water and a final tadka (tempering) of butter, red chilli powder and

coriander powder are added to impart an aromatic and richer taste, reminiscent of traditional Lucknowi cuisine.

AMRITSARI DHABA BUTTER CHICKEN

INGREDIENTS

For the Marinade:
Chicken, boneless: 1 kg
Mustard oil: 2 tbsp
Kashmiri red chilli powder: 2 tbsp
Ginger garlic paste: 2 tbsp
Coriander powder: 1 tbsp
Cumin powder: 1 tsp
Turmeric powder: ½ tsp
Fenugreek leaves: 1 tsp
Dried mango powder: 1 tsp
Black salt: ½ tsp (or to taste)
Garam masala: 1 tsp
Fresh mint: 1 tbsp
Fresh coriander: 1 tbsp
Salt to taste
Thick curd (hung curd): ½ cup
Lemon juice: 1 tbsp

For the Makhani Gravy Base:
Ghee: 2 tbsp
Cumin seeds, whole: 1 tsp
Onions, medium, sliced: 3–4
Garlic: 10–15 cloves
1-inch ginger, roughly chopped
Green chillies: 3–4
Kashmiri red chilli powder: 2 tbsp
Coriander powder: 1 tbsp
Turmeric powder: ½ tsp

Fenugreek leaves: ½ tsp

Kashmiri red chillies, whole: 6–7

Green cardamom: 3–4

Tomatoes, roughly chopped: 1 kg

Cashew nuts: ⅓ cup

Coriander stems and roots: A small handful

Salt to taste

Butter: 2 tbsp

For the Tadka

Oil: 1 tsp

Onion, medium, chopped: 1

Garlic, chopped: 3 tbsp

Ginger, chopped: 1 tbsp

Green chillies, slit: 2–3

Kashmiri red chilli powder: 1 tbsp

STEPS

1. Follow the same steps as in the above Butter Chicken recipe for marinating the chicken, preparing the makhani gravy, and combining everything.
2. Grill or bake the marinated chicken, and add it to the prepared makhani gravy. Add hot water as needed to adjust the consistency of the gravy.
3. The recipe also includes a tadka (tempering) of butter, chopped onion, garlic, ginger and green chillies, which should be added to the gravy.

MUMBAI-STYLE BUTTER CHICKEN

INGREDIENTS

Chicken breast, boneless: 1 kg

Ginger garlic paste: 2½ tbsp

Red chilli powder: 2½ tbsp
Salt to taste
Oil to pan fry

For the Gravy:
Tomatoes, roughly slit: 1 kg
Onions, medium, roughly cut: 267 gm (about 2)
Garlic paste: 2½ tbsp
Cashew nuts: 133g
Fenugreek leaves: 2½ tsp
Garam masala: 1 tsp
Sugar: 5 tbsp
Kashmiri chilli powder: 5 tbsp
Butter: 12 tbsp
Cream: 8 tbsp
White vinegar: 4 tbsp
Salt to taste

STEPS

1. For preparing the Mumbai-style butter chicken, follow the same steps as mentioned in the above Butter Chicken recipe for marinating the chicken, preparing the gravy, and combining all the elements.
2. Pan-fry the marinated chicken pieces until they are fully cooked and slightly charred, then add them to the gravy.

Note: This version includes additional ingredients such as white vinegar for acidity and extra sugar for a characteristic sweet and tangy flavour profile.

Iyenger Uncle's Butter Chicken

Ingredients

Chicken thighs: 1 kg
Coconut oil (for frying the chicken): 3 tbsp
Hung curd: ½ cup
Ginger, minced: 2 tbsp
Garlic, minced: 3 cloves
Turmeric powder: 1½ tsp
Kashmiri red chilli powder: 3 tsp
Meat masala: 2 tbsp
Salt to taste

For the Gravy:
Ghee: 3 tbsp
Black mustard seeds: 1½ tsp
Cumin seeds: ½ tsp
Green cardamom: 3
Black cardamom: 2–3
1-inch cinnamon stick
Star anise: 2
Curry leaves: 2 sprigs
Onion, thinly sliced: ½ cup
Ginger, minced: 2–3 tbsp
Garlic, minced: 6 cloves
Tomatoes, medium, quartered: 6
Coconut milk: 135 ml
Meat masala: 2 tbsp
Red chilli powder: 1 tbsp
Fenugreek leaves, crushed: 1 tbsp
Dried mango powder: 1 tbsp
Salt to taste

Steps

1. Follow the steps mentioned in the above butter chicken recipe for marinating the chicken, preparing the sauce, and combining the components.
2. In this version, pan-fry the marinated chicken in coconut oil for added flavour, and use curry leaves for a south Indian touch.
3. The addition of coconut milk also brings a distinct richness to the gravy that is characteristic of South Indian cooking.
4. Use the same preparation and cooking techniques, adjusting the ingredients to include masala, dried mango powder and fenugreek leaves for an authentic Iyenger Uncle's true flavour.

Bohri Chicken Curry

Ingredients

Kashmiri red chillies: 20
Black pepper: 60–70
Star anise: 8
Turmeric powder: 4 tsp
Fresh coconut, grated: 8 tbsp
Coriander seeds: 8 tsp
Cashew nuts: 30–35
Fennel seeds: 4 tsp

Steps

1. Dry roast all the spices separately, ensuring they don't burn.
2. Blend them in a mixer-grinder to a fine powder.
3. Store in an airtight container.

Chicken Haldi Ghati

Ingredients

Black pepper powder: 1 tsp
Salt: 1 tsp (or to taste)
Coriander seeds: 2 tsp
Black pepper: 20
Turmeric powder: ½ tsp
Cashew nuts: 8
Cumin seeds: 1 tsp
Coriander powder: 1 tsp
Kashmiri red chilli powder: 1 tsp
Garam masala: 1 tsp

Special Additions

Add onion, curd, ginger, garlic, green chillies, vinegar and fresh cream

Steps

1. Gather all the spices and ingredients for the spice blend.
2. Dry roast the coriander seeds, black pepper, cumin seeds and cashew nuts on medium heat for about 3–4 minutes until aromatic.
3. Let the roasted spices cool completely, then blend them into a smooth powder.
4. Mix in the powdered ingredients (black pepper powder, salt, turmeric powder, coriander powder, Kashmiri red chilli powder, garam masala).
5. Store the blend in an airtight container in a cool, dark place for up to 3–6 months to maintain its freshness and potency.

6. The special additions (onion, curd, ginger, garlic, green chillies, vinegar and fresh cream) as per the recipe requirements to complete the dish.

Hyderabadi Mutton Curry

Ingredients

Green chillies: 13
Salt: 4 tsp (or to taste)
Turmeric powder: 2½ tsp
Red chilli powder: 5 tsp
Coriander powder: 8 tsp
Red chillies, whole: 5
Mace blades: 3
Black pepper: 2½ tsp
Cloves: 1½ tsp
Black cardamom: 5
Green cardamom: 5
1-inch cinnamon sticks: 3

Steps

1. Dry roast all the spices separately, ensuring they don't burn.
2. Blend them in a mixer-grinder to a fine powder.
3. Store in an airtight container.

Note: This recipe also asks for ginger, garlic, green, onions, tomatoes and curd.

Bohri Curry Powder

Ingredients

Raw peanuts: 33 gm
Cashew: 25 gm
Chana dal: 40 gm
Poppy seeds: 26 gm
Sesame seeds: 50 gm
Black pepper: 1 tsp
Coriander seeds: 1 tsp
Fenugreek seeds: 1 tsp
Mustard seeds: 1 tsp
Fennel seeds: 1 tsp
Cumin seeds: 1 tsp
Cardamom: 3–4
1-inch cinnamon stick
Cloves: 5–6

Steps

1. Dry roast all the spices separately, ensuring they don't burn.
2. Blend them in a mixer-grinder to a fine powder.
3. Store in an airtight container.

Mangalorean Special Curry Masala

Ingredients

Kashmiri chilli: 30 gm
Pandi chilli: 30 gm
Coriander seeds: 15 gm
Curry leaves: 8–10
Cloves: 2–3
Green cardamom: 2–3

Cumin seeds: 2½ tsp
Black pepper: 2½ tsp
Fenugreek seeds: 1 tsp
Turmeric powder: 1 tsp
Fennel seeds: 1½ tsp
Black cardamom: 1
Bay leaf: 1
1-inch cinnamon stick
Salt: ½ tsp (or to taste)

STEPS

1. Dry roast all the spices separately, ensuring they don't burn.
2. Blend them in a mixer-grinder to a fine powder.
3. Store in an airtight container.

BUNTS-STYLE KUNDAPUR POWDER

INGREDIENTS

Byadgi chillies: 37
Coriander seeds: 3 ½ tbsp
Cumin seeds: 1 tbsp
Fenugreek seeds: 1 tsp
Black pepper: 1 tsp
Coconut oil: 1 tbsp
Garlic powder: 1 tsp

STEPS

1. Dry roast all the spices separately, ensuring they don't burn.
2. Mix with the coconut oil and blend them in a mixer-grinder to a fine powder.
3. Store in an airtight container.

Bafat Masala Powder

Ingredients

Kashmiri chilli: 15 gm
Long red chillies (kumta chilli or byadgi dried chillies): 30 gm
Madras chillies: 15 gm
Coriander: 35 gm
Cumin seeds: 1 tsp
Black pepper: 1 tsp
Turmeric powder: 1 tsp

Steps

1. Dry roast all the spices separately, ensuring they don't burn.
2. Blend them in a mixer-grinder to a fine powder.
3. Store in an airtight container.

Yeti Gassi

Ingredients

Byadgi chillies: 10
Coriander seeds: 1½ tbsp
Cumin seeds: ½ tsp
Fenugreek seeds: ½ tsp
Black pepper powder: ½ tsp
Garlic: 6 cloves
Chilli powder: 1 tsp
Turmeric powder: 1 tsp
Coconut, grated: ½ cup
Mustard seeds: ½ tsp
Dried curry leaves: ½ tsp

Carom seeds: ½ tsp
Salt to taste

1. Dry roast all the spices separately, ensuring they don't burn.
2. Blend them in a mixer-grinder to a fine powder.
3. Since this masala contains fresh coconut and garlic, it should be stored in an airtight container in the refrigerator and used within 1–2 weeks to maintain freshness.

Note: The moisture content in coconut and garlic reduces the shelf life compared to a dry spice blend. This recipe also has kokum, onions, ginger paste and green chilli.

KITCHEN KING

INGREDIENTS

Dried red chillies: 10–12
Bay leaves: 5
Mace blades: 3
1-inch cinnamon sticks: 5
Cloves: 15–17
Green cardamom: 10–12
Black cardamom: 3
Star anise: 3–4
Black pepper: 1 tbsp
Coriander seeds: ¼ cup
Cumin seeds: 2 tbsp
Nigella seeds: 1 tbsp
Fennel seeds: 1 tsp
Split chickpeas: 1 tbsp

Split black gram (urad dal): 1 tbsp
Mustard seeds: 1 tsp
Dried fenugreek leaves: 1 tbsp
Black salt: ½ tsp
Salt: ½ tsp (or to taste)
Dried mango powder: 1 tsp
Dried ginger powder: 1 tsp
Asafoetida: ¼ tsp
Turmeric powder: 1 tsp
Nutmeg powder: ⅛ tsp
Garlic powder: 1 tsp

STEPS

1. Dry roast all the spices separately, ensuring they don't burn.
2. Blend them in a mixer-grinder to a fine powder.
3. Store in an airtight container.

BHUPINDER'S MULTIPURPOSE MASALA

INGREDIENTS

Onion powder: 40 gm
Garlic powder: 20 gm
Ginger powder: 10 gm
Coriander, whole: 2 tbsp
Cumin seeds: 1 tbsp
Kashmiri red chilli, whole: 7–8
Bay leaves: 3–4
Green cardamom: 3–4
Black cardamom: 1
Black peppers: 2 tsp
1-inch cinnamon stick

Cloves: 1 tsp
Fenugreek seeds: ½ tsp
Star anise: 1
Fenugreek leaves: 3 tbsp
Caraway seeds: 1 tsp
Turmeric powder: ½ tsp
Salt: 1 tsp (or to taste)
Black salt: ½ tsp
Asafoetida: 1 tsp
Citric acid (tatri): 3 gm
Sugar: 1 tsp
Nutmeg: 3 gm
Mint powder: 1 tsp

STEPS

1. Dry roast all the spices separately, ensuring they don't burn.
2. Blend them in a mixer-grinder to a fine powder.
3. Store in an airtight container.

DHABA MUTTON

INGREDIENTS

Bay leaves: 2
Black cardamom: 2
Star anise: 1
Green cardamom: 3
Cloves: 4
Black pepper: ½ tsp
Coriander powder: 1 tbsp
Cumin powder: ½ tbsp
Garam masala: ½ tbsp

Red chilli powder: ½ tbsp
Cumin seeds: ½ tbsp
Turmeric powder: ¼ tsp
Degi mirch powder: ½ tbsp
Salt: ½ tbsp (or to taste)
Coriander powder: ½ tbsp
Cumin powder: ½ tbsp
Garam masala: ½ tbsp
Red chilli powder: ½ tsp
Dried fenugreek leaves: ½ tbsp

STEPS

1. Dry roast all the spices separately, ensuring they don't burn.
2. Blend them in a mixer-grinder to a fine powder.
3. Store in an airtight container.

CHAMPARAN MUTTON/AHUNA

INGREDIENTS

Kashmiri red chilli powder: 1 tsp
Spicy red chilli powder: ½ tsp
Coriander powder: 1 tsp
Turmeric powder: ¼ tsp
Cumin powder: ½ tsp
Garam Masala: 1 tsp
Red chillies, whole: 3–4
1-inch cinnamon stick
Black pepper: 2–3
Green cardamom: 1–2
Black cardamom: ½
Bay leaf: 1
Salt to taste

1. This dish requires you to toss in all the spices together while cooking, without preparing a pre-ground spice blend.
2. The whole spices (red chillies, cinnamon stick, black pepper, green cardamom, black cardamom, bay leaf) are added directly to the dish to release their flavours gradually.
3. Add the powdered spices (Kashmiri red chilli powder, spicy red chilli powder, coriander powder, turmeric powder, cumin powder, garam masala and salt) directly to the pot while cooking.
4. For Champaran mutton/ahuna, no prior roasting or grinding of the spices is necessary. The unique flavours come from cooking all the spices together during the preparation of the dish, allowing the flavours to meld directly into the mutton.

Punjabi Mutton Curry

Ingredients

Turmeric powder: 2 tsp
Red chilli powder: 1 tsp
Fennel seeds: ¼ tsp
Green cardamom: 1
Clove: 1
1-inch cinnamon stick
Black cardamom: 1
Black pepper: 2–3
Kashmiri chilli powder: ¼ tsp
Coriander powder: ½ tsp
Cumin powder: ¼ tsp
Garam masala powder: 1 tsp
Dried fenugreek powder, roasted and crushed: 3 tsp
Salt to taste

STEPS

1. Dry roast all the spices separately, ensuring they don't burn.
2. Blend them in a mixer-grinder to a fine powder.
3. Store in an airtight container.

KHOTACHIWADI EAST INDIAN BOTTLE MASALA

INGREDIENTS

Coriander seeds: 2 tbsp
1-inch cinnamon stick
Cumin seeds: 1 tbsp
Sesame seeds: 1 tbsp
Poppy seeds: 1 tbsp
Yellow mustard seeds: 1 tbsp
Stone flower: ½ tbsp
Black pepper: 1 tsp
Star anise: 2
Maipatri (patri): ½ tbsp
Fennel seeds: 1 tsp
Fenugreek seeds: 1 tsp
Black cumin seeds: 1 tsp
Cloves, whole: ½ tsp
Nutmeg, whole, crushed: ¼
Mace blade: 1
Bay leaves: 1 tsp
Kashmiri chilli powder: 1 tbsp
Whole wheat flour: 1 tbsp
Turmeric powder: 1 tbsp

STEPS

1. Dry roast all the whole spices separately, ensuring they don't burn.

2. Blend in a mixer-grinder, with the powdered spices, to a fine powder.
3. Store in an airtight container.

VADOUVAN*

INGREDIENTS

Coriander seeds: 2½ tbsp
Fenugreek seeds: 1 tbsp
Cumin seeds: 1 tbsp
Black mustard seeds: 1 tbsp
Cardamom: ½ tbsp
Nutmeg powder: 1¼ tsp
Turmeric powder: 1½ tsp
Black pepper, freshly ground: 1 tsp
Red chilli flakes: 1 tsp
Cloves, crushed: ½ tsp
Salt: 1½ tbsp (or to taste)
Dried curry leaves: 15–20 tbsp

STEPS

1. Dry roast all the whole spices separately, ensuring they don't burn.
2. Blend in a mixer-grinder, with the powdered spices, to a fine powder.
3. Store in an airtight container.

---

* Vadouvan is a French-inspired Indian spice blend that combines classic curry spices with a milder and aromatic twist, making it great for adding nuanced flavour to a variety of dishes, including stews, marinades and roasted vegetables.

Machher Kalia[*]

Ingredients

Dried red chillies: 4
Bay leaves: 4
Cardamom: 4
Cloves: 4
Cinnamon: 2
Cumin seeds: 1 tsp
Turmeric: 1 tsp
Kashmiri red chilli powder: 1 tsp
Cumin powder: 1 tsp
Bengali gorom moshla: ½ tsp

Steps

1. This recipe requires whole spices. You don't have to roast them separately. Use the combination when you are cooking the dishes.

Dimer Dalna[†]

Ingredients

Dried red chillies, whole: 4–6
Bay leaf, whole: 6
Cardamom, whole: 6
Cloves, whole: 6
1-inch cinnamon, whole: 2

---

[*] Machher Kalia is a traditional Bengali fish curry that combines whole and ground spices to create a rich, aromatic flavour profile typical of Bengali cuisine.
[†] Dimer Dalna is a classic Bengali egg curry where the aromatic phoron tadka forms the foundation of the flavour.

Cumin seeds: 1 tbsp
Cumin powder: 1 tbsp
Coriander powder: 1 tbsp
Turmeric powder: 1 tbsp
Red chilli powder: 1 tbsp
Salt to taste
A pinch of sugar

Steps

This recipe requires the addition of spices in two steps.

1. **Phoron Tadka/Tempering:** In hot oil, prepare a tempering mix using the dried red chillies, bay leaves, cardamom, cinnamon, cloves and cumin seeds. Allow the spices to sizzle and release their aromatic flavours.
2. After the tempering, add the powdered spices—cumin powder, coriander powder, turmeric powder, red chilli powder, salt and a pinch of sugar—into the dish. Mix well to ensure the spices blend evenly. This step helps build the rich, layered taste that makes this dish truly satisfying.

Mutton Kosha

Ingredients

Cumin powder: 4 tbsp
Coriander powder: 4 tbsp
Bengali shahi garam masala powder: 4 tbsp
Asafoetida: 1 tsp
Red chilli powder: 3 tbsp
Turmeric powder: 1½ tbsp
Sugar: 2 tbsp
Bay leaves: 4
Dried red chillies: 4

Cloves: 4

Black cardamom: 2

Green cardamom: 4

1-inch cinnamon stick

STEPS

1. You can either marinate your meat with Bengali shahi garam masala powder or put it in the pot while cooking.
2. The whole spices may be tempered at the beginning, in the oil, before adding the meat.
3. The powdered spices can go on top after the meat is roasted in the pot.
4. Alternatively, you can add it all in a pot and cook everything together.

BIYEBARIR MUTTON CURRY[*]

INGREDIENTS

Spices for Marination:
Coriander powder: 2 tsp
Cumin powder: 2 tsp
Bengali garam masala powder: 2 tsp
Red chilli powder: 2 tsp
Sugar: 2 tsp
Salt: 2 tsp (or to taste)

Spices for Cooking:
Poppy seeds: 1 tbsp
Melon seeds: ½ tbsp

---

[*] Biyebarir Mutton Curry is a traditional Bengali wedding-style mutton curry. Proper marination and slow cooking help to enhance the flavours, making it perfect for celebratory occasions.

Turmeric powder: 1 tsp
Coriander powder: 1 tsp
Cumin powder: 1 tsp
Bengali garam masala powder: 1 tsp
Red chilli powder: 1 tsp
Sugar: 1 tsp
Salt: 1 tsp (or to taste)

For Tempering:
Dried red chillies: 6
Bay leaves: 4
Black cardamom: 3
Green cardamom: 3
1-inch cinnamon sticks: 2

STEPS

1. Mix the mutton with the spices for marination (coriander powder, cumin powder, Bengali garam masala powder, red chilli powder, sugar and salt).
2. Allow it to marinate for at least 2 hours, or overnight for better flavour absorption.
3. Heat oil in a heavy-bottomed pot and add the tempering spices (dried red chillies, bay leaves, black cardamom, green cardamom, and cinnamon sticks). Let them sizzle in the oil to release their aromatic flavours.
4. Add the marinated mutton to the pot and cook on medium heat until the mutton starts browning. Then, add the spices for cooking (poppy seeds, melon seeds, turmeric powder, coriander powder, cumin powder, Bengali garam masala powder, red chilli powder, sugar and salt) and stir well to coat the mutton evenly.
5. Add water as needed and let the mutton curry simmer on low heat until the mutton is tender and the flavours meld well together.

Uralikizhan Moru Kozhambu[*]

Ingredients

Chana dal, rinsed and drained: 1½ tbsp
Fenugreek seeds: ½ tsp
Mustard seeds: ½ tsp
Coriander, chopped: 2½ tbsp
1-inch fresh ginger, peeled and chopped
Fresh coconut, grated: 150 gm

Steps

1. Place the fenugreek seeds in a *kadahi* or a small, sturdy and dry skillet set over medium heat. Toast them for 1–2 minutes or until they emit a roasted aroma.
2. Once roasted, move the fenugreek seeds from the pan to a compact blender.
3. Add all other ingredients into the blender, including the pre-soaked chana dal and 4 tbsp of water.
4. Blend everything together until you obtain a uniformly smooth paste.

Aloo Matar Rasedar

Ingredients

Asafoetida: 2 gm
Cumin seeds: 40 gm
Cloves: 5 gm

---

[*] This Uralikizhan Moru Kozhambu is a traditional South Indian yogurt-based curry, with a blend of coconut, spices, and ginger that adds an aromatic and creamy texture to the dish. This blend forms the base of the flavourful gravy.

Chilli powder: 30 gm
Kashmiri garam masala: 40 gm
Coriander powder: 40 gm

STEPS

1. Mix all the powdered spices together (chilli powder, Kashmiri garam masala, coriander powder) and store them in an airtight container.
2. When preparing the dish, start by heating oil in a pan. Add asafoetida and cumin seeds to the hot oil and allow them to release their aroma.
3. Once the cumin seeds are fragrant, add the other ingredients for the dish, and then add the spice blend to enhance the flavour.

ALOOGADDA VEPUDU*

INGREDIENTS

Ghee: 3 tbsp
Mustard seeds: ½ tsp
Cumin seeds: ½ tsp
Salt to taste

For the Masala:
Coriander seeds: 15 gm
Cumin seeds: 1 tsp
Black pepper, whole: 10–12
Dried red chillies: 4
Green cardamom: 4
Cloves: 3

---

* Aloogadda Vepudu is a traditional Andhra-style potato stir-fry that relies on a fragrant, freshly roasted spice blend.

1-inch cinnamon stick
Turmeric powder: 1 tsp
Lemon powder: 2 tsp

For the Tempering:
Oil: 2 tsp
Onion, sliced: 1
Curry leaves: 15–20

STEPS

1. Place a tawa or small skillet, over very low heat, roast the following until fragrant—coriander seeds, cumin seeds, black pepper, dried red chillies, green cardamom, cloves and the cinnamon stick—for about 3 minutes.
2. Transfer all the roasted spices to a blender, add 1 tsp turmeric powder and 2 tsp lemon powder, and blend until ground.

To Cook:
1. In a large pan, heat ghee over medium heat, add mustard seeds and cumin seeds, and stir-fry until they begin to splutter.

ALOO KI TARKARI

INGREDIENTS

Dried fenugreek leaves: 3 tbsp
Turmeric powder: 1 tsp
Cumin powder: 1 tsp
Kashmiri red chilli powder: 1 tsp
Dried mango powder: ½ tsp
Asafoetida: A small pinch
Cloves: 6

Bay leaves: 3
Fresh ginger, peeled and crushed: 30 gm
Salt to taste

Steps

1. Add the dried fenugreek with turmeric powder, cumin seeds, Kashmiri red chilli powder and dried mango powder in a bowl. Mix with a little water to form a paste.
2. In a kadahi, heat the oil over medium heat. Add the asafoetida and fry for about 10 seconds.
3. Toss in the cloves and bay leaves while continuing to stir-fry.
4. Add the prepared spice paste to the pan and cook while stirring.

Achari Mushroom

Ingredients

Mustard seeds: ½ tsp
Nigella seeds: ½ tsp
Coriander seeds, crushed: 1 tsp
Cumin seeds: ½ tsp
Dried red chillies, crushed: 1 tsp
Garlic, coarsely chopped: 5 cloves
Dried mango powder: 1 tsp
Rock salt: 1 tsp
Salt to taste

Steps

1. Dry roast all the raw spices over low heat until aromatic.
2. Roughly grind them with garlic (while ensuring to not make a smooth powder).

3. Add dried mango powder, rock salt and salt, and mix thoroughly.
4. Keep in an airtight container and use in any achari preparation from meat to fish, potato, cauliflower etc.

Murgir Lal Jhol

Ingredients

Dried red chillies: 4
Kashmiri red chillies: 2
Ginger garlic powder: 15 gm
Bay leaves: 2
Salt: 2 tbsp (or to taste)
Turmeric: 1 tsp
Sugar: 1 tbsp
1-inch cinnamon stick
Cloves: 3
Cardamom: 4

Steps

1. Dry roast all the raw whole spices, apart from bay leaves.
2. Grind them to a powder of your desired consistency.
3. Keep in an airtight container.

Note: When cooking murgir lal jhol, add the bay leaves whole at the beginning to temper the oil. Use curd for the gravy instead of tomato to achieve the rich, traditional flavour typical of Bengali red curries.

Macher Jhol

Ingredients

Ginger garlic powder: 2 tsp
Nigella seeds, whole: 1 tsp
Turmeric powder: ¾ tsp
Kashmiri chilli powder: 1½ tsp
Cumin powder: ½ tsp
Coriander powder: 1 tbsp
Cardamom: 10
Cloves: 10
1-inch cinnamon sticks: 2

Steps

1. Mix the first 6 spices in the list as you dry roast and powder the last 3.
2. Grind all the spices together to a fine powder.
3. Keep in an airtight container.

Note:

- Use whole nigella seeds—don't powder them. Add them directly to the mustard oil.
- All other spices should be in powdered form.
- Toast the leftover whole spices and then grind them into a powder.
- Use tomatoes as the base for the gravy.
- You can replace ginger garlic powder with fresh paste if you prefer.

Macher Jhol 2

Ingredients

Turmeric powder: 2 tbsp
Kashmiri red chilli powder: 1 tbsp
Cumin powder: 1 tbsp
Bengali garam masala: 2 tbsp

Steps

1. Mix and combine all the powders together.
2. Keep in an airtight container.

Note: You can also opt to roast whole spices (corresponding to these powders) before grinding them, which can enhance the aroma and flavour of the macher jhol.

The roasting step brings out the essential oils of the spices, providing an added depth to the dish.

Handi Murgh Curry

Ingredients

Ginger garlic powder: 10 gm
Bay leaf, large: 1
Black cardamom: 4
Green cardamom: 4
Kashmiri chilli powder: 1 tsp
Turmeric powder: ½ tsp
Coriander powder: 3 tbsp
Salt: 2½ tsp (or to taste)

1. Dry roast the whole spices for enhanced flavour and aroma.
2. While cooking the dish, first, add the bay leaf into the oil/ghee.
3. Keep a blend of the rest of the spices to use when you are cooking.
4. Keep in an airtight container.

Note: You can use curd to create a rich, creamy base. Alternatively, using tomato will add a deeper and tangier flavour to the curry, giving it a different character that balances well with the spice blend.

DELHI DOPIAZA

INGREDIENTS

Mutton: 1 kg
Ghee: 200 gm
Onions, sliced: 300 gm
1-inch ginger, finely chopped
Salt to taste
Cumin seeds: 2 tsp
Coriander seeds: 3 tsp
Black pepper: 1 tsp
Cloves: 8–10
Green cardamom: 10–15
Water: 500 ml

STEPS

1. Rinse the mutton pieces under cold water and set aside.
2. In a large pan, heat the ghee over medium heat. Add the sliced onions and sauté until golden brown.

3. Stir in the chopped ginger and continue to cook for another 1–2 minutes.
4. Add the mutton to the pan and fry until the pieces are well browned and any liquid has evaporated.
5. In a dry skillet, lightly roast the cumin seeds, coriander seeds, pepper and cloves just until they start to release their aromas.
6. Grind the roasted spices into a fine powder.
7. Sprinkle the ground spices, salt and cardamom over the browned mutton and mix thoroughly.
8. Pour in 500 ml of water, then cover the pan. Reduce the heat to low and let the mutton simmer gently for about 90 minutes or until the meat is tender and the flavours have melded together.
9. Serve the tender mutton with a side of rice or bread for a complete meal.

AIN-I-AKBARI DOPIAZA[*]

INGREDIENTS

Meat (middling fat): 10 seer[†]/kg
Ghee: 2 seer/kg
Onions: 2 seers/2 kg
Salt: ¼ seer/250 gm (or to taste)
Fresh pepper: ⅛ seer/125 gm

---

[*] This historical dish was served at Akbar'scourt (c. 1600).
[†] The terms 'seer', 'dam' and 'misqal' are old units of measurement used in South Asia, particularly during the Mughal era, to weigh ingredients. In this recipe for Dopiaza, from the *Ain-i-Akbari*, both seer and dam are used to specify quantities of different ingredients. Here's a breakdown:

- 1 seer is roughly equivalent to 1 kg.
- Dam is a smaller unit of measurement, typically used for spices. It is about 20 grams.
- Misqal is an even smaller unit of measurement. 1 m (misqal) is 6 gm.

Cumin seeds: 1 dam/20 gm
Coriander seeds: 1 dam/20 gm
Cardamom: 1 dam/20 gm
Cloves: 1 dam/20 gm
Black pepper: 2 dams/40 gm

1. To prepare this historical dish, you can follow the recipe above but remember this is for 10 kg of meat.

DOPIAZA I

INGREDIENTS

Coriander powder: 4 tbsp
Turmeric powder: 2 tsp
Fennel seeds, crushed: 2 tsp
Black pepper, crushed: 1 tsp
Red chilli powder: 2 tsp
Salt: 2 tsp (or to taste)

STEPS

1. Combine all the listed spices in a mixing bowl. Stir them together until they are well mixed.
2. Transfer the blend to an airtight container to maintain freshness.
3. When preparing your DoPiaza, use this spice blend according to the taste preferences noted in your recipe to enrich the dish with enhanced flavours.

Dopiaza 2

Ingredients

Coriander seeds: 4 tsp
Turmeric powder: 1 tsp
Cumin seeds: 2 tsp
Cloves: 1 tsp
1-inch cinnamon sticks: 3
Dried Kashmiri red chillies: 10
Black pepper: 1 tsp
Green cardamom: 6

Steps

To prepare approximately 100 gm of this spice blend and use it in your cooking:

1. Lightly roast the coriander seeds, cumin seeds, cloves, dried Kashmiri red chillies, black pepper and green cardamom pods in a dry pan over medium heat until they are fragrant. This enhances their flavours.
2. Cool the spices and then grind them, along with the turmeric powder and cinnamon sticks, in a spice grinder or mortar and pestle to a fine powder.
3. Store your freshly made spice blend in an airtight container to keep it fresh.
4. Use the spice blend as part of the cooking process detailed in the original Dopiaza recipe. This blend will impart a robust flavour that enhances the natural taste profiles of the other ingredients.

Jewish-Style Chicken/Paneer Dopiaza

Ingredients

Cumin seeds seed: 2½ tsp
Coriander: 2½ tsp
Turmeric powder: 2½ tsp
Salt: 2 tsp (or to taste)
Black pepper: ¼ tsp
Cloves: 6
1-inch cinnamon stick
Green cardamom: 4
Bay leaves: 2
Dried hot red chilli: ½ tsp

Steps

1. Dry roast the whole spices and let them cool.
2. In a jar, add all the spices with the powdered spices and blend till you get a smooth aromatic powder.
3. Keep in an airtight container.

Jewish Murgi Alaa Curry

Ingredients

Cumin seeds seed: 4 tsp
Coriander: 4 tsp
Turmeric powder: 2 tsp
Salt: 3–4 tsp (or to taste)
Garam masala: 4 tsp
Bay leaves: 5

1. Dry roast the whole spices and let them cool.
2. In a jar, add all the spices with the powdered spices and blend till you get a smooth aromatic powder.
3. Keep in an airtight container.

Note: Use tomato (and not curd) for the base, as it adds a tangy and vibrant flavour.

Kofta Curry

Ingredients

Turmeric powder: 1½ tsp
Salt: 1½ tsp (or to taste)
1–inch cinnamon stick: 5
Green cardamom: 2 tbsp
Cloves: 2 tbsp

Steps

1. Dry roast the whole spices and let them cool.
2. In a jar, add all the spices with the powdered spices and blend till you get a smooth aromatic powder.
3. Keep in an airtight container.

Note: The Jewish version uses tomato to add the tang to the dish. You can also add brown onions to get a deeper flavour and mint leaves for freshness.

Anglo-Indian Keema Curry

Ingredients

Ginger powder: 2 tsp
Garlic powder: 2 tsp
Dried hot red chilli flakes: 1 tsp
Turmeric powder: ½ tsp
Dried mint powder: 2 tbsp
Salt: 1 tsp (or to taste)
Cloves, whole: 4
Green cardamom: 2
Black cardamom: 2
1-inch cinnamon stick

Steps

1. Dry roast the whole spices and let them cool. Mix them with the powdered spices and blend to a smooth powder.
2. Keep in an airtight container.

Xacuti*

Ingredients

Kashmiri dried red chillies, chopped (seeds removed for a milder curry): 6 gm
Dried coconut flakes: 30 gm
Cumin seeds: 1 tbsp
Coriander seeds: 1 tbsp

---

* Xacuti Masala is a complex spice blend, characteristic of Goan cuisine. It combines the earthy warmth of coriander and cumin with the fragrant fennel and subtle sweetness from dried coconut flakes.

Carom seeds: 1 tsp
Fennel seeds: 1 tbsp
Black poppy seeds: 1 tbsp
Cloves: 7
Black pepper: 1 tbsp
Cinnamon sticks: 7 gm
Star anise: 4
Turmeric powder: ½ tsp

STEPS

1. Dry roast the whole spices and let them cool. Mix them with the powdered spices and blend to a smooth powder.
2. Keep in an airtight container.

LAHORI CHANA GOSHT

INGREDIENTS

Green cardamom: 2
Black cardamom: 1
Black pepper: 8–10
Cloves: 3–4
1-inch cinnamon sticks: 2
Star anise: 1
Carom seeds: ¼ tsp
Red chilli, crushed: 1½ tsp
Cumin powder: 1 tsp
Coriander powder: 1 tsp
Garam masala powder: 1 tsp
Salt: 1 tsp (or to taste)

STEPS

1. Dry roast the whole spices and let them cool. Mix them with the powdered spices and blend to a smooth powder.
2. Keep in an airtight container.

Note: Only use curd to make the base gravy. If you want an added kick, add green chillies.

ANGLO-INDIAN ESSENTIAL CURRY PASTE

INGREDIENTS

Malt or wine vinegar: ¼ cup
Coriander seeds: 2 tbsp
Cumin seeds: 2 tsp
Red chillies: 4–6
Fresh garlic, peeled: 2 tsp
Fresh ginger, cleaned and chopped: 2 tsp
Red chilli powder: 1 tbsp
Turmeric powder: ½ tsp
Garam masala: 1 tsp
Mustard seeds, whole: 1 tsp
Sugar: 1 tsp
Salt: 1 tsp (or to taste)

STEPS

1. Dry roast the whole spices and let them cool.
2. In a blender, add all the whole spices, herbs and powder along with the vinegar.
3. Make a smooth paste and use it in any of your Anglo-Indian dishes. You can deep freeze this blend as well.

Anglo-Indian Vindaloo Paste

Ingredients

Malt or wine vinegar: ¼ cup
Fresh garlic, cleaned and chopped: 2 tbsp
Fresh ginger, peeled and chopped: 2 tbsp
Cumin seeds, whole: 3 tbsp
Red chillies: 10
Chilli powder: 2 tbsp
Curry leaves, stalk included: about 10
Mustard seeds, whole: 1 tbsp
Fenugreek seeds: ½ tsp
Sugar: 1 tsp
Salt: 1 tsp (or to taste)

Steps

1. Dry roast the whole spices and let them cool.
2. In a blender, add all the whole spices, herbs and powder along with the vinegar.
3. Make a smooth paste and use it in any of your vindaloo dishes. You can deep freeze this blend as well.

Goan Vindaloo Paste

Ingredients

Kashmiri red chillies: 15–20
1-inch cinnamon stick
Cloves: 6–8
Cumin seeds: 1 tsp
Black pepper: 10–12
Black mustard seeds: ¼ tsp

Turmeric powder: ½ tsp
Ginger garlic paste: 50 gm
Goa Vinegar (or substitute with red wine vinegar or malt vinegar): ¼ cup

STEPS

1. Dry roast the whole spices and let them cool.
2. In a blender, add all the whole spices, herbs and powder along with the vinegar.
3. Make a smooth paste and use it in any of your vindaloo dishes. You can deep freeze this blend as well.

Note: Soak the Kashmiri chillies in water before you make the paste.

GOAN RECHEADO*

INGREDIENTS

Kashmiri red chillies, soaked and de-seeded: 60 gm
Cumin seeds: 2 tsp
Black pepper: 1 tsp
Cloves: 15–20
1–inch cinnamon sticks: 3
Turmeric powder: 1½ tsp
Sugar: 1½ tsp
Salt: 1½ tsp (or to taste)
Garlic: 15 medium cloves
2-inch ginger piece
Goa vinegar/red wine vinegar: 1 cup

---

* Goan Recheado Masala is a spicy and tangy paste, integral to Goan cuisine.

1. Soak the Kashmiri red chillies in warm water until soft. De-seed them for a milder spice level.
2. Dry roast the cumin seeds, pepper, cloves and cinnamon sticks over medium heat until they release their fragrance. Allow them to cool completely.
3. In a blender, combine the soaked Kashmiri red chillies, roasted whole spices, turmeric powder, sugar, salt, garlic cloves, ginger and vinegar.
4. Blend everything until you achieve a smooth, aromatic paste.
5. Transfer the masala to an airtight container and store it in the refrigerator for future use.
6. Store this recheado masala in an airtight container in the refrigerator for up to 2 weeks. For longer storage, freeze it in portions, and it will keep well for several months.

Maharashtrian Curry Powder

Ingredients

Onion powder: 50 gm
Dried coconut powder: 70 gm
Black cumin seeds: 1 tsp
Star anise: 2
Red chillies, whole: 4–6
Coriander seeds: 1 tbsp
Cumin seeds: 1 tsp
Turmeric powder: ½ tsp
Garam masala: 1 tsp
Ginger garlic powder: 2 tbsp

1. Dry roast all the whole spices (black cumin seeds, star anise, red chillies, coriander seeds and cumin) over medium heat until they release their aroma. Allow them to cool completely to room temperature.
2. Mix the roasted whole spices with all the powdered spices (onion powder, dried coconut powder, turmeric powder, garam masala and ginger garlic powder).
3. Blend the mixture to a fine powder using a spice grinder.
4. Transfer the curry powder to an airtight container to maintain its freshness.
5. Store this curry powder in an airtight container in a cool, dark place. It will stay fresh for up to 3-6 months, retaining its flavour and aroma when stored properly.

Konkani Shaguto

Ingredients

Dried bay leaves: 2
Salt: 2 tsp (or to taste)
1-inch cinnamon stick
Cloves: 4
Black pepper: 4–6
Coriander seeds: 1 tsp
Cumin seeds: 2 tsp
Dried stone flower: 1 tbsp
Dried red byadgi or Kashmiri chillies, seeds removed: 8–10
Cashew nuts, raw and unsalted: ¼ cup
White poppy seeds: 2 tsp
Dried coconut, grated: ½ cup

STEPS

1. Dry roast all the whole spices and bring to room temperature.
2. Mix all the powdered spices with the whole spices.
3. Blend to a fine powder.
4. Keep in an airtight container.

Note: Use fresh coconut for a richer flavour.

MANGALOREAN PORK INDAD PASTE

INGREDIENTS

White wine vinegar: 200 ml
Onions, medium, sliced: 5
Cumin powder: 1½ tbsp
Dried Kashmiri chillies: 20
Black pepper: 2 tbsp
Sultana (golden) raisins (kishmish), soaked: 100 gm
Garlic: 8–10 cloves
Green chillies: 4
Mint leaves: 5 gm
Cloves: 12
Cinnamon powder: ½ tsp

STEPS

1. Roast the dried Kashmiri chillies, pepper and cloves over medium heat until they release their aroma. Let them cool to room temperature.
2. Blend the roasted spices with the onions, white wine vinegar, raisins, garlic, green chillies, mint leaves, cumin powder and cinnamon powder until smooth. Do not add

water while blending, as the vinegar and onions provide sufficient moisture.

3. Use this paste for your Mangalorean pork indad or freeze it in portions for later use.
4. Store the paste in an airtight container in the refrigerator for up to 2 weeks. It can also be frozen for several months.

RUFINA SHROTRI'S PORK INDAD PASTE

INGREDIENTS

Dried red chillies: 8
Green chillies: 3
Onion: 1 and ½
Cumin seeds: ½ tsp
Turmeric powder: ¼ tsp
Tamarind, cherry-sized: 1
Garlic: 8–10 cloves
Black pepper: 5
Cloves: 5
1-inch cinnamon
Vinegar: 1 tsp
Sugar: 1 tsp
Salt: ½ tsp (or to taste)

STEPS

1. Roast the dried red chillies, cumin seeds, pepper, cloves and cinnamon stick over medium heat until aromatic. Let them cool to room temperature.
2. Blend the roasted spices with the onion, green chillies, turmeric powder, tamarind, garlic, vinegar, sugar and salt until smooth. Do not add water.
3. Use this paste in your pork indad or freeze it for future use. Store it in an airtight container in the refrigerator for up to 2 weeks or freeze it for several months.

Parsi Curry

Ingredients

Dried red chillies (mixture of Kashmiri, Goa and any local chillies): 10 gm
Turmeric: ½ tbsp
Dried ginger powder: 1 tbsp
Dried garlic powder: 1 tbsp
Cumin seeds: 4 tbsp
Bay leaves: 1 tsp
Dried curry leaves: 1 tsp
Coriander seeds: 4 tbsp
Mustard seeds: 1½ tbsp
Fenugreek seeds: 2 tbsp
Poppy seeds: 2 tbsp
Gram, roasted: 3 tbsp
Star anise: 3–4
Black sesame seeds: 1 tbsp
1-inch cinnamon sticks: 3
Cloves: 4–6
Green cardamom seeds, peeled: ¼ tsp
Black pepper: ½ tsp
Nutmeg, grated: ¼ tsp
Salt: ¼ tsp (or to taste)
Oil: ¼ tsp

Steps

1. Dry roast each ingredient individually on low heat until they release their aromatic oils and are lightly browned. Allow them to cool completely.
2. Grind the roasted ingredients to a fine powder.
3. Combine and mix thoroughly to ensure an even distribution of flavours.

4. Heat the oil until very hot, then sprinkle it onto the spice powder and mix well. This step helps preserve the masala for a longer time, preventing spoilage.

5. Store the spice blend in an airtight glass container in a cool, dry place. Proper storage will maintain the blend's freshness and potency for several months.

Sabzi Masala

Ingredients

Oil: 2 tsp
Garlic: 7 cloves
Peanuts: 50 gm
Dried coconut, grated: 2 tbsp
Curry leaves: 15–20
Coriander Seeds: ½ cup
Cumin seeds: 2 tbsp
Fennel seeds: 1 tbsp
Sesame seeds: 2 tbsp
Chilli powder: 2 tbsp
Turmeric powder: 1 tbsp
Dried mango powder: 2 tbsp
Garam masala: 1 tbsp
Dried fenugreek leaves: 2 tbsp
Sesame seeds: 2 tbsp
Salt: 2 tbsp (or to taste)

Steps

1. In a pan, heat 2 tsp of oil and roast 7 cloves of garlic until they turn golden brown. Remove and set aside.

2. In the same pan, add peanuts and roast until they turn crunchy. Remove and set aside.

3. Add dried coconut and a few curry leaves to the pan. Keeping the flame on low, roast until they turn golden brown. Transfer all the roasted ingredients to a plate and allow them to cool completely.

4. In a separate pan, take coriander seeds, cumin seeds, fennel seeds and sesame seeds. Roast on a low flame until the spices turn aromatic. Cool completely, then grind to a coarse powder. Transfer the powder to a large bowl.

5. To the bowl with the ground spices, add chilli powder, turmeric powder, dried mango powder, garam masala, dried fenugreek leaves, sesame seeds and salt. Mix well, ensuring everything is well combined.

6. Store the sabzi masala in an airtight container.

Notes: This sabzi masala can be used to prepare any dry, *bharwa* (stuffed) or gravy-based dishes.

Archana's Gujarati Dal

Ingredients

Dried coriander seeds: 5 tbsp
Red chilli powder: 4 tbsp
Mustard seeds: 1 tsp
Fenugreek seeds: 1 tsp
Cumin seeds: 1 tsp
Turmeric powder: 2 tbsp
Asafoetida: ½ tsp

Steps

1. Grind the dry coriander seeds, mustard seeds, fenugreek seeds, cumin seeds and turmeric powder into a fine powder using a spice grinder or mortar and pestle.

2. In a large bowl, combine the ground spices with red chilli powder and asafoetida. Mix thoroughly to ensure even distribution of all the spices.

3. Store the Gujarati dal masala in an airtight container in a cool, dry place. Proper storage will maintain its freshness and potency for several months.

Chef Kunal Kapur's Madras Curry Powder

Ingredients

Bay leaves, whole: 3
Dried red chillies, whole: 8
Coriander seeds: 2½ tbsp
Black pepper: 1 tbsp
Fenugreek seeds: 1 tsp
Fennel seeds: 1½ tbsp
2-inch cinnamon sticks: 3
Salt: 1 tsp (or to taste)
Cumin seeds: 1 tbsp
Turmeric powder: 1¼ tsp
Ginger powder: 1 tbsp
Garlic powder: 2 tsp

Steps

1. Dry roast all the spices except turmeric, ginger powder and garlic powder in a pan over medium heat, stirring frequently until fragrant (around 3–5 minutes). Be careful not to burn the spices.

2. Cool the spices completely. This is important to prevent any loss of flavour.

3. Grind the cooled spices into a fine powder using a mortar and pestle or a spice grinder.

4. Mix the ground spices with turmeric powder, ginger powder and garlic powder.
5. Store the Madras curry powder in an airtight container for up to 6 months.

KADAHI MASALA

INGREDIENTS

Coriander seeds: 6 tbsp
Cumin seeds: 1½ tsp
Dried red chillies: 6–7
Green cardamom: 10
Black cardamom: 2
Black pepper: 25–30

STEPS

1. Dry roast all the spices in a pan over medium heat, stirring frequently until fragrant (around 3–5 minutes). Be careful not to burn the spices.
2. Cool the spices completely. This is important to prevent any loss of flavour.
3. Grind the cooled spices into a coarse powder using a mortar and pestle or spice grinder.
4. Store the blend in an airtight container for up to 6 months.

BANGDA TIKHLA MALVANI PASTE

INGREDIENTS

Coconut, dried: 100 gm
Byadgi chillies: 7
Turmeric powder: ¼ tsp

Onion Powder: 2 tbsp
Tirphal (a type of schezwan pepper): 4
Kokum, dried: 6
Black pepper: ½ tsp
Coriander seeds: ¾ tsp

1. Blend all the ingredients to a fine powder to use in the Bangda Tikhla dish.
2. If you are making it fresh, replace the dried coconut, onion powder and dried kokum with fresh coconut, fresh onion and fresh kokum. Blend everything to make a smooth paste. In the final step of cooking, add the kokum to the fish gravy.

MRS BEETON'S INDIAN CURRY POWDER[17]

INGREDIENTS

Coriander seeds: 3 tbsp
Turmeric: 2 tbsp
1-inch cinnamon sticks: 3
Red chilli powder: 1 tsp
Mustard seeds: 1 tsp
Ginger powder: 1 tsp
Allspice powder (kababchini): 1 tsp
Fenugreek seeds: 1½ tbsp

STEPS

1. Lightly dry roast the whole spices separately on a medium to low flame until aromatic. Allow to cool completely.

163

2. Transfer the cooled spices to a spice grinder or mortar and pestle. Grind to a fine powder.

3. Store the Indian curry powder in an airtight container in a cool, dry place. Proper storage will maintain its freshness and potency for several months.

TUNGRYMBAI (FERMENTED SOYBEAN) AXONE/AKHUNI

INGREDIENTS

Fermented soybean: 500 gm
Onion, grated: 1 cup
Black sesame seeds/perilla seeds paste: 4 tbsp
Turmeric: 1 tsp
Pork cut into small pieces (optional): 2
Ginger, sliced: 2 tbsp
Oil to fry
Dried king chilli: 1
Salt to taste

STEPS

1. Mash the fermented soybean paste until smooth and set aside.
2. Heat 2 tbsp of oil in a pan over medium heat.
3. Add the grated onion and fry until it turns translucent.
4. Stir in 1 tsp of turmeric powder and salt to taste.
5. Add the mashed soybean paste to the pan and mix well.
6. Once the aroma of the soybean paste starts to come through, add the sliced ginger.
7. Pour some water (enough to create a thick mixture, but not too watery).

8. Let the mixture cook and boil for 25–30 minutes, stirring every 2–3 minutes to prevent sticking.
9. When the mixture becomes a thick paste, your tungrymbai/axone is ready to eat! Enjoy it as a savoury accompaniment to your meal.

Madurai Drumstick Curry (Madurai Murungakkai Kari Kozhambu)

Ingredients

Coriander powder: 4 tbsp
Chilli powder: 1 tbsp
Turmeric powder: ½ tsp
Black pepper powder: ½ tsp
Cumin seeds: 1 tsp
Fennel seeds: 1 tsp
Mustard seeds: ½ tsp
Fenugreek seeds: ½ tsp
Asafoetida: A pinch
Salt: 1½ tsp (or to taste)

Steps

1. Lightly dry roast the whole spices separately on a medium to low flame until aromatic. Allow to cool completely.
2. Transfer the cooled spices to a spice grinder or mortar and pestle. Grind to a fine powder.
3. Store the masala powder in an airtight container in a cool, dry place. Proper storage will maintain its freshness and potency for several months.

Green Masala Mutton Curry (Masala Kari Kurma)

Ingredients

Ghee: 2 tsp
Cloves: 3
1-inch cinnamon stick
Fennel seeds: ¼ tsp
Coriander seeds: 1 tbsp
Onion powder: 4 tbsp
Guntur red chilli, whole: 3
Coconut: ½ cup
Poppy seeds: 2 tsp

Steps

1. Heat the ghee in a pan. Add cloves, cinnamon, Fennel seeds, coriander seeds and red chilli. Roast until aromatic.
2. In a grinder, add the roasted spices with onion powder, coconut and poppy seeds. Grind to a fine paste.
3. Transfer the ground spice blend to an airtight container. Store in a cool, dry place.

Meatball Curry (Kyma Urundai Kari Kozhambu)

Ingredients

For the Meatballs:
Meat, minced: 500 gm
Turmeric powder: ¼ tsp
Bengal gram powder, fried, roasted: ¼ cup
Chilli powder: ½ tsp

Coriander powder: 1 tsp
Cloves, finely pounded: 2
1-inch cinnamon, finely pounded: 2
Ginger garlic paste: 1 tsp
Egg, beaten: 1
Salt: ½ tsp (or to taste)

For Tempering:
Oil: 2 tbsp
Curry leaves: 8
Cloves: 2
1-inch cinnamon sticks: 2
Cardamom: 2
Onions, large, finely chopped: 2
Chilli powder: 1½ tsp
Coriander powder: 2 tsp
Ginger garlic paste: 3 tsp

For Grinding:
Tomatoes, large: 2
Coconut: ¼ cup
Poppy seeds: 2 tsp
Cumin seeds: 2 tsp
Salt: 1 tsp (or to taste)
Lemon, juiced: 1

For the Garnish:
Coriander leaves, chopped: ¼ cup

STEPS

1. Wash the minced meat, place on a sieve and squeeze out the water.
2. Add turmeric powder, ginger garlic paste, chilli powder, coriander powder, cloves and cinnamon.

3. Add fried Bengal gram, beaten egg and salt to taste.
4. Knead the mixture well and form small, compressed lemon-sized balls. Set it aside.

For Cooking the Meatballs:

1. Heat oil in a heavy vessel, then add curry leaves and whole spices followed by chopped onions.
2. Sauté until the onions are translucent.
3. Add chilli and coriander powders, along with ginger garlic paste. Keep cooking on low heat till the oil rises to the surface.

For Preparing the Gravy:

1. Grind the ingredients listed and add to the above, blending well. Add enough water to make it a pouring consistency.
2. Let the gravy simmer for 10 minutes, and carefully add the meatballs one by one.
3. Cover the vessel and cook for 10 minutes on low heat until the meatballs are cooked and the curry thickens.
4. Add lime juice, remove from heat and garnish with chopped coriander leaves.

ANGLO-INDIAN KOFTA 'BALL' CURRY

INGREDIENTS

For the Koftas:
Lean meat, ground: 1 kg
Onion, medium, finely chopped: 1½
Curry leaves, finely chopped: 3
Green chillies, finely chopped: 2
Green coriander, finely chopped: 1 small bunch

Salt to taste
Oil for frying the koftas
Masala paste (recipe below): ½ portion

Masala Paste:
Cumin powder: 4 tbsp
Fresh ginger garlic paste: 3 tbsp
Kashmiri red chilli: 3 tbsp
Red chilli powder: 2 tsp
Fresh ground coconut or coconut powder: 2 tbsp
Garam masala: 2 tsp

For the Curry:
Oil: ½ cup
Onion, medium, finely sliced: 1
Curry leaves: 20
Tomato, medium, finely chopped: 1
Coconut milk: 1 can
Curd, whisked: ¼ cup
Tamarind paste: ½ tsp
Salt to taste

STEPS

1. Mix ground meat, onion, curry leaves, green chillies and coriander with half the masala paste. Form into balls and set aside.
2. Place a heavy-bottomed pan with oil over a moderate flame and fry the koftas to a rich brown colour. Drain and transfer to the pot of simmering curry gravy.
3. Heat the oil and add curry leaves. Fry the onions until golden. Add the remaining masala paste and fry until fragrant.

4. Stir in tomato, coconut milk, curd and tamarind purée.
5. Add the koftas to the curry, along with potatoes, and simmer for 15 minutes.
6. Garnish with fresh coriander. Serve with coconut rice.

Rana Safvi's Kofta Curry[18]

Ingredients

For the Koftas:
Meat, minced: 1 kg
Poppy seeds: 2 tsp
Black cardamom: 4
Red chilli, whole: To taste
Black pepper: 4 tsp
Onions, small: 4
Cumin seeds: 2 tsp
Gram flour, roasted: 6 tsp
Salt to taste

Curry Masala:
Mustard oil (for frying)
Fenugreek seeds: 1 tsp
Onions, large, chopped: 4
Garlic: 20–24 cloves
4-inch piece of ginger
Turmeric powder: 4 tsp
Red chilli powder to taste
Coriander powder: 4 tsp
Salt to taste
Water (as needed)
Fresh coriander for garnish

1. Dry roast all the spices and grind them into a coarse powder.
2. Grind the onions and mix them with the minced meat.
3. Add the ground spices and roasted gram flour. Mix well.
4. Shape the mixture into small balls (koftas).
5. Heat mustard oil in a pan until it starts smoking, then turn off the heat and let it cool slightly.* Reheat the oil, add fenugreek seeds and fry until dark brown.
6. Add chopped onions, garlic, ginger, turmeric powder, red chilli powder, coriander powder and salt. Sauté until golden brown.
7. Add water to the curry base and bring it to a boil. Gently add the koftas to the curry.
8. Simmer on low heat for 35–40 minutes until the koftas are cooked through.
9. Garnish with freshly chopped coriander. Serve hot with rice or bread.

CHIGOOR KA SALAN

INGREDIENTS

Turmeric powder: 1 tsp
Ginger powder: 2 tsp
Garlic powder: 3 tsp
Cumin powder, dry roasted: 4 tsp
Tender leaves and flowers of the tamarind tree (chigoor): 50 gm
Curry leaves: 2 sprigs
Salt: 2 tsp (or to taste)
Red chilli powder: 2½ tsp

---

* Mustard oil has a strong, sharp taste and aroma when uncooked. Gently heating it until it starts to smoke often helps with the sharpness, making it more suitable for cooking and giving it a more balanced, less intense flavour.

STEPS

1. In a grinder, add turmeric powder, ginger powder, garlic powder, roasted cumin powder, tender chigoor, curry leaves, salt and red chilli powder. Grind until a fine powder is formed.
2. Transfer the blend to an airtight container. Store in a cool, dry place.

HYDERABADI KORMA

INGREDIENTS

Green cardamom: 12
Cloves: 10
1-inch cinnamon sticks: 2
Onion powder: 8–9 tbsp
Ginger garlic powder: 2 tbsp
Turmeric powder: ¼ tsp
Red chilli powder: 3 tbsp
Nigella seeds: 1½ tsp
Charoli seeds (chironji): 1½ tsp
Almonds, peeled: 12
Poppy seeds: 1½ tsp
Dried coconut: 1½ tsp
Salt: 1½ tsp (or to taste)
Saffron: ¾ tsp

STEPS

1. In a grinder, add green cardamom, cloves, cinnamon, onion powder, ginger garlic powder, turmeric powder, red chilli powder, caraway seeds, chironji, almonds, poppy seeds, dried coconut, salt and saffron.
2. Grind to a coarse powder.

3. Transfer the blend to an airtight container. Store in a cool, dry place.

Korma Asafjahi

Ingredients

Almonds, blanched and sliced: 25
Raisins, whole: 20
Onion, finely chopped: 12 tbsp
Red chilli powder: 2 tsp
Black pepper: 15
Garam masala powder: 1 tsp
Sugar: 1 tsp
Green chillies, finely chopped without seeds: 5 tbsp
Saffron: A pinch, diluted in warm water
Ghee/oil to fry

Steps

1. In a pan, fry the almonds and raisins separately in ghee until golden. Set aside.
2. In the same ghee, fry the chopped onions until golden brown.
3. Add red chillies, black pepper, garam masala powder, sugar and green chillies to the onions. Cook with 2 tbsp of water, stirring well until the water dries up.
4. Add the fried almonds, raisins and saffron to the mixture. Mix well.
5. Use this spice paste with curd and meat to create a delicious dish.
6. It can be stored in an airtight container in the refrigerator for up to 1 week. For longer storage, it can be frozen in portions for several months.

Kashmiri Pandit Roghan Josh

Ingredients

For the Curry:
Meat (preferably from the front leg or *dast*): 1 kg
Ghee or vegetable oil: 300 gm
Curd, divided into two portions: 250 gm and 25 gm
Salt to taste
Cloves: 4
Asafoetida: A pinch
Dried ginger powder: 1 tsp
Red chilli powder (preferably roghni lal mirch): 1 tsp
1-inch cinnamon stick
2-inch fresh ginger, ground
Sugar: 1 tsp
Garam masala: 2 tsp
Saffron: A pinch
Kewra water: 1 tsp
Mawa (khoya): 100 gm
Almonds, soaked and skinned: 25 gm
Water: Approximately 3 cups

Steps

1. In a heavy-bottomed *degchi*,* heat the ghee or vegetable oil. Add the cloves, asafoetida, cinnamon stick, meat pieces, 250 gm curd, ginger powder, red chilli powder and dried ginger powder. Cover the pot and simmer on low heat until all the water evaporates and a reddish sediment begins to appear. Stir occasionally to prevent burning.

---

* A broad-rimmed, curved-bottomed cooking utensil.

2. Add 2 tbsp of water, cover again and let it simmer. After a few moments, scrape the sediment with a spatula, turning the meat continuously. Repeat this process until the meat turns reddish brown.
3. Once the meat is reddish brown, add sugar and water. Cook for at least half an hour or until the meat becomes tender.
4. When the meat is tender, add garam masala and saffron (ground to a paste with some kewra water). Cover the pot and let it cook for another 10 minutes.
5. Thin the mawa with the remaining 25 gm of curd and add it to the pot along with the almond paste. Place the vessel on a low flame and cook for a few more minutes.
6. Once the gravy has thickened and the mawa is red, remove from heat. Serve hot with naan or rice, garnished with additional almonds or fresh coriander leaves, if desired.

QALYA

INGREDIENTS

Salt: 1 tbsp (or to taste)
Asafoetida: ½ tsp
Cloves: 1 tsp
Red chilli powder: 2½ tsp
Ginger powder: 2½ tsp
Turmeric powder: 3 tsp
Fennel seeds: 2½ tsp
Garam masala: 4 tsp
Sugar: 1 tsp

1. Combine salt, asafoetida, cloves, red chilli powder, ginger powder, turmeric powder, fennel seeds, garam masala and sugar in a bowl. Mix the spices thoroughly and store the spice blend in an airtight container to keep it fresh until use.
2. If cooking fresh, first, add asafoetida in curd with cloves, salt, red chilli powder, ginger powder and dried ginger powder.
3. Turmeric powder goes in next, once the meat is browned.
4. Add fennel seeds in a small muslin bag or directly towards the end of the cooking process. Eventually, add garam masala and sugar.

Note: The consistency of the gravy should be thin but not watery.

KASHMIRI CURRY

INGREDIENTS

Mustard oil: 2 tbsp
Dried red chillies, broken into pieces: 12
Garlic, minced: 6 cloves
Fennel seeds: ½ cup
Cumin seeds: ¼ cup
Fenugreek seeds: ¼ cup
Black cardamom: 2 tbsp
Green cardamom: 2 tbsp
Bay leaves, coarsely broken: 10
Saffron threads: 1 tsp
Ginger powder: 3 tbsp
Chilli powder: 1 tbsp

Cinnamon powder: 2 tsp
Clove powder: 1 tsp
Mace powder: 1 tsp
Nutmeg powder: ½ tsp

Steps

1. In a cast-iron or non-stick wok or skillet, heat the oil over medium heat. Add the broken red chillies and minced garlic. Sauté for 1 minute, stirring frequently until fragrant and golden brown.
2. Add the fennel seeds, cumin seeds, fenugreek seeds, black cardamom seeds, green cardamom and coarsely broken bay leaves to the pan. Sauté and stir the mixture constantly for about 2 minutes. Watch closely to ensure the spices don't burn, but allow them to darken slightly and release their aromas.
3. Remove the pan from heat and stir in the saffron threads. Let the mixture cool completely.
4. Once cool, grind all the ingredients together in a spice or coffee grinder until a very fine powder is obtained. Alternatively, use a mortar and pestle for a more traditional approach.
5. Transfer the ground spice blend to a bowl and mix with the ginger powder, paprika, cinnamon, cloves, mace and nutmeg. These pre-ground spices enhance the flavour profile without needing further grinding.
6. Store your home-made masala in an airtight container in a cool, dark place. It will stay fresh for about 1 week at room temperature or up to 1 year in the refrigerator.

Dhana-Jeera

Ingredients

Cumin seeds: ¼ cup
Coriander seeds: 1 cup
Cloves: 4
Dried jwala chilli, whole: 10–12

Steps

1. In a medium cast-iron or non-stick skillet, heat the pan over medium heat. Add the cumin seeds and dry roast them, stirring constantly for 2–3 minutes.
2. Reduce the heat slightly and add the coriander seeds and cloves to the pan. Roast them for about 1 minute, stirring occasionally until they're just heated through.
3. Remove the pan from heat, toss in chillies and let the mixture cool completely. Once cool, transfer the mixture to a spice grinder or coffee grinder and grind to a fine powder.
4. Store your freshly ground masala in an airtight container in a cool, dark place. It will stay fresh for about 1 month at room temperature or up to 1 year in the refrigerator.

GARAM MASALA

◌

GARAM MASALA IS OFTEN REVERED AS THE QUEEN of all spices, a title bestowed upon it by Mukhiya Singh, a seasoned spice shop owner in Khari Baoli, Delhi's renowned spice market and the largest in Asia. His claim was bold, and I couldn't let it slip without probing deeper. I asked him why garam masala, in particular, was dubbed the queen rather than the king of spices. He chuckled, taken aback by my inquiry.

'I call garam masala the queen because everyone desires it,' he began, 'whether they use just a pinch or a whole packet. Just as every queen has her unique charm, the queen of a state is the epitome of grace. Similarly, garam masala possesses a delicate elegance, the *nazakat* of a *mallika* (queen).' His reasoning was compelling, at least for the northern regions of India, where garam masala is a staple in kitchens. Garam masala is more than just a spice blend—it is a symbol of cultural heritage and culinary artistry. This aromatic mix of spices varies across regions, religions and families based on tradition and taste.

One of the most fascinating aspects of garam masala is its diversity. While the core concept remains the same, the ingredients and proportions vary significantly across different regions of India. Each regional variation of garam masala reflects the local palate, available ingredients and culinary traditions.

For a fair taste test, I gathered spices from various brands and local varieties from different states. My selection ranged from well-known brands like MDH, Catch, Shan, National, Noorie, MTR Masala, Priya Masala to Zoff Spices. I also explored the blends crafted at Khari Baoli and INA Market, and finally, included my own blend, which is also featured in this book. Each blend had a similar composition but varied in proportions—some offered a more rustic and robust flavour, while others leaned towards a floral note. My version struck a balance between the two. The base spices used make a significant difference—using more cumin seeds and coriander lends an earthy tone and darker colour, whereas a balanced mix brings out the floral notes of cinnamon or star anise. Personally, I like to add stone flower to my spice blend, a choice driven by my own taste rather than any scientific method.

I see garam masala as a very fluid blend; almost every spice mix can be considered a derivative of this earthy combination. Whether it's nihari, biryani or a delectable kabab, garam masala is a common thread. In my conversation with Mukhiya Singh, I realized the fascination with 'shahi' garam masala. Contrary to popular belief, the modern version of garam masala did not exist during the Mughal or 'Shahi' era. However, the term 'shahi' gives chefs the freedom to include a variety of spices, making it a comprehensive blend. What is a comprehensive blend? One that doesn't require any additional spices, like kitchen king, sabzi masala or chicken curry masala. Just add onions, ginger, garlic and a base of curd or tomato, and the dish is complete. The shahi blend, in my opinion, serves as a one-stop-shop, a secret spice blend that every cook, whether in a restaurant or street-side shop, swears by.

Margaret Shaida, in *The Legendary Cuisine of Persia*,[1] explains that 'garam masala' comes from the Persian words 'garm', meaning warmth, and 'masaleh', meaning ingredients. The 'hot' in the garam masala refers to the warming nature of the spices traditionally used, such as black pepper, cardamom, cloves, cinnamon, nutmeg and mace. While she doesn't assert that garam masala is originally Persian, she does draw a parallel to Persian spice blends known as *advieh*, a term that translates to medicine in Arabic, reinforcing the relationship between cooking and healing. Interestingly, the advieh mixtures she describes bear a striking resemblance to the garam masala recipes.

Nutrition consultant and cookbook author Sangeeta Khanna shares her personal connection with this queen of spice blends. During our conversation, she recalls that her family used garam masala mostly in the winter for its warming effect, often making 'garam masala ka surua' (garam masala soup) with just water and the spice blend. She also mentions thanda masala, the opposite of garam masala, which helps keep the body cool. Thanda masala primarily consists of coriander and cumin seeds, with additions like Fennel seeds, tej patta and poppy seeds to enhance its flavour profile. When used in curries, it is often complemented by tempering with fenugreek seeds, asafoetida (hing) and chillies. This blend is commonly used in light summer curries, often with mint or coriander leaf paste for a refreshing touch. There are two schools of thought regarding the grind size of the blend. Sangeeta prefers a coarser grind to ensure the spices don't lose their aroma too quickly once ground into a fine powder.

When examining the basic composition of garam masala through the recipe provided below, you will notice that most north Indian blends feature cumin seeds and coriander as the primary base. In contrast, these ingredients are often absent in south Indian blends. To understand the composition of a store-bought spice blend, it's important to know that manufacturers list ingredients in order of quantity, from highest to lowest. For example, if cumin seeds is used in large amounts, it will be listed first.

Interestingly, Nancie McDermott's book, *The Curry Book: A Celebration of Memorable Flavors and Irresistible Recipes*,[2] describes garam masala as 'a dry preparation made of cinnamon, pepper, cloves and other spices'. This suggests that her recipe might contain more cinnamon, as cumin seeds isn't mentioned. Curious to see for yourself? Read on—I have included her recipe in the following section.

Food book author Charmaine O'Brien offers valuable insights on various spices, particularly garam masala. She mentions the Mughal chefs, who travelled to India, brought their spices and incorporated them into local dishes to enhance the dining experience for the royals. While they may not have specifically called it garam masala, they certainly had a similar blend in their repertoire. O'Brien also notes the regional logic behind spice usage, suggesting that the health properties of spices may have shaped taste preferences, leading to the creation of standard spice blends.

Noted food historian, author and restaurant consultant, Salma Husain recalls that during her childhood, her family never used pre-packaged spices. Instead, they had a house help who ground fresh spices daily, tailored to the family's cooking needs. This spice blend was typically in a paste form since it included freshly ginger powder and chillies along with other spices, rather than the more common powdered format. Even in the books she has translated, she never mentions the use of 'garam masala' but instead mentions various types of masala for numerous dishes.

Over time, the availability of pre-packaged garam masala has made cooking more accessible and appealing, allowing home cooks to easily incorporate complex Indian flavours into their dishes without the need for sourcing, measuring and blending individual spices by hand.

Nowadays, people simply grab a box from the cupboard and presto—masala magic happens. The traditional practice of roasting and blending your own garam masala is becoming increasingly rare. But I also know it's not the same ritual because we are juggling work, laundry, and a hungry self and family; and that little box brings with it the promise of no-fuss cooking.

The confusion surrounding garam masala begins here. Many food enthusiasts and modern historians claim that Ayurveda advises on garam masala and extols its benefits. However, Vikram Doctor, journalist and food history expert, in one of his articles, presents a different perspective. Along with questioning the origins of garam masala from the Ayurvedic route, he also examines why this blend is strangely absent in south India if it is so popular across the country and in Ayurveda.[3] Having a primarily north Indian concentration suggests that it was likely introduced by Indo–Islamic rulers influenced by Persian and Ottoman courts. The use of expensive trade spices like cinnamon and cardamom instead of cheaper, locally grown ones indicates its initial use in noble kitchens. Over time, as wealth increased and courts declined, garam masala was adopted by home cooks. Rarely the main source of flavour in dishes, it is most effective when added towards the end of the cooking process, enhancing the aroma of dishes like curries and meat-based preparations without overpowering other flavours. Its unique blend of spices brings depth and complexity to the final dish, acting as a fragrant finishing touch. Interestingly, garam masala is less frequently used in poultry and biryani recipes, and rarely incorporated into vegetable or fish preparations. The reason for adding it at the end is quite practical—doing so avoids the potential bitterness that prolonged heat can cause, thus preserving the warm, aromatic notes that define this spice blend.[4] Adding it at the end is perfect for that final sweet-spice whiff you get when you uncover a cooking pot—it makes that moment aromatic and memorable.

However, as a cook, I find myself somewhat uncertain about its use in a strictly defined way, as suggested above. Garam masala is a versatile blend used both to enhance flavour and elevate aroma. In many dishes, you may use some or all the spices in the blend at different stages of cooking. For instance, whole spices like cloves or cinnamon may be added in the beginning to flavour the oil, while other components may be used in different combinations later. Ultimately, it depends on the desired effect of the blend and the nature of the dish being prepared. And honestly, if it smells right, tastes right and makes your neighbour jealous, you're probably doing it right.

On the internet, one can find numerous articles touting the 'authentic' and 'original' garam masala and its health benefits. One such write-up by Garima Arora states, 'it can stimulate the digestive system to produce digestive enzymes that help in the breakdown of fat, protein, carbs and fibre. Without sufficient digestive enzymes, you are likely to experience indigestion, bloating, gut issues, etc.'[5] However, she also advises those with acidity and gut issues to avoid garam masala. These health benefits, she notes, are not unique to garam masala but are attributable to many spices used in traditional 'desi' cooking. The other most common misconception is regarding the usage. We often hear from cooks and chefs to use garam masala in meat-based dishes. However, cookbook author and lecturer Yamuna Devi's *Lord Krishna's Cuisine—The Art of Indian Vegetarian Cooking* gives the recipe for vegetarian dishes that include garam masala. One of her recipes for this blend curiously contains dried shredded coconut, which is unique compared to the popular recipe for the blend.[6]

Independent journalist and food writer Priyadarshini Chatterjee delves into the intricate layers of this spice blend. She writes, 'Interestingly, many recipes for garam masala (like my mother-in-law's) feature spices like coriander, cumin seeds, and fennel seeds that are actually cooling spices.'[7] This may confuse some, given the name garam masala implies a warming blend. Chatterjee explains that this nuance is central to Indian subcontinental cooking, where spice blends not only add flavour but also ensure bodily balance and gut health.

She further elaborates, 'The flavour of garam masala depends on the combination and proportions of spices, how the spices are treated, and even the method of pounding. Recipes for garam masala vary not only by region but also by kitchen and cook. This ranges from the basic mix of three spices popular in Bengal to extravagant recipes listing over 30 spices, often considered chef's secrets or family heirlooms passed down generations.'

The timing of adding garam masala to a dish can vary—it may be added either at the start of cooking or towards the end. For me, this decision largely hinges on whether the spices have been roasted prior to grinding.

Oindrila Bala, a Kolkata-based baker and *MasterChef 2019* runner-up, shares that her family insists on making everything fresh. She explains, 'The Bengali version of garam masala is quite different from what you find in Delhi or other northern regions. 'Our garam masala consists of just three spices: cinnamon, clove and cardamom. We use this blend at home all the time, gently heating the spices before grinding them. Other spices like cumin seeds, coriander, long pepper and nutmeg are added separately depending on the dish we are cooking.' It was only after she married into a Punjabi family that she began making garam masala with 15 different spices.

Oindrila further recalls that in her family, powdered spice blends are a relatively recent development. She grew up watching her grandmother and mother prepare pastes on a *sil batta*, a traditional grinding stone, and only making enough for three to four days. This method is similar to the preparation done in restaurants. Her story reminded me of my family in Sasaram, Bihar. Every time I visit my paternal and maternal homes, I notice a house help or a family member making a paste by grinding various spices with ginger and garlic. This paste is prepared daily and used in various dishes or those that call for garam masala.

Sangeeta Khanna mentions a similar practice, noting that historically, people did not prepare spice blends in advance. She also talks about the modification in the spice blend, where people add chillies, salt and all sorts of other ingredients— something that I too found in my research. In my opinion, this was likely due to factors such as limited storage options, fewer people to feed, less commercialization and the scarcity of expensive spices. Unlike modern times, they had the luxury and gift of time, allowing them to prepare their blend or paste fresh each day. *Can you do this now?* Certainly! That's why you have this book. Take some time to prepare your blends, or make them in advance and store them.

I agree with Nancie McDermott when she writes, 'Recipes for garam masala are many, varying by region, over the course of time, and from cook to cook. This is not surprising in a land where the ability to cook well and season food imaginatively is a source of pride and cause for respect.'[8] It is also the reason you will find so many different spice blends for the same dish throughout this book—every individual takes pride in their own version of the blend, using the same ingredients but altering the ratios.

Chandrima Sarkar's Bengali Garam Masala

Ingredients

Green cardamom: 4 tbsp
1-inch cinnamon stick: 8
Cloves: 2 tbsp

Steps

1. Dry roast all the whole spices. Be careful not to burn the spices.
2. Once the spices have cooled down, grind them into a fine powder using a mortar and pestle or a spice grinder.
3. Store the garam masala in an airtight container in a cool, dark place for up to 6 months.

Shahi Bengali Garam Masala

Ingredients

1-inch cinnamon sticks: 4
Cloves: 15–18
Green cardamom: 35–40
Black cardamom: 6
Nutmeg, grated: 1 tsp
Mace blades: 6
Bay leaves: 20
Dried red chillies: 14
Black pepper: 3 tbsp

1. Lightly dry roast the spices (except nutmeg and mace) on a medium to low flame until aromatic. Allow them to cool completely.
2. Transfer all cooled spices to a spice grinder or mortar and pestle. Grind to a fine powder.
3. Store the spice blend in an airtight container in a cool, dry place. Proper storage will maintain its freshness and potency for several months.

BENGALI GARAM MASALA

INGREDIENTS

Cardamom: 8 tbsp
Cloves: 3 tbsp
1-inch cinnamon stick: 5

STEPS

1. Lightly dry roast the cardamom, cloves and cinnamon separately on a medium to low flame until aromatic. Allow it to cool completely.
2. Transfer all the ingredients to a spice grinder or mortar and pestle. Grind to a fine powder.
3. In a large bowl, combine all the ground spices. Mix thoroughly to ensure even distribution.
4. Store the spice blend in an airtight container in a cool, dry place.

ANGLO-INDIAN GARAM MASALA

INGREDIENTS

Black pepper: 3 tbsp
Cardamom: 3 tbsp
1-inch cinnamon stick: 3
Cloves: 12–15
Mace blade: 1
Nutmeg, grated: 1 tsp

STEPS

1. Lightly dry roast all the spices on a medium to low flame until aromatic. Allow it to cool completely.
2. Transfer all the ingredients to a spice grinder or mortar and pestle. Grind to a fine powder.
3. In a large bowl, mix all the ground spices thoroughly to ensure even distribution.
4. Store the spice blend in an airtight container in a cool, dry place.

CHEF JYOTI VISHNANI'S SINDHI GARAM MASALA*

INGREDIENTS

1-inch cinnamon sticks: 10
Cumin seeds: 3 tbsp
Black pepper: 2 tsp
Nutmeg: 1 tsp
Nigella seeds: 1 tbsp
Cardamom: 6–8
Cloves: 12–15
Bay leaves: 12–13

---

* Chef Jyoti Vishnani's is a freelance consultant chef and an expert in Regional Sindhi cuisines.

1. Dry roast the spices together, stirring continuously until they emit a sweet aroma. Be careful not to burn the spices.
2. Once the spices emit a sweet aroma, remove them from the heat and set them aside to cool completely.
3. Once cooled, transfer the roasted spices to a grinder. Grind to a fine powder.
4. Store the Sindhi garam masala in an airtight container in a cool, dry place. Proper storage will maintain its freshness and potency for several months.

JUNAID AALAM'S PURANI DILLI GARAM MASALA

INGREDIENTS

Cloves: 15
Green cardamom: 10–12
1-inch cinnamon sticks: 2
Black cardamom: 4
Coriander seeds: 2 tbsp
Cumin seeds: 2 tbsp
Dried ginger: 2 tbsp
Mace blades: 2
Long pepper: 5
Bay leaves: 8
Black pepper: 2 tsp
Nutmeg, grated: 1 tsp

STEPS

1. Dry roast the spices together, stirring continuously until they emit a sweet aroma. Be careful not to burn the spices.
2. Once the spices emit a sweet aroma, remove them from the heat and set them aside to cool completely.

3. Once cooled, transfer the roasted spices to a grinder. Grind to a fine powder.
4. Store the garam masala in an airtight container in a cool, dry place. Proper storage will maintain its freshness and potency for several months.

Easy Garam Masala

Ingredients

Coriander seeds: 6 tbsp
Cumin seeds: 4 tsp
Cloves, whole: 4 tsp
Black pepper, whole: 2 tsp
1-inch cinnamon sticks: 3
Bay leaves: 10–12

Steps

1. Dry roast the spices together, stirring continuously until they emit a sweet aroma. Be careful not to burn the spices.
2. Once the spices emit a sweet aroma, remove them from the heat and set them aside to cool completely.
3. Once cooled, transfer the roasted spices to a grinder. Grind to a fine powder.
4. Store the garam masala in an airtight container in a cool, dry place. Proper storage will maintain its freshness and potency for several months.

Chef Jatin Khurana's Punjabi Garam Masala

Ingredients

Coriander seeds: 6 tbsp
Cumin seeds: 3 tsp

Cloves, whole: 4 tsp
Black pepper, whole: 2 tsp
1-inch cinnamon sticks: 3
Bay leaves: 8
Long pepper: 3–4
Black cardamom: 2
Green cardamom: 4
Dried ginger powder: 1 tsp

STEPS

1. Dry roast the spices together, stirring continuously until they emit a sweet aroma. Be careful not to burn the spices.
2. Once the spices emit a sweet aroma, remove them from the heat and set them aside to cool completely.
3. Once cooled, transfer the roasted spices to a grinder. Grind to a fine powder.
4. Store the garam masala in an airtight container in a cool, dry place. Proper storage will maintain its freshness and potency for several months.

HOME-MADE GARAM MASALA

INGREDIENTS

Coriander seeds: 7 tbsp
Cumin seeds: 1½ tsp
Black cardamom, whole: 3
Stone flower: 1 tbsp
Black pepper: 1 tbsp
1-inch cinnamon stick
Green cardamom: 4
Cloves: 2
Star anise: 2
Mace blade: 1

Bay leaves: 4
Salt: ¼ tsp (or to taste)

STEPS

1. Dry roast the spices together, stirring continuously until they emit a sweet aroma. Be careful not to burn the spices.
2. Once the spices emit a sweet aroma, remove them from the heat and set them aside to cool completely.
3. Once cooled, transfer the roasted spices to a grinder. Grind to a fine powder.
4. Store the garam masala in an airtight container in a cool, dry place. Proper storage will maintain its freshness and potency for several months.

MUMTAZ'S GARAM MASALA

INGREDIENTS

Coriander seeds: 7 tbsp
Cumin seeds: 3 tbsp
Black pepper: 1 tsp
Turmeric powder: ½ tsp
Fennel seeds: 1 tsp
Salt: ½ tsp (or to taste)
Nutmeg, whole: 1
Dried ginger powder: ½ tsp
Asafoetida: ¼ tsp
Boriya chillies: 4
Kashmiri chillies: 4
Bay leaves: 2
Cloves: 4–6
Black cardamom: 2
1-inch cinnamon stick
Star anise: 2

STEPS

1. Dry roast the spices together, stirring continuously until they emit a sweet aroma. Be careful not to burn the spices.
2. Once the spices emit a sweet aroma, remove them from the heat and set them aside to cool completely.
3. Once cooled, transfer the roasted spices to a grinder. Grind to a fine powder.
4. Store the garam masala in an airtight container in a cool, dry place. Proper storage will maintain its freshness and potency for several months.

ALADIN'S GOAN GARAM MASALA

INGREDIENTS

Coriander seeds: 3 tbsp
Cumin seeds: 1 tbsp
Black pepper: 2 tbsp
Fennel seeds: 1 tbsp
Black cardamom: 4
1-inch cinnamon sticks: 2
Cloves: 8–10
Bay leaves: 6
Green cardamom: 6
Nigella seeds: 1 tsp
Star anise: 2
Nutmeg, grated: ½
Mace blade: 1

STEPS

1. Dry roast the spices together, stirring continuously until they emit a sweet aroma. Be careful not to burn the spices.

2. Once the spices emit a sweet aroma, remove them from the heat and set them aside to cool completely.
3. Once cooled, transfer the roasted spices to a grinder. Grind to a fine powder.
4. Store the garam masala in an airtight container in a cool, dry place. Proper storage will maintain its freshness and potency for several months.

Chef Kunal Kapur's Garam Masala

Ingredients

Bay leaves: 3
1½-inch cinnamon stick
Black cardamom, whole: 2
Nutmeg, whole:
Green cardamom: 12–15
Black pepper: 1½ tbsp
Mace, whole: 1
Cloves: 1 tbsp
Fennel seeds: 1½ tbsp
Cumin seeds: 2 tbsp
Coriander seeds: 4 tbsp
Nigella seeds: 1 tbsp
Stone flower: 2
Rose petals, dried: 1 tbsp
Ginger powder: 1½ tbsp

Steps

1. Dry roast all the whole spices (excluding ginger powder and rose petals, dried) in a pan over medium heat, stirring frequently until fragrant (for around 3–5 minutes). Be careful not to burn the spices.

2. Cool the spices completely.
3. Mix the ginger powder and rose petals, dried.
4. Grind the spices into a fine powder using a mortar and pestle or a spice grinder.
5. Sift the ground spices to remove any coarse particles (optional).
6. Store the garam masala in an airtight container in a cool, dark place for up to 6 months.

CHEF OINDRILA BALA'S GARAM MASALA

INGREDIENTS

Bay leaves: 7–8
Kewra water: 6 drops
Meetha attar (an edible essential oil): 2 drops
Allspice powder: 20
Nutmeg, whole: ⅓
Mace blades: 4
Poppy seeds: 2 tbsp
Cashew nuts: 15
Black cardamom: 2
Cloves: 12
Cardamom: 10
1-inch cinnamon sticks: 3
Chilli powder: 2 tsp

STEPS

1. Heat a pan on a medium to low flame. Dry roast the bay leaves, allspice powder, nutmeg, mace, poppy seeds, cashews, black cardamom, cloves, green cardamom and cinnamon sticks separately until they become aromatic. Be careful not to burn the spices.

2. Remove the spices from the pan and allow them to cool completely.
3. Transfer the cooled spices to a spice grinder or mortar and pestle. Grind to a fine powder.
4. In a large bowl, combine the ground spice mixture with the chilli powder.
5. Add 6 drops of kewra water and 2 drops of meetha attar. Mix thoroughly to ensure even distribution.
6. Store the spice blend in an airtight container to maintain its freshness and potency for 6 months.

AMAN'S AGRA GARAM MASALA

INGREDIENTS

Nigella seeds: 1 tbsp
Coriander seeds: 2 tbsp
Black pepper: 1 tbsp
Cumin seeds: 1 tsp
Black cardamom: 4
Green cardamom: 5
Fennel seeds: 1 tsp
Cloves: 1 tsp
Mace blade: 1
Star anise: 4
1-inch cinnamon sticks: 2
Fenugreek leaves: 1 tsp
Bay leaves: 6
Stone flower, small: 1
Nutmeg, grated: ¼ tsp
Red chillies, whole: 8–10
Dried ginger: 2

1. Lightly dry roast the spices (except nutmeg and mace) on a medium to low flame until aromatic. Allow them to cool completely.
2. Transfer all cooled spices to a spice grinder or mortar and pestle. Grind to a fine powder.
3. Store the spice blend in an airtight container in a cool, dry place. Proper storage will maintain its freshness and potency for several months.

Neha Gupte's Konkani Garam Masala

Ingredients

Lawangi or paandi red chillies: 20
Kashmiri red chillies: 10
Coriander seeds: 5 tbsp
Black cardamom: 3
Green cardamom: 10
1–inch cinnamon sticks: 2
Cloves: 6
Black pepper: ½ tbsp
Turmeric powder: ½ tsp
Fenugreek seeds: ½ tsp
Fennel seeds: 1 tsp
Cumin seeds: 1 tsp
Poppy seeds: 1 tbsp
Sesame seeds (optional): ½ tsp
Mace blade, small: 1
Stone flower: 1 tsp
Bay leaves: 4
Star anise: 1
Nigella seeds: ½ tsp
Nutmeg, small: ¼

STEPS

1. Lightly dry roast the spices (except turmeric powder, poppy seeds, sesame seeds and nutmeg) separately on a medium to low flame until aromatic. Allow to cool completely.
2. Transfer the cooled spices to a spice grinder or mortar and pestle. Grind to a fine powder.
3. Store the spice blend in an airtight container in a cool, dry place. Proper storage will maintain its freshness and potency for six months.

KHALAJAAN'S SPECIAL GARAM MASALA

INGREDIENTS

Green cardamom: 2 tbsp
Black cardamom: 10
1-inch cinnamon sticks: 6
Star anise: 4
Cloves: 12–15
Black pepper: 1 tsp
Nutmeg, whole: 1
Mace blades: 3
White pepper: 1 tsp
Nigella seeds: 1 tbsp
Fennel seeds: 1 tbsp

STEPS

1. Transfer all the spices to a spice grinder or mortar and pestle. Grind to a fine powder.
2. Store the spice blend in an airtight container in a cool, dry place. Proper storage will maintain its freshness and potency for several months.

Easy Garam Masala 2

Ingredients

Black cardamom: 7
Green cardamom: 10–12
Nutmeg: ½
Mace blades: 2
Black pepper: 1½ tbsp
Cumin seeds: 4 tbsp
Cloves: 10
1-inch cinnamon sticks: 3

Steps

1. Transfer all the spices to a spice grinder or mortar and pestle. Grind to a fine powder.
2. Store the spice blend in an airtight container in a cool, dry place. Proper storage will maintain its freshness and potency for several months.

Mehjabeen's Basic Garam Masala

Ingredients

Fennel seeds: 6 tbsp
1-inch cinnamon sticks: 4
Cardamom: 3 tbsp
Cloves: 3 tbsp

Steps

1. Lightly dry roast the spices (except nutmeg and mace) on a medium to low flame until aromatic. Allow to cool completely.

2. Transfer all the cooled spices to a spice grinder or mortar and pestle. Grind to a fine powder.
3. Store the spice blend in an airtight container in a cool, dry place. Proper storage will maintain its freshness and potency for several months.

Kashmiri Garam Masala

Ingredients

1-inch cinnamon sticks: 4
Nutmeg, grated: ½
Green cardamom: 2 tbsp
Black pepper: 2 tbsp
Cumin seeds: 1½ tbsp
Dried ginger: 1 tbsp
Nigella seeds: 1 tbsp
Bay leaves: 3
Cloves: 2 tbsp
Fennel seeds: 1 tbsp
Mace: 2

Steps

1. Dry roast each spice individually on a low flame for a few seconds to a minute, or until the distinct aroma of each spice is released. Ensure not to overcook, as burning will result in a bitter taste.
2. If you accidentally burn one spice, you can replace and roast it again separately rather than wasting the entire batch.
3. Once all the spices are roasted, combine them and grind into a smooth powder.
4. Store the spice blend in an airtight container for future use.

Nawabi Garam Masala

Ingredients

Cumin seeds: 2 tbsp
Nigella seeds: 1 tbsp
Kashmiri red chilli: 4
Black pepper: 1 tbsp
Nigella seeds: 1 tbsp
Cloves: 1½ tbsp
Mace: 2
Nutmeg, grated: ½
1-inch cinnamon sticks: 3
Green cardamom: 1 tbsp
Allspice powder: 1 tbsp

Steps

1. Ensure the pan is completely dry and free of moisture before beginning.
2. Dry roast all the spices together in a large pan over a low flame for a few minutes, stirring continuously until the distinct aroma of the spices is released.
3. Remove the spices and allow them to cool.
4. Grind the roasted spices together in a blender until you achieve a fine powder.
5. Store the spice blend in an airtight container or bottle to retain freshness.

Vijayalakshmi's Tamil Nadu Garam Masala

Ingredients

Coriander seeds: 4 tbsp
Cumin seeds: 2 tbsp

Bay leaves: 5
1-inch cinnamon sticks: 4
Dried mundu chilli: 6
Long pepper: 8
Nutmeg, whole: ½
Green cardamom: 1 tbsp
Star anise: 4
Mace blades: 4–5
Black cardamom: 7
Black pepper: ½ tbsp
Cloves: ½ tbsp

STEPS

1. Transfer all the spices to a spice grinder or mortar and pestle. Grind to a fine powder.
2. Store the spice blend in an airtight container in a cool, dry place. Proper storage will maintain its freshness and potency for several months.

KERALA GARAM MASALA

INGREDIENTS

Fennel seeds: ¼ cup
Green cardamom: 50–55
Black pepper, whole: 40
1-inch cinnamon sticks: 2
Mace blade, whole: 1
Nutmeg, whole: 1
Star anise: 2
Cloves: 35

Steps

1. Dry roast all the ingredients on low heat until they are fragrant, stirring continuously.
2. Transfer all the spices to a spice grinder or mortar and pestle. Grind to a fine powder.
3. Store the spice blend in an airtight container in a cool, dry place. Proper storage will maintain its freshness and potency for several months.

Malabari Garam Masala

Ingredients

Fennel seeds: 12 tbsp
Green cardamom: 1 tbsp
Black pepper, whole: 1
1-inch cinnamon sticks: 2
Star anise: 4
Cloves: 2 tbsp

Steps

1. Dry roast all the ingredients on low heat until they are fragrant, stirring continuously.
2. Transfer all the spices to a spice grinder or mortar and pestle. Grind to a fine powder.
3. Store the spice blend in an airtight container in a cool, dry place. Proper storage will maintain its freshness and potency for several months.

CHANDANI'S RANCHI GARAM MASALA

INGREDIENTS

Black pepper: 5 tbsp
Cloves: 1½ tbsp
Black cardamom: 8–10
Green cardamom: 1 tbsp
Cinnamon powder: 1½ tbsp
Nutmeg powder: ½ tbsp
Mace powder: 1 tbsp

STEPS

1. Dry roast all the whole ingredients on low heat until they are fragrant, stirring continuously.
2. Transfer all the spices to a spice grinder or mortar and pestle. Grind to a fine powder.
3. Store the spice blend in an airtight container in a cool, dry place. Proper storage will maintain its freshness and potency for several months.

BHAGEL'S GUJARATI FAMILY GARAM MASALA

INGREDIENTS

Star anise: 8–10
Black pepper: 1 tbsp
Green cardamom: 1 tbsp
Cloves: 1 tbsp
Cobra saffron (nagkesar): ½ tbsp
Nigella seeds: 1 tbsp
1-inch cinnamon sticks: 2
Mace: 2
Stone flower: 30 gm

Bay leaves: 10–12
Coriander seeds: 2 tbsp

1. Dry roast the spices until their aroma. Make sure not to over-roast to avoid burning.
2. You can also roast the spices individually. This allows for easy replacement if one spice gets burnt, saving time and resources.
3. Once all the spices are roasted, allow them to cool.
4. Grind the roasted spices together into a fine powder using a blender.
5. Pass the powder through a fine sieve to achieve a very fine consistency.
6. Store the spice blend in an airtight jar or bottle to maintain freshness.

MADRAS GARAM MASALA

INGREDIENTS

Fennel seeds: 4 tbsp
Cloves: 4 tsp
Cardamom: 4 tsp
1-inch cinnamon sticks: 3
Star anise: 2
Mace: 1
Dried kanthari chilli: 3

STEPS

1. Dry roast all the ingredients on low heat until they are fragrant, stirring continuously.

2. Transfer all the spices to a spice grinder or mortar and pestle. Grind to a fine powder.
3. Store the spice blend in an airtight container in a cool, dry place. Proper storage will maintain its freshness and potency for several months.

Georgy Santhosh's North Kerala Garam Masala

Ingredients

Fennel seeds: 4 tbsp
Cumin seeds: 2 tbsp
Green cardamom: 2 tbsp
Cloves: 2 tbsp
1-inch cinnamon sticks: 3
Star anise, whole (optional): 1
Nutmeg, grated (optional): ¼ tsp
Mace blade (optional): ¼

Steps

1. Dry roast all the ingredients on low heat until they are fragrant, stirring continuously.
2. Transfer all the spices to a spice grinder or mortar and pestle. Grind to a fine powder.
3. Store the spice blend in an airtight container in a cool, dry place. Proper storage will maintain its freshness and potency for several months.

Harjot's Peshawari Garam Masala

Ingredients

Cumin seeds: 2½ tbsp
Nigella seeds: 1 tbsp

Cloves: 1 tbsp
Rose petals, dried: 2 tbsp
Green cardamom: 1 tbsp
Black cardamom: 4
Black pepper: 1 tbsp (or 6 gm)
Bay leaves: 8
1-inch cinnamon sticks: 2
Mace: 1
Nutmeg, grated: ½ tsp
Dried ginger: 1 tsp
Saffron: A pinch

STEPS

1. Dry roast all the ingredients (apart from saffron and rose petals, dried) on low heat until they are fragrant, stirring continuously.
2. Transfer all the spices, saffron and rose petals, dried to a spice grinder or mortar and pestle. Grind to a fine powder.
3. Store the spice blend in an airtight container in a cool, dry place. Proper storage will maintain its freshness and potency for several months.

GARAM MASALA FROM PRASHAD: COOKING WITH INDIAN MASTERS[9]

INGREDIENTS

Green cardamom: 3 tbsp
Black cardamom: 6
Cloves: 12–15
1-inch cinnamon sticks: 5
Bay leaves: 8
Mace blade: 1

1. Dry roast all the ingredients on low heat until they are fragrant, while stirring continuously.
2. Transfer all the spices to a spice grinder or mortar and pestle. Grind to a fine powder.
3. Store the spice blend in an airtight container in a cool, dry place. Proper storage will maintain its freshness and potency for several months.

NANCIE MCDERMOTT'S GARAM MASALA

INGREDIENTS

Cardamom (black or green): 3 tbsp
1-inch cinnamon sticks: 5
Cloves, whole: 3 tbsp
Black pepper: 2 tbsp

STEPS

1. Measure all the ingredients. Lightly crush the cardamom pods, if necessary, to facilitate grinding.
2. Transfer all the ingredients to a spice grinder and grind to a fine powder.
3. Store the garam masala in an airtight container in a cool, dry place for 3 months.

Note: This recipe includes the option to use either black or green cardamom. Choosing one over the other will affect both the flavour and colour of your spice blend.

Jennifer Brennan's Aromatic Garam Masala

Ingredients

Allspice powder: 2 tbsp
Cinnamon powder: 1 tbsp
Nutmeg powder: 2 tsp
Clove powder: 2 tsp
Ginger powder: 1 tsp

Steps

1. Combine all the measured spices in a bowl.
2. Mix thoroughly until well combined.
3. Store the aromatic masala in an airtight container.

KABAB

∾

WHEN DOES A DISH EARN THE TITLE OF 'LEGENDARY' OR become an 'emotion'? Hard to pinpoint exactly, but perhaps it's when a dish or ingredient weaves itself into daily conversations or graces the verses of legendary poets. Consider when Mir Taqi Mir, the *khuda-e-sukhan* (god of poetry), wrote, '*Aatish-e-Gam men dil bhunaa shaayad der se buu kabab ki si hai*' (It seems my heart has been seared in the flames of sorrow; For quite some time now, it has smelled like a roasting kabab), or when the last Mughal Bahadur Shah Zafar penned, '*Jigar ke tukde hue, jal ke dil kabaab hua, ye ishq jaan ko mere koi azaab hua*'(My heart shattered into pieces, charred and turned to ash; This love has become a relentless torment for my soul).

For me, kababs and biryani epitomize emotion, though, for others, it might be a steaming cup of tea, a chilled glass of lassi or a rich navratan korma. Emotions are subjective, just like our preferences for food. You might relish bottle gourds or round gourds, while I might not. Our tastes and emotions vary, and that's perfectly fine. But when it comes to kababs, I've rarely met anyone who doesn't delight in these grilled or pan-fried delicacies, whether they're made from meat, vegetables or even fruits.

The experience of enjoying kababs extends beyond their taste—it's about immersing yourself in the simplicity and richness of the surroundings. I remember wandering the lively lanes of Chowk, a market in Lucknow, while savouring the famed galawat ke kabab at Tunday Kababi. In these narrow alleys, where you might accidentally bump into someone if you're not careful, you find yourself enveloped in a medley of aromas—from attar shops to the tantalizing scents of kababs, biryani, nihari, halwa and pani batasha. It's as if you are marinating in this sensory delight.

After soaking in the atmosphere, when you find a seat at Tunday Kababi, you eagerly shout your order, '*Ek* plate *kabab, do paratha lagana!*' (One plate of kababs and two parathas, please!). You might add a bottle of water or a soft drink. When I was savouring the blend of over 128 spices (as is claimed) and herbs in the meat, my friend asked which dish I would describe myself as. Taking a big bite of the kabab, I instinctively replied, 'Kabab.' Simple yet possessing a layered complexity and depth of flavour, kababs have the qualities that I like to think exist in me as well.

In *Persia As It Is* by Charles James Wills, the author describes two kinds of kababs in Persia that highlight a socio-economic divide in the food culture of the region during the time:[1]

The kababs intended for the wealthier classes are more elaborately prepared. The meat (often lamb, the size of a walnut) is skewered on a slender rod of iron, mixed with pieces of lean and a piece of fat from the tail of the oriental sheep. The kabab is then cooked over a fierce fire, occasionally enhanced with a topping of garlic or onion sauce, and sometimes served with pillows of boiled rice, venison, or fowl. This variant of kabab is described as richly smothered in a luxurious sauce and often served with a squeeze of lemon to enhance the flavours.

In contrast, the kabab available to the lower classes or poorer sections of society is mentioned in passing as part of a broader discussion on the varied and inexpensive diet of the working classes, which also includes items like beef (though it is noted that beef is never eaten by the well-to-do). The richer kababs are clearly more complex and served in a more lavish style compared to the simpler versions available to the general populace.

Long before the Mughal era elevated kababs to the culinary spotlight in India, the art of grilling meat was already in practice, as evinced in the historical texts from the 13th century. Amir Khusrau's references in Volume II of the *Risail-ul-Ijaz* about kababs served with sirka (vinegar) illuminate this rich tradition.[2] Walking through the busy lanes of Matia Mahal in Old Delhi, I found myself pausing to pick up a bottle of jamun sirka, which led to an intriguing conversation. When my companion was puzzled about its use, I shared how, traditionally, sirka isn't just a condiment for Asian dishes or something used to get rid of extra weight, but a delightful enhancement for kababs that offers a tangy contrast to the smoky flavours of the grilled meat. This use of vinegar with kababs goes back to Khusrau's days when the flavours were perhaps more pronounced and integral to culinary experiences.

In the historical record *Ain-i-Akbari*,[3] kabab is categorized as part of a broader class of foods that involves cooking meat with various accompaniments. In a discussion, food historian and author Salma Hussain introduced the concept of Kunduazizi, a kabab that dates far beyond the Mughal era, almost reaching antiquity. The recipe for this ancient dish involves using fowl as the primary meat, which is then marinated in citrus fruit, seasoned with crushed black pepper and then cooked using a traditional spit grilling technique.* If we flip through K.T. Achaya's work, we would find that the roasting of meat is not a new thing for the Indian subcontinent. According to him,

---

* Spit grilling is a technique used in traditional barbecue. It involves slowly cooking meat, poultry, or seafood in a pit or on a spit over hot coals or flavoured wood chips.

roasting pieces of meat on spits over an open fire has been described in various Sanskrit works of literature as well. He also writes about shula and bhadritakas, dishes which can also be termed kababs.[*4]

But how do you define a kabab or paint a picture for people who have never heard of kababs? There are a few ways, one being to straightforwardly tell them that it is simply grilled meat that they may or may not add spices and other ingredients to, to enhance the flavour. In fact, the essence of kababs can be traced back to the very origins of cooking itself.[5] The practice of grilling meat began soon after humans first tamed fire. Physical evidence indicates that the earliest methods of cooking involved heating food on hot stones. As culinary techniques evolved, around 30,000 years ago, humans in central Europe developed 'earth ovens' that were essentially pits lined with stones and filled with hot coals and ashes. Food, presumably wrapped in leaves to retain moisture and flavour, was placed atop the ashes, and then covered with earth to roast slowly. This method allowed tough meats, like those from mammoths, to cook slowly, breaking down the collagen in connective tissues into gelatin, rendering the meat tender and more digestible. Such slow cooking techniques are the precursors to today's barbecue methods, where meats are seasoned and cooked slowly to enhance flavour and tenderness. Kababs, at their core, embody this ancient art of slow-cooking meat, a culinary practice that dates back to the dawn of human civilization.

Alternatively, I might describe kababs as a culinary soap opera unfolding in the courtyard of our grand house in Sasaram, where

---

[*] In *The Story of Our Food* by K.T. Achaya, the author details various traditional meat dishes, particularly those befitting royalty. The text describes how pigs were roasted whole, and the portions obtained were called 'sunthakas'. The Rajput royalty of Rajasthan continues to prepare this item under the name 'shula'. Additionally, the author mentions 'bhadritakas', which were pieces of meat first roasted and then fried, resulting in a dish resembling kababs.

the women of my family—my *naani*, ammi, *khala* and *maami*[*]—were the deft directors of the scene. Each played her part—one crafted the spice blend with *aabi hakmat* (ancestral wisdom), another expertly sliced the meat into thin pasanda cuts, the third threaded these slices onto skewers and the fourth grilled it. But always remember, '*Kabab lagaye jaate hai aur kabab seke jaate hai*'—the charm of the line is lost in translation, so I'd rather let it shine in its original form.

As the kababs sizzled on a coal-fired *sigdi* (barbecue), I, alongside my cousins, would gather around the fire, our eager eyes reflecting the dancing flames. The ritual of grilling was a spectacle of sparks and aroma, where the thrill of snatching the freshly grilled seekh straight from the fire was worth every singe. Our impatience often led to burned mouths, but the joy of biting into the succulent Bihari Kabab—a family favourite that reigned supreme over all other varieties—was unmatched. In the wide world of kabab traditions, this beloved recipe from my childhood stood out and helped me embrace a deep understanding of flavours that only a home could foster.

Indeed, the versatility of kababs means there isn't a specific time or exclusive pairing that defines when or how they should be enjoyed. Kababs adapt seamlessly to a variety of serving preferences—some savour them with rice, while others prefer them tucked inside bread or savoured on their own with a side of chutney. As academic, food critic and historian Pushpesh Pant eloquently puts it, 'Kababs are a quintessential classy snack—elegant morsels of either meat or vegetables with a meaty texture that can be served at any time. They can be served as starters or wrapped in a roti to make a light meal on the run. They can be roasted on a skewer or pan-grilled like a patty. Some varieties are cooked on a griddle or in a handi.'[6] This flexibility in preparation

---

[*] Maternal grandmother, mother and maternal aunts (mother's sister and uncle's wife).

and presentation highlights the universal appeal of kababs, making them a beloved choice for any meal, whether as a light snack or as part of a substantial feast.

When the Moroccan explorer Ibn Battuta visited India during Muhammad bin-Tughlaq's era of the Sultanate period (1206–1526), he noted that chicken kababs were a delicacy served to royals, while the common folk often enjoyed kababs with paratha for breakfast. Shami kababs paired with paratha remain a popular dish even today, though it's unclear if they are served as a typical breakfast item. Unfortunately, finding 'real' shami kababs has become increasingly rare, as the recipes vary significantly from one city to another, including Delhi, Lucknow and personal household variations.

Nowadays, kababs have predominantly become an evening snack in many street-side eateries, though they are available throughout the day in restaurants. This shift reflects both their enduring popularity and the evolving dining habits of contemporary life, where the traditional time and manner of eating certain dishes have been adapted to modern rhythms.

In the 9th century, it was common to cook skewered meat over an open charcoal fire, much like it is done in modern practice. However, the culinary texts from that era, such as the *Kitab al-Tabikh* written by Muhammad bin Hasan al-Baghdadi in 1226, often describe roast meat being cooked in a *tannuur* (or tandoor).[7] Unlike the smaller cuts typically seen in shish kababs today, larger cuts such as whole stuffed kid or spice-encrusted racks of lamb were traditionally prepared in this manner.

Fish preparation in the tannuur was also noted for its unique cooking method, as described in *Kitab al-Tabikh*. A distinctive recipe involved roasting the head, baking the body and frying the tail of the fish, a technique that was later adopted in medieval European cuisine.

The text highlights a particularly celebrated dish called juudhaab (or juudhaabah), where meat was served atop a sweet pudding. This pudding was strategically placed at the bottom of the tannuur to soak up the meat's succulent drippings during cooking.

While fried meats were common and enjoyed, they were generally considered less sophisticated and prestigious compared to roasted or stewed preparations. Reflecting on my experiences with whole meat kababs in Karnataka and Kerala, I find that the fried versions there don't quite meet my expectations of what a kabab should be, both in terms of texture and taste. The frying method alters the flavour profile significantly, which does not align well with my palate. Despite this, I admit to enjoying several types of fried kababs, such as chapli kabab, shami kabab and keema goli from Delhi, charpa from Jharkhand, and kacche keeme ke kabab from Uttar Pradesh. This preference might seem contradictory since these dishes also deviate from the traditional grilling method. However, these kababs usually consist of minced meat, seasoned with whole spices and herbs, creating a flavour harmony that appeals to me despite the cooking method. I am purposefully keeping kababs like galawat ke kabab and shami kabab from Lucknow out of this list since they are pan-shallow fried and not deep-fried like the ones I have mentioned above.

In *Medieval Cuisine of the Islamic World: A Concise History with 174 Recipes*, kababs are mentioned as one of the many meat dishes enjoyed in medieval Islamic cuisine. The book describes various types of meat used in kababs (grilled meat), including mutton, chicken and sometimes beef. The preparation often involved marinating the meat in vinegar and spices, such as coriander, cumin seeds, black pepper and cinnamon, before cooking it on a spit or in an oven.[8] One of the dishes that I fancy is Sabbath tharid. Tharid, a dish originally associated with the Sabbath and great feasts after fasting, remains significant in Andalusian cuisine, a region known for its blend of Islamic, Christian and Jewish influences. Originally linked to the Prophet Muhammad, it also became a feast dish for Persians, Jews and Christians, reflecting Andalusia's rich cultural heritage.

Similar to korma, when it comes to kabab, the list is endless—the popular, not-so-popular, known and unknown kababs being incredibly difficult to cover. Below, you will find all such spice blends and kababs from different regions, families and eras. You can make it in the 'authentic' way it is mentioned or tweak it to suit your taste buds and create your own version. One thing I am sure that all kabab lovers would agree with is the pairing of kababs with green coriander and mint chutney, a squeeze of lime/lemon or drops of natural vinegar along with freshly sliced onions.

Rana Safvi's Shami Kabab[9]

Ingredients

Mutton, minced: 500 gm
Split Bengal gram: 100 gm
1-inch ginger: 1
Red chillies, whole: To taste
Onions, small: 2
Bay leaves: 2
Cloves: 4
Black cardamom: 2
Black pepper: 14–16
Cumin seeds: ½ tsp
Potatoes, large: 2
Salt to taste

For the Stuffing:
Onions, small, finely chopped: 2
Fresh coriander leaves, chopped
Fresh mint leaves, chopped
Green chillies, chopped

Steps

1. Wash the mince and chana dal thoroughly.
2. Peel and chop the ginger into small pieces.
3. Peel and dice the potatoes into small chunks.
4. In a large pot, combine the mince, chana dal, ginger, red chillies, 2 small onions, bay leaves, cloves, black cardamom, black pepper, cumin seeds, potatoes and salt.
5. Add enough water to cover the ingredients and bring to a boil.
6. Cook until all the ingredients are tender and the water has evaporated. Ensure the mixture is dry when done.

7. Remove and discard the cooked onions and bay leaves from the mixture.
8. Transfer the remaining mixture to a grinder and grind to a smooth paste.
9. Take small portions of the mixture and shape them into kababs.
10. Make a small indentation in each kabab and stuff it with the finely chopped onions, fresh coriander leaves, mint leaves and green chillies.
11. Seal the kababs properly to keep the stuffing inside.
12. Heat oil in a frying pan over a medium to low flame.
13. Fry the kababs on a slow flame until they are golden brown and cooked through.
14. Serve the kababs hot, garnished with additional chopped coriander and mint leaves if desired. They can be served with chutney or a side salad.

Notes: Ensure the water is completely evaporated before grinding to achieve a smooth paste. Frying on a slow flame ensures the kababs are cooked evenly and do not burn. You can adjust the number of red chillies based on your spice preference.

AWADHI SHAMI KABAB

INGREDIENTS

For Boiling, Masala A:
Goat or lamb meat, minced: 500 gm
Bengal gram: 125 gm
½-inch ginger
Garlic: 5 cloves
Red chillies: 4
Black pepper: 4
Black cardamom: 4

Cinnamon: 1 tsp
Salt to taste
Water: Approximately ½ l

Masala B:
Garam masala: 1 tsp
Mace powder: ½ tsp
Green cardamom powder: ½ tsp
Kewra water: 1 tsp
Meetha attar: 2 drops

For the Filling, Masala C:
Mint leaves: 50 gm
Green chillies: 10
1-inch ginger
Onions, medium: 3
Salt: ¼ tsp (or to taste)
Ghee: 250 gm

STEPS

1. Clean the minced meat and set it aside. Chop the ginger and squeeze the juice from the garlic cloves.
2. In a deep pot, add all the ingredients listed under Masala A. Cover and cook until the chana dal is tender. Uncover and keep stirring until all the water evaporates and the mixture starts sticking to the sides of the pot. Remove from heat and grind everything into a smooth paste.
3. Add the ingredients from Masala B to the paste and blend well. Divide the mixture into sixteen equal portions and set aside.
4. Wash and finely chop the mint leaves, green chillies and onions. Slice the ginger into thin slivers. Mix everything with salt using your fingers.

5. Take each portion of the mince paste, flatten it slightly and place a small amount of the filling in the centre. Shape the paste around the filling into patties.

6. Grease a tawa with about 50 gm of ghee and place the kababs on it. Cook on a very low flame. Melt the remaining ghee and pour it over the kababs. When the sides turn light brown, gently flip them to cook until they are golden brown on all sides.

7. Serve the kababs hot with fresh mint chutney and roomali roti or warqui paratha.

BIHARI SHAMI KABAB

INGREDIENTS

Mutton, boneless: 1 kg
Split Bengal gram, husked: 10 tbsp
Green cardamom: 16
Black cardamom: 8
1-inch cinnamon sticks: 8
Red Kashmiri chilli powder: 2 tsp
Dried ginger powder: 2 tsp
Garlic, finely chopped: 8–12 cloves
Salt: 6 tsp (or to taste)
Green chillies, finely chopped: 2 tsp
Fresh coriander leaves, finely chopped: 4 tbsp
Ginger, finely chopped: 4 tsp
Nigella seeds:2 tsp
Turmeric powder: 2 tsp
Ghee/oil for deep frying
Chaat masala powder: 4 tsp
Onions, large, sliced: 4

1. Wash, trim and drain the meat. Cut it into large chunks.
2. In a large pan, combine the meat, chana dal, green cardamom, black cardamom, cinnamon sticks, red Kashmiri chilli powder, dried ginger powder, garlic and salt.
3. Add just enough water to cover the ingredients. Cook on low heat until the water evaporates and the meat is tender.
4. Remove the pan from heat and let it cool.
5. Discard the whole spices.
6. Grind the mixture in a food processor until it becomes a fine paste. Taste and add more salt if needed.
7. Lightly grease your hands. Divide the kabab mix into equal portions. Roll each portion into balls and flatten them slightly to form round patties.
8. Heat oil in a frying pan. Shallow-fry the kababs on medium heat until they are golden brown on both sides.
9. Arrange the kababs on a serving platter. Serve hot with onion slices and chutney.

Purani Dilli Special Shami Kabab

Ingredients

Mutton, minced: 1 kg
Bengal gram: 100 gm (½ cup)
Garlic: 12–15 cloves
2-inch ginger, chopped
Cloves: 10
1-inch cinnamon sticks: 2
Green cardamom: 6–8
Bay leaves: 4
Salt: 2 tsp (or to taste)

Eggs, lightly beaten: 2
Ghee/oil for frying: 250 gm (1¼ cups)

For the Stuffing/Filling:
Green chillies, chopped: 2–3
3-inch ginger, finely chopped
Fresh coriander leaves, chopped: 4 tbsp
Almonds, blanched and chopped: 25 gm (approx. 20)

STEPS

1. Put the minced meat, the next eight ingredients and 500 ml of water in a big pot. Cook until all the water has evaporated and the mince is soft (for about 1 to 1½ hours).
2. Take out the cinnamon sticks and bay leaves, then pulse the ingredients into a fine paste. Beat and mix in the eggs.
3. Grease your hands just a little. Using a tiny bit of the mince mixture, ball it up. Form a depression in the middle and stuff with a little filling. Pinch the edges together to contain the filling, then use your palms to gently flatten the ball. Repeat to prepare each kabab.
4. Heat the ghee in a frying pan. Fry the kababs till they are golden brown on both sides.
5. Assemble the kababs with mint sprigs, lime wedges and onion rings.

DILLI 6 SHAMI KABAB

INGREDIENTS

Mutton, boneless pieces: 1 kg
Split chickpeas: 200 gm
Coriander seeds: 1 tsp
Cumin seeds: 1 tsp

Dried red chillies: 8
Garlic: 10 cloves
Red chilli powder: ½ tsp
Coriander powder: ½ tsp
Turmeric powder: ½ tsp
Salt: 1 tsp (or to taste)
Ginger paste: 1 tsp
Water: ½ l
Garam masala: ½ tsp
Chaat masala: ½ tsp
Eggs: 2
Fresh coriander leaves, chopped
Oil for frying

Steps

1. In a pressure cooker, combine the boneless mutton pieces, split chickpeas, coriander seeds, cumin seeds, dried red chillies, garlic cloves, red chilli powder, coriander powder, turmeric powder, salt, ginger paste and water.
2. Cook in a pressure cooker until the mutton and split chickpeas are tender (for approximately 20–25 minutes).
3. Allow the mixture to cool slightly. Remove the whole spices if desired.
4. Transfer the cooked mixture to a food processor and grind to a fine paste. Transfer the paste to a large mixing bowl.
5. Add garam masala, chaat masala, chopped fresh coriander leaves and eggs to the mixture. Mix well to combine.
6. Lightly grease your hands. Take a small portion of the mixture and form it into a ball. Gently flatten it to form a round patty. Repeat the process to make all the kababs.
7. Heat oil in a deep frying pan or wok over medium heat. Fry the kababs in batches until they are golden brown and crisp on both sides.

8. Drain on kitchen paper to remove excess oil. Arrange the kababs on a serving platter.
9. Serve hot with onion rings, lime wedges and mint chutney.

BULANDSHEHAR CHICKEN SHAMI KABAB

INGREDIENTS

Split Bengal gram, soaked for 2 hours: 150 gm
Water: 3–4 cups
Boneless chicken, cut into cubes: ½ kg
Button red chillies: 8–10
Ginger garlic paste: 1½ tbsp
Salt: ½ tsp (or to taste)
Coriander seeds, roasted and crushed: 1 tbsp
Cumin seeds, roasted and crushed: 1 tbsp
Fresh coriander leaves: ¼ cup
Fresh mint leaves: ¼ cup
Green chillies: 2–3
Garam masala powder: 1 tsp
Curd: 1 tbsp
Eggs: 1–2
Oil for frying

STEPS

1. Put the split Bengal gram that has been soaked in water in a pressure cooker along with the chicken pieces, ginger garlic paste, roasted and crushed cumin seeds and coriander seeds, button red chillies, and salt. Stir thoroughly.
2. Put green chillies, fresh mint leaves and fresh coriander leaves in a blender. Pulverize them in a grinder.
3. Cook until the chicken and split Bengal gram are well cooked. It should take 3–4 whistles on a medium flame.

4. Once done, open the lid and wait for the water to evaporate by cooking on a high flame. Allow it to cool. Ensure the mixture becomes dry.
5. Stir in curd, eggs, the cooked chicken combination and garam masala powder. Grind to a smooth paste until thoroughly mixed.
6. Use water to wet your hands. Divide the mixture into parts and form them into kababs of the same size.
7. In a frying pan, heat the oil. The kababs should be fried until golden brown on all sides.
8. Along with onion rings, lime wedges and chutney, serve hot.

Kathal Shami Kabab

Ingredients

Raw jackfruit (kathal), boiled and mashed: 700 gm
Gram flour, roasted: 150 gm
Onion, chopped: 1
Fresh mint leaves, chopped: ¼ cup
Fresh coriander leaves, chopped: ¼ cup
Ginger and garlic, crushed: 2 tbsp
Garam masala powder: 1½ tbsp
Green chillies, chopped: 1½ tbsp
Chilli flakes: 1½ tbsp
Nutmeg, grated: ½ tsp
Black pepper, crushed: 1 tbsp
Lemon, juiced: 1
Salt as per taste
Water as required (to shape the kabab)
Ghee/oil for shallow frying

1. Mash the boiled jackfruit thoroughly in a dish.
2. Add all the remaining ingredients like salt, onion, fresh mint, fresh coriander, roasted gram flour, red chilli powder, garam masala powder, etc. Thoroughly blend it.
3. Form equal amounts of the mixture into kababs.
4. In a non-stick skillet, heat enough oil. Add the prepared kababs and shallow-fry them until brown and crispy. Drain over absorbent paper.
5. Serve hot with green chutney and onion slices.

Tarana Husain Khan's Kacche Gosht ki Tikiya[10]

Ingredients

Meat, finely minced: 1 kg
Ghee or oil: 1 cup
Green papaya paste: ½ tbsp
Tenderizer powder: 1 tsp
Bengal gram, roasted, shelled and powdered: 50 gm
Onion, large, finely diced: 1
Ginger paste: 1 tbsp
Garlic paste: 1 tbsp
Red or yellow chilli powder: 1–2 tsp
Green cardamom: 10
Black cardamom: 3
Black pepper: 1 tsp
Cumin seeds: 1 tsp
Egg: 1
Salt to taste

For the Stuffing:
Onions, diced into tiny square pieces: 2

Green chillies, finely chopped: 5–6
Coriander leaves, finely chopped: 1 bunch

1. Fry the onions in ghee till they turn golden. Drain and remove them. Grind them with the garam masalas (cumin seeds, black pepper and cardamom) and reserve the mix.
2. Take the minced meat in a large bowl and add ginger garlic paste, chilli powder (in Rampur, yellow chillies are used), roasted Bengal gram powder, papaya paste and salt. Knead them well. Grind the minced meat if it appears too rough.
3. Add the fried onions and garam masala paste. Mix them thoroughly and add the egg.
4. Add the stuffing and mix well. Shape into palm-sized, flat, thin patties. The shapes can be irregular.
5. Heat some oil in a frying pan or thick, flat-bottomed pan and fry one patty on simmer to check the softness. If it is too tough, add ½ tsp of tenderizer and mix it well. In case the patty breaks and is impossible to fry, add breadcrumbs to the mixture.

DAHI WALE KABAB

INGREDIENTS

Mutton, minced (80 per cent lean, 20 per cent fat): 1 kg
Onions, medium, finely chopped: 3
Curd: 1–1½ cups
Salt: 1¼ tsp (or to taste)
Garlic, minced: 3 cloves
Garlic powder: ½ tsp
Green chillies, finely chopped: 4

Red chilli powder: 1 tsp
Red chilli flakes: 2 tsp
Cumin seeds: 1 tsp
Cumin powder: 1 tsp
Coriander seeds: 2 tsp
Wheat flour: 3 tbsp
Ghee or oil: 1 cup

STEPS

1. Finely chop the onions and green chillies. Mince the garlic cloves.
2. In a large pot, combine the minced mutton, onions, curd, salt, minced garlic, garlic powder, green chillies, red chilli powder, red chilli flakes, cumin seeds, cumin powder and coriander seeds.
3. Mix well and let it sit for 60–90 minutes.
4. Grease your hands lightly. Take a small portion of the mixture and form it into a ball. Gently flatten it to form a round patty. Repeat the process to make all the kababs.
5. Heat ghee or oil in a frying pan.
6. Fry the kababs on medium heat until they are golden brown and crisp on both sides.
7. Drain on kitchen paper.
8. Serve the kababs with onion rings, lime wedges and chutney.

AWADHI PATILI KABAB

INGREDIENTS

Coconut, desiccated: 100 gm
Charoli seeds: 2 tbsp
Poppy seeds: 50 gm
Allspice powder: 1 tsp
Mace blades: 4

Nutmeg, grated: ½ tsp
Green cardamom: 15
Black cardamom: 6
Cloves: 10–12

STEPS

1. In a dry pan over medium heat, dry roast all the ingredients until they turn aromatic.
2. Allow all the roasted ingredients to cool completely.
3. Using a spice grinder or a powerful blender, grind the cooled roasted ingredients into a fine powder. Do this in batches, if necessary, to ensure a consistent texture.
4. Transfer the blended spice mix to an airtight container. Store it in a cool, dry place to maintain its freshness and potency.

PURDANASHEEN KABAB

INGREDIENTS

Raw papaya paste: 50 gm
Ginger paste: 25 gm
Garlic paste: 25 gm
Red chilli powder: 2 tsp
Salt: 2 tsp (or to taste)
Curd: 50 gm
Cloves: 5
Green cardamom: 5
Black cardamom: 2
Mace blade: 1
Black pepper: 1 tsp
Allspice powder: 1 tsp
Gram flour, roasted: 1 tbsp
Lazzat-e-taam (p. 321): 1 tsp

Kewra water: 1 tbsp
Meetha attar: 2 drops

STEPS

1. In a blender, add raw papaya paste, ginger paste, garlic paste, red chilli powder, salt and curd. Blend until smooth.
2. In a dry pan, roast cloves, green cardamom, black cardamom, mace, black pepper and allspice powder until aromatic.
3. Allow the roasted spices to cool slightly, then grind them into a fine powder using a spice grinder or mortar and pestle.
4. Mix the blended paste with the ground spice powder thoroughly in a large mixing bowl.
5. Stir in 1 tbsp roasted gram flour, 1 tsp lazzat-e-taam, 1 tbsp kewra jal and 2 drops of meetha attar. Mix well until all the ingredients are fully incorporated.
6. Use this mixture to marinate your kabab mixture. Ensure the meat is well coated and let it marinate for at least 2 hours or preferably overnight for best results.

KACCHE KEEMA KI TIKIA

INGREDIENTS

Mutton, minced (with 20 per cent fat): 1 kg
Raw papaya paste: 1 tbsp
1-inch ginger, ground
Salt: 2 tsp (or to taste)
Thick curd, hung for an hour in muslin: 100 gm
Ghee: 2 tbsp
Onions, medium, finely sliced: 2
Parched gram, roasted and ground: 100 gm

Poppy seeds, roasted and ground: 3 tbsp
Charoli seeds, roasted and ground: 2 tsp
Garam masala powder: 1½ tsp
1-inch cinnamon stick
Ghee/oil for frying: 250 gm (1¼ cups)

For the Filling:
3-inch ginger, finely chopped
Green chillies, finely chopped: 2–3
Fresh coriander, chopped: 4 tbsp

STEPS

1. Prepare the mince: Mix the minced mutton with ghee, papaya paste, ginger and salt. Let it marinate for one hour.
2. In a skillet, heat ghee/oil and fry the onions until golden. Cool and grind.
3. Combine the ground onions, parched gram, poppy seeds, charoli seeds, garam masala and cinnamon into the marinated mince.
4. Mix chopped ginger, green chillies and fresh coriander together.
5. With greased hands, take small portions of the mince mixture, form into balls, make a depression in the centre, fill them with a bit of the filling mixture, then seal and flatten slightly.
6. Heat some ghee on a griddle over low heat. Place the kababs on the griddle, cover with a lid and cook for about 5 minutes on each side until golden, adding a bit more ghee as needed during cooking.
7. Garnish the cooked kababs with onion rings and fresh coriander.

Chobi Kabab[11]

Ingredients

Mutton or beef (pasande or thinly sliced): 1 kg
Onion, small: 2
Garlic: 4 cloves
1-inch ginger: 2
Poppy seeds: 2 tbsp
Bengal gram, roasted: 2 tbsp
Garam masala: 2 tbsp
Red chilli powder: 2 tbsp
Salt to taste
Nutmeg, grated: ¼ tsp
Mace blade: 1
Ghee for frying: As needed

Steps

1. Grind all the spices finely. First, lightly fry the onion in ghee until golden, remove it and then grind it finely.
2. After washing the meat slices, coat them well with the spice mixture and let them marinate for 20 minutes.
3. Grease a skewer or a thick wooden stick with ghee. Wrap 3–4 seasoned meat slices around the skewer and place it on a barbeque, rotating it occasionally.
4. Keep lightly basting the meat with ghee using a cloth wrapped around a stick. Once the meat turns golden brown, wrap another 3–4 slices around the skewer and continue cooking, adding more ghee as needed.
5. Continue this process until all the meat is cooked. Once done, remove the meat from the skewer, slice it and serve.

Mahi Machli Kabab

Ingredients

Mahi fish pieces, boneless: 500 gm
Curd, whisked: 250 gm
Onion: 1
Lemons, juiced: 2
Eggs: 2
Chickpea flour, roasted: 2½ tbsp
Cream, whisked: 2 tbsp
1-inch cinnamon stick
Cloves: 4–6
Cardamom: 4–6
Black pepper: 15–20
Red chilli flakes: 1 tbsp
Salt to taste
Ghee as needed

Steps

1. Use a pointed tool to pierce the fish pieces. Rinse the fish pieces with garlic-infused water.
2. Mix lemon juice and salt. Rub this mixture onto the fish pieces and rinse again to ensure the flavours infuse well and any excess marinade is washed off.
3. In a pan, heat ghee and fry thinly sliced onions until golden. Remove the onions and grind them with the rest of the spices to form a paste.
4. Break eggs into the spice paste and whisk together. Mix the curd and cream to blend thoroughly.
5. Submerge the fish pieces in the prepared spice mixture.
6. Place the seasoned fish on an iron skewer. Set the skewer over coals and continuously turn while basting

with ghee for even cooking. You can also grill these on a grill pan.

7. Once the fish is cooked and has a slight char, serve it hot with green chutney.

AWADHI GOLA KABAB

INGREDIENTS

Meat, minced: 1 kg
Eggs: 2
1-inch ginger: 2
Red chilli, crushed: 1 tbsp
Black pepper: 1 tbsp
Nutmeg: ¼ tsp
Mace blade: 1
Nigella seeds: 1 tbsp
Saffron: ¼ tsp
Gram flour, roasted: ½ cup
Onions: 1 cup
Garlic: 8–10 cloves
Bay leaves: 4
Green caradamom: 6–8
Green chillies: 10

STEPS

1. Begin by heating a 3 tbsp ghee in a pan and frying the onions until they turn golden. Once they are golden, add garlic water and remove from heat.

2. After 20 minutes, add the minced meat and chickpea lentils to the same pan.

3. As the minced meat nears full cooking, break two eggs into the pan. Continue cooking until the meat is completely tender.

4. Finely grind the cooked meat mixture and incorporate all the spices and salt.
5. Rinse the onions twice after massaging them into thin slices.
6. Finely chop the onions, salt, ginger, mint, and red chilli, mix them into the meat, and fill this stuffing into the minced meat to form kababs.
7. To prepare the kababs, apply a bit of milk/water/oil to your hands to form each kabab, ensuring they are quite large; roughly 16 kababs should be made from 1 kg of minced meat.
8. Fry the kababs in ghee.

Dilliwale Arvi ke Patte ke Kabab

Ingredients

Taro leaves (arvi ke patte), medium: 10
Gram flour: 10 tbsp
Garam masala: 1 tsp
Onion, medium, finely chopped: 1
Red chilli flakes: 2 tbsp
Yellow chilli flakes: 1 tbsp
Salt to taste

Steps

1. Wash the taro leaves thoroughly.
2. In a bowl, finely grind the onions, garam masala, salt and chilli. Mix these spices into the gram flour. Add water to make a thick batter (similar in consistency to minced meat for kababs).
3. Spread the batter evenly over each taro leaf. Fold the leaves to form kababs.

4. In a large pot, boil water. You can either tie a thick cloth over the pot or place a bamboo basket to hold the kababs. Place the kababs on the cloth or basket, cover them with a lid or another suitable object and let them steam.
5. Once the leaves are cooked, cut them into shapes similar to shami kababs. Fry them in ghee or oil until crispy.
6. Drain the fried kababs on a paper towel to remove excess oil and serve hot with green chutney.

Murgh aur Keema ke Kabab

Ingredients

Chicken, skinless and clean: 1 whole (about 1 kg)
Meat, minced: 250 gm
Curd (for marinating): 250 gm
Ghee: 250 gm (125 gm for cooking minced meat and 125 gm for basting)
Onions, medium, finely chopped: 2
Garlic, minced: 1
Garam masala: 1 tbsp
Cumin powder: 1 tbsp
Cardamom powder: 1 tsp
Clove powder: 1 tsp
Cinnamon powder: 1 tsp
Red chilli powder: 1 tsp
Black pepper powder: 1½ tsp
Salt to taste
Green chillies, finely chopped (optional, for extra heat): 10

Steps

1. In a large bowl, mix the curd with garam masala, cumin seeds, cardamom, clove, cinnamon, red chilli powder, black pepper and salt.

2.   Clean the chicken thoroughly. Rub the marinade all over the chicken and inside the cavity. Let it marinate in the refrigerator for at least 4 hours, preferably overnight.

3.   Heat half the ghee (125 gm) in a pan. Add minced meat and cook until browned and cooked through. Set aside.

4.   After marination, stuff the chicken's cavity with cooked minced meat, some chopped onions and optional green chillies for added spice.

5.   Preheat your oven to 375°F (190°C) for about 20 minutes. Place the stuffed chicken in a roasting pan. Drizzle with some of the remaining ghee.

6.   For those without an oven, cook the marinated and stuffed chicken in a large, covered pot with a bit of water over low heat for about 1½–2 hours, basting occasionally with ghee until the meat is tender and fully cooked.

7.   As the chicken roasts, baste it periodically with the remaining ghee mixed with a bit of curd to keep it moist and flavourful. Roast the chicken for about 1–1½ hours or until the juices run clear and the chicken is golden brown.

8.   Serve the murgh aur keema ke kabab hot, garnished with slices of raw onion and freshly chopped coriander. Lemon wedges can be served alongside for squeezing over the chicken.

Sweet Kabab[12]

Ingredients

Meat, minced: 1 kg
Sugar: 250 gm
Ghee for cooking: 250 gm
Onion, finely chopped: 250 gm
Curd, whisked: 250 gm
Egg, beaten: 1
Fresh coriander, chopped: 4–5 tbsp

1-inch ginger: 2
Poppy seeds: 1½ tsp
Chickpea flour: 2½ tbsp
Cloves: 8
Cardamom: 6
1-inch cinnamon stick
Red chilli powder: 1 tbsp
Salt: 3 tbsp (or to taste)
Lemons, juiced: 2

STEPS

1. In a pot, mix 250 gm of sugar with sufficient lemon juice to create a thick syrup. This is your base for the sweet kababs.
2. Take the minced meat and incorporate it into the sweet syrup. At this stage, add your aromatic spices, such as garam masala, cloves, cardamom and cinnamon to infuse the meat with rich flavours.
3. Transfer the spiced meat and syrup mixture into a pot. Seal the pot tightly to ensure that the flavours are well-contained and place it in a preheated oven or gas stove. Cook until the meat absorbs the syrup and is tender.
4. Once the meat is cooked and flavoured with the sweet syrup, form it into small patties. Coat each patty in beaten egg, then shallow or deep-fry them in ghee until golden brown on both sides.

GALAWAT KE KABAB

INGREDIENTS

Mutton, minced: 1 kg (with an additional 200 gm fat)
Brown onion paste: 1 tsp
Brown cashew paste: 1½ tbsp

Ghee: 2 tbsp (plus extra for frying)
Salt to taste
Ginger garlic juice: 1 tbsp
Raw papaya paste, with skin: 2 tbsp
Prepared galawat ka masala: 1 tbsp
Kewra water: 1 tsp
Rose water: 1 tsp
Red chilli powder: A pinch
Sprinkles of ghee
Sprinkles of milk

For Galawat ka Masala:
Betel leaf root: 1
Vetiver root (khus ki jad): 20 gm
Long pepper: ¼ tsp
Allspice powder: ¼ tsp
Black pepper: 1 tsp
Black cumin seeds: 1 tsp
Cloves: 4–5
Green cardamom: 5–6
Star anise: 1
Bay leaves: 2
Rose petals, dried: 1 tbsp
Stone flower: 1 tbsp
Nutmeg, small: ¼ tsp
Mace blade: 1
Black cardamom: ½ tsp
Saffron: A pinch
1-inch cinnamon stick
½-inch sea foam
Wild berries dried: 1–2

STEPS

1. Mix the minced mutton and fat thoroughly.

2. Pass the mixture through a meat grinder or use a food processor until well minced. Repeat, if necessary, to ensure fine texture.

3. Combine all the spices listed under 'For Galawat ka Masala' in a spice grinder. Grind to a fine powder to ensure that the flavours meld well.

4. In a large mixing bowl, combine the minced meat with the ground spice mix, brown onion paste, cashew paste, ginger garlic juice, raw papaya paste, kewra water, rose water, and a pinch of salt and red chilli powder.

5. Mix well to ensure all the ingredients are evenly distributed.

6. Let the mixture marinate for at least 2 hours or, ideally, overnight in the refrigerator.

7. Heat a flat pan over medium heat and add some ghee for shallow frying.

8. Moisten your hands with water, take small portions of the marinated meat and form patties directly in the pan.

9. Cook each patty until a golden crust forms on both sides and the kababs are cooked through.

10. Serve the kababs hot with green chutney, paratha, sliced onions and lemon wedges.

PUSHPESH PANT'S GALWATI KE KABAB[13]

INGREDIENTS

Lamb, finely minced: 750 gm
Raw papaya paste: 100 gm
Gram flour, roasted: 4 tbsp
Garam masala: 1 tsp
Ghee: 4 tbsp
Green cardamom, lightly crushed: 4
Salt to taste

1. Mix the minced lamb and raw papaya paste in a bowl. Set aside to marinate in the refrigerator for at least 1 hour.

2. Add the roasted gram flour, garam masala, ghee, green cardamom and salt to the marinated lamb. Mix well.

3. Divide the mixture into equal portions and shape into patties.

4. Heat a pan over medium heat and add ghee. Fry the patties until golden brown and cooked through (for about 3–4 minutes on each side).

5. For a smoky flavour, place a small bowl with hot coals in the pan, add cloves and ghee, cover, and let it smoke for a few minutes.

6. Serve hot with green chutney, paratha, onion rings and lemon wedges.

GHILAFI KABAB

INGREDIENTS

Lamb, minced: 600 gm (with an additional 100 gm fat)
Ginger garlic paste: 3 tbsp
Onion, chopped: 4 tbsp
Spring onion, chopped: 4 tbsp
Tomato, chopped: 4 tbsp
Bell pepper, chopped: 4 tbsp
Green chilli, chopped: 2 tbsp
Coriander, chopped: 3 tbsp
Red chilli powder: 2½ tbsp
Allspice powder: ½ tsp
Garam masala: 2 tbsp
Lemon juice: 2 tbsp
Butter, melted (for basting): 2 tbsp

1. Mix the minced lamb with ginger garlic paste, chopped onion, spring onion, tomato, bell pepper, green chilli, coriander, red chilli powder, allspice powder, garam masala, lemon juice and salt. Ensure the mixture is well combined.
2. Divide the mixture into equal portions. Shape each portion into a long sausage shape around skewers, pressing firmly to ensure the mixture sticks well.
3. Preheat a grill to medium heat. Place the skewers on the grill and cook for about 5–6 minutes, turning each occasionally to cook evenly.
4. Baste with melted butter during the cooking process to keep the kababs moist.
5. Serve hot with lemon and fresh, sliced onions.

SEEKH KABAB

INGREDIENTS

Mutton, minced (20 per cent fat): 900 gm
Button red chillies: 6–7
Coriander seeds: 1½ tbsp
Cumin seeds: 1½ tbsp
Carom seeds: 1 tsp
Cloves: 5–6
1-inch cinnamon stick
Mint leaves: A handful
Fresh coriander: A handful
Onion, fried: ½ cup
Green chillies: 6–8
Garlic: 7–8 cloves
2-inch piece of ginger

Lemon juice: ½ tbsp
Red chilli powder: 1 tsp
Garam masala: 1 tsp
Salt: 2 tsp (or to taste)
Kashmiri red chilli powder: 1 tsp
Ghee: 1–2 tbsp

STEPS

1. In a frying pan, add button red chillies, coriander seeds, cumin seeds, carom seeds, cloves and the cinnamon stick. Mix well and dry roast until fragrant. Let it cool.

2. In a spice grinder, add the roasted spices and grind to a coarse powder. Set aside.

3. In a chopper, combine mint leaves, fresh coriander, fried onion, green chillies, garlic, ginger, lemon juice, red chilli powder, garam masala powder, salt and Kashmiri red chilli powder.

4. Chop until well combined into a paste.

5. In a bowl, mix the minced meat with ground spices and the prepared paste. Add ghee and mix well. Cover the bowl with a plastic wrap and refrigerate for 2 -3 hours.

6. Form the marinated meat mixture into oblong shapes around skewers. Ensure the meat is firmly packed around the skewer. Let this marinated meat sit and refrigerate for another 30 minutes.

7. Preheat the grill to medium to high heat. Place the kababs on the grill. Cook one side for 5–7 minutes, then turn the kababs and cook for another 5–7 minutes until they are cooked from all sides.

8. Once cooked, remove the kababs from the grill. Slide the meat off the skewers and serve on warmed naan with sliced onions and green chutney.

Bazarwale Dilli ke Seekh Kabab

Ingredients

Coriander seeds: 2 tbsp
Red chilli, crushed: 1½ tbsp
Red chilli powder: 1 tsp
Garam masala powder: 2 tsp
Cumin powder, roasted: 1 tbsp
Turmeric powder: ½ tsp
Salt: 1½ tsp (or to taste)
Onion, large: 1
Green chillies: 8–10
Lemon, juiced: 1
Ginger garlic paste: 2 tsp
Fresh coriander: 1 cup
Kachri powder or papaya paste: 1 tbsp
Onion, fried: ½ cup

Steps

1. Coarsely pound the coriander seeds and mix with crushed red chilli, red chilli powder, garam masala powder, roasted cumin powder and turmeric powder. Set aside.
2. Finely chop 1 large onion, 8–10 green chillies and 1 cup fresh coriander.
3. Combine the chopped ingredients with the coarsely pounded spice mix in a large bowl.
4. Add salt, lemon juice, ginger garlic paste, kachri powder or papaya paste, and fried onion to the bowl. Mix thoroughly.
5. Use this mixture in 1 kg of chicken or minced mutton to make Delhi market-style seekh kabab.

Kashmiri Seekh Kabab

Ingredients

Kashmiri red chilli powder: 4 tsp
Salt: 3 tsp (or to taste)
Black cardamom seeds, powdered: 1 tsp
Eggs, lightly beaten: 2
Black cumin seeds: ¾ tsp
Saffron, ground with some water or milk: 1¼ tsp
Coriander leaves, finely chopped: 1 tbsp
Dried mint leaves: 1 tsp

Steps

1. Grind the black cardamom seeds and black cumin seeds into a fine powder using a spice grinder or mortar and pestle.
2. Soak the saffron threads in a small amount of warm water or milk until they release color.
3. In a bowl, combine the Kashmiri red chilli powder, salt, ground black cardamom, and ground black cumin seeds.
4. Add the soaked saffron (including the liquid), chopped coriander leaves, and dry mint leaves to the bowl.
5. Mix everything thoroughly until the ingredients are evenly combined and the saffron is well incorporated. This blend is used during the preparation process to infuse the meat with flavour before cooking.

Note: To make these or any good kabab, I prefer meat from the hind legs of lambs. This recipe calls for 1 kg meat.

Andhra Boti Kabab

Ingredients

Red chilli powder: 4 tsp
Ginger powder: 4 tsp
Garlic powder: 4 tsp
Nutmeg, grated: ½ tsp
Allspice powder: 2 tsp
Charoli seeds: 2 tbsp
Poppy seeds: 2 tbsp
Nigella seeds: 2 tbsp
Gram flour, roasted: 3 tbsp

Steps

1. Dry roast charoli seeds, poppy seeds and caraway seeds on a low flame until fragrant. Let them cool. Dry roast gram flour until golden and fragrant.
2. Combine the roasted charoli seeds, poppy seeds, caraway seeds, red chilli powder, ginger powder, garlic powder, grated nutmeg and allspice powder in a grinder.
3. Grind to a coarse powder. In a mixing bowl, combine the ground spice mixture with the roasted gram flour.
4. Store the prepared spice blend in an airtight container. Use as needed for marinating meat for Andhra boti kabab.

Awadhi Boti Kabab

Ingredients

Raw papaya paste: 3 tbsp
Onions, fried: 2
Curd: ½ cup
Ginger garlic paste: 1 tbsp

Gram flour: 1 tbsp
Red chilli powder: 1 tsp
Almonds: 14–15
Salt: 1 tsp (or to taste)
Fennel seeds: 1 tsp
Cloves: 4–5
Green cardamom: 4
Mace blade: 1
1-inch cinnamon stick
Black cardamom seeds: 1
Black pepper: 8–10
Cumin seeds: ½ tsp
Coriander seeds: 1 tbsp

STEPS

1. Roast all the dry spices with gram flour and grind them to a fine powder.
2. Add curd, fried onion and ginger garlic paste to 500–600 gm meat. Use this marinade along with raw papaya paste and salt for chicken or mutton, based on your preference.
3. Grill the marinated meat on a sigdi or cook in a pan until done.

BENGALI BOTI KABAB

INGREDIENTS

Salt: 1 tsp (or to taste)
Chilli flakes: 1 tsp
Garam masala: 1 tsp
Red chilli powder: 1 tsp
Coriander powder: 1 tsp
Garlic paste: 1 tsp
Ginger paste: 1 tsp
Onion paste: 2 tbsp

Poppy seed paste: 1 tsp
Curd: 4 tbsp
Onions, fried: 2–3 tbsp
Papaya paste: 1 tsp
Gram flour, roasted: 2½ tsp
Mustard oil: 2 tbsp

STEPS

1. In a large bowl, add salt, chilli flakes, garam masala, red chilli powder, coriander powder, garlic paste, ginger paste, onion paste, poppy seed paste, curd, fried onions, papaya paste, roasted gram flour and mustard oil.
2. Mix all the ingredients thoroughly to form a smooth marinade.
3. Add the marinade to the meat of your choice (such as mutton or beef). Cover the bowl and refrigerate for at least 2 hours or overnight for best results.
4. Once marinated, grill or cook the meat until tender and juicy.

DILLI BOTI KABAB

INGREDIENTS

Cumin seeds: 1 tsp
Poppy seeds: 1 tsp
Nutmeg, whole: ¾
Black pepper: 8–10
Mace blade: 1
Green cardamom: 8
Cloves: 10
1-inch cinnamon stick: 2
Onion, fried: ½ cup
Turmeric powder: 1 tsp
Red chilli powder: 3 tsp

Chilli flakes: 2 tsp
Garam masala: 3 tbsp
Salt: 1 tsp (or to taste)

STEPS

1. In a dry pan, roast cumin seeds, poppy seeds, nutmeg, black pepper, mace blade, green cardamom, cloves and cinnamon until aromatic. Let them cool.
2. In a grinder, add the roasted spices and grind to a fine powder.
3. Mix the ground spices with fried onion, turmeric powder, red chilli powder, chilli flakes, garam masala and salt.
4. Transfer the spice blend to an airtight container and store in a cool, dry place.
5. Use this with curd and papaya paste to marinate the kababs. Cook on a tawa or sigdi.

ANDHRA DUM KABAB

INGREDIENTS

1-inch cinnamon stick: 2
Cardamom: 10–12
Cloves: 10–12
Green chillies: 1 tsp
Nigella seeds: 1 tsp
Charoli seeds: 1 tsp
Poppy seeds: 2 tsp
Dried coconut: 1 tsp
Garlic powder: 2 tsp
Ginger powder: 1½ tsp
Dried red chillies: 4 tsp
Salt: 2 tsp (or to taste)
Allspice powder: 1 tsp
Gram flour, roasted: 2½ tsp

STEPS

1. In a grinder, add cinnamon, cardamom, cloves, green chillies, black caraway seeds, charoli seeds, poppy seeds, dried coconut, garlic powder, ginger powder, dried red chillies, salt, allspice powder and roasted gram flour.
2. Grind until a fine powder is formed.
3. Transfer the blend to an airtight container. Store in a cool, dry place.

CHATPATA BOTI KABAB

INGREDIENTS

Garam masala: 2 tbsp
Cumin powder: 1½ tbsp
Black salt: 1 tsp
Chilli flakes: 2 tbsp
Coriander powder: 2 tbsp
Black pepper powder: 1 tsp
White pepper powder: 1 tsp
Ginger garlic powder: 2 tbsp
Carom seeds: 1 tsp
Nutmeg, grated: ½ tsp
Fenugreek leaves, dried and crushed: 2 tbsp
Chaat masala: 2 tbsp
Kashmiri red chilli powder: 2 tbsp

STEPS

1. Combine all the spices in a bowl. Ensure they are thoroughly mixed to create a uniform spice blend.
2. Rub the spice mix all over the meat, ensuring every piece is well-coated.

3. Allow the meat to marinate for at least 2-4 hours, or overnight in the refrigerator for deeper flavour infusion.
4. Cook the marinated meat as desired, either by grilling or baking.
5. Adjust the seasoning and spice level after the initial cooking stage as per your taste.

Bihari Boti Kabab

Ingredients

Gram flour, roasted: 4 tbsp
Red chilli powder: 4 tbsp
Degi red chillies: 4 tbsp
Coriander seeds, whole: 2 tbsp
Poppy seeds: 2 tbsp
Kachri powder: 1 tbsp
Salt: 1 tbsp (or to taste)
Allspice powder: 1 tbsp
Nutmeg, grated: ½ tbsp
Mace, whole: ½

Steps

1. In a dry pan, lightly roast gram flour, degi red chillies, coriander seeds and poppy seeds over medium heat until they are fragrant. This enhances the flavours.
2. Allow the roasted spices to cool. Then, place all the ingredients, including the non-roasted ones (kachri powder, salt, allspice powder, nutmeg and mace), into a spice grinder.
3. Grind everything together until it becomes a fine, consistent powder. Make adjustments based on your texture preference.
4. Transfer the spice blend to an airtight container and store it in a cool, dry place to maintain its freshness and potency.

5. Rub the spice mix all over the meat, ensuring every piece is well-coated.
6. Allow the meat to marinate for at least 2–4 hours or overnight in the refrigerator for deeper flavour infusion.
7. Cook the marinated meat as desired, either by grilling or baking.

Rajasthani Boti Kabab

Ingredients

Raw papaya paste: 2 tbsp
Ginger paste: ¾ tbsp
Garlic paste: ¾ tbsp
Mathaniya red chilli paste: 4 tbsp
Ghee: 4 tsp
Hung curd: 250ml
White pepper powder: 2 tbsp
Lemon juice: 2 tbsp
Garam masala powder: 3 tbsp
Mustard oil: 3 tbsp
Salt to taste

Steps

1. Combine all marinade ingredients in a large bowl. Add the meat of your choice and ensure each piece is well-coated. Cover and marinate for 5 hours to allow the flavours to meld.
2. Preheat a charcoal grill or a moderate oven to 200°C (400°F). Thread the marinated meat onto skewers.
3. Grill the skewered meat for about 25 minutes, turning and basting with melted butter until the meat is cooked through.
4. Serve hot, accompanied by slices of onion and lemon wedges.

Bhopali Kacche Keema ke Kabab

Ingredients

Mutton, pounded: 1 kg
Onions, medium, sliced and fried to a golden brown: 6 (approx. 400 gm)
Garlic, made into a paste: 1½ tbsp
Ginger, made into a paste: 1 tbsp
Poppy seeds, soaked and ground to a paste: 2 tbsp
Roasted chickpeas (bhuna chana), ground to a powder: 4 tbsp
Red chilli powder: 2 tsp
Salt: 2 tsp (or to taste)
Charcoal, small pieces: 2–3

For the Kabab Masala:
Black pepper, whole: 10–12
Black cardamom, large: 2
Green cardamom: 4–6
Cloves: 4
Bay leaf, broken: 1
1-inch cinnamon stick, broken into pieces
Nigella seeds: ½ tsp
Nutmeg, grated: ¼
Mace, whole: ½

For the Fresh Mix:
Mint leaves, chopped: 60 gm
Coriander leaves, chopped: 60 gm
Green chillies, chopped: 40–60 gm
Lemons, juiced: 6

1. In a large bowl, combine the pounded mutton with fried onions, garlic paste, ginger paste, poppy seed paste, ground roasted chickpeas, red chilli powder, salt and the prepared kabab masala. Mix well until all ingredients are evenly distributed. Let this mixture rest for 30 minutes to meld the flavours.

2. Prepare an onion by peeling and hollowing out the centre. Place 2–3 small pieces of burning charcoal in the onion.

3. Position the onion in the centre of the mutton mixture, pour 1 tbsp of ghee over the charcoal and cover the bowl tightly. Allow it to smoke for 10–15 minutes to infuse a smoky flavour.

4. Remove the onion and charcoal. Add the chopped mint, coriander, green chillies and lemon juice to the smoked mutton mixture. Stir well to ensure all flavours are thoroughly combined.

5. Lightly shape the mixture into roundels, ensuring they are not packed too tightly to maintain a tender texture.

6. Heat a frying pan with oil or ghee and shallow-fry the kababs over a low flame. Cook each side until they develop a darkish brown crust, which should take about 20 minutes.

7. Serve the kababs hot, garnished with sliced onions, mint and lemon slices. Accompany with green chutney if desired, though the flavourful kababs may stand well on their own.

Easy Kacche Keema ke Kabab

Ingredients

Coriander seeds, roasted and crushed: 3 tbsp
Cumin powder: 3 tsp
Garam masala: 3 tsp
Kashmiri red chilli, crushed: 2 tsp
Degi red chilli, crushed: 4 tsp
Sugar, powdered: 2 tsp

Steps

1. Begin by dry roasting the coriander seeds until they release their aroma. Cool them and crush finely.
2. In a bowl, combine the crushed coriander seeds with cumin powder, garam masala, both forms of red chilli and powdered sugar.
3. Stir all the ingredients together until well-mixed.
4. Keep the spice blend in an airtight container in a cool, dry place. Use as required in your kabab recipes.

Razia's Kacche Keema ke Kabab[14]

Ingredients

Gram flour, roasted: 6–8 tbsp
Poppy seeds, roasted and ground: 3 tbsp
Charoli seeds, roasted and ground: 2 tsp
Garam masala powder: 2 tsp
Cinnamon powder: 2 tsp

1. Dry roast chana, poppy seeds, and charoli seeds separately until fragrant. Allow them to cool and then grind each to a fine powder.
2. Combine the ground parched gram, poppy seeds, charoli seeds, garam masala and cinnamon in a mixing bowl.
3. Stir the mixture thoroughly to ensure even distribution of all the spices.
4. Transfer the spice blend to an airtight container. Store in a cool, dry place.

DILLI KACCHE KEEMA KABAB (KEEMA GOLI)

INGREDIENTS

Black pepper, crushed: 3 tsp
Cumin seeds: 3 tbsp
Coriander, crushed: 3 tbsp
Red chilli, whole, crushed: 3 tbsp
Mango powder: 3 tsp
Chaat masala powder: 3 tsp
Garam masala: 3 tsp
Salt: 3 tsp (or to taste)

STEPS

1. Dry roast the whole spices. Use a spice grinder to coarsely grind all the ingredients together. The blend should be rough and coarse, not a fine powder.
2. Ensure all the spices are evenly mixed to distribute flavours uniformly.
3. Keep the blend in an airtight container in a cool, dry place.

Jharkhand Keema Kabab (Tikiya)

Ingredients

Gram flour, roasted: 6–8 tbsp
Poppy seeds: 1½ tbsp
Coriander seeds: 1½ tbsp
Garam masala: 2 tbsp
Degi red chilli powder: 2 tbsp

Steps

1. Dry roast the poppy seeds and charoli seeds in a pan until fragrant. Set aside to cool.
2. Mix all the ingredients in a bowl. Grind the mixture to a coarse consistency using a food grinder.
3. Store the blend in an airtight container to maintain freshness.

Special Kathi Kabab

Ingredients

Boneless mutton, cut into 1-inch cubes: 1 kg
2-inch dried kachri or raw papaya, ground (use papaya only if kachri is not available)
Dried figs: 4
Onions, medium: 4
Garlic: 8 cloves
1-inch ginger, ground
2-inch raw papaya, ground
Black pepper: 12
Yellow mustard seeds: 2 tbsp
Cumin seeds: 1 tsp

Curd: 4 tbsp
Ghee: 4 tbsp
Onion rings and lime wedges for garnish

1. Soak the kachri (or papaya) and figs in water for 4 hours (it isn't necessary to soak papaya). Drain the soaked items and blend them with onions, garlic, ginger and papaya into a fine paste.
2. Separately roast the pepper, mustard seeds and cumin seeds on a griddle until aromatic. Grind them into a fine powder.
3. Stir the roasted spice mix into the wet masala paste. Add curd and mix thoroughly.
4. Coat the mutton cubes with the masala paste and refrigerate overnight to marinate.
5. Thread the marinated meat onto skewers. Cook under a grill or on a barbecue, turning frequently until evenly browned. Continue to cook for an additional 10 minutes, basting with melted ghee occasionally.
6. Before serving, transfer the cooked kababs to a greased frying pan and heat thoroughly.
7. Garnish with onion rings and lime wedges.

Easy Kathi Kabab

Ingredients

Nutmeg, grated: ½
Green cardamom: 20–25
Mace, whole: 1
Garam masala: 2 tbsp
Cloves: 8
Mango powder: 2 tbsp

1. Dry roast the whole spices on a griddle until aromatic.
2. Combine all the spices in a mixing bowl, ensuring a uniform blend. Grind the spices together to achieve a finer consistency.
3. Transfer the spice blend to an airtight container and store in a cool, dry place.

Kolkata's Nizam-Style Kathi Kabab

Ingredients

Nutmeg powder: 1 tsp
Mace powder: 1½ tsp
Cloves: 2½ tsp
Ginger and garlic powder: 3 tbsp
Cumin powder, roasted: 2 tsp
Red chilli powder: 2 tsp
Kashmiri red chilli powder: 1 tsp
Salt: 1 tbsp (or to taste)
Black salt: 2 tsp

Steps

1. Mix the nutmeg powder, mace, cloves, ginger and garlic powder, cumin powder, red chilli powder, Kashmiri red chilli powder, salt and black salt.
2. Blend this spice mixture that works wonderfully as a rub for the kabab.
3. Add hung curd and green papaya paste to the meat to create a good kabab marinade.

KOLKATA-STYLE CHICKEN KATHI KABAB

INGREDIENTS

Salt: 5 tbsp (or to taste)
Black salt: 1½ tbsp
Mango powder/tartaric acid: 1½ tbsp
Bengali garam masala: 3 tsp
Kashmiri red chilli powder: 2 tsp
Ginger powder: 2 tsp
Garlic powder: 2 tsp

STEPS

1. Mix salt, black salt, mango powder/tartaric acid, Bengali garam masala, Kashmiri red chilli powder, ginger powder and garlic powder.
2. Blend this spice mixture that works wonderfully as a rub for the kabab.
3. Add hung curd and mustard oil/ghee to the chicken to create a good kabab marinade.

VEG KATHI KABAB

INGREDIENTS

Turmeric powder: 1 tbsp
Kashmiri red chilli powder: 2 tbsp
Coriander powder: 2 tbsp
Bengali garam masala: 2 tbsp
Coriander powder: 5 tbsp
Salt: 2 tbsp (or to taste)
Chaat masala: 2 tbsp
Mango powder/tartaric acid: 1½ tbsp

Ginger powder: 1 tbsp
Garlic powder: 2 tbsp
Black salt: 1 tbsp (or to taste)

Steps

1. Mix salt, black salt, mango powder/tartaric acid, Bengali garam masala, Kashmiri red chilli powder, ginger powder and garlic powder.
2. Blend this spice mixture, which works wonderfully to prepare veg kathi kabab and roll.
3. Use vegetables like tomato, carrot, peas, potato, onions, etc. to prepare your kathi kabab and use the blend mentioned above.
4. For extra zing, add lemon juice.

Chapli Kabab

Ingredients

For the Spice Blend:
Coriander seeds, crushed: 1 tbsp
Red chilli, crushed: 2 tsp
Cumin powder: 1 tsp
Garam masala powder: 1 tbsp
Carom seeds, crushed: 1½ tsp
Black pepper, crushed: 1 tsp
Dried pomegranate seeds, crushed: 1 tbsp
Salt: 1 tbsp (or to taste)
Black salt: 1 tbsp

Other Ingredients

Cooking oil: 2 tsp
Eggs, whisked: 4
Onions, medium, chopped: 3

Green chillies, chopped: 10–12
Meat, minced: ½ kg (with an additional 30 per cent fat)
Ginger garlic paste: 1 tbsp
Fresh coriander, chopped: 2 tbsp
Egg: 1
Maize flour: 1 cup
Tomatoes, medium, de-seeded and chopped: 2

STEPS

1. Combine all the spice blend ingredients (crushed coriander seeds, crushed red chilli, cumin powder, garam masala powder, crushed carom seeds, black pepper powder, crushed dried pomegranate seeds, salt and black salt) in a bowl and mix well.
2. Dice onions in small pieces and green chillies.
3. In a large bowl, combine the minced meat, chopped onions, green chillies, 1 tbsp ginger garlic paste, 2 tbsp chopped fresh coriander and the prepared spice blend. Mix well until combined.
4. Add 1 cup maize flour and mix thoroughly.
5. Before frying, add 2 medium chopped tomatoes and a cooked omelette of 2 eggs (optional) to the mixture. Mix until well combined. Cover and refrigerate for 30 minutes.
6. Dip your hands in ice-cold water, grease them with oil and take a portion of the mixture to form the kababs (approximately 120 gm each). Shape them into equal sizes.
7. Heat the rendered fat and fry the chapli kababs on a medium to low flame until done.

Roshni's Chapli Kabab

Ingredients

Coriander seeds: 1½ tbsp
Cumin seeds: 2 tsp
Black pepper: 25–30
Black cardamom seeds: 3
Chilli flakes: 2 tsp
Dried pomegranate seeds: 2 tsp
Carom seeds: ½ tsp

Steps

1. Dry roast the coriander seeds, cumin seeds, black pepper, black cardamom seeds, chilli flakes, dried pomegranate seeds and carom seeds in a pan on medium heat until fragrant.
2. Allow the roasted spices to cool completely. Grind the cooled spices to a coarse powder.
3. Use this spice blend for this version of chapli kababs. Mix thoroughly with the meat and let it marinate.
4. Dip your hands in ice-cold water, grease them with oil and take a portion of the mixture to form the kababs (approximately 120 gm each). Shape them into equal sizes.
5. Heat the rendered fat or ghee/oil and fry the chapli kababs on a medium to low flame until done.

AQIB'S CHAPLI KABAB

INGREDIENTS

Meat, minced
Coriander seeds, crushed: 2½ tbsp
Cumin seeds, crushed: 1 tbsp
Pomegranate seeds: 1½ tsp
Red chilli, crushed: 2 tsp
Cumin powder: 1 tsp
Garam masala powder: 1 tsp
Black pepper: ½ tsp
Carom seeds, crushed: 1 tsp
Salt: 1 tbsp (adjust to taste)

STEPS

1. Combine all the dry ingredients (crushed coriander seeds, crushed cumin seeds, pomegranate seeds, crushed red chilli, cumin powder, garam masala powder, black pepper, and crushed carom seeds) in a bowl.
2. Mix thoroughly with the minced meat and other wet ingredients (ginger garlic paste, onions, green chillies, fresh coriander, tomatoes, egg and plain flour) to form a cohesive mixture.
3. Allow the meat mixture to marinate for at least 30 minutes before forming into kababs.
4. Heat oil in a frying pan and fry the kababs on a medium to low flame until done.

Patili Kabab

Ingredients

Meat, minced: 1 kg
Raw papaya paste: 3 tbsp
Onions, medium: 3
1-inch ginger

Masala A:
Desiccated coconut: 8 tbsp
Poppy seeds: 3 tbsp

Masala B:
Cumin powder: 1 tbsp
Coriander powder: 1 tbsp

Other Ingredients:
Ghee: 1 cup
Salt to taste
Curd: 1 cup
Kewra water: 2 tbsp
Meetha attar: 4–5 drops
Gram flour: 3–4 tbsp
Coal, small: 2

Steps

1. Wash the minced mutton in muslin cloth under running water. Tie up the cloth and hang for 15 minutes to drain water. Mix the drained mince with crushed raw papaya and salt. Set aside for 30 minutes.
2. Slice the onions finely and fry in 2 tbsp ghee until golden brown. Remove and grind with curd. Grind the ginger into a fine paste.

3. Lightly roast the Masala A ingredients and grind into a paste. Roast the cumin seeds and coriander seeds from Masala B and grind to a fine powder.

4. Mix the marinated mince with Masala A paste, Masala B powder and roasted gram flour.

5. Place the mixture in a shallow dish. Place half a peeled onion and a live coal in the centre. Pour 1 tbsp ghee over the coal and immediately cover to infuse the smoke. Let it sit for 15 minutes.*

6. Heat the remaining ghee in a pot. Add the mince mixture and cook on a slow flame, stirring for 5 minutes. Cover and cook, stirring occasionally to prevent sticking.

7. When ghee starts to appear on the sides, add kewra water and meetha attar drops. Simmer for 5 more minutes.

8. Serve hot with warqui paratha.

---

* An alternative for this would be to burn a cinnamon stick and pour some ghee on top.

Shaheen Qureshi's Patili Kabab

Ingredients

Green cardamom: 3 tbsp
Cloves: 2 tbsp
Nutmeg, grated: 1 tsp
Black cardamom: 1 tbsp
Mace blade: 1
Cumin seeds: 3 tbsp
Allspice powder: 3 tbsp
Coriander seeds: 3 tbsp
Charoli seeds: 3 tbsp
Poppy seeds: 4 tbsp
Desiccated coconut: 6 tbsp
Gram flour, roasted: 6 tbsp

Steps

1. Dry roast the spices and cool completely.
2. Grind all the roasted spices into a coarse powder using a spice grinder or mortar and pestle.
3. Combine the ground spices with 6 tbsp roasted gram flour. Store the spice blend in an airtight container.
4. Use this spice blend to season 1 kg of mutton for kababs. Add it along with other ingredients like salt and ginger garlic paste, and marinate the meat as per your kabab recipe.

Mohsina Khan's Patili Kabab

Ingredients

1-inch cinnamon sticks: 2
Nutmeg: 1
Mace blades: 2
Green cardamom: 2 tbsp
Black pepper: 2 tsp
Cumin seeds: 2 tbsp
Rose petals, dried: 4 tbsp
Poppy seeds: 3 tbsp

Steps

1. Grind all the roasted spices into a coarse powder using a spice grinder or mortar and pestle.
2. Store the spice blend in an airtight container.
3. Use this spice blend to season 1 kg of mutton mince for kababs. Add it along with other ingredients like salt, ginger garlic paste, papaya paste and marinate the meat as per your kabab recipe.

Jennifer Brennan's Peshawari Pasande[15]

Ingredients

Lamb, trimmed of fat and skin: 1½ kg
Curd, whisked: 500 ml
Ginger, ground: 1 tsp
Garlic, smashed, peeled and finely chopped: 2 cloves
Salt: 1 tsp (or to taste)
Ghee: 3 tbsp
Coriander powder: 1 tbsp

Onions, medium, ground to a paste: 3-4
Turmeric powder: 1 tsp
Clove powder: 1 tsp
Black pepper, freshly ground: 1 tsp
Cardamom, ground: 1 tsp
Hard-boiled eggs, peeled and sliced: 3

STEPS

1. Slice the lamb thinly and beat the slices until they are about ⅛ inch thick.
2. In a large bowl, mix curd, ginger, garlic and salt. Add the lamb slices to the bowl and mix well. Marinate for 3 hours.
3. Heat ghee in a large saucepan. Fry the onions over medium heat until they are brown and crisp. Drain the onions and blot them dry with paper towels. Once cooled, grind the onions into a powder.
4. Remove the lamb from the marinade. In the same saucepan, fry the fried onions with coriander, chillies (adjust quantity to taste) and turmeric.
5. Add the lamb slices and reduce the heat to a simmer. Cook for 30 minutes until the meat is tender and the gravy has evaporated.
6. Add the onion powder from Step 3, the remaining curd marinade, ground poppy seeds, almonds and saffron to the pan. Cook uncovered over medium to low heat, stirring occasionally until the gravy is thick.
7. Transfer the pasande to a serving dish. Garnish with slices of hard-boiled eggs.

Abbas Iftekhar's Pasande Kabab

Ingredients

Ginger powder: 3 tbsp
Garlic powder: 3 tbsp
Black pepper powder: ½ tsp
Salt: 1 tsp (or to taste)
Red chilli powder: 3 tsp
Green cardamom powder: 3 tsp
Garam masala: 4½ tsp

Steps

1. In a bowl, combine the ginger powder, garlic powder, black pepper powder, salt, red chilli powder, green cardamom powder and garam masala.
2. Stir the spices until they are well mixed and form a uniform blend.
3. Use this spice blend to season the lamb for pasanda kabab. Add it along with other ingredients like salt, papaya paste, lemon and curd. Marinate and cook the meat as per your kabab recipe.

Awadhi Pasande Kabab

Ingredients

Cumin seeds: 1 tbsp
Black pepper: 2 tbsp
Black cardamom: 5
Green cardamom: 7
Cloves: 1 tbsp
1-inch cinnamon stick: 2
Red chillies: 2 tbsp

Poppy seeds: 2 tbsp
Almonds: 2 tbsp
Gram flour, roasted: 3 tbsp
Nutmeg, small: 1
Mace blade: 1
Salt: 1 tsp (or to taste)

STEPS

1. Grind all the roasted spices into a coarse powder using a spice grinder or mortar and pestle.
2. Combine all the ground spices in a bowl and mix well. Store the spice blend in an airtight container.
3. Use this spice blend to season 1 kg of meat for kababs. Add it along with other ingredients like hung curd, ginger garlic paste, lemon and papaya paste. Marinate and cook the meat as per your kabab recipe.

DUM KE KABAB

INGREDIENTS

Meat, minced: 500 gm
Cashews: ¼ cup
Almonds: ¼ cup
Coriander powder: 2 tsp
Cloves: 3
1-inch cinnamon sticks: 2
Green cardamom: 6
Black cumin seeds: 1 tsp
Onions, medium: 2
Red chilli powder: 1 tsp
Turmeric powder: ½ tsp
Salt to taste
Mint, chopped: 2 tbsp

Coriander, chopped: 2 tbsp
Green chillies, chopped: 4
Oil or ghee

STEPS

1. Blanch and peel the almonds and cashews.
2. Slice the onions and fry them in hot oil until golden brown. Set aside.
3. Combine cashews, almonds, grated coconut, coriander powder, cloves, cinnamon and cardamom in a blender.
4. Add about ½ cup of water and blend until smooth.
5. In a bowl, mix the lamb mince with fried onions, red chilli powder, turmeric and salt.
6. Add the blended paste and mix well. Let it marinate for at least 30 minutes.
7. Spread the marinated mince on a tray, forming a small well in the centre.
8. Place hot charcoals in the well, pour a bit of oil over them and cover for 10 minutes. Remove the cover and mix in the chopped mint, coriander and green chillies.
9. Skewer the kababs and cook them in a moderately hot tandoor or over a charcoal grill.
10. Alternatively, shape the mixture into round patties, heat oil on a tawa and shallow-fry the patties until cooked through and golden brown.

RAJVEER ASTHANA'S GALAWATI KABAB

INGREDIENTS

Fennel seeds: 1½ tbsp
Cumin seeds: 2 tbsp
Nigella seeds: 1 tbsp

Black salt: 1 tbsp

Fenugreek seeds: 1 tbsp

Poppy seeds: 1 tbsp

Coriander seeds: 3 tbsp

Celery seeds: 1 tbsp

Black pepper: ½ tbsp

White pepper: ½ tbsp

2-inch cinnamon sticks: 8

Black cardamom, large: 10–12

Star anise: 6

Dried ginger root: 1 tbsp

Allspice powder: 1 tbsp

Green cardamom: 2 tbsp

Dried red chillies: 6–7

Bay leaves: 6–7

Long pepper: 10

Cloves: ½ tbsp

Nutmeg: 1

Mace blades: 3

STEPS

1. Grind all the roasted spices into a coarse powder using a spice grinder or mortar and pestle.
2. Combine all the ground spices in a bowl and mix well. Store the spice blend in an airtight container.
3. Use this spice blend to season 1 kg of minced meat for kababs. Add it along with other ingredients like ginger garlic paste, ghee and papaya paste. Marinate and cook the meat as per your kabab recipe.

Galawati Kabab

Ingredients

Coriander seeds: 2 tsp
Cumin seeds: 1 tsp
Green cardamom: 6
Black cardamom: 2
Red chilli, whole: 12
1-inch cinnamon stick
Mace blades: 4–6
Cloves: 8
Nutmeg: 1
Gram flour, roasted: 9 tbsp
Salt: 1½ tsp (or to taste)

Steps

1. Grind all the roasted spices into a coarse powder using a spice grinder or mortar and pestle.
2. Combine all the ground spices in a bowl and mix well. Store the spice blend in an airtight container.
3. Use this spice blend to season 700 gm of minced meat for kababs. Add it along with other ingredients like ginger garlic paste, ghee and papaya paste. Marinate and cook the meat as per your kabab recipe.

Kakori Kabab

Ingredients

Mutton, minced: 1 kg
Onion, chopped: ¾ cup
Onion paste, fried: ¼ cup

Raw papaya, grated: ¼ cup
Cashew nuts, ground to a paste: 3 tbsp
Garam masala: 1 tsp
Poppy seeds: ¼ cup
Black pepper powder: 1 tsp
Red chilli powder: 1 tsp
Green cardamom powder: 1 tsp
Clove powder: ½ tsp
Saffron: 1 tsp soaked in 1 tsp of warm milk
Kewra attar: 2 drops
Gram flour, roasted: 7 tbsp
Butter, melted for basting: 15–20 tbsp
Desi ghee: 4 tsp

STEPS

1. Give your mutton a double grind for a smooth texture. On the third go-round, add the desi ghee to help create a silky soft mixture.

2. In a bigger bowl, toss together the ground mutton with all the other ingredients. Mix it all up with your hands until everything is evenly distributed.

3. Let the kabab mixture rest for 90–120 minutes. This allows all the flavours to mix well with each other and create a symphony of taste. After 90–120 minutes, give it another quick knead.

4. Divide the mixture into equal portions. With a little oil on your hands to prevent sticking, mould each portion into a long, sausage-like shape around a skewer. Aim for kababs that are about 4–5 inches long.

5. Get your charcoal grill nice and hot or build a low charcoal fire. Place the skewers with the kababs on the grill and cook for about 5 minutes.

6. Brush the kabab with melted butter for added richness. Continue cooking for another 4 minutes, turning

the skewers regularly to ensure even browning and cooking throughout.

7. Enjoy your succulent kababs hot off the grill, served with refreshing onion rings and a cooling mint chutney.

BANGALORE EMPIRE RESTAURANT-STYLE FRIED CHICKEN KABABS

INGREDIENTS

Chicken (legs and wings), with bones: ½ kg
Cornflour: 2 tbsp
Ginger garlic paste: 1 tbsp
Cumin powder: ½ tbsp
Garam masala: 2 tsp
Coriander powder: 1 tsp
Lemon juice: 2 tbsp
Green chillies, finely chopped: 3
Red food colour (optional): ¼ tsp
Salt to taste
Oil for deep frying

STEPS

1. In a bowl, whisk together all the ingredients except the chicken and oil. If the batter is too thick, add a little water to achieve the desired consistency.
2. Add the chicken pieces to the spice batter and mix well to coat them evenly. Let it marinate for 3–4 hours, or preferably overnight, in the refrigerator.
3. Heat the oil in a deep-bottomed vessel over medium heat.
4. Once the oil is hot, add the marinated chicken pieces in batches, ensuring not to overcrowd the pan. Fry for 3–4

minutes, turning the pieces occasionally until they are golden brown and cooked through.

5. Remove the fried chicken pieces and drain them on paper towels. Serve hot with lime wedges and onion rings.

Jose's Kerala Fried Chicken Kabab

Ingredients

Chicken on the bone, cut into medium or bite-sized pieces: 700 gm
Ginger paste: 1 tbsp
Garlic paste: 1 tbsp
Curry leaves, finely chopped: 2 sprigs
Black pepper, crushed: ½ tsp
Green chilli paste: 1 tsp
Kashmiri red chilli powder: 2 tbsp
Coriander powder: 2 tsp
Hung curd: 2 tsp
Garam masala: 1½ tsp
Salt: 1 tsp (or to taste)
Cornflour: 7 tbsp
Oil for frying
Chaat masala for sprinkling

Steps

1. In a large bowl, add the chicken pieces. Then, add the garlic paste, curry leaves, ginger paste, pepper powder, green chilli paste, Kashmiri red chilli powder, coriander powder, curd, garam masala powder and salt. Mix everything well to coat the chicken evenly. Cover and refrigerate for at least 2 hours.

2. After marinating, add the cornflour to the chicken and mix well to ensure the pieces are well-coated.
3. Heat oil in a deep pan or kadahi over medium-high heat.
4. Once the oil is hot, carefully slide in the marinated chicken pieces in batches, making sure not to overcrowd the pan. Fry until the chicken is golden brown and cooked through, turning occasionally for even cooking.
5. Remove the fried chicken kabab pieces and drain them on paper towels to remove excess oil. Sprinkle chaat masala over the chicken kabab for added flavour.
6. Serve hot with onion slices and lemon wedges on the side.

Easy Kerala Chicken Fry Kabab

Ingredients

Black pepper powder: 1 tsp
Kashmiri red chilli powder: 1 tbsp
Kanthari chilli: 1 tbsp
Cumin powder: 1 tsp
Garam masala powder: 1 tsp
Black salt: ½ tsp
Salt: 1 tsp (or to taste)

Steps

1. Grind the black pepper, kashmiri red chilli, kanthari chilli, cumin seeds, garam masala, salt and black salt into a fine powder using a spice grinder or mortar and pestle.
2. Use this spice blend to create an easy Kerala chicken fry kabab following the steps above.

His Highness Maharajadhiraj Hari Singhji's Shikampuri Kabab[16]

Ingredients

Lean mutton from leg or shoulder: 1½ kg
Split gram: 36 gm
Salt: 36 gm (or to taste)
Red chillies, whole: 6 gm
Green chillies, whole: 36 gm
Black cardamom, whole: 6
Bay leaves, whole: 6
1-inch cinnamon sticks: 6
Cloves, whole: 12
Curd: 115 gm
Garam masala powder: 6 gm
Green chillies, finely chopped with seeds: 75 gm
Fresh coriander leaves, finely chopped: 36 gm
Lime juice: 45 ml
Clotted cream (malai): ½ kg
Eggs, lightly beaten: 3
Ghee for frying kababs

Steps

1. Keep clotted cream in the refrigerator for 8–10 hours until firm. Remember to take it out just before using it to help shape the kababs.
2. In a large pot, add the minced mutton, split gram, salt, whole red chillies, whole green chillies, black cardamom, bay leaves, cinnamon sticks and cloves.
3. Add about 8 cups of water and boil for 1 hour until the water is completely evaporated. Discard the red chillies, green chillies and whole spices.
4. Finely grind the boiled meat mixture.

5. Add curd, lightly beaten eggs, garam masala powder, finely chopped green chillies, coriander leaves and lime juice to the ground meat. Mix and knead well until all ingredients are thoroughly combined.

6. Divide the meat mixture and clotted cream into 18 equal parts each.

7. Take a portion of meat, place a portion of clotted cream inside and shape it into a 4-inch-long sausage-like shape. Wet your hands with a little water to give the kababs a smooth and even shape.

8. Heat ghee in a frying pan over medium heat.

9. Deep-fry the kababs, three at a time, until they turn golden brown.

10. Drain the kababs on paper towels and serve hot.

Zohaib Ali's Orange Shikampuri Kabab

Ingredients

Meat (*raan* or hind leg), minced: 1 kg
Chana dal: 250 gm
Arrowroot: 5 tbsp
Salt: 1½ tbsp (or to taste)
Coriander powder: 3 tsp
Red chilli powder: 2 tsp
Ghee: 250 gm
Sugar: 1 tsp
Garam masala: 1½ tsp
3-inch ginger, diced
Fresh coriander leaves, finely chopped: ½ cup
Green chillies, finely chopped: 6
Orange, peeled, segmented, skinned and crumbled: 1
Raisins: 20
Onion, fried: ½ cup

STEPS

1. In a large pot, combine the minced meat, chana dal and 4 cups of water. Boil until the meat and dal are tender, and the water has evaporated.
2. Grind the boiled meat and dal mixture finely on a grinding stone or in a food processor.
3. Add 2 tbsp arrowroot, salt, coriander powder, red chilli powder and garam masala to the ground mixture. Mix well.
4. Mix the finely chopped green chillies, fresh coriander leaves, diced ginger, crumbled orange segments, raisins, fried onion and sugar into the meat mixture. This forms the filling.
5. Take small portions of the meat mixture in one hand, flattening them with the other.
6. Place ½ tsp of the filling in the centre of each portion and roll it into a ball about 1 inch in diameter. Continue until all the meat mixture is used.
7. Roll each ball in the remaining arrowroot to coat. Heat ghee or oil in a kadahi and deep-fry the kababs until light brown.
8. Drain on paper towels and serve hot with your favourite chutneys or dips.

Easy Shikampuri Kabab

Ingredients

Garlic powder: 3 tsp
Salt: 1 tsp (or to taste)
Chilli powder: 2 tsp
Garam masala powder: 2 tsp

For the Filling:
Hung curd: 200 gm
Mint leaves, ground: 2 tbsp
Salt: 1 tsp (or to taste)
Black pepper: 1 tsp

STEPS

1. Use the given spice blend for 500 gm minced meat and the filling, as specified. Use all the other ingredients as mentioned in the other Shikampuri kababs.
2. Follow the recipe steps mentioned above for Shikampuri kabab.

ABHIMANYU SHARMA'S SHIKAMPURI KABAB

INGREDIENTS

Kashmiri dried red chillies: 6
Guntur dried red chillies: 6
Cumin powder, roasted: 2 tsp
Garam masala: 2 tsp
Salt: 2 tsp (or to taste)

For the Filling:
Hung curd or cream cheese: ¼ cup
Onion, finely chopped: ½
Coriander leaves, finely chopped: 1 tbsp
Green chillies, finely chopped: ½ tsp

STEPS

1. Use the given spice blend for 500 gm minced meat and the filling, as specified. Use all the other ingredients as mentioned in the other Shikampuri kababs.

2. Follow the recipe steps mentioned above for Shikampuri kabab.

Ammi's Shikampuri Kabab (Guler Kabab)

Ingredients

Coriander powder: 3 tsp
Red chilli powder: 2 tsp
Garam masala: 1½ tsp
Allspice powder: 2 tbsp
Black pepper: 2 tbsp

For the Filling:
Onion, fried: ½ cup
Sugar: 3 tsp
Salt: 1 tsp (or to taste)
Raisins, fried and sliced: 20
Almond, fried and sliced: 20
Poppy seeds, roasted: 3 tbsp

Steps

1. Dry roast the spices and mix in the minced meat.
2. Use the given spice blend for 500 gm minced meat and the filling, as specified. Use all the other ingredients as mentioned in the other Shikampuri kababs.
3. Follow the recipe steps mentioned above for Shikampuri kabab.

Chef Kunal Kapur's Chicken Tikka Kabab

Ingredients

For the First Marinade:

Chicken leg, boneless: 500 gm
Salt to taste
Lemon, juiced: 1
Ginger and garlic paste: ½ tbsp

For the Second Marinade:

Mustard oil: 5 tsp
Kashmiri chilli powder: 1½ tbsp
Curd: 1 cup
Additional salt to taste
Lemons, juiced: 1½
Ginger and garlic paste: ½ tbsp
Chaat masala: A pinch
Fenugreek powder: ½ tsp

Steps

1. First marinade: Combine chicken with salt, lemon juice, and ginger and garlic paste. Let it marinate for at least 30 minutes.

2. Second marinade: Heat mustard oil, add Kashmiri chilli powder, then mix in curd, lemon juice, additional ginger and garlic paste, chaat masala and fenugreek powder. Add the chicken and ensure it's well-coated.

3. Grill the chicken in a preheated grill or oven at 200°C for 20–25 minutes or pan-grill, turning it occasionally until fully cooked.

4. Serve hot with a sprinkle of chaat masala and lemon wedges on the side.

Tikka Masala

Ingredients

Coriander seeds: 3 tbsp
Cumin seeds: 3 tbsp
Black pepper: 2 tsp
Degi red chillies: 20
Black cardamom: 6
Green cardamom: 8
1-inch cinnamon stick: 2
Cloves: 8
Turmeric powder: ½ tsp
Dried mango powder: 2 tbsp
Kashmiri red chilli powder: 2 tsp
Fenugreek powder: 2 tsp

Steps

1. Lightly roast coriander, cumin seeds, black pepper, black and green cardamom, cloves and cinnamon in a dry pan until aromatic.
2. Cool the roasted spices and then grind them into a fine powder using a spice grinder.
3. Mix the turmeric powder, dried mango powder and Kashmiri red chilli powder with the freshly ground spices.
4. Transfer the spice mix into an airtight container for future use as a seasoning in various dishes. This blend will give a different flavour to your tikka. Follow your recipe or as written above.

Shadab's Purani Dilli Tikka

Ingredients

Cumin seeds: 2 tbsp
Red chilli powder: 4 tbsp
Nutmeg, grated: ½ tsp
Mace blades: 3
Turmeric powder: 1½ tbsp
Ginger powder: 2 tbsp
Garlic: 2 tbsp
Black pepper: 2 tbsp
Long pepper: 4
1-inch cinnamon stick: 2
Star anise: 3
Valaiti saunf: ½ tsp
Black cardamom: 3
Citric acid: ½ tsp
Papaya powder: 1 tsp
Red food colour (optional): ½ tsp
Salt: 4 tbsp (or to taste)
Black salt: 1 tsp

Steps

1. Lightly roast all the spices apart from salt, chilli powder, citric acid, food colour and papaya powder.
2. Cool the roasted spices and grind them into a fine powder, including the ones left out.
3. Transfer the spice mix into an airtight container for future use as a seasoning in various dishes. This blend will give a different flavour to your tikka. Follow your recipe or as written above.

Benazir Naqvi Tikka

Ingredients

Dried Kashmiri chillies: 8–10
Dried red chillies: 8–10
Bay leaves: 4–6
Coriander seeds: 5 tbsp
Cumin seeds: 2 tbsp
Black pepper: 2 tsp
1-inch cinnamon stick: 2
Black cardamom: ½ tbsp
Cloves: 8 tbsp
Green cardamom: 10 tbsp
Star anise: 2
Nutmeg, grated: ¼ tsp
Mace blades: 3–4
Turmeric powder: 1½ tsp
Ginger powder: 1½ tbsp
Garlic powder: 1½ tbsp
Raw mango powder: 1½ tbsp
Salt: 1½ tsp (or to taste)

Steps

1. Lightly roast all the whole spices in a dry pan until aromatic.
2. Cool the roasted spices and then grind them into a fine powder using a spice grinder.
3. Mix the turmeric powder, dried mango powder, and ginger and garlic powder with the freshly ground spices.
4. Transfer the spice mix into an airtight container for future use as a seasoning in various dishes. This blend will give a different flavour to your tikka. Follow your recipe or as written above.

Special Tikka

Ingredients

Black cardamom: 3–4
Green cardamom: 6–8
Clove: ½ tsp
1-inch cinnamon stick
Black pepper: ½ tsp
Fenugreek seeds: ½ tsp
Fennel seeds: ½ tsp
Bay leaves: 2
Fenugreek leaves: ½ tsp
Red chilli, whole: ½ tsp
Mace blades: 3–4
Nutmeg, grated: ⅛ tsp
Dried ginger: 1 tsp
Carom seeds: ½ tsp
Long pepper: 3
Stone flower: ½ tsp
Coriander seeds: 1 tsp
Star anise: 4
Cumin seeds: 1 tsp
Nigella seeds: 1 tsp

Steps

1. Roast the spices: In a dry skillet over medium heat, roast black cardamom, green cardamom, cloves, cinnamon sticks, black pepper, fenugreek seeds, Fennel seeds, bay leaves, fenugreek leaves, whole red chilli, mace, nutmeg, dried ginger, carom, long pepper, stone flower, whole coriander, star anise, cumin seeds and caraway seeds. Stir frequently and roast until fragrant (for about 2–3 minutes).

2. Allow the roasted spices to cool completely.

3. Transfer the cooled spices to a spice grinder. Grind the spices to a fine or coarse powder, depending on your preference.

4. Transfer the spice blend to an airtight container and store it in a cool, dry place to preserve its flavours.

Malai Tikka

Ingredients

Cashew nuts: ½ cup
Poppy seeds: ¼ cup
Processed cheese: ¼ cup
Green chillies: 5
Hung curd: 4 tbsp
Butter: 2 tbsp
Green cardamom: 4–6
Salt: 1 tsp (or to taste)
Fenugreek powder: 1 tsp
White pepper powder: 1 tsp
Saffron: A few strands
Fresh cream: 3 tbsp

Steps

1. Soak the cashew nuts and poppy seeds in warm water for 10–15 minutes to soften them. Drain the water and transfer the cashew nuts and poppy seeds to a grinder.

2. Add the green chilli and processed cheese to the grinder. Grind until you get a smooth paste. Add hung curd to the mixture and blend again until smooth. Add butter, green cardamom, salt, fenugreek leaves, white pepper powder and saffron to the grinder.

3. Blend until all the ingredients are well combined into a smooth paste.
4. Add the fresh cream to the paste and give it a final blend to ensure a creamy consistency.
5. Transfer the prepared paste to an airtight container and store in the refrigerator until ready to use.

Mutton Charpa

Ingredients

Meat, minced (20 per cent fat): 500 gm
Salt: 1½ tsp (or to taste)
Red chilli powder: 1 tbsp
Cumin seeds, roasted: 1 tsp
Garam masala powder: 2 tsp
Black pepper powder: 1 tsp
Ginger garlic paste: 1 tbsp
Short-grain rice: 1 cup (soaked in water for 1 hour)
Chana dal: ½ cup (soaked in water for 1 hour)
Green chillies, chopped: 2
Coriander, chopped: ½ cup
Oil for frying
Water as required

Steps

1. In a large bowl, add 500 gm of minced meat, salt, red chilli powder, roasted cumin powder, garam masala powder, black pepper powder and ginger garlic paste.
2. Mix well and massage the spices into the meat until evenly distributed.
3. Drain the soaked chana dal and rice. Transfer them to a blender and blend to a smooth paste, adding water as needed to achieve the right consistency.

4. Add the blended chana dal and rice paste to the spiced minced meat. Mix thoroughly to combine all the other ingredients.
5. Take small portions of the mixture and shape them into small patties.
6. Heat oil in a deep frying pan over medium heat. Once the oil is hot, carefully add the patties to the pan. Deep-fry the patties until they are golden brown and crispy on both sides.
7. Remove the patties from the oil and drain on paper towels.
8. Serve hot with fresh lemon wedges, vinegar and onion.

Bihari Kabab

Ingredients

Meat, thinly sliced and pounded (pasanda cut): 1½ kg
Curd: ¾ cup
Raw papaya with skin, finely grated: 6 tbsp
Onions, fried: ¾ cup
Ginger, freshly grated: 4 tsp
Garlic, chopped: 4 tsp
Nutmeg powder: 1 tsp
Cinnamon powder: 1 tsp
Cumin powder, roasted: 1½ tsp
Red chilli powder: 4 tsp (or to taste)
Bihari kabab garam masala (recipe below): 6 tsp
Mustard oil: ¾ cup
Gram flour, roasted: 5 tbsp
Salt to taste

For the Bihari Kabab Masala:
Allspice powder: 2 tsp
Fennel seeds: 2 tsp
Star anise: 2

Black pepper, whole: 4 tsp
Cloves: 2
Green cardamom: 10
Coriander seeds, whole: 2 tbsp
Cumin seeds: 2 tbsp
Dried red chillies: 12
Poppy seeds: 2 tsp

STEPS

1. Dry roast and grind allspice powder, fennel seeds, star anise, whole black pepper, cloves, green cardamom, whole coriander seeds, cumin seeds, poppy seeds and dried red chillies into a fine powder.

2. In a big bowl, mix curd, finely grated raw papaya with skin, fried onions, grated ginger, chopped garlic, nutmeg powder, cinnamon powder, roasted cumin powder, paprika powder, red chilli powder, Bihari kabab garam masala, roasted gram flour and mustard oil. Add salt to taste and mix well.

3. Marinate the thinly sliced and pounded meat in this mixture.

4. Cover and refrigerate for at least 24 hours.

5. Thread the marinated meat onto skewers. Grill the meat on skewers until tender.

6. Heat a coal on the grill. Drop a few drops of oil on the heated coal, then cover the grill with a metal lid to infuse the meat with the smoky flavour.

7. Remove the meat once tender and cooked through.

8. Serve the Bihari kababs with green chutney, sliced onions and paratha or naan.

9. Store the unused portion of the masala in an airtight jar for future use.

Nusrat Arif's Bihari Kabab

Ingredients

Long pepper: 7
Allspice powder: 7
Salt: 2 tbsp (or to taste)
Coriander powder: 2 tbsp
Red chilli powder: 1½ tbsp
Kashmiri red chilli: 1½ tbsp
Chaat masala: 1½ tbsp
Turmeric powder: 2 tbsp
Garam masala powder: 3 tbsp
Cumin powder: 2 tsp
Gram flour: 3 tbsp

Steps

1. Dry roast all the spices and combine them in a mixing bowl.
2. Grind to a fine powder and mix with the roasted gram flour.
3. Store the spice blend in an airtight container to preserve its freshness.
4. Follow the recipe of your Bihari kabab for the other steps.

Pathar ke Gosht

Ingredients

Lamb meat, boneless, cut into medium-sized pieces and flattened: 1 kg
Hung curd: 1 cup
Garam masala powder: 1 tsp
Cardamom powder: ½ tsp
Green chillies, ground into a paste with a bit of salt: 10–15
Raw papaya peel paste, for softening meat pieces: 1 tbsp
Ghee: As required
Salt: 1 tsp (or to taste)

Steps

1. In a large bowl, place the flattened lamb pieces. Mix the hung curd, green chilli paste, garam masala powder, cardamom powder, raw papaya peel paste and salt together in another bowl.

2. Pour this mixture over the lamb pieces, ensuring they are well-coated. Marinate for 1½–2 hours.

3. Use a seasoned granite stone, about 2–2½ feet long and 4–6 inches thick. Heat the stone by placing live charcoal underneath it until it is hot. If you don't have a granite stone, a charcoal grill or griddle can be used instead.

4. Place the marinated meat pieces on the hot stone. Sprinkle some ghee on each side of the meat pieces.

5. Keep turning the pieces until they become crisp and brown. Serve the cooked lamb hot, garnished with onion rings and lemon wedges.

Pushpesh Pant's Pathar ke Gosht[17]

Ingredients

Green chillies, de-seeded: 8–10
Lamb, boneless, cut into flat steaks, about ½ inch thick: 800 gm
Allspice powder: 1 tsp
Black pepper powder: 1 tsp
Ginger paste: 1½ tsp
Garlic paste: 1½ tsp
Green papaya paste: 1½ tsp
Raw papaya paste: 1½ tsp
Vegetable oil for brushing
Salt to taste

Steps

1. Grind the de-seeded green chillies into a fine paste. In a bowl, combine the allspice powder, ground black pepper powder ginger paste, garlic paste, green papaya paste, raw papaya paste and salt.
2. Place the lamb steaks on a clean surface and pound them to flatten to about ½-inch thickness. Rub the prepared marinade onto the lamb steaks, ensuring each piece is well coated. Cover and refrigerate the marinated lamb for 3–4 hours to allow the flavours to meld.
3. Heat a granite stone with live charcoals underneath. If you don't have a granite stone, a charcoal grill or griddle can be used instead.
4. Place the marinated lamb steaks on the heated surface.
5. Brush the meat with vegetable oil and cook, turning occasionally until the lamb is tender and has a nice char, ensuring it cooks evenly on both sides.

6. Once cooked, remove the kababs from the heat. Serve hot, garnished with sliced onions, lemon wedges, mint leaves and fresh mint chutney.

Thatti ka Gosht

Ingredients

Lamb meat, boneless, cut into 3-inch pieces and flattened (pasanda cut): 1 kg
Garam masala powder: 2 tsp
Green chillies: 10–15
Coriander leaves: 2 tbsp
Mint leaves: 2 tbsp
Ghee: As required
Salt to taste

Steps

1. Make a paste of green chillies, coriander leaves and mint leaves, adding a little salt to enhance the flavour.
2. In a bowl, combine the lamb pieces with the prepared masala paste, garam masala powder and salt. Mix well to ensure the lamb pieces are evenly coated with the marinade. Cover and let the meat marinate for 2–3 hours in the refrigerator.
3. Place the marinated meat pieces between the rods of a Hyderabadi grill.* If you don't have one, use a similar grill or skewer method.
4. Cook the meat over live charcoal, turning it frequently. Brush the meat with ghee while cooking to keep it moist and enhance the flavour.

---

* A Hyderabadi grill is a rectangular or square grill made of iron rods fixed on one side, with a clamp to hold the marinated meat pieces in between.

5. Continue grilling until the lamb pieces are crisp and brown on the outside.

6. Once the kababs are cooked, remove them from the grill. Serve hot, garnished with onion rings and lemon wedges.

Asma Khan's Eid ke Murgh Kabab[18]

Ingredients

Chicken thighs, skinless and boneless, cut into 5-cm pieces: 1 kg
Full-fat Greek-style curd: 200 gm
Lemon juice: 2 tbsp
Garlic cloves, finely chopped: 6
Onion, large, sliced: 1
2-inch fresh ginger, grated
Salt: 1 tsp (or to taste)
Chilli powder: ½ tsp
Sugar: 1 tsp
Ghee: 4 tbsp
Rose water: 1 tsp
Lemon wedges to serve

Steps

1. In a large bowl, combine the chicken, curd, lemon juice, garlic, onion, ginger, salt, chilli powder, sugar and rose water. Mix well to coat the chicken pieces thoroughly.

2. Cover the bowl and marinate the chicken in the fridge overnight.

3. Remove the chicken from the fridge and let it come down to room temperature before cooking.

4. Preheat the grill to medium and thread the chicken pieces onto skewers. Ensure the skewers are not packed tightly to allow even cooking.

5. Grill the chicken for 7–10 minutes, turning frequently until the chicken is cooked through and slightly charred.
6. Serve hot, garnished with lemon wedges.

Easy Seekh Kabab

Ingredients

Garam masala: 3 tbsp
Phaphda chilli, crushed: 3 tbsp
Nutmeg, grated: ½ tsp
Yellow chilli powder: 2 tbsp
Salt: 1 tbsp (or to taste)

Steps

1. Combine garam masala, phaphda chilli, grated nutmeg, yellow chilli powder and salt in a bowl.
2. Mix the spices thoroughly to ensure an even distribution.
3. Store the spice blend in an airtight container to keep it fresh until use.
4. To cook the dish, follow the steps given above or your own recipe.

Kabab Murgh Shirin (Sweet)[19]

Ingredients

Chicken, skinned and boned: ½ kg
Milk: 1 l
Mawa: 115 gm
Egg: 1
Almonds, blanched and chopped: 50 gm
Charoli seeds, blanched and chopped: 50 gm

Raisins, chopped: 50 gm
Sugar: ½ kg
Saffron: A good pinch diluted in warm water
Kewra water: 30 ml
Ghee for frying the kababs

STEPS

1. Mince the chicken and boil it in milk until tender. Continue boiling until the milk is completely absorbed.
2. Finely grind the chicken and mix in the mawa and egg. Divide this mixture into 16 equal portions.
3. Mix the almonds, charoli seeds and raisins. Divide this mixture into 16 equal portions.
4. Take each portion of the chicken mixture and flatten it. Place one portion of the stuffing in the centre, shape it into a ball and then flatten it again. Wet your hands with a little water to give the kababs a smooth and even shape.
5. Heat ghee in a frying pan. Deep-fry the kababs, a few at a time, until they are dark brown.
6. In a separate pan, combine sugar and 4 cups of water. Cook, stirring until the syrup reaches a one-thread consistency. Add saffron and kewra water to the syrup.
7. Place the fried kababs into the syrup. Heat the mixture until it starts boiling, then remove from heat.
8. Serve the kababs hot or cold, as desired.

MAAS KE SULE

INGREDIENTS

Mutton (or any other of your choice), cleaned, deboned and cut into 2-inch pieces: 1 kg
Ghee for basting

For the First Marinade:
Raw papaya, peeled and roughly cut: ½ cup (75 gm)
Garlic paste: 5 tsp
Red chilli powder: 2 tsp
Salt to taste

For the Second Marinade:
Curd, whisked: ½ cup
Onions, peeled and sliced evenly: ¾ cup
Garlic, peeled and sliced evenly: 3 tbsp
Ginger, peeled and roughly cut: 1½ tsp
Clove powder: ½ tsp
Ghee for deep-frying
Salt to taste

For Smoking:
Cloves: 10
Charcoal, small: 2
Ghee: 1 tbsp

Steps

1. Blend the raw papaya into a fine paste. Mix the papaya paste with garlic paste, red chilli powder and salt. Rub this mixture onto the venison pieces (boṭi) and refrigerate for 10 hours.
2. Drain the excess moisture and marinate the meat for another 2 hours.
3. Whisk the curd in a bowl. Deep-fry the onion and garlic slices in ghee until golden brown. Grind the fried onions and garlic with ginger, clove powder, salt and a little water into a fine paste.
4. Mix this paste with the curd and rub it on to the marinated meat. Keep aside for 2 hours.
5. Preheat the oven to 350°F (180°C).

6. Skewer the marinated meat pieces, leaving at least an inch between each piece. Keep a tray underneath to collect the drippings.

7. Roast the skewered meat in a moderately hot tandoor or charcoal grill for 10–12 minutes or a preheated oven for 18–20 minutes.

8. Remove and hang the skewers to allow the excess moisture to drip off (approx. 5–6 minutes). Baste with ghee and roast again for 8–10 minutes.

9. Serve the maas ke sule hot, garnished with your choice of accompaniments.

SAHIL SINGH'S SULA

INGREDIENTS

Red chilli powder: 7 tbsp
Dried sour cucumber (kacchri), ground: 1½ tbsp
Clove powder: 1 tbsp
Chaat masala: 1½ tbsp

STEPS

1. Ensure all the spices are ground to a fine powder if not already in that form. Combine all the measured spices in a mixing bowl. Stir thoroughly to ensure the spices are well blended.

2. Store the spice blend in an airtight container to preserve its flavour and freshness.

3. Use the prepared spice blend with the steps mentioned in the maas ke sule recipe above to achieve a different flavour profile. The blend should be added during the marination process and incorporated throughout the cooking to infuse the meat with its unique taste.

KABARGAH

INGREDIENTS

Mutton from ribs with fatty layer and skin intact (2–3 rib bones per piece, 25–30 pieces per kg): 1 kg
Ghee: 250 gm
Curd: 1 cup
Red Kashmiri chilli powder: 2 tsp
Ginger powder: 1 tsp
Aniseed powder: 1 tsp
Turmeric: 1 tsp
Asafoetida: A pinch
Garam masala: 1 tsp
Salt: 2 tsp (or to taste)
Milk: 1 l
Cloves: 2

STEPS

1. In a large pot (*patila*, about 3-l capacity), pour milk (you can do half-milk, half-water, too). Add turmeric, ginger powder, aniseed powder, cloves, 1 tsp salt and asafoetida. Stir well and add the mutton pieces. Boil on medium heat for about 30 minutes until the meat becomes tender and the water is absorbed. Remove from heat and let it cool slightly.

2. In a bowl, mix curd, chilli powder, garam masala and 1 tsp salt to make a batter by beating with a spoon or hand churner.

3. Remove the cooked mutton pieces from the gravy (the leftover gravy can be strained and used for soup or mixed with the batter). Set the mutton aside.

4. Heat ghee in a wok over low heat. Dip each meat piece in the prepared batter and deep-fry, one by one, until brown. Serve the kabargah pieces hot.

Rukhsaar Sayeed's Kashmiri Tujji

Ingredients

Mutton, cut into cubes: 1 kg
Red chilli powder: 2 tbsp
Fennel powder: 1 tbsp
Dhania powder: 2 tbsp
Meat masala: 2 tsp
Turmeric powder: 1 tsp
Cumin powder: 1 tsp
Curd: 1–1½ cups
Salt: 1 tsp (or to taste)
Vinegar: 1½ tbsp
Ginger garlic paste: 1 tbsp
Ghee: 2 tbsp

Steps

1. Mix all the spice blend ingredients in a bowl.
2. In a separate bowl, take 1 kg mutton cubes and coat them with 1–1½ cups curd, 1½ tbsp vinegar and 1 tbsp ginger garlic paste.
3. Add the prepared spice blend to the mutton and mix well to ensure the meat is evenly coated.
4. Add 2 tbsp ghee to the mixture and mix again.
5. Marinate the meat for at least 2 hours, preferably overnight.

Enhance your culinary experience by using the marinated mutton to prepare the Kashmiri tujji recipe detailed above.

KASHMIRI MUTTON KANTI

INGREDIENTS

Mutton (boneless and cubed): ½ kg
Onion, medium, cut into rings: 2
Curd: 5 tbsp
Garam masala: 1 tsp
Ginger garlic paste: 1 tbsp
Tomatoes, large, cubed: 2
Green chillies: 5–6
Turmeric powder: ½ tsp
Chilli powder: 2 tsp
Coriander powder: 2 tsp
Cumin seeds: 1 tsp
Cardamom: 2
Cloves: 2
1-inch cinnamon stick: 2
Coriander leaves, chopped: ½ cup
Salt to taste
Oil for frying

STEPS

1. Wash the mutton pieces thoroughly and drain well. Marinate the mutton with curd, ginger garlic paste, and half of each of the spices (garam masala, turmeric powder, chilli powder, coriander powder, cumin seeds, cardamom, cloves and cinnamon). Refrigerate the marinated meat in a covered container overnight.

2. Bring the marinated meat to room temperature before cooking. Heat oil in a pan and shallow-fry the mutton cubes one by one until they are browned. Remove and set aside.

3. In another pan, heat some oil and add the onion rings, tomato cubes, and the remaining spices. Sauté until the onions turn golden and the tomatoes soften.

4. Add the fried mutton cubes and green chillies to the pan. Stir well and add soy sauce (if using) along with some water. Cover with a lid and cook until the water is absorbed and the mutton is tender.

5. Garnish with chopped coriander leaves and serve hot with naan.

LOCAL SPICES
OF STATES

∾

J UST LIKE EVERY HOME, LOCALITIES AND COMMUNITIES ALSO
have their own spice blends, and every state is popular for
their version of it. These are the unique blends that add extra
local flavour to a particular dish—be it lazzat-e-taam from
Lucknow, goda masala from Maharashtra, ver masala from
Kashmir and so on. Their popularity is mostly limited to their
state and the people of that state who have travelled around.

When I was travelling across the country for this book, my
major focus was to try food and spices on the streets or visit the
grocery stores and explore their local spice blends. In one of
my interesting explorations in Jaipur, I found a few delicious
food stalls amid the beautiful shoes, clothes and jewellery sold
in the famed Bapu Bazar. When I walked into one such store
and asked for the local spice blend, they looked at me as if I had
asked for something that did not even exist. The vendor said,
'Everything is local, what do you want?' His question left me
puzzled. On the flip side, when I was in Lucknow and asked
the shop owner at Mata Badal Pansari, Aminabad, to suggest the
local spice, he gave me a range of spices from lazzat-e-taam—
one was made by him, while the other was branded. He also had
thandai masala, garam masala and so on. One can only imagine
how many stories must be buried within this 166-year-old

spice shop in Lucknow. During my interaction with Dheeraj Gupta, the current owner of the shop, I got to know about a legacy which started in 1857 in Lucknow that has served many legends, including modern chefs like Vikas Khanna, Ranveer Brar, Sanjeev Kapoor as well as the late Imtiaz Qureshi.

Local spice shops and spice blends like these add a unique flavour, which, in turn, becomes the 'secret' spice blend that any spice enthusiast (like me) who travels, always asks for.

Just like in Lucknow, when I was in Jodhpur, every local, tourist guide and internet search sent me to MV Spices near Mehrangarh Fort. As I walked through the historical street, the aroma led me to the shop (I also had Google Maps on and people to ask directions from). Renowned for its rich legacy and vibrant home-made local spices, MV Spices is currently run by Kavita Gehani and her family.

I was welcomed warmly into the shop; perhaps this was their way of welcoming people or perhaps it was our mutual love for spices. When I enquired about its origins, I was told that Mohanlal, the late founder, was a scientist and inventor who meticulously tested each spice to create the perfect masala blends. His scientific approach was complemented by the matriarch, Bhagvanti, who ensured each blend passed her rigorous taste tests. This meticulous process has since been passed down, with Kavita and her sisters continuing the tradition with the same dedication and care.

As we moved through the shop, Kavita told me that they don't use any preservatives or flavour enhancers. 'Everything is natural, just like it was when my father started the business,' she said. This commitment to authenticity is what sets MV Spices apart.

The most popular masala, I was told, was the maharaja masala, a blend that has garnered acclaim not just locally but globally, and is particularly used in vegetarian delicacies.

As I left MV Spices, I felt a deep appreciation for the legacy they uphold. It's not just about selling spices—it's about preserving a heritage and sharing a piece of their heart with every blend. Jodhpur's streets may be filled with many spice shops, but MV Spices stands out as a true mistress of spices, blending history, love and tradition into every packet.

Similar to these spices in Jodhpur, you will find Lalbaugh Spice market in Mumbai, Mapusa Market in Goa, Mattancherry Spice Market in Kerala or my favourite and Asia's biggest spice market, Khari Baoli in Delhi. All of these have stories to narrate, with the majority of their stores being as old as sliced breads. A few patterns can be seen noticeably—shops are being run by the third or fourth generation, all have the local popular spices, each of them has their version of garam masala and a mountain of various kinds of chillies outside the shop to attract the customer (fascinatingly, the capsaicin in red chilli repels insects and mites but attracts humans).

Usually, the local spice blends are used as one blend '*Rām-bān*'* which takes care of everything. Goda masala adds a subtle sweetness, garam masala adds aroma, earthy and floral flavour, lazzat-e-taam adds a unique rustic and aromatic flavour, Rampuri khushboo masala (as the name suggests) adds aroma, and Goan xacuti and recheado spices add tang, heat and sharpness.

Kashmir uses ver masala, which is usually a blend of shallots, garlic, other spices and mustard oil. This blend is then made into some roundels (tikkiya), sundried and used for at least a year.[†] These tikkiyas can be used in anything and everything. For instance, I like mixing a portion in my omelette—to many, this might be pushing the envelope, but the whole idea is to be able to use the spices the way we want in our dishes to enhance the flavour.

---

* The term 'राम-बाण' (Rām-bāṇ) in Hindi literally means 'the arrow of Rama'. Figuratively, it represents a powerful, definitive solution to a problem—similar to a highly effective remedy or cure.
† Ver masala is dried to be stored for almost one year probably because of the cold weather. Drying the spices or ingredients is a known technique for places that have less sunlight throughout the year.

In the maximum city, Mumbai, a unique spice exists within the East Indian Catholic community. Unlike many who go out to buy spice blends for the dishes, in this community, families hold dear the practice of making their own 'bottle masala'. This isn't just any spice mix—it's a yearly ritual, a fragrant legacy passed down through generations. This orange-red-hued spice blend got its name because of the families that would create and store it in dark beer bottles. The masala includes fiery chillies alongside the floral and earthy turmeric and cumin seeds, as well as fennel seeds. Traditionally, asafoetida can also be added to help the spice blend last long.

One of my favourite books on spices, *The Flavour of Spice* by Marryam H. Reshii, explores multiple spice stories—one of them is the Nadar coriander powder. 'Even though what they call coriander powder is actually a spice blend consisting of coriander seeds roasted till they are very dark along with curry leaves, dried ginger, urad dal, asafoetida and fenugreek,' she writes.[1]

The cuisine favoured by the Nadar trading community can effortlessly challenge any preconceived ideas you might hold about southern Indian fare. To begin with, it's a misconception that all dishes from the south are laden with spice. Instead, the meals are characteristically gentle in flavour, providing a balanced selection of meats, fish and vegetables. This culinary style emphasizes a milder, more nuanced taste profile that caters to a diverse palate.[2]

The beauty of hyperlocal spices lies in their availability, seasonality and connection to the local climate. From north to south, east to west, each region of India has its own distinct spice blends, often crafted to suit the local weather and seasonal ingredients. These blends are rarely known beyond their regions of origin, creating a unique culinary signature that reflects the identity of each community. For instance, the spicy podis of Andhra Pradesh, the distinctive karuveppilai podi of Tamil Nadu, and the unique chammanthi podi of Kerala are all examples of regional culinary pride. To the uninitiated, the cuisines of the southern states may seem similar, but each blend is different; deeply rooted in local tradition and flavour.

Colleen Taylor Sen explains that spices serve multiple purposes in gastronomy, such as adding flavour, texture and excitement to dishes, particularly for those with otherwise monotonous diets. She notes that even simple dishes can use a few spices, while more complex recipes may require over a dozen, added at different stages of cooking.[3]

Many of these hyperlocal spice blends and the story of spices exist as one of collaboration—rarely is a spice found alone, for each one brings out the best in its companions. There is no definitive recipe; instead, each cook and family create their own unique combination. This varied use of hyperlocal spices illustrates how the Indian masala dabba relies on subtle alchemy. It is this intricate interplay that makes Indian cuisine or rather the subcontinent endlessly fascinating to me.

Rampuri Khushboo Masala

Ingredients

Nutmeg, whole: 1
Mace blades: 2
Green cardamom: 3 tbsp
Cloves: 10
1-inch cinnamon stick: 2

Steps

1. Dry roast all the ingredients on low heat until they are fragrant, stirring continuously.
2. Transfer all the spices to a spice grinder or mortar and pestle. Grind to a fine powder.
3. Store the spice blend in an airtight container in a cool, dry place. Proper storage will maintain its freshness and potency for several months.

Azmat Ali's Kashmiri Ver

Ingredients

Shallots (pran): 50 gm
Garlic: 50 gm
Kashmiri red chilli, whole: 50 gm
Fennel powder: 1 tsp
Dried ginger powder: 1 tsp
Dried coriander seeds: 1 tsp
Nigella seeds: 1 tsp
Salt: 1 tsp (or to taste)
Black cardamom: 4–6
Green cardamom: 2
Black pepper: 8–10
1-inch cinnamon stick

Cloves: 4–6

Mustard oil, smoked: 50 ml

1. Blend the garlic and shallots into a paste. Place the paste in an airtight container and let it sit overnight.
2. The next day, add the red chilli powder to the paste. Mix thoroughly until the mixture is smooth and homogenous.
3. Mix all the remaining spices into the paste. Blend until you achieve a smooth, consistent paste.
4. Smoke the mustard oil (preferably cold-pressed) and let it cool naturally.
5. Add the cooled mustard oil to the spice paste. Mix well, then knead the mixture into a dough-like consistency.
6. Transfer the mixture to a new airtight container. Store it away from direct sunlight for 7 days.
7. After 7 days, open the container and knead the spice blend again. You can either use it as it is or proceed to the next step.
8. Shape the mixture into small rounds (tikkis) with a slight indentation in the centre. Cover them with a muslin cloth and let them dry in the sun.
9. Use this spice blend in your Kashmiri dishes or Kashmiri-inspired recipes for a local flavoured dish.

NADAR CORIANDER POWDER/NADAR POWDER

INGREDIENTS

Coriander seeds: 6 tbsp

Star anise: 4–6

Poppy seeds: 2 tbsp

Bengal gram: 1 tbsp

Dried ginger powder: 1 tbsp
Black pepper: 1 tbsp
Raw rice: 1 tbsp

STEPS

1. Dry roast all the ingredients together.
2. Thoroughly combine all the ingredients in a bowl to ensure even distribution.
3. For a finer blend, grind the whole spices and rice until you achieve a smooth powder.
4. Store the spice blend in an airtight container in a cool, dry place. This will help maintain its freshness and potency for several months.

EAST INDIAN BOTTLE MASALA

INGREDIENTS

Bedki chillies: 10
Kashmiri chillies: 10
Cloves: 8–10
Turmeric: 3 tbsp
Coriander seeds: 2 tbsp
Cumin seeds: 2 tbsp
Sesame seeds: 1½ tbsp
Poppy seeds: 1½ tbsp
Fennel seeds: 1 tbsp
Mustard seeds: 2 tsp
Nigella seeds: 1 tsp
Green cardamom: 1 tsp
2-inch cinnamon stick

1. Dry roast the above ingredients individually on low heat until they release their aromatic oils and are lightly brown.
2. Allow the roasted spices to cool completely, then grind them into a fine powder using a spice grinder or mortar and pestle.
3. Store the ground spice blend in a clean, airtight container to maintain its freshness and potency.

Lazzat-e-Taam (Potli ka Masala)

Ingredients

Clove: 1 tsp
Green cardamom: 3–4
Nutmeg, whole: ¼
Mace blade: 1
2-inch cinnamon sticks: 2
Black pepper: 1 tsp
Coriander seeds: 1 tsp
Allspice powder: 1 tsp
Cumin seeds: 1 tsp
Nigella seeds: 1 tsp
Bay leaf, cut into small bits: 1
Poppy seeds: 1 tsp
Fennel seeds: 1 tsp
Star anise: 1
White pepper: 1 tsp
Barberry (baobeer): 1 tsp
½-inch dried galangal
Vetiver roots, chopped: 1 tsp
Sandalwood powder: ½ tsp
Rose petals: 1 tsp

Dried lemongrass (jarakhush): 1 tsp
Dried fennel seeds leaves: 1 tsp
15-inch x 15-inch muslin cloth to make the bouquet garnish
Kewra: 1 tsp
Meetha attar: 1 tsp
A 20-inch-long twine (optional)

STEPS

1. Lightly toast the clove, cardamom, nutmeg, mace, cinnamon, black pepper, coriander, allspice powder, cumin seeds, caraway seeds, bay leaf, poppy, fennel seeds, star anise, white pepper, barberry, galangal and vetiver roots on a griddle or large frying pan for 2–3 minutes on a very low flame until aromatic. Remove from heat.
2. Once the spices are cool, mix with the sandalwood powder, rose petals, dried lemongrass and dried fennel seeds leaves. In a blender, dump all the spices and grind to a smooth powder.
3. Store the ground spice blend in a clean, airtight container to maintain its freshness and potency.

SHEEBA IQBAL'S POTLI MASALA

INGREDIENTS

Coriander seeds: 1½ tbsp
Fennel seeds: 1 tsp
Cumin seeds: 1 tsp
Black pepper: 1 tsp
Cloves: 5
Green cardamom: 5
Black cardamom: 3
Bay leaves: 2

STEPS

1. Either crush these spices roughly or use them whole.
2. Combine all the ingredients in a spice bag or a piece of muslin cloth tied securely.
3. Use it in yakhni or korma or dishes of your choice.

VALSAD

INGREDIENTS

4-inch ginger
Garlic: 8–10 cloves
Turmeric powder: 2 tsp
Dried red chillies: 10–15
Cumin seeds: 2 tsp
Coriander seeds: 1 tbsp
2-inch cinnamon stick
Cloves: 6–7
White cardamom, peeled: 5–6
Black pepper: 8–10
Poppy seeds: 1 tbsp
Salt: 3 tsp (or to taste)

STEPS

1. Dry roast the whole spices on a low heat until they release their aromatic oils and are lightly brown.
2. Grind all the ingredients with ginger and garlic. Mix them well and store them in an airtight jar.
3. It can be kept for 6–8 days, and longer in the refrigerator.

Buffath

Ingredients

Ginger and garlic powder: 50 gm
Red chillies: 10 gm
Mustard powder: 1 tsp
Cumin powder: 1 tsp
Garam masala: 1 tsp
Chilli powder: ½ tsp
Kashmiri chilli powder: 1 tbsp
Turmeric powder: ½ tsp
Salt: 1 tsp (or to taste)
Sugar: 1 tsp

Steps

1. Dry roast all the whole spices and bring down to room temperature.
2. Mix all the powdered and whole spices together.
3. Blend to a fine powder.
4. Keep in an airtight container.

Chef Anahita Dhondhy's Dhansak

Ingredients

Sambhar masala: 3 tsp
Dhana-jiru masala: 2 tsp
Red chilli powder: 2 tsp
Turmeric powder: 1 tsp
Cumin powder: 1 tsp
Garam masala (optional): 1 tsp

1. Combine all the ingredients in a bowl and mix thoroughly to ensure an even distribution of flavours.
2. Store the blended masala in an airtight container in a cool, dry place to maintain freshness.

CHEF ANAHITA DHONDHY'S DHANA JIRU

INGREDIENTS

1-inch turmeric
Coriander seeds: 8 tbsp
Cumin seeds: 4 tbsp
Black pepper: 3½ tbsp
Curry leaves: 3 tbsp
Fenugreek seeds: 2 tbsp
Poppy seeds: 2 tbsp
Nigella seeds: 1 tbsp
1-inch cinnamon stick
Cloves: 4–6
Green cardamom: 4–6
Bay leaves: 4–6
Dried orange peel: 2 tbsp
Dried sweet lime peel: 2 tbsp

STEPS

1. Roast each ingredient individually with 1–2 tsp of oil on a tawa until aromatic.
2. Cool the roasted ingredients, then grind them to a fine powder.
3. Combine all the ground spices in a large bowl and mix thoroughly.

4. Store the masala in an airtight container. This can be kept for up to a year.

Chef Anahita Dhondhy's Parsi Sambhar

Ingredients

Kashmiri red chillies: 15–20 (or chilli powder: 3 tbsp)
Fenugreek seeds: 3 tbsp
Mustard seeds: 2 tbsp
Asafoetida powder: 1 tsp
1-inch cinnamon stick
Cloves: 5–6
Black pepper: 1 tbsp
Star anise: 6–8
Salt: ¼ tsp (or to taste)
Oil: 2 tbsp

Steps

1. Grind all the spices individually, except asafoetida, to a fine powder.
2. Transfer the ground spices to a large thali and mix thoroughly. Make a well in the centre and place the asafoetida in it.
3. Heat the oil till very hot and pour it over the asafoetida. Crush the asafoetida completely with a wooden spoon and mix well with the other spices.
4. Let the masala cool completely, then store it in an airtight glass jar.

Kerala Sambhar

Ingredients

Coriander seeds: 2 tbsp
Dried red chillies: 20 gm
Split pigeon peas: 3 tbsp
Split chickpeas: 1 tbsp
Turmeric powder: 1 tsp
Fenugreek seeds: 1 tsp
Cumin seeds: 2 tsp
Black pepper: 1 tbsp
Asafoetida: ½ tsp
Curry leaves: ½ cup
Coconut oil: 1 tsp

Steps

1. In a pan, dry roast the lentils on low heat for 5 minutes until they release their aroma and turn golden. Remove and set aside.
2. Add all the whole spices, apart from the chillies, and roast on a low flame. Once they are nicely toasted and aromatic, remove and set them aside.
3. Add ½ tsp of oil to the pan and sauté the red chillies on a low flame, ensuring each one gets lightly coated with oil. Sauté for just 20–25 seconds. Remove and set aside.
4. Allow all the roasted ingredients to cool completely. Mix all the roasted ingredients together with the turmeric powder. Grind the mixture to a fine powder.
5. Spread the ground spice blend on a paper to cool before storing. Store the blend in a dry, airtight container.
6. This samhbar powder stays fresh for 6 months when stored properly on the countertop and up to a year when kept in the freezer.

Bihari Masala

Ingredients

Gram flour, roasted: 2 tbsp
Poppy seeds: 1 tbsp
Coriander seeds: 1 tbsp
Cumin seeds: 2 tbsp
Nutmeg powder: ½ tsp
Mace blade: 1
Cloves: 6
Black pepper: 1 tsp
Black cardamom: 1
Green cardamom: 4
1-inch cinnamon stick: 2
Star anise: 1
Long pepper: 1–2
Allspice powder: 8
Black salt: ½ tsp
Tartaric acid: 2 pinches
Red chilli powder: 1 tbsp
Kashmiri red chilli powder: 1 tbsp
Salt: 1½ tsp (or to taste)
Turmeric: ½ tsp

Steps

1. Dry roast all the whole ingredients (except the powders and salts) in a pan over low heat until they release their aromatic oils and become lightly brown. Remove from heat and let them cool completely.
2. Grind the roasted ingredients finely using a spice grinder or mortar and pestle.
3. Combine the ground spices with salt, red chilli powder and turmeric powder. Mix thoroughly to ensure an even distribution of all the ingredients.

4. Store the spice blend in an airtight container in a cool, dry place. This will help maintain its freshness and potency for several months.

Note: Adjust the quantities of red chilli powder and salt to suit your taste preferences.

CHEF SAI PRIYA'S BESARA PASTE*

INGREDIENTS

Black mustard: 4 tbsp
Garlic cloves: 10
Green chillies: 4
Cumin seeds: 1 tbsp

STEPS

1. Soak the mustard and cumin seeds in water for 15 minutes.
2. Add the soaked mustard and cumin seeds, garlic and green chillies to a blender. Add a little water and blend into a fine paste.
3. Leave the paste aside for 15 minutes before using it in the curry of your choice.

KOLHAPURI ONION GARLIC MASALA

INGREDIENTS

Kashmiri red chillies: 6
Byadgi red chillies: 4
Lavangi mirch: 8

---

* Chef Sai Priya is a food researcher showcasing Odia cuisine and temple foods.

Coriander seeds: 6 tbsp
Cumin seeds: 2 tbsp
Nigella seeds: ½ tsp
Fennel seeds: 2 tsp
Mustard seeds: 2 tsp
Sesame seeds: 2 tsp
Poppy seeds: 2 tsp
Bay leaves: 2
½-inch cinnamon stick
Star anise: 1
Cloves: 3–5
Black pepper: 1 tsp
Black cardamom: 1
Green cardamom: 2
Mace blades: 2
Triphala: ½ tsp
Mesua ferrea: ½ tsp
Oil: 1 tbsp
Turmeric: 2 tsp
Asafoetida: ¼ tsp
Fenugreek seeds: ½ tsp
Stone flower: ½ tsp
Onions, sliced: 2 tbsp
Garlic: 6 cloves
Fresh coriander, chopped
Fresh coconut: 2 tbsp
Salt: 2 tsp (or to taste)
Ginger powder: 2 tsp
Nutmeg powder: ¼ tsp

STEPS

1. Set a pan on medium heat until moderately hot.
2. Dry roast the coriander seeds on a low flame until aromatic. Remove and allow to cool.

3. Add cumin seeds, caraway seeds and fennel seeds to the pan. Stir and dry roast on a low flame until aromatic. Transfer to the same bowl as the coriander seeds.
4. Add mustard seeds, sesame seeds and poppy seeds. Dry roast until aromatic and transfer to the same bowl.
5. Cool all the roasted ingredients completely. Mix all the roasted ingredients with turmeric powder, salt and ginger powder. Grind the mixture into a fine powder.
6. Mix the ground spices with the red chilli powder in a large bowl.
7. Heat the oil until very hot, then sprinkle it onto the spice powder. Mix well to coat the spices and enhance their preservation.
8. Store the spice blend in an airtight glass container in a cool, dry place. Proper storage will maintain the blend's freshness and potency for several months.

Notes: Use three different types of whole red chillies for the blend: Kashmiri and byadgi chillies for colour and lavangi chillies for spice.

MALVANI MASALA

INGREDIENTS

Byadgi chillies: 10
Sankeshwari chillies: 2
Pandi chillies: 2
Coriander seeds: 5 tbsp
Cumin seeds: 1½ tbsp
Nigella seeds: 1 tbsp
Fennel seeds: 2 tbsp
Mustard seeds: 1 tbsp
Poppy seeds: 2 tbsp
Black pepper: 2 tbsp

Cloves: 4–6 tsp
Cobra saffron (nagkesar): 1 tsp
Allspice powder: ½ tsp
Star Anise: ½ tsp
Triphala: ½ tsp
Black cardamom: 3
Green cardamom: 6
Mace blade: 1
Stone flower: 1
1-inch cinnamon stick
Nutmeg, grated: ¼ tsp
Turmeric powder: 1 tsp
Asafoetida: ½ tsp
Bay leaves: 2
Fenugreek seeds: ½ tsp

STEPS

1. Dry roast the chillies in a large kadahi. Remove the stalks from the chillies and grind them into a fine powder. Transfer the chilli powder to a large bowl.

2. Set a kadahi over a low to medium flame and add the coriander seeds, cumin seeds, caraway seeds, fennel seeds, mustard seeds and poppy seeds. Mix well and dry roast the spices until they become fragrant. Transfer the roasted spices to a bowl.

3. Add the remaining whole spices (black pepper, cloves, cobra saffron, allspice powder, star anise, triphala, black cardamom, green cardamom, mace, wild mace, stone flower, cinnamon stick, nutmeg, turmeric, asafoetida, bay leaves, fenugreek seeds) to the kadahi and dry roast them, stirring frequently until they become fragrant. Transfer these spices to the same bowl and allow them to cool completely.

4. Transfer all the roasted spices into a mixer grinder jar and grind them to a fine powder. Transfer the ground spice mix into the bowl with the chilli powder.

5. Mix the ground spices with the chilli powder. Strain the mixture through a sieve into a large plate to ensure a fine consistency.

6. Transfer the malvani masala into an airtight jar. The masala can be used for up to a year if stored correctly.

Konkani Masala

Ingredients

Sankeshwari red chillies, dried
Coriander seeds: 3 tbsp
Bay leaves: 3
Star anise: 2
Cloves: 6
Black pepper: 1 tsp
Mace, whole: 1
1-inch cinnamon stick: 2
Green cardamom: 4
Fennel seeds: 1 tbsp
Poppy seeds: 1 tbsp
Triphala: ½ tsp
Nutmeg, grated: ¼ tsp

Steps

1. Remove the stalks from the chillies and grind them into a fine powder. Transfer the chilli powder to a large bowl.

2. Set a kadahi over a high flame and heat it well. Lower the flame and add the coriander seeds, bay leaves, star anise, cloves, black pepper, mace, cinnamon stick, green cardamom, fennel seeds, poppy seeds and triphala. Mix well and dry roast the spices until they become fragrant. Transfer the roasted spices to a bowl and allow them to cool completely.

3. Transfer all the roasted spices into a mixer grinder jar and grind them to a fine powder. Transfer the ground spice mix into the bowl with the chilli powder.
4. Mix the ground spices with the chilli powder. Strain the mixture through a sieve into a large plate to ensure a fine consistency.
5. Transfer the konkani masala into an airtight jar. Store it in a cool, dry place. The masala can be used for up to a year if stored correctly.

SONAL AGARWAL'S BIKANERI NAMKEEN

INGREDIENTS

Red chilli powder: 2 tbsp
Longi chilli powder: 1 tbsp
Turmeric powder: 1 tbsp
Coriander powder: 4 tbsp
Salt: 1 tbsp (or to taste)
Black salt: 1 tsp
Chaat masala: 1 tsp
Mango powder: ½ tsp
1-inch cinnamon stick
Bay leaves: 3
Nigella seeds: ½ tsp
Garam masala: 1 tbsp

STEPS

1. Combine all the ingredients in a large bowl. Mix thoroughly to ensure even distribution of all the spices.
2. Store the Bikaneri masala in an airtight container in a cool, dry place. Proper storage will help maintain its freshness and potency for several months.

Maharashtrian Ghati

Ingredients

Sankeshwari red chillies, dried: 10
Kashmiri red chillies: 10
Coriander seeds: 4 tbsp
Star anise: 4
1-inch cinnamon stick: 4
Cumin seeds: 1 tbsp
Nigella seeds: 1 tsp
Cloves: 6–8
Green cardamom: 15
Mace blade: 1
Black cardamom: 5
Black pepper: 1 tsp
Nutmeg: ½
Stone flower: 1
Bay leaves: 2
Garlic: 4 cloves
Dried coconut, grated: 3 tbsp
Salt: 1 tsp (or to taste)
Poppy seeds: 1 tbsp
Onions, fried: 3 tbsp

Steps

1. Set a pan or kadahi over medium heat. Dry roast each ingredient separately until they become fragrant and slightly darker. Transfer to a plate to cool.
2. Once all the roasted ingredients have cooled, transfer them to a grinder. Grind to a fine powder.
3. Combine all the ground spices in a bowl. Mix thoroughly to ensure even distribution.

4.   Store the ghati masala in an airtight container in a cool, dry place. Proper storage will help maintain its freshness and potency for several months.

AGRI KOLI

INGREDIENTS

Byadagi red chillies: 5
Shankeshwari red chillies: 5
Kashmiri red chillies: 5
Panda red chillies: 5
Bay leaves: 3
Mace blade: 1
Green cardamom: 3
Mustard seeds: 1 tsp
Coriander seeds: 3 tbsp
Black cumin seeds: 1 tbsp
Cloves: 10–12
Cobra saffron: 1 tsp
Stone flower: 1 tbsp
Cumin seeds: 1 tbsp
1-inch cinnamon stick: 6
Black pepper: 10–12
Triphala, de-seeded: 10–12

STEPS

1.   Dry roast the chillies in a large kadahi. Remove the stalks from the chillies and grind them into a fine powder.
2.   Set a pan or kadahi over medium heat. Dry roast each of the following ingredients separately until they become fragrant and slightly darker—bay leaves, mace blade, green cardamom pods, mustard seeds, coriander seeds, black

cumin seeds, cloves, cobra saffron, stone flower, cumin seeds, cinnamon sticks, black pepper and triphala. Transfer each roasted ingredient to a plate to cool.

3. Once all the roasted ingredients have cooled, transfer them to a grinder. Grind to a fine powder.

4. Combine all the ground spices in a bowl. Mix thoroughly to ensure even distribution.

5. Store the Agri masala in an airtight container in a cool, dry place. Proper storage will help maintain its freshness and potency for several months.

ANDHRA KARVEPAKU KARAM

INGREDIENTS

Curry leaves: 40
Oil: 3 tbsp
Coriander seeds: 1 tbsp
Cumin seeds: 1 tsp
Dried red chillies: 3
Dried garlic, chopped (or garlic powder): 1 tsp
Black gram, husked: 2 tbsp
Asafoetida: A pinch
Black pepper: 1 tsp
Salt to taste

STEPS

1. Heat 3 tbsp of oil in a pan. Add 40 curry leaves and fry until they are crisp. Remove the fried curry leaves and set aside.

2. In the same oil, add 1 tbsp of coriander seeds, 1 tsp of cumin seeds, 3 dried red chillies, 1 tsp of chopped dried garlic or garlic powder, 2 tbsp of husked black gram, a

pinch of asafoetida, and 1 tsp of black pepper. Fry these ingredients until they are light brown.

3. Add the fried curry leaves and salt to the pan. Mix well.
4. Transfer the mixture to a grinder and grind to a fine powder.
5. Add more salt if needed. Mix thoroughly to ensure even distribution.
6. Store the spicy powdered flavouring in an airtight jar.

Note: This spicy powdered flavouring can be sprinkled on curd or used to enhance the flavour of any lightly flavoured dish.

BHAJA

INGREDIENTS

Cumin seeds: 5 tbsp
Fennel seeds: 5 tbsp
Coriander seeds: 3 tbsp
Cardamom: 12–14

STEPS

1. Heat a pan on a medium to low flame and add the whole spices to the pan.
2. Dry roast them evenly on all sides, stirring continuously for about 8 minutes. Ensure that the spices are roasted thoroughly.
3. Add the roasted spices to a grinder and blitz them until you have a fine powder. Alternatively, you can use a mortar and pestle to grind the spices by hand.
4. Store the bhaja masala powder in an airtight container in a cool, dry place.

Sylvia Davis's Rasam Podi

Ingredients

Red gram (masoor dal): 3 tbsp
Bengal gram: 4 tbsp
Black gram, husked: 2 tbsp
Coriander seeds: 3 tbsp
Oil: 2 tbsp
Dried red chillies: 5
Black pepper: 1 tbsp
Asafoetida: ¼ tsp
Cumin seeds: 2 tsp
Fenugreek seeds: 1 tsp

Steps

1. Heat a pan on a medium to low flame and dry roast the red gram, Bengal gram, husked black gram, and coriander seeds until they become aromatic and slightly brown. Remove from the pan and set aside.
2. In the same pan, heat 2 tbsp of oil. Add dried red chillies, black pepper and asafoetida. Fry until the chillies are crispy and the spices are fragrant. Remove from the pan and set aside.
3. Once all the roasted and fried ingredients have cooled completely, transfer them to a grinder. Add the cumin seeds and fenugreek seeds.
4. Transfer the ground powder to a large bowl and mix thoroughly to ensure an even distribution of all the spices.
5. Store the spice mix in an airtight container in a cool, dry place. Proper storage will maintain its freshness and potency for several months.

Jaunsari Pahadi

Ingredients

Sichuan pepper (timru/timut): 1 tbsp
Cobra saffron: ½ tbsp
Carom seeds: ½ tbsp
Cumin seeds: 1 tbsp
Spikenard (kadar jadi): ½ tbsp
Star anise: 2
Black pepper: 1 tbsp
Nutmeg, grated: ½ tbsp
1-inch cinnamon stick
Black cardamom: 1
Green cardamom: 4–6
Bay leaves: 4
Dried ginger powder: ½ tbsp
Triphala: ½ tbsp
Dried curry leaves: ½ tbsp

Steps

1. Heat a pan on a medium to low flame. Dry roast each ingredient separately until they become aromatic and slightly brown. This helps to release their essential oils and enhance their flavours. Remove from the pan and let them cool completely.
2. Once all the ingredients have cooled, transfer them to a grinder. Grind to a fine powder.
3. In a large bowl, combine all the ground spices. Mix thoroughly to ensure an even distribution of all ingredients.
4. Store the pahadi masala in an airtight container in a cool, dry place. Proper storage will maintain its freshness and potency for several months.

Mewati Chaas

Ingredients

Cumin seeds: ¼ cup
Coriander seeds: ¼ cup
½-inch cinnamon stick
Black pepper: 25–30
Carom seeds: ½ tsp
Fennel seeds: ½ tsp
Dried mint: 1½ tbsp
Black salt: ½ tsp
Asafoetida: ¼ tsp
Dried mango powder: 1½ tsp
Salt: ½ tsp (or to taste)

Steps

1. Heat a pan on a medium to low flame. Dry roast the cumin seeds, coriander seeds, a cinnamon stick, black pepper, carom seeds and fennel seeds until they become aromatic and slightly brown. Remove from the pan and let them cool completely.
2. Once all the roasted ingredients have cooled, transfer them to a grinder. Add the dried mint, black salt, asafoetida, dried mango powder and salt.
3. Grind the mixture to a fine powder.
4. Mix thoroughly to ensure an even distribution of all ingredients.
5. Store the spice mix in an airtight container in a cool, dry place. Proper storage will maintain its freshness and potency for several months.

NIHARI

॰

WHEN WE FLIP THE PAGES OF CULINARY HISTORY, we find stories of royal dishes that eventually made their way into the lives of common folk, gracing the bustling streets with a taste of the palace. Among these, the narrative of nihari is particularly striking. What started as a humble nourishment for the poor, rose through the culinary ranks to grace the royal table. In the royal kitchens, the recipe was refined and enriched, yet the essence of the dish—the texture and the depth of flavour—remained untouched. I believe nihari to be not just a dish but a symbol of aspiration, embodying the journeys of individuals who rose from obscurity to prominence and inspired countless others.

Growing up, the anticipation of Eid-ul-Azha (Bakrid) always brought with it the promise of home-made nihari, a dish immersed in our family tradition. Each year, we would journey to our maternal and paternal house in Sasaram to partake in it. *Chote Mamu** would call the *naanbai* (bread maker), providing him with the ingredients to craft the khamiri naan—the perfect companion to nihari in my opinion.

Meanwhile, the women of the house—Ammi, Khala and Mami—along with our ever-reliable house help, Baby Aunty, would take charge of the nihari preparation. They meticulously cleaned the feet and claws, and selected the finest cuts of meat

---

* Younger uncle.

from the calf muscle, neck and other choice parts. The masala was freshly prepared, and everything was placed into a large *degh*,* which was then sealed and left to slow-cook over the gentle heat of coal through the night.

As dawn broke, the degh would be opened, releasing an intoxicating aroma that signalled the magic of freshly cooked nihari. Us kids would eagerly lay out the *dastarkhwan*,† ensuring every plate had a bowl and spoon, and a smaller plate for the bones. The flavours of nihari were elevated with the addition of julienned ginger, freshly chopped coriander leaves, green chillies and a squeeze of lime—all of which we ensured were available in abundance.

Gathering around the dastarkhwan, the family would share a hearty breakfast, dipping the freshly baked khamiri naan into the rich, aromatic nihari. The warmth of the dish was the perfect antidote to the chilly winter mornings. Even as we grew older and Eid-ul-Azha occasionally fell outside of winter, the tradition continued. The family would come together and invite neighbours to share in the meal and laughter, embodying the spirit of togetherness and celebration. The essence of those mornings—family unity, communal preparation and shared enjoyment—remains etched in my heart.

However, there remains a layer of complexity woven around nihari that is encapsulated in two persistent questions: Is it nihari or nahari? And was it born in Delhi or Lucknow? To the first, I would say, the distinction lies in its etymology and consumption habits. 'Nihari' originated from the Persian *nahar*, meaning morning, highlighting its traditional role as a hearty breakfast for labourers after morning prayers, particularly in the cold winters of Delhi. Abu Sufiyan from Old Delhi's Shahjahanabad always offers a clever twist to this query, saying, '*Jise nihar ke khayi jaaye wo nihari aur jise nahar mooh khayi jaye*

---

* Cauldron.
† Tablecloth.

wo nahari' (That which is eaten after admiring is nihari, and that which is eaten with a flowing mouth is nahari). For the sake of history here, let's stick to nihari as the main word, which can also be pronounced as nahari.

The debate intensifies when the origins of nihari are discussed, with proponents from both Delhi and Lucknow vying for the culinary crown. The dish, infused with black pepper and history, was, according to writer Anoothi Visha, initially prepared in the streets of Shahjahanabad (old Delhi) to protect against the diseases borne by the cold waters of the Yamuna.[1] This story from Delhi adds to the rich narrative, embedding the dish deeply within the cultural and historical fabric of the city. The story in the lanes of Lucknow, however, is that they created the dish during the construction of the Imambara complex by Asaf-ud-Daula, Nawab of Awadh, in 1784. This essentially means that there was a 145-year difference between the origin stories—I am more inclined to believe the Delhi version.

When we compare the two versions of nihari—Delhi's and Lucknow's—I find that the former is a little thick compared to the latter, which, in turn, tells me many things. First, it was perhaps the prototype created to feed the people who were creating the city and working throughout the day (with whole wheat flour as a thickening agent, adding a hearty consistency to this beloved dish). The origins of this spiced bone-meat broth are believed to have descended from Afghani shorwa with Babar. Enhanced with a spice blend to balance its rich meatiness, this broth incorporated ingredients like curd and coriander, transforming it into a dish that boosted both flavour and worker immunity.[2] However, when nihari made its way to Lucknow, it underwent a delectable transformation. In the early 1800s, during a severe famine, the *khansamas** of Lucknow refined the recipe to create a version that was thinner, smoother, milder and more aromatic than its robust Shahjahanabad counterpart.

---

* Royal chefs.

What set the Lucknow nihari apart was the incorporation of shanks (nalli) and trotters (paya), which gave the broth a unique, sticky texture and rich, savoury flavours. This variation also introduced paan ki jhad, khus ki jhad, and gilla masala—a blend of brown onions, ginger and other spices—that elevated its complexity. When this culinary gem travelled to Bhopal, the begums there adapted it to suit local tastes, making the thinned broth even thinner.

According to Abdul Halim Sharar in *Guzishta Lucknow*, nihari was one of the most iconic dishes of Lucknow. This rich, aromatic beef stew was prepared overnight, allowing the flavours to deepen and blend into a sumptuous delicacy. Sharar notes that nihari was so exceptional that even the wealthiest aristocrats would frequent the stall of Mahumdu, the famous vendor who perfected it.[3]

In Delhi, some of the best niharis have found a home in Matia Mahal. Matia Mahal, a street echoing the resonant past of a bygone era, was once synonymous with the grandeur and opulence that epitomized Mughal Delhi. Positioned adjacent to the Jama Masjid, this historical thoroughfare was a vibrant enclave, where nobles and royalty indulged in the luxuries of Mughal life. The street was named after a Mughal Begum and was famed for its refined culture, hosting an array of shops selling exotic perfumes and luxurious goods. The perfumers of Matia Mahal were not mere traders—they were artists who captivated the senses with their aromatic concoctions, that lingered in the air, weaving tales of romance and splendour.

At the zenith of its splendour, Matia Mahal was also known for its *hammams*—luxurious public baths that nobles and courtiers would retreat to in order to escape Delhi's harsh, sweltering heat. These hammams were not just about cleanliness; they represented opulence and served as places where hidden treasures and stories of wealth added to their mystique.

Today, the opulence of the past has faded, and the street has transformed significantly. Matia Mahal is now renowned, not for perfumes or palatial baths, but for its vibrant culinary scene. It has become a gastronomic destination, famous for its array of street food, where the scents of kababs, curries and breads fill the air, drawing both locals and tourists alike. It's a haven where the legacy of the Mughals flavours meets the dynamism of regular people.

Traditionally, the meat used in nihari has remained consistent. Street vendors often serve it with beef or buffalo meat, while upscale restaurants prefer mutton or lamb. The choice of cooking fat could be robust mustard oil or ghee. Traditional Lucknow nihari has whole spices packed in a small potli of muslin cloth to give only the flavour and not stay in the dish. The potli gets discarded once the dish is ready.

In Agra, nihari often features bone-in-meat, a tradition that extends to Bihar and Jharkhand. The essence of nihari is intertwined with beef or buffalo meat, while paya refers to its mutton or lamb counterpart. Each region adds its unique touch, yet all versions agree on the inclusion of red meat. Interestingly, in Lucknow's treasured culinary heritage, you can also find chicken and quail nihari.

Unlike its crimson counterparts, Lucknow's nihari boasts a yellowish hue, courtesy of the saffron and yellow food colour. This golden variation stands in stark contrast to the deep red gravies preferred in Delhi and other states, where such a colour might be considered unacceptable. What is acceptable, however, in Delhi is the 'taar', which means leftover nihari from the previous day/cauldron being mixed in the fresh batch to maintain the continuity and depth of flavour in the new batch. Regardless of these variations, a generous ghee tadka graces every bowl, adding a rich, buttery finish that is universally adored.

In November 2023, I had the pleasure of meeting Manzilat Fatima, the great-granddaughter of Wajid Ali Shah and owner of Manzie in Kolkata. She graciously hosted me at her restaurant, offering a lavish spread of her finest dishes. Among them was her rendition of nihari, served with dal puri—a surprising pairing for someone accustomed to enjoying nihari with khamiri roti, kulcha or simply khushka/phulka. Her version was milder, echoing the subtleties of Lucknow nihari. As a descendant of the nawabs, Manzilat seemed the perfect custodian of this magnificent dish. She suggested that I try the dish in Metiabruz, which closely resembles what nawab sahab might have savoured. Intrigued by her unique spice blend, I asked about the secret behind her spectacular nihari. She responded with a smile and served me some mutton chap.

Even with different variations or versions, one thing will always remain the same (luckily)—nihari will be slow-cooked overnight in large pots to ensure the flavour is absorbed into the meat. One benchmark, while preparing this dish, is that the meat should disintegrate and blend with the gravy. From Delhi's Kallu nihari, Haji Shabrati to Lucknow's Rahim nihari to Kala Khan nihari House in Rawalpindi and Zahid nihari in Karachi—all follow the same template. While a standard accompaniment is khamiri roti, you can also ask for maghaz (brain) and extra butter or ghee on top.

NIHARI MASALA

INGREDIENTS

For Masala 1:
Ghee: 1¼ cups
Meat shank and neck, with bone: 2 kg
Salt to taste
Garam masala powder: 3 tsp
Red chilli powder: 3 tsp
Coriander powder: 4 tsp
Ginger, minced: 1½ tbsp
Garlic, minced: 1½ tbsp
Turmeric powder: 1½ tbsp
Wheat flour: 6 tbsp
Onions, medium, sliced: 2

For Masala 2:
Long pepper: 2 sticks
Coriander seeds: 2½ tbsp
Mace powder: ½ tsp
Nutmeg powder: ½ tsp
Bay leaves: 2
1-inch cinnamon sticks: 2
Black cardamom: 4
Cloves: 20
Green cardamom: 10
Cumin seeds: 1 tsp
Black pepper: 1 tbsp
Fennel seeds: 4 tbsp
Star anise seeds: ¼ tsp

For Garnishing:
Fresh coriander, chopped
Fresh green chillies, sliced

Ginger, julienned

Lemons, cut into wedges

STEPS

1. In a large pot, heat 1¼ cups of oil on high heat. Add the meat and sear it until evenly browned on all sides.
2. Mix the garam masala, red chilli, coriander, ginger, garlic and turmeric. Cook until the meat is well-coated with the spices.
3. Pour 10 glasses of water over the meat. Separately, dissolve the wheat flour in 4 glasses of water and stir it into the pot. Ensure the meat is fully submerged, adding more water if needed, and bring to a boil.
4. Grind the ingredients listed under Masala 2 into a fine powder.
5. Once the meat mixture is boiling, add the freshly ground spice mix. Reduce the heat to medium and let it simmer for 6–7 hours, partially covered.
6. In a separate pan, fry the sliced onions in ¼ to ⅓ cup oil until golden brown and then add them to the simmering nihari.
7. Continue to simmer for another 15–20 minutes to integrate the flavours fully.
8. Serve the nihari hot, garnished with fresh coriander, green chillies, julienned ginger, lemon wedges and fried onions.
9. Accompany with hot khamiri naan.

ROCKY MOHAN'S NIHARI

INGREDIENTS

Lamb/mutton shanks: 500 gm

Garlic paste, finely ground: 6 tbsp

White butter (safed makhan): 4 tbsp

Red chilli powder: 3 tsp
Coriander powder: 3 tsp
Ginger paste: 4 tsp
Salt: 1 tsp (or to taste)
Milk: ¼ tsp
Refined flour: 6 tbsp

For the Bhagar (Flavouring):
White butter: 4 tbsp
Onions, finely sliced: 4 tbsp
Green cardamom, powdered: ¾ tsp
Black pepper, powdered: ¼ tsp
2-inch cinnamon sticks: 2
Lemon juice: 4 tsp

STEPS

1. Boil the lamb/mutton in 1 cup of water for 15 minutes. Drain the meat pieces and keep aside, reserving the stock. Add half of the finely ground garlic paste to the stock and stir well.
2. In a pot, heat the white butter. Add red chilli powder, coriander powder and ginger paste. Stir well and add the drained meat. Cook for 5 minutes.
3. Add the remaining garlic paste and mix. Continue to stir until the oil is released from the masala.
4. Add the refined flour and mix well. Pour the reserved stock and stir continuously to avoid lumps. Simmer for about 20 minutes, stirring occasionally.
5. In a separate pan, heat white butter and add the sliced onions. Fry until golden brown. Remove and mix with the powdered cinnamon, cardamom and black pepper. Add the fried onions to the main pot and mix well.

6. Reduce heat to low and simmer. Add the cinnamon sticks. Simmer until the meat is tender and the flavours have blended well. Add lemon juice before serving.
7. Once cooked, serve hot, garnished with fresh coriander leaves.

Rana Safvi's Nihari[4]

Ingredients

1-inch cinnamon sticks: 2
Bay leaves: 4–6
Green cardamom: 8–10
Cloves: 8–10
Turmeric powder: 1 tbsp
Red chilli powder: 1 tbsp
Coriander powder: 2 tbsp
Garam masala: 1 tbsp
Fennel seeds: 1 tsp
Black pepper: 1 tsp
Cumin seeds: ½ tsp
Nutmeg, grated: ½ tsp
Salt: 1 tsp (or to taste)

Steps

1. In a dry pan over medium heat, lightly roast the whole spices—cinnamon, bay leaves, cardamom, cloves, fennel seeds, black pepper, cumin seeds and nutmeg—until they become fragrant. This should take about 1–2 minutes, being careful not to burn them.
2. Allow the roasted spices to cool completely. Then, transfer them to a spice grinder and grind them to a fine powder.

3. In a bowl, combine the freshly ground spices with turmeric powder, chilli powder, coriander powder and garam masala. Mix thoroughly to ensure an even blend.

4. Transfer the spice blend to an airtight container and store it in a cool, dry place.

5. Use this spice blend for cooking nihari by following the steps previously provided or with your own preferred recipe. This spice blend aims to enhance the deep, aromatic flavours typical of nihari.

DELHI NIHARI

INGREDIENTS

1-inch cinnamon stick
Fennel seeds: 1 tsp
Coriander seeds: ½ tsp
Cumin seeds: ¼ tsp
Bay leaves: 2
Black pepper: ½ tsp
Cloves: 3
Nutmeg: ¼ tsp
Green cardamom: 3
Black cardamom: 1
Long pepper: 2
Allspice powder: ¼ tsp
Mace blades: 3
Star anise: 2
Ginger powder: 1 tsp
Kashmiri chilli powder: 1 tsp
Chilli powder: 1 tsp
Salt: 1 tsp (or to taste)
Turmeric powder: ½ tsp
Coriander powder: ½ tsp

Steps

1. In a dry pan over medium heat, add the cinnamon stick, bay leaf, cardamom pods (both green and black), cloves, fennel seeds, pepper, cumin seeds and nutmeg. Roast for 1–2 minutes, stirring constantly until fragrant. Be careful not to burn the spices.
2. Allow the roasted spices to cool completely. Then, transfer them to a spice grinder and grind them into a fine powder.
3. In a bowl, combine the freshly ground spices with the mace blade, turmeric powder, Kashmiri chilli powder, chilli powder, coriander powder, allspice powder and salt. Mix thoroughly to ensure an even distribution of flavours.
4. Transfer the spice blend to an airtight container and store it in a cool, dry place. This will help preserve the aroma and flavour of the spices.
5. This home-made nihari masala can be used in your favourite nihari recipe to create a deep, aromatic flavour profile. You can adjust the amount of spice blend according to your taste preference.

Purani Dilli Nihari

Ingredients

Coriander seeds: 2½ tbsp
Fennel seeds: 1½ tbsp
Black pepper: 1 tsp
Green cardamom: 10–12
Cloves: 20
Black cardamom: 2
Star anise: 3–4
Long pepper: 3
Bay leaves: 4
Nutmeg, whole: ½

Mace blades: 8–10
Dried ginger powder: 1 tbsp
Boriya chilli powder: 15–20
Kachri powder: 1½ tbsp
Red chilli powder: 1 tbsp
Salt: 1 tsp (or to taste)

Steps

1. In a dry pan over medium heat, add the coriander seeds, anise seeds, black pepper, green cardamom pods, cloves, black cardamom pods, star anise, long pepper and bay leaves. Roast for 1–2 minutes, stirring constantly until fragrant. Be careful not to burn the spices.
2. Allow the roasted spices to cool completely. Then, transfer them to a spice grinder and grind them into a fine powder.
3. In a bowl, combine the freshly ground spices with the nutmeg, mace, dried ginger powder, boriya chilli powder, kachri powder/papaya paste, red chilli powder and salt. Mix thoroughly to ensure an even distribution of flavours.
4. Transfer the spice blend to an airtight container and store it in a cool, dry place. This will help preserve the aroma and flavour of the spices.
5. This home-made nihari masala can be used in your favourite nihari recipe to create a deep, aromatic flavour profile. You can adjust the amount of spice blend according to your taste preference.

Lucknow's Nihari Khas[5]

Ingredients

Mutton (preferably seena and kareli): 1 kg
Onion: 500 gm
Garlic: 20 gm

Ginger: 20 gm
Turmeric powder: 1 tbsp
Red chilli powder: 1 tbsp
Coriander powder: 2 tbsp
1-inch cinnamon stick
Black cardamom: 10
Black pepper: 10
Cloves: 1 tbsp
Mace blades: 3–5
Nutmeg, grated: ½ tsp
Nigella seeds: ½ tsp
Kewra water: 1 medium-sized cup
Salt to taste
Curd: ½ cup
Gram flour, roasted: 1 cup
Mustard oil: 400 gm
All-Purpose flour (maida): 1 tbsp

For Yakhni:
Trotters (paya): 12
Mutton: ½ kg
Onion: 200 gm
Black pepper: 10
Bay leaves: 5
Water: 3 large cups

Steps

1. Wash and clean the mutton and paya. In a pressure cooker or deep vessel, combine all yakhni ingredients with three cups of water. Cook covered for 30 minutes or until very tender.
2. Peel and finely slice onions. Grind ginger to a paste. Extract garlic juice. Dry-grind or pound spices from cinnamon to caraway seeds.

3. Heat mustard oil to a smoking point in a patila. Carefully add garlic juice off the stove, then turn the heat on and fry onions until golden and crisp. Remove, crush finely and set aside.

4. Halve the oil quantity, add the mutton pieces, ginger paste, turmeric, coriander, chilli powder, curd, ground spices and salt. Stir over medium heat until the meat is half-cooked and the oil begins to separate.

5. Add the crushed onions back to the pan, cover and set aside. Prepare the yakhni by mashing the mutton and straining the stock prepared earlier.

6. In a separate vessel, heat the remaining oil and roast the gram flour and all-purpose flour until light brown. Gradually add the yakhni, stirring continuously. Once blended, add the semi-cooked mutton, stirring for five more minutes.

7. Cover and simmer on low heat until the meat is tender. Finish with kewra water, simmering for an additional 15 minutes.

8. Serve hot with kulcha or khamiri roti.

AWADHI AAM NIHARI

INGREDIENTS

Green cardamom: 10
Cloves: 10
1-inch cinnamon sticks: 3
Bay leaves: 6
Coriander powder: 4 tsp
Red chilli powder: 2 tsp
Turmeric: 1 tsp
Salt: 1½ tsp (or to taste)

STEPS

1. In a dry skillet over medium heat, roast the green cardamom, cloves, cinnamon sticks and bay leaves until they become fragrant. This will take about 1–2 minutes, and you should stir constantly to prevent burning.
2. Once the whole spices are roasted, allow them to cool and then grind them to a fine powder using a spice grinder or mortar and pestle.
3. Combine the freshly ground spices with the coriander powder, red chilli powder, turmeric and salt in a bowl. Stir well to ensure a uniform mixture.
4. Transfer your spice blend to an airtight container and store it in a cool, dry place to maintain freshness.
5. To prepare nihari with this spice blend, use the nihari cooking steps previously discussed or your own preferred method. This blend will give the dish a distinct and personalized flavour profile.

FARHEEN'S HYDERABADI NIHARI POTLI

INGREDIENTS

Balchar: 15 gm
Vetiver roots: 20 gm
Sandalwood (chandan) powder: 2 tbsp
Coriander, whole: 5 tbsp
Green cardamom: 6 tbsp
Cloves: 2 tbsp
Black pepper: 2 tbsp
Mace blade: 1
Bay leaves: 4
Nutmeg: ½
Black cardamom: 12–15
Fennel seeds: 1½ tbsp

1-inch cinnamon sticks: 6
Nigella seeds: 4 tbsp
Rose petals, dried: 1 tbsp
Allspice powder: 2 tsp
Dried galangal (paan ki jad): 1½ tbsp
Long pepper: 2 tsp
Stone flower: 2 tsp

STEPS

1. Collect all the spices as per the list. There's no need to roast them. Maintain their natural essence.
2. Put the spices in a muslin or thin cotton cloth and tie it securely to create a *potli* (spice bag).
3. This potli masala can be used to prepare 1 kg of nihari. This blend will give you a complex flavour without overwhelming the dish.

HYDERABADI NIHARI

INGREDIENTS

Fennel seeds: 4 tbsp
Ginger powder: 1 tbsp
Nutmeg, grated: 1
Mace blade: 1
Black pepper: 1 tbsp
Green cardamon: 10–12
Black cardamom: 6
1-inch cinnamon stick: 4
Star anise: 6
Long pepper: 4
Cloves: 1 tbsp
Nigella seeds: 1 tsp

Cumin seeds: 1 tsp
Bay leaves: 2
Kashmiri red chilli powder: 4 tbsp
Guntur chilli: 3 tbsp
Salt: 1 tbsp (or to taste)

STEPS

1. Stir all the ingredients together until evenly mixed. This blend does not require roasting as the raw qualities of these spices will infuse directly into the nihari, creating a depth of flavour once cooked.
2. Store the masala in an airtight container to keep it fresh and use it within a few months for the best flavour.
3. Incorporate this masala into your nihari recipe as per your usual method or by following the steps provided above for other nihari recipes. Adjust the amount of masala according to the intensity of flavour desired and the quantity of meat being used.

ZEBA'S NIHARI

INGREDIENTS

Green cardamom: 5–6
Cloves: 5–6
Black pepper: 1 tsp
Black cardamom: 2
Star anise: 2
Mace blade: 1
Nutmeg, grated: ¼
Dried ginger, crushed: 2
Fennel seeds: 1½ tbsp
Cumin seeds: 1 tbsp
Long pepper: 3–4

Bay leaves: 2
Coriander seeds: 1 tbsp
1-inch cinnamon sticks: 2
Carom seeds: ½ tsp
Salt: 1 tsp (or to taste)
Red chilli powder: 1 tbsp
Turmeric powder: 1 tsp
Kashmiri red chilli powder: 1 tbsp

STEPS

1. Blend all the spices thoroughly in a bowl to ensure even mixing. Since this blend is for use in traditional cooking, no roasting or grinding is required before adding to your dish.
2. Transfer the spice blend to an airtight container to preserve freshness and potent flavours. Use within a few months to ensure maximum flavour.
3. Utilize this spice blend according to the requirements of your dish, adjusting quantities based on the desired spice level and the volume of other ingredients. Follow your recipe or existing cooking methods to achieve a vibrant and flavourful outcome.

PARATHA

୶

LONG BEFORE THE ERA OF MUESLI, CEREALS AND various egg or sandwich options, Indians cherished the simple pleasure of parathas, with the potato-stuffed version being a favourite. Stuffed parathas are akin to our version of sandwiches—you can fill them with whatever delights your taste buds and serve them with chutney, pickles, creamy butter and thick curd. The renowned Paranthe Wali Gali in Chandani Chowk, Old Delhi, quite literally translates to the lane of flatbreads. According to the loyal patrons of this lane, the first shop, established by Pandit Gaya Prasad Shiv Charan Paranthewala in 1872, laid the foundation for a rich culinary history.

By the 1960s and 70s, several other paratha shops had sprung up in the vicinity, all driven by a common goal—to offer a hearty meal to travellers, refugees and merchants. This lane then became synonymous with affordable, satisfying meals. A leisurely stroll down this busy lane reveals three more prominent establishments—Pandit Kanhaiyalal Durga Prasad Dixit's shop from 1875, Pandit Dayanand Shivcharan's from 1882 and Pandit Baburam Devidayal Paranthewala's from 1886. All share a family lineage, with generations dedicated to serving delectable parathas to food enthusiasts.

Today, people from far and wide flock to this lane, brushing shoulders with fellow food lovers, shoppers and content creators. After navigating the labyrinthine streets, they eventually find their way to their favourite paratha shop. What's intriguing, though, is the method of cooking—these parathas are deep-fried in small, heavy cast iron pans, using ghee or oil. The range of fillings is extensive, from the standard potatoes and cauliflower to exotic choices like bananas, apples and rabdi.

In 2022, the Bulgaria-based food website, Taste Atlas, recognized our humble paratha as one of the top five street foods in the world.[1] It's no surprise that the fans of this stuffed bread extend far beyond our borders.

In the heart of Delhi's Moolchand area, people line up in the dead of night to relish piping-hot parathas cooked on flat tawas. Some might argue that in the wee hours, it's the lovers, students or partygoers who stand before these wooden carts or get the plates to enjoy their parathas in the comfort of their cars. For a few, it might even be a romantic evening with parathas accompanied by the soulful tunes of Mohammed Rafi.

In the realm of stuffed parathas, we mustn't overlook Punjab, where a similar delight is known as Amritsari kulcha, cooked in a tandoor rather than on a flat pan. With a crispy exterior and a soft interior, it hails from Amritsar but is savoured in many parts of India. In Delhi, it often goes by the name 'chur chur naan'. To clarify, Amritsari kulcha is distinct from the kulche and chole found on the streets of Delhi. The secret lies in the smoky flavour imparted by the tandoor and the intricate process of dough preparation, similar to that of the puff pastry or croissant. Layers are created through kneading, adding ghee and folding the dough multiple times. It is then shaped into small balls and stuffed with various fillings like onions, potatoes and cauliflower before being baked in the tandoor.

One such kulcha vendor (and my favourite) is Pehalwan Kulchewala in Amritsar in Nimak Mandi. With people queuing up outside, they start making this crispy bread at 7 a.m. and by 2 p.m., they wrap up. The masala has a distinctive tang, which is only accentuated by the sprinkling of coriander seeds and fresh coriander leaves on top of the bread before baking it. You might overlook the sign outside the shop, which has turned black from years of exposure to smoke, but the crowd of people will lead you to the enticing aroma of the kulchas. The story of the shop goes back to 1952, when Pehalwan Atma Ram, a professional wrestler, around 60 at the time, took the concept of the Peshawari khameeri roti (sourdough naan) and turned it around to create the Amritsari naan. Since sourdough wasn't suitable for the warm climate of north India, he used maida dough and stuffed it with boiled potatoes to present it as a whole meal. The combination of chana and tamarind-onion chutney was added later.

In culinary history, we find intriguing references to the beloved paratha that challenge conventional wisdom. *Punjab Under the Sultans* by Bakhshish Singh Nijjar, a publication from 1979 that spans India's history from 1000–1526 CE, sheds light on the deep-seated fondness for parathas in Punjab, enjoyed not only by Muslim nobles but also by Hindu aristocrats. In the Kannada prose *Vaddaradhane* (920 CE) by Shivakotiacharya, the term 'paratha' makes its appearance, indicating its presence in the culinary landscape of that era.[2]

To trace the etymology of the term, we journey back to Sanskrit. The word finds its origin in 'parat' and 'aata', referring to layers of dough. An enlightening reference comes from the 12th-century Sanskrit encyclopaedia *Manasollasa*, compiled by Someshvara III, a Western Chalukya king reigning in present-day Karnataka. This book vividly describes a flatbread crafted from wheat flour, jaggery and gram paste—a culinary innovation that laid the foundation for regional favourites like puran poli in Maharashtra and Gujarat. The text also explores other stuffed wheat flatbreads such as vestika, manda/mandaka and polika, the latter evolving into the savoury angarapolika.[3] Centuries later, the Gujarati text *Varanaka Samuchaya* (1520 CE) highlighted the popularity of spicy flatbreads like methi thepla, relished with refreshing raita.[4] But beyond its history, my understanding of the paratha came from a much simpler, more personal source—my grandmother, at our dining table. It was 2017 or 2018, and we were savouring bites of paratha with mango pickle and jaggery. Out of nowhere, she asked, 'Sadaf, you talk so much about history, but do you know why it's called paratha?' I was stumped—I didn't have an answer. She smiled and explained, 'It's because it means *parat aur aata*— layered dough.' That simple explanation felt like a revelation, one of those moments that tied the food on my plate to its name, its essence and its story.

While the Mughals undoubtedly added their distinctive twist to the paratha, it's uncertain whether they had any involvement in the creation of the Calcutta 'Moglai' paratha. A delectable delight, this paratha stands out with its predominant ingredients—finely chopped onions expertly blended with ginger garlic paste, generous quantities of diced green chillies and fresh cilantro leaves. This vibrant mixture is skilfully fried to create a flavourful masala. The magic unfolds as this tantalizing stuffing is spread across a thinly rolled maida sheet on a tawa, followed by the addition of a beaten egg. The paratha is then deftly folded, fried to perfection on both sides and served with a delicately spiced turmeric-based alu curry.

In his article, Sumit Paul talks about how the Mughlai paratha made its debut during the reign of Jehangir, who grew weary of ordinary parathas with 'qeema' (not to be confused with 'kheema', which is a corrupted form of the Arabic 'qeema').[5]

In pursuit of culinary innovation, Jehangir entrusted his cook, Adil Hafiz Usman, with a challenge. He granted Usman a mere ten days to devise something extraordinary. On the ninth day, Usman unveiled the 'zabir-fala' or 'anda-roti' (where 'zabir' signifies egg and 'fala' translates to bun in Pehlavi). This creation, known as the Mughlai paratha, delighted Jehangir to such an extent that he bestowed upon Usman a generous reward of 1001 gold coins.

Usman's culinary legacy hails from Burdwan, which is situated in present-day West Bengal. Interestingly, he chose not to disclose the complete recipe for the Mughlai paratha and reserved that knowledge for his son. As Burdwan emerged as the Mughal empire's official revenue-collection centre for Bengal during Shah Jahan's era, eateries specializing in Mughlai cuisine began to flourish.

Usman's son, Farogh, embarked on a journey of culinary experimentation with Mughlai parathas in Burdwan, while carefully guarding the secret recipe. As his descendants ventured into the world of culinary arts in 19th-century Calcutta, the Mughlai parathas became an intrinsic part of the city's culinary heritage.

To this day, I have yet to meet someone who does not like a good stuffed paratha—it is what makes breakfast special, long journeys special and the first thing one orders at a dhaba. There are endless ways to make it, with every state adding its own twist.

Home-Made Potato (Aloo) Paratha

Ingredients

For the Dough:
Whole wheat flour (atta): 2 cups
Water: As required to knead the dough
Salt: A pinch (optional)
Ghee or oil for frying the parathas

For the Filling:
Potatoes, medium, boiled, peeled and mashed: 3–4
Green chillies, finely chopped: 2
1-inch ginger, grated
Red chilli powder: ½ tsp
Garam masala: ½ tsp
Cumin seeds: ½ tsp
Fresh coriander leaves (cilantro), finely chopped: A handful
Dried mango powder: ½ tsp
Salt to taste

Steps

For the Dough:
1. In a large bowl, mix the whole wheat flour with a pinch of salt.
2. Slowly add water to make a smooth and pliable dough. The dough should be neither too hard nor too soft.
3. Cover the dough and let it rest for at least 20–30 minutes.

For the Filling:
1. In a mixing bowl, combine the mashed potatoes and all the other filling ingredients. Mix everything well until you get a smooth and uniform mixture.

2. Check the seasoning and adjust it according to your taste.

Making the Parathas:
1. After the dough has rested, divide it into equal-sized balls.
2. Take a ball of dough and roll it out a bit. Place a good amount of the potato filling in the centre.
3. Gather the edges of the dough and seal the filling inside. Flatten it gently with your fingers.
4. Dust it with some flour and roll it out gently to the size of a regular roti or chapati. Ensure the filling spreads evenly.
5. Heat a tawa or griddle and place the rolled paratha on it. Cook on one side until you see tiny bubbles.
6. Flip the paratha and apply some ghee or oil. Once the bottom side has golden spots, flip it again and apply ghee or oil to the other side.
7. Cook both sides until they have nice golden-brown spots and are well-cooked.

Serving:
Serve the parathas hot with plain curd, pickle and butter. Some also enjoy it with a side of fresh salad or raita.

Notes: The key to a good aloo paratha lies in its filling. Ensure the potatoes are not watery. It's best to boil them until they are just done and not overcooked. Adjust the spices according to your preference. Use ghee for frying for an authentic taste.

OTHER VERSIONS OF STUFFED PARATHAS

1. **Aloo paratha:** Stuffed with spicy mashed potatoes; this is perhaps the most popular of all.
2. **Gobi paratha:** Stuffed with grated cauliflower seasoned with various spices.

3. **Paneer paratha:** Filled with crumbled or grated paneer (Indian cottage cheese) mixed with spices.

4. **Mooli paratha:** It is stuffed with spicy grated radish, sometimes with radish leaves.

5. **Methi paratha:** These parathas are made using fresh fenugreek leaves mixed directly into the dough. Sometimes, they can also be used as stuffing.

6. **Pyaz paratha:** Made with a spicy onion filling.

7. **Palak paratha:** Incorporated with a stuffing made of spiced spinach paste or sometimes mixed directly into the dough.

8. **Keema paratha:** Popular among non-vegetarians, this is stuffed with minced meat (usually mutton or chicken) that's been cooked with spices.

9. **Peas paratha:** Filled with a mixture of mashed or coarsely ground green peas spiced up with seasonings.

10. **Dal paratha:** Stuffed with cooked and spiced lentils, often using leftover dal from a previous meal.

11. **Egg paratha:** For those who eat eggs, this involves breaking an egg over the half-cooked paratha, folding it in and cooking it further.

12. **Cheese paratha:** A modern twist to traditional parathas, filled with cheese, often combined with other ingredients like spinach, corn or paneer.

13. **Sattu paratha:** Popular in the state of Bihar, it's stuffed with roasted gram flour mixed with spices.

14. **Mixed vegetable paratha:** A mix of various vegetables like carrots, peas and beans, finely chopped or grated, are seasoned and used as filling.

15. **Coconut paratha:** A sweet paratha made with freshly grated coconut mixed with jaggery or sugar.

16. **Gur paratha:** A sweet version stuffed with jaggery, often seasoned with fennel seeds and cardamom.

Amritsari Kulcha

For the Dough:
All-purpose flour: 2 cups
Yogurt: ¼ cup
Baking powder: 1 tsp
Baking soda: ¼ tsp
Sugar: 1 tsp
Salt: ½ tsp (or to taste)
Water: As needed for kneading
Butter or ghee for brushing

For the Filling:
Potatoes, boiled and mashed: 3 medium-sized
Coriander seeds, toasted and crushed: 1 tbsp
Cumin seeds, toasted and crushed: 1 tbsp
Onions, finely chopped: 2
Green chillies, chopped: 2–3
Fresh coriander leaves, chopped: ¼ cup
Dried mango powder: 1 tsp
Salt to taste

Steps

1. In a mixing bowl, combine all-purpose flour, baking powder, baking soda, sugar and salt. Add curd and mix well. Gradually add water and knead into a soft and smooth dough. Cover the dough with a damp cloth and let it rest for 1–2 hours.

2. In a separate bowl, mix mashed potatoes with crushed coriander seeds, crushed cumin seeds, chopped onions, green chillies, fresh coriander leaves, dried mango powder and salt until evenly combined.

3. Divide the dough into small portions and flatten each portion slightly. Take a portion of the potato stuffing and place it in the centre of the flattened dough. Bring the edges together to seal the stuffing inside, and gently roll it into a round or oval shape using a rolling pin.

4. Preheat a tawa or oven on a high flame. Place the rolled kulcha on the hot tawa and cook on one side until bubbles start to appear. Flip and cook the other side, pressing gently with a kitchen towel or spatula. Alternatively, cook the kulcha in a tandoor or an oven at high heat until it turns golden brown.

5. Once cooked, brush the kulcha with butter or ghee. Serve hot with chole (chickpea curry), raita and pickled onions.

Cauliflower (Gobi) Paratha

Ingredients

Turmeric powder: ¼ tsp
Red chilli powder: ½ tsp
Coriander powder: ½ tsp
Garam masala: ¼ tsp
Cumin seeds: ½ tsp
Carom seeds (optional): ½ tsp
Salt to taste

Steps

1. Dry roast the cumin seeds and carom seeds (if using) in a pan over medium heat until they release their aroma. Let them cool completely.

2. Combine the roasted seeds with turmeric powder, red chilli powder, coriander powder, garam masala and salt.

3. Mix thoroughly to create a uniform blend.

4. Store the blend in an airtight container in a cool, dry place.
5. The spice blend can be stored for up to 3-4 months in an airtight container to maintain its freshness and potency.
6. To make the cauliflower paratha, please refer to the detailed paratha-making steps above. Use this spice blend with finely grated cauliflower to prepare an amazing and flavourful paratha.
7. Enjoy it hot with butter and a side of curd and pickle.

COTTAGE CHEESE (PANEER) PARATHA

INGREDIENTS

Red chilli powder: ½ tsp
Garam masala: ¼ tsp
Cumin powder: ½ tsp
Dried mango powder: ¼ tsp
Salt to taste

STEPS

1. Measure out the red chilli powder, garam masala, cumin powder, dried mango powder and salt.
2. Combine all the ingredients in a mixing bowl and mix thoroughly until well blended.
3. Store the blend in an airtight container in a cool, dry place.
4. The spice blend can be stored for up to 3–4 months in an airtight container to maintain its freshness and flavour.
5. To make the paneer paratha, please refer to the detailed paratha-making steps above. Use this spice blend with crumbled paneer to prepare an amazing and flavourful paratha. Enjoy it hot with butter and a side of curd and pickle.

Radish (Mooli) Paratha

Ingredients

Red chilli powder: ½ tsp
Coriander powder: ½ tsp
Carom seeds: ½ tsp
Fennel seeds, crushed: ½ tsp
Green chillies, chopped: 1
Salt to taste

Steps

1. Dry roast the carom seeds and fennel seeds until they release a fragrant aroma. Let them cool completely.
2. Combine the roasted seeds with red chilli powder, coriander powder, chopped green chillies and salt.
3. Mix thoroughly to create a uniform blend.
4. Store the blend in a cool, dry place for up to 3–4 months in an airtight container to maintain its freshness and flavour.

Note: Make sure to squeeze out the excess water from the grated radish before mixing in the spice blend.

Fenugreek (Methi) Paratha

Ingredients

Red chilli powder: ½ tsp
Turmeric powder: ¼ tsp
Carom seeds: ½ tsp
Black sesame seeds: 1 tsp
Garlic, chopped: 1 clove
Salt to taste

1. Dry roast the carom seeds and black sesame seeds until fragrant. Let them cool.
2. Mix the roasted seeds with red chilli powder, turmeric powder, chopped garlic, and salt.
3. Blend everything together to create an even mix.
4. Store in an airtight container for up to 3 months.

ONION PARATHA (PYAZ KA PARATHA)

INGREDIENTS

Red chilli powder: ½ tsp
Garam masala: ¼ tsp
Cumin seeds: ½ tsp
Chaat masala: ¼ tsp
Dried mint leaves: 1 tsp
Salt to taste

STEPS

1. Dry roast the cumin seeds until aromatic. Allow them to cool.
2. Combine with red chilli powder, garam masala, chaat masala, dried mint leaves, and salt.
3. Mix well to create a uniform blend.
4. Store in an airtight container for up to 3–4 months.

Minced Meat (Mutton Keema) Paratha

Ingredients

Red chilli powder: ½ tsp
Garam masala: ½ tsp
Coriander powder: ½ tsp
Cumin powder: ½ tsp
Fenugreek leaves, crushed: 1 tsp
Mint leaves, chopped: 1 tbsp
Salt to taste

Steps

1. Combine red chilli powder, garam masala, coriander powder, cumin powder, crushed kasuri methi and salt.
2. Mix thoroughly. Add the chopped mint leaves to the blend just before marinating.
3. Store the dry blend in an airtight container.

Peas (Matar) Paratha

Ingredients

Red chilli powder: ½ tsp
Garam masala: ¼ tsp
Dried mango powder: ¼ tsp
Pomegranate seeds: ½ tsp
Cumin powder, roasted: ½ tsp
Salt to taste

Steps

1. Combine red chilli powder, garam masala, dried mango powder, crushed pomegranate seeds and salt.

2. Add roasted cumin powder and mix well.
3. Store in an airtight container. The blend can last for 3–4 months in a cool, dry place.

LENTIL (DAL) PARATHA

INGREDIENTS

Red chilli powder: ½ tsp
Asafoetida: A pinch
Garam masala: ¼ tsp
Cumin seeds: ½ tsp
Carom seeds: ¼ tsp
Garlic, chopped: 1 clove
Salt to taste

STEPS

1. Dry roast the cumin seeds and ajwain until aromatic. Let them cool.
2. Combine all the spices including asafoetida, red chilli powder, garam masala and chopped garlic.
3. Mix well.
4. Store the blend in an airtight container.
5. It can be stored for up to 3–4 months.

MURTABAK/EGG PARATHA

INGREDIENTS

For the Dough:
Maida flour: 500 gm
Sugar: 1 tsp
Milk: ¾ cup
Salt: 1 tsp (or to taste)

Baking soda: ½ tsp

Onions, medium, chopped: 2

Chicken, minced: 500 gm

Ginger garlic paste 1 tbsp

Turmeric powder: ½ tsp

Salt to taste

Red chilli powder: 1 tsp

Red chilli, crushed: ½ tsp

Cumin seeds, roasted and crushed: 1½ tsp

Green chillies, chopped: 2–3

Eggs: 5

Black pepper powder: 1 tsp

Tomato, medium, de-seeded and chopped: 1

Green onion, chopped: 1 cup

Fresh coriander, chopped: ½ cup

STEPS

Prepare the Dough:

1. In a mixing bowl, combine maida flour, sugar, salt, baking soda, and milk.

2. Mix until a soft dough forms. Divide the dough into lemon-sized balls.

3. Coat each ball lightly with oil and let it rest for 1 hour.

Prepare the Stuffing:

1. Cook Minced Chicken: Heat 1 teaspoon of oil in a pan over medium heat. Add the minced chicken and cook for about 5 minutes until lightly browned.

2. Add ginger garlic paste, turmeric powder, red chilli powder, crushed red chilli, cumin seeds (roasted and crushed), and salt. Cook for another 3-4 minutes until the chicken is well seasoned and any raw aroma is gone.

3. Add the chopped onions, tomatoes, green chillies, green onions, and fresh coriander. Stir well and let it cook for about 5-6 minutes until the vegetables soften.
4. In another pan, scramble the eggs with a little oil and black pepper powder. Once scrambled, add them to the chicken mixture. Mix thoroughly and set aside.
5. Shape the murtabak
6. Take each dough ball and roll it out on a floured surface into a thin flat sheet.
7. Place a handful of the prepared minced chicken mixture in the center.
8. Fold the dough from all four sides to make a square-shaped murtabak.
9. Cook the murtabak.
10. Heat oil in a skillet over medium heat.
11. Place the murtabak in the skillet, cooking each side for 3-4 minutes until golden brown and crispy.
12. Apply a little oil around and over the murtabak while cooking to enhance crispiness.
13. Once cooked, drain on a paper towel.
14. The crispy murtabak pairs well with chutneys or gravies and makes a perfect hearty meal.

CHEESE PARATHA

INGREDIENTS

Red chilli flakes: ½ tsp
Dried berries powder: ½ tsp
Salt to taste
Garlic, chopped and fried: 2 tbsp
Spring onions (green part), chopped: ½ cup
Black pepper powder: ½ tsp
Coriander, chopped: 2 tbsp

STEPS

1. Combine red chilli flakes, dried berries powder, salt, black pepper powder and chopped coriander in a mixing bowl.
2. Mix thoroughly to ensure even distribution of flavours.
3. Store in an airtight container.

GRAM FLOUR PARATHA

INGREDIENTS

Whole gram flour, roasted: 1½ cups
Nigella seeds: 2 tsp
Cumin seeds: 1 tsp
Roasted fennel seeds: ½ tsp
Green chilli, chopped: 2
Ginger, chopped: 2tsp
Onion, chopped: ¼ cup
Coriander, chopped: A handful
Lemon juice: 3 tbsp
Mango pickle, chopped: 4 tbsp
Mustard oil: 1 tbsp
Salt to taste

STEPS

1. Dry roast the cumin seeds, fennel seeds, and let them cool.
2. Combine all the ingredients, including gram flour, nigella seeds, chopped green chilli, ginger, onion, coriander, mint leaves and salt. Mix thoroughly.
3. Store in an airtight container or use it fresh.

Mixed Vegetable Paratha

Ingredients

Red chilli powder: ½ tsp
Garam masala: ¼ tsp
Turmeric powder: ¼ tsp
Coriander powder: ½ tsp
Spinach, chopped: ¼ cup
Pomegranate seeds, crushed: ½ tsp
Salt to taste

Steps

1. Dry roast the turmeric powder and allow it to cool.
2. Combine red chilli powder, garam masala, coriander powder, chopped spinach, and crushed pomegranate seeds.
3. Mix well. Store the blend in an airtight container.

Sweet Kobbary Andhra-Style Coconut Paratha

Ingredients

Green cardamom powder: ¼ tsp
Fresh coconut, grated: 1 cup
Jaggery, grated or powdered: ¾ cup
Cinnamon powder: A pinch
Pistachios, chopped: 1 tbsp
Mixed nuts, roasted: 2 tsp

Steps

1. Combine cardamom powder, cinnamon powder, grated coconut, jaggery, roasted mixed nuts and chopped pistachios.

2. Mix thoroughly until all the ingredients are well combined.
3. Store in an airtight container, for up to 2 months.

Punjabi Jaggery (Gur) Paratha

Ingredients

Jaggery powder/jaggery, finely chopped: ¾ cup
Cardamom powder: ¼ tsp
Almonds, crushed: 15–20
Coconut, desiccated: ¼ cup
Sesame seeds: 1 tsp
Fennel seeds, crushed: ½ tsp

Steps

1. Combine cardamom powder, crushed fennel seeds, jaggery powder, crushed almonds, desiccated coconut and sesame seeds.
2. Mix thoroughly. Store the mixture in an airtight container.

Sugar Paratha

Ingredients

Sugar: ¾ cup
Green cardamom powder: ½ tsp
Coconut powder: 2 tbsp
Poppy seeds, roasted: 1 tsp
Nutmeg powder: A pinch
Saffron: A pinch
Salt: A pinch

1. In a bowl, combine sugar, green cardamom powder, nutmeg powder, saffron, salt, coconut powder and roasted poppy seeds.
2. Mix until all the ingredients are well combined.

Mawa Paratha

Ingredients

Mawa, grated: ¾ cup
Fennel seeds: 1½ tbsp
Mixed nuts, chopped: 2 tbsp
Coconut powder: 2 tbsp
Nutmeg powder: ¼ tsp
Green cardamom powder: ½ tsp
Dried rose petals, crushed: 2 tbsp
Jaggery, chopped: ¼ cup

Steps

1. Combine grated mawa, fennel seeds, chopped mixed nuts, green cardamom powder, dried rose petals, chopped jaggery, coconut powder and nutmeg powder in a bowl.
2. Mix all the ingredients thoroughly until well blended.

PICKLE

⌒

FOR ME, HERITAGE AND PICKLES ARE ALMOST THE SAME. Both carry a sense of preservation, patience and tradition that connects us to our roots. Just as a pickle preserves the essence of fresh ingredients, heritage safeguards the culture, stories and memories passed down through generations. Both need time, care and patience to mature, and when done right, they become richer with layers of complexity and depth.

Pickles offer a taste of traditional recipes, a glimpse into the past, much like heritage allows us to revisit old customs and legacies.

To me, they are both reminders that some things in life are worth preserving—not just for ourselves but for the generations that follow. Both are a celebration of what makes us unique and rooted.

The Indian subcontinent is a place of celebration, and every celebration is connected with stories, folklore, myths and anecdotes. Like every food, pickles have stories too. In our subcontinent; if a woman in her youth asks for a lot of pickles, it often could mean that the girl is pregnant and hence craving for something *chatpata*. There isn't a single English word to translate chatpata; it is a mix of spicy, sour and tangy.

When I think about pickles, particularly in the sweltering heat of summer, I think of my mother, a master at the craft, who expertly blends raw mangoes with mustard oil, chillies and colourful spices. From the Chinese salting their vegetables to the Mesopotamians immersing theirs in vinegar, the science of pickling has been perfected over thousands of years and is still used in our kitchens today.

More than just a method of preserving food, pickling is an ancient practice steeped in culture and tradition. It is, at its core, a defence against time. When bacteria, yeasts and moulds, the unseen enemies, cause fresh food to spoil, an acidic environment—created through brine, vinegar or citrus juice—halts their advance. This process prevents the growth of harmful microorganisms and preserves the integrity of the food, ensuring flavours endure long after the harvest season. Yet, of all the global variations, nothing compares to the pickles of the Indian subcontinent. They carry with them the bold heat of mustard oil, the smoky intensity of toasted spices and the rich history of family traditions passed down from one generation to the next.

As I've come to appreciate over time, along with preserving food, pickles also preserve memories, flavours and our connection to home. They perfectly embody the essence of preserving memories—for instance, when I lost my mother, it was her mango pickles that calmed me in my solace. Before this, I had never made aged pickles—I had always relied on my ammi. When we lost her, I wanted to recreate the same pickle, but I failed miserably. I rang up my aunts, and while one of them said she had never made pickles, another gave me the recipe. Abbi, who used to work with ammi in making pickles, knew the process but not the ingredients or their ratio. Naturally, everything was then left to be analysed and figured out by me. I started by getting 3 kg of sliced mangoes and figuring out the recipes from books, online videos and people with expertise. Even though the pickle turned out good, it was not the one ammi used to make. In the process, I failed to recreate the same flavour but succeeded in learning how to make pickles with care, attention and patience. Another pickle ammi used to make was that of flat beans (sem) and potatoes. Many of her recipes are lost, but they are now replaced by my ratio. The pickles will never have the same flavour, but they will keep her memory alive.

Salman Rushdie's *Midnight's Children* comes to mind when reflecting on pickling as more than just a culinary process. In the novel, the protagonist, Saleem Sinai speaks of his own special blends of pickles and refers to the 'chutnification of history', a striking metaphor that likens the pickling of food to the preservation and blending of time. As he stirs his spices and immerses ingredients in brine or oil, he is simultaneously digging into his own past, bottling fragments of memories, moments and histories. The pungent smells and the sharp tastes all work in concert to trigger recollections, helping him recapture the events that shaped his life. Saleem reflects how history, much like pickles, is subjective—a blend of flavours, spices and interpretations, each unique to the person crafting it. I have always heard stories from people around me that the mood or mindset of the person preparing the pickle can influence its taste and preservation. If someone is angry or upset while making it, the pickle might spoil; maybe this reflects the idea that positive energy should go into making food, but I would think this idea of mindset is not only for pickle but anything that you do.

The other common myth suggests that the success of a batch of pickles depends on the alignment of stars and planets. Some households begin the pickling process on auspicious days to ensure the pickle ferments correctly and lasts longer. I am unsure about the facts or the logic, but this is one of those customs and traditions.

Something that I believe should be scrapped but still persists is the myth in some traditions that women should not make pickles during their menstrual cycle, as it is thought to spoil the batch. This belief, though entirely unscientific, stems from historical taboos and superstitions surrounding menstruation. What fascinated me most during my discussions with the older women of Amritsar while writing this book was how, in many communities, pickling sessions served as informal spaces for women to exchange knowledge, discuss family matters and share folklore. These gatherings became hubs for preserving not just food, but also social bonds and cultural cohesion.

'Can everything that grows under the sun be pickled?' asks Pooja Pilai in her story for *Indian Express*:[1]

> Even a cursory survey of Indian pickles indicates that this may indeed be the case. Unripe mangoes? Of course. Limes and lemons? But obviously. These are some of the most popular types of pickles that the Indian subcontinent produces, consumes and exports. Then there are the only slightly less popular pickles made of red chillies, green chillies, Indian gooseberry (*amla*), garlic and some that use a medley of seasonal vegetables, such as the staple north Indian winter pickle made of cauliflower, carrots and turnips (*gobhi, gaajar, shalgam ka achar*).

Usually, as a practice, the pickles that last long and through all seasons are made in the summer—when there is less humidity, and the sun can do its job in cooking the vegetables, fruits or meat. Fresh ingredients like carrots, etc. are usually made in the winter and have to be consumed quickly or in the same season. Age-old wisdom and basic logic will tell you to not pickle anything in the monsoon. Rain will spoil any pickle you make with water and humidity. At its core, achar is about preservation, and with India's vast regional diversity, people pickle whatever local produce or meat is readily available.

Jan Davison in her book, *Pickles, A Global History*, writes, 'Throughout history, pickling has been relied upon both to conserve foods and add to their savour.' While pickles were an intrinsic part of dining among the elite in imperial Rome and medieval Baghdad, pickling provided essential food for the masses as well. In ancient China, pickled vegetables sustained workers building the Great Wall, and, in much of Europe, pickled fish, cabbage and cucumbers once formed the mainstay of the diet —so much so that the Lithuanians created Roguszys, the god of pickles.[2]

She further writes:

In India, Pakistan and Bangladesh, pickles are prepared in mustard or sesame oil combined with salt and spices. The most popular pickles prepared this way, and exported the world over is mango . . . Often, the fruit and vegetables are salted and dried out in the sun before being packed in jars with spices and oil. The jars of pickles are placed back in the sun for up to one month, which aids preservation: the light and heat destroy mould spores and bacteria.

Madhur Jaffrey's *An Invitation to Indian Cooking* provides a fascinating glimpse into how pickles can become deeply ingrained in family traditions. Jaffrey's grandmother often brought her home-made pickles on long car journeys to the summer resorts of Simla and Mussoorie. As Jaffrey describes, 'When tossing and turning at the never-ending and ever-climbing hairpin bends made our taste buds turn green,' her grandmother would magically appear with a small brown crockpot filled with her lime pickles. These pickles were sour, pungent and dark with age. Taking just a small bite would initially pucker the mouth, but the aftertaste left a feeling of complete refreshment.[3]

In *A Historical Dictionary of Indian Food*, K.T. Achaya delves into the history of pickles in India. He cites the work of Nemichandra, who, in his Lilavati (around 1170 CE), describes serving King Nilapati a variety of pickles made from fruits, vegetables and roots, all flavoured with camphor. Achaya also mentions the *Lingapurana of Gurulinga Desika* (1594 CE), from modern-day Karnataka, which lists 50 different types of pickles.

Additionally, the Gujarati text, *Varanaka-Samuchaya* (1520 CE), details pickles such as the distinctive athanu, goondas and chundo, known for their sweet-sour flavour and the addition of cardamom and cloves.[4]

The simplest pickle that one can make is that of lemon, which my bade mama makes the best bottles of (and I often end up taking some from him). The simplest way to make a lemon pickle is to wash, dry and toss the lemon with salt in proportion to its weight, sun-dry and then bottle it. This is the simple version, but if you want to be creative, you can slice the lemons and include sugar, jaggery powder, chilli, asafoetida, turmeric, fennel seeds and whatever else you enjoy the most. The simple one usually goes wonderful with khichdi or is given to those who feel nauseated or have motion sickness. I remember, as a kid, every time my family travelled long distances, they would always keep some nimbu achar for me.

But what is the science? Over a phone conversation, Krish Ashok emphasizes the importance of dehydration in the pickling process, explaining that removing water is crucial for preserving food. India's intense sun or even simple fans can be effective tools for achieving this. Dehydration helps to inhibit the growth of bacteria and fungi. Additionally, acidic environments, such as those created by vinegar or citric acid (naturally found in citrus fruits), are hostile to microbes.

To prevent oxidation, Ashok recommends reducing oxygen levels. This is where oil comes into play. Pickled raw mangoes submerged in oil can last for several years, though not indefinitely, as the oil itself may eventually become rancid. He clarified that the term 'probiotic' refers to the presence of beneficial microbes. He highlighted that pickles intended to last for decades must have a sterile environment, free from any microbes.

Pickling has been a part of human history for thousands of years, but the word 'pickle' itself made its debut in the English language around the 15th century. Initially, as noted by the *Oxford English Dictionary*, it referred to a spicy sauce served alongside meat. Over time, the term evolved to describe a salty or acidic liquid used to preserve fruits and vegetables. Eventually, the process of soaking food in this brine became known as 'pickling' and the preserved product was called a 'pickle' or 'pickled' food.

The word 'pickle' is derived from the Middle Dutch *pekel*, which lexicographer Grant Barrett explains as meaning 'to prick or pierce'.[5] This interpretation metaphorically reflects the sensation one experiences when tasting the spicy and salty brine. Although achar (derived from the Persian word Āchār, meaning preserved or salted meats, pickles or fruits in salt, vinegar, honey or syrup) might appear to be a simple side dish, its role in South Asian cuisine has endured for generations.

The phrase 'in a pickle', commonly understood today as being in a predicament, gained popularity in the 1600s after appearing in William Shakespeare's *The Tempest*. However, Shakespeare likely used it to convey a sense of intoxication rather than a dilemma. How the phrase shifted to its modern meaning remains somewhat mysterious.

Lexicographer Kory Stamper suggests that its figurative use may have originated as early as 1562 when John Heywood's poem used 'pickle' to describe a predicament or an undesirable situation, contributing to the broader linguistic development of the term.[6] Additionally, a Dutch phrase from 1561, loosely translated to 'sitting in the pickle', could imply being in an embarrassing or disagreeable situation, though its exact meaning remains debated.[7] In the subcontinent, *achar daalna* translates to 'to pickle something'. However, in Hindi idiomatic usage, it refers to neglecting something, leaving it unused, or allowing it to spoil due to carelessness or disuse.

Growing up, achar was more than just a side dish at our table. While ammi's pickles were always delicious, I was particularly fond of the ones my aunt, Hoori phuphi, made in Ranchi. I eagerly looked forward to visiting her every other month—not just for her company but also for her incredible pickles. She would always have a few small bottles out on the table, but the real treasures—the larger jars—were carefully stored away in her *kothri*.* During a visit in March 2024, she remembered how much I loved her mango pickle and gave me a few small bottles to take home.

Achars offer a spectrum of flavours, ranging from sweet to spicy and salty, based on the ingredients used. For instance, raw mangoes, with their naturally sour taste, lend themselves equally well to both sweet and spicy variations. However, they are not limited to just mango or lemon; pickles are made throughout the country using diverse ingredients. Be it mesu pickle from Sikkim, axone pickle from Nagaland, desert berries beans achar from Rajasthan or the fish pickles thriving in coastal regions—the variety is immense.

Pickle is like life—it takes time to reach its best. Rush it, and it may get spoiled, or worse, completely ruined. Patience is the secret to both, letting flavours and moments unfold in their own time. Pickle-making is an art—one that can't be rushed or modernized with shortcuts. Not everyone can easily master it either. Being such an ancient tradition, it's also surrounded by folklore and myths. There are beliefs that making achar in the first year of marriage can cause the relationship to sour or that accepting achar for free can harm friendships unless you pay at least a token amount. Some even say that a broken pickle jar signals bad luck or that stirring pickles with a knife can bring family discord. It's interesting how many superstitions are tied to achar, but what remains undisputed is that it enhances meals and carries memories passed down through generations. The process of pickling, then, becomes a powerful symbol of how we preserve time itself, immortalizing moments through taste and memory.

---

* Storeroom.

FRUIT PICKLES

MANGO PICKLE (AAM KA ACHAR)

INGREDIENTS

Raw mango, chopped: 2 kg
Fenugreek: 100 gm
Nigella seeds: 50 gm
Fennel seeds: 100 gm
Turmeric powder: 50 gm
Mustard oil: 1½ l
Chilli powder : To taste
Salt to taste

STEPS

1. First, cube the mangoes and then dry them.
2. Once you have dried the mangoes, combine all the spices in a bowl. Add oil and salt to the bowl before mixing the ingredients together.
3. Next, add the dried mango chunks to the bowl and mix well to ensure they are coated in the spices and oil.
4. Now, place the coated mango chunks in a completely dry glass jar. Pour the remaining spices and oil mixture from the bowl into the glass jar.
5. Seal the jar. You will need to store the pickle jar in a dry place for 7 days until it is ready.
6. Serve the mango pickle with paratha, roti or rice. More unconventionally, add it to a plate of Maggi.

Mamidi Avakaya (Andhra Pradesh)

Ingredients

Raw green mangoes: 1 kg
Mustard powder: 100 gm
Garlic, peeled (optional), ¼ cup
Red chilli powder: 150 gm
Fenugreek seeds: 1½ tsp
Salt to taste
Oil: 375 ml

Steps

1. Clean the mangoes, remove the pit and cut them into smaller pieces.
2. In a large bowl, place the chopped mangoes and add chilli powder, mustard powder, salt and fenugreek seeds to it. You can also add garlic to this, depending on your preference. Mix well.
3. Now, add the oil to the mixture. Mix well.
4. Transfer the mixture to a dry glass jar. Seal the container properly and leave it unattended in a dry place for 3–4 days.
5. Open the jar and mix the pickle mixture with a dry spoon. By the next day, you should see a layer of oil floating on top of the pickle. This will mean the pickle is now ready to be served.

Rekha Kumari's Bihari-Style Mango Pickle (Aam ka Kucha)

Ingredients

Raw mangoes (tangy and firm): 2–3
Mustard seeds: ¼ cup
Fenugreek seeds: ¼ cup
Fennel seeds: ¼ cup
Salt: ¼ cup (or to taste)
Red chilli powder: ¼ cup (or to taste)
Turmeric powder: ¼ cup
Coriander powder: ¼ cup
Mustard oil (you can adjust the quantity as per your taste)
Sugar (optional but not recommended): 1 tbsp

Steps

1. Wash the raw mangoes thoroughly and pat them dry. Cut the mangoes into very small cubes or grate them.
2. In a pan, dry roast the mustard seeds, fennel seeds and fenugreek seeds until aromatic. Allow them to cool down.
3. Once cooled, grind them coarsely in a mortar and pestle or a spice grinder.
4. In a large mixing bowl, combine the mango cubes or grated mangoes with salt, red chilli powder and turmeric powder. Keep this bowl in the sun for 12–14 hours. Add the coarsely ground spices now.
5. Add the mustard oil and mix everything well so that the mango pieces are well coated with the spices. Let it rest in the sun again for 14–16 hours for the mangoes to unravel its sourness.
6. Transfer the mixture to a clean, dry glass jar. Ensure it is sealed tightly.

7.   You can place the jar in sunlight for a few hours each day for about 2–3 days to enhance the flavours. It helps in marinating the mangoes properly.

8.   After 3–4 days, the pickle is ready to be served. You can store it in the refrigerator for a longer shelf life.

Sun-Dried Mango Pickle
(Magaya Pachadi, Andhra Pradesh)

Ingredients

Raw mango slices: 6
Salt: ½ cup (or to taste)
Red chilli powder: ½ cup
Garlic pods: ¼ cup
Fenugreek powder, roasted: 3 tsp
Turmeric powder: 2 tsp

For tempering:
Sesame oil: ¾ cup
Curry leaves
Dried red chilli: 6
Asafoetida: 3 tbsp
Mustard: 3 tsp
Fenugreek seeds: ¼ tsp

Steps

1.   Clean the mangoes, peel the skin and cut into medium-sized pieces.

2.   Add turmeric and salt to the mangoes in a bowl and mix well. Once the mangoes are coated with it, cover the bowl and leave aside for 3 days.

3.   After 3 days, squeeze the mango slices and separate them from the masala that is left behind.

4. Now, sun-dry the pieces for about 12 hours and sun-dry the masala for roughly an hour.

5. Add the mango slices and the masala to a mixing bowl. Add red chilli powder, garlic pods and roasted fenugreek powder to the mixture. Mix well.

6. In a pan, heat sesame oil. Add mustard, fenugreek seeds, curry leaves, dried red chilli and asafoetida. Mix and turn the heat off.

7. Once the oil mixture cools completely, add it to the dry mango mixture and mix them together.

8. Let the mixture rest in a dry, airtight glass jar for 3 days.

9. After 3 days, the pickle is ready to be served with a hot serving of rice.

MISKUT (GOA)

INGREDIENTS

Raw green mangoes, chopped: 8
Fenugreek seeds: 1 tsp
Sesame oil: 1 cup
Asafoetida: ¼ tsp
Sea salt: ½ cup
Mustard seeds: ¼ cup
Chilli powder: ½ cup
Turmeric powder: 1 tsp

STEPS

1. Cut the mangoes after thoroughly washing and drying them.

2. Add mustard and fenugreek seeds to a pan and dry roast. Remove the spices from the pan and crush them coarsely.

3. Now, heat up some oil in the same pan and add asafoetida. Turn off the heat.
4. Add the crushed spices with chilli powder and salt to the bowl of cubed mangoes. Mix well.
5. Now, add the oil to this mixture after ensuring it has cooled down. Mix again.
6. You will now need to store this mixture in an airtight jar in a dry place for around 2 weeks before it is ready to be consumed.

Baby Mango Pickle (Maavadu/Vadu Mangai, Tamil Nadu and Kerala)

Ingredients

Raw baby mangoes (vadu manga): 1 kg
Red chilli, whole: 30
Turmeric powder: 1 tsp
Fenugreek seeds: 1 tsp
Mustard seeds: 2 tsp
Asafoetida: ¼ tsp
Salt to taste
Curry leaves: 15–20 leaves
Sesame oil: 2 tbsp

Steps

1. Soak the mangoes in salted water. After 2 days, drain the water and dry the mangoes.
2. After drying, marinate the mangoes with chilli and turmeric powder.
3. Heat up the oil and temper it with curry leaves, fenugreek mustard seeds and asafoetida.
4. Add the baby mangoes next and cook them for a couple of minutes. Mix well.

5. After that, take it off the heat and let the mixture cool down.
6. Store the mixture in an airtight jar for 8–10 days. Shake the bottle daily.

Odia Instant Dry Mango Pickle (Ambula Acharo)

Ingredients

Raw mangoes (small and dried): 8
Mustard oil: 2 tbsp
Blend of cumin seeds, nigella, fenugreek, radhuni and fennel seeds (panch phoran): 1 tbsp
Red chillies, whole: 2
Asafoetida
Tamarind paste: 1 tbsp
Mustard seeds: 1 tbsp
Jaggery: 1 cup
Paste of tomato: 1
Turmeric powder: ½ tsp
Red chilli powder: 1 tsp
Cumin powder: 1 tsp
Sugar: Very little, adjust to taste
Salt to taste
Curry leaves

Steps

1. First, soak the mangoes in water for 4 hours. After soaking, boil them for 10 minutes.
2. Heat some oil in a pan. Add panch phoran, red chillies, asafoetida, curry leaves, tamarind paste, mustard seeds and jaggery. Cook until the jaggery melts.
3. Add salt, turmeric, cumin seeds and red chilli powder. Cook on a low flame.

4. Add the tomato paste to the pan. Mix together before adding the boiled mangoes.
5. Add a little bit of sugar and more water, depending on the consistency you prefer.
6. Let the pickle cool down before serving. Store in an airtight container.

Gujarati-Style Instant Pickle
(Aam ka Chunda)

Ingredients

Raw mango, grated: 1
Salt: 1 tsp (or to taste)
Jaggery: 1 cup
Chilli powder: 1 tsp
Cumin powder: 1 tsp

Steps

1. Start by sautéing the grated mangoes over a low flame. After a few minutes, add jaggery and salt.
2. Add chilli and cumin powder once the jaggery begins to melt. Mix everything together.
3. Once the jaggery melts entirely, take the pan off the heat.
4. Once the mixture cools down, transfer the pickle to an airtight container and enjoy with your meals.

Assamese Gooseberry Pickle
(Amlokhir Asar)

Ingredients

Gooseberry: 500 gm
Fennel seeds: 1 tsp
White mustard seeds: 1 tsp
Celery seeds: 1 tsp
Red chilli powder (optional): 1 tsp
Vinegar: ½ cup
Salt to taste
Turmeric powder: 1 tsp
Mustard oil: 1 cup

Steps

1. Clean and chop the gooseberries. Add them to a bowl. Add vinegar and around 2–3 tsp of salt. Mix well and keep aside for 10–12 hours.
2. After letting it rest, drain the excess water. Add them to a bowl.
3. To the bowl of gooseberries, now add turmeric and some salt. Next, spread out the gooseberries and allow them to sun-dry for around 4 hours.
4. Now, mildly roast the spices in a pan and grind them once roasted.
5. Add all the spices to the sun-dried gooseberries along with the chilli powder before finally adding oil to the mixture. Mix well.
6. Let the mixture rest for 3 days before it is ready to serve.

Andhra Gooseberry Pickle (Usiri Uragaya)

Ingredients

Gooseberries, large: 10
Oil: 4 tbsp
Lemon juice: 3 tbsp
Mustard seeds: 2 tsp
Fenugreek seeds: 1 pinch
Red chilli powder: 3 tsp
Turmeric powder: ¼ tsp
Salt: 1 tsp (or to taste)
Garlic clove, large (optional): 1

Steps

1. Wash and dry the gooseberries. You can either chop the gooseberries or make slices in them without cutting them all the way.
2. Meanwhile, blend mustard and fenugreek seeds to form a fine powder.
3. Now fry the gooseberries in oil until they turn slightly golden. You can add the garlic cloves before taking the gooseberries off the heat.
4. Let the pan cool down a little before adding the previously prepared powder, red chilli powder, turmeric and salt.
5. Once the pan has cooled down completely, add the lemon juice. Mix well.
6. After mixing, you can taste the mixture to check for salt. Add more salt as and if required.
7. Transfer the mixture to an airtight glass jar and let it sit for 3 days before using.
8. You can enjoy the pickle with a range of food items, including rice and dosa.

Rajasthani Desert Berries and Beans Pickle (Ker Sangri Achar)

Ingredients

Desert berry (ker): 150 gm
Beans (sangri): 150 gm
Fenugreek seeds: ½ tsp
Fennel seeds: 1½ tsp
Nigella seeds: ½ tsp
Dried mango powder: 1 tsp
Asafoetida: ¼ tsp
Turmeric powder: ½ tsp
Mustard seeds: 2 tsp
Red chilli powder: 1 tsp
Salt to taste
Oil: ¼ cup
Bay leaf: 1

Steps

1. Wash the dried desert berries and beans thoroughly before soaking them in water overnight.
2. The next morning, drain the excess water and boil the desert berries and beans in different pans. Once they are tender, allow them to dry properly.
3. Take a pan and add some oil to it. Add in fenugreek seeds, fennel seeds, asafoetida, nigella seeds and bay leaf once the oil is heated. Reduce the flame when the spices begin to heat up.
4. Add the boiled desert berries and beans. Next, add turmeric, mustard seeds, red chilli powder, dried mango powder and salt. Mix and cook it for a few minutes.
5. After removing the pan from the heat, mix everything again. Now store this mixture in an airtight jar for a few days before serving it.

Bengali, Assamese-Style Jujube Pickle
(Kuler Achar/Bogorir Asar)

Ingredients

Dried jujube: 500 gm
Jaggery: 250 gm
Mustard oil: ½ cup
Cumin seeds: 1 tsp
Coriander seeds: 2 tsp
Aniseeds: 2 tsp
Blend of cumin seeds, nigella, fenugreek, radhuni and Fennel
seeds: 2 tsp
Dried chillies: 3
Chilli powder: 1 tsp
Salt: 2 tsp (or to taste)

Steps

1. Clean the jujube and make small incisions on them.
2. Put the oil in a pan and mildly roast all the spices, except chilli powder and salt. To the same pan of roasted spices, add jaggery with a cup of water.
3. Add in the jujube once the jaggery starts to melt. Mix together.
4. Add in the chilli powder and salt. Now, reduce the heat and stir repeatedly for a few minutes before adding around ¾ cup of water. Stir again for a couple of minutes.
5. The consistency of the syrup should be somewhat runny and not too thick as it will thicken once it is cooled.
6. After removing from heat, wait until the mixture cools down completely before storing in an airtight glass jar. This sweet, hot and tangy pickle is ready to be enjoyed.

Sohphie Pickle (Local seasonal berries pickle, Meghalaya)[8]

Ingredients

Sohphie fruits: 250 gm
Fenugreek seeds, crushed: 1 tsp
Mustard seeds, crushed: 2 tbsp
Turmeric powder: ½ tsp
Red chilli powder: ½ tbsp
Fennel seeds, crushed: ½ tbsp
Salt: 1 tbsp (or to taste)
Mustard oil: ½ cup

Steps

1. Let the sohphie dry for a day after washing it.
2. The next day, combine all the spices and salt in half a portion of oil. Add the sohphie to this mixture and mix thoroughly.
3. Now, deposit the mixture into a dry container. Add the remaining oil to the container, seal the lid and shake the bottle well.
4. Allow the jar to sit in the sun for 10 days and keep shaking the jar occasionally. The pickle can be served once this step is complete.

Orange Tholi Instant Pickle (Kerala)

Ingredients

Orange peel, chopped: 1 cup
Tamarind, small, pulped: 1
Dried red chillies: 2
Red chilli powder: 2 tsp

Asafoetida powder: ¼ tsp
Fenugreek powder: ¼ tsp
Mustard seeds: ¼ tsp
Salt to taste
Sesame oil
Curry leaves

Steps

1. In a pan, heat some oil before adding mustard seeds.
2. Next, add in the curry leaves and dried red chillies when the mustard seeds start to sputter. Let it cook for a minute.
3. Now, shallow fry the orange peel for a minute or two.
4. To the pan, add combined red chilli, fenugreek, turmeric and asafoetida powder. Now, add salt. Stir to mix the ingredients.
5. The last ingredient to be added to the pan is the tamarind pulp. Take the mixture off the heat once the water dries out.
6. Once it has cooled, store it in a dry container.

Deepa Kulkarni's Tomato Pickle (Bissi Upinkai, Raichur, Karnataka)

Ingredients

Tomatoes, chopped: 4–6
Sesame oil/groundnut oil: 3–4 tbsp
Fenugreek powder: ⅕ tsp
Mustard powder: 1–1½ tsp
Asafoetida: A pinch
Red chillies, whole: 3–4
Curry leaves: 1 sprig
Tamarind paste: 1½ tsp

Jaggery: ¼ tsp
Salt to taste
Red chilli powder: To taste

STEPS

1. Heat oil and add mustard seeds to crackle, then asafoetida, curry leaves and the whole red chillies.
2. Then, add tomatoes that are not too finely chopped but also not too chunky. Stir well and let it cook. Ensure that it doesn't stick to the pan. Cook over a medium heat so that it doesn't burn.
3. Add salt and tamarind paste. Let it cook till the water from the tomatoes evaporates. Add the rest of the spices and jaggery, and let it cook for a minute or two. If you feel that the oil is less, add some more and cook for a couple of minutes.
4. The pickle is ready and can be consumed immediately. If it is stored in the fridge, the pickle can stay up to a week.

NORTH INDIAN INSTANT JACKFRUIT PICKLE (KATHAL KA ACHAR)

INGREDIENTS

Jackfruit, cut: 250 gm
Raw mango, chopped: 100 gm
Turmeric powder: 1 tsp
Fennel seeds: 2 tbsp
Fenugreek seeds, powdered: 2 tbsp
Yellow mustard seeds: 2 tbsp
Nigella seeds: 2 tbsp
Asafoetida: ¼ tsp
Vinegar: 1 tbsp
Mustard oil: 400ml

Red chilli powder: To taste
Salt to taste

STEPS

1. Boil some water in a saucepan. While the water is still being heated, add jackfruit pieces to it.
2. Once the jackfruit is boiled, strain it and let it air-dry.
3. In a new pan, dry roast all the spices. Once they are roasted, add the fenugreek and asafoetida. Place all of the roasted spices in a dry bowl.
4. To the spice bowl, add turmeric and red chilli powder. Next, add the jackfruit and mango chunks. Mix well.
5. The last step is to add vinegar to the mixture. Mix it again.
6. Now, deposit the mixture in an airtight container, letting it sun-dry for a day. After one day, pour some oil on the pickle. It will be ready to serve.

HILL LEMON PICKLE (HIMACHAL PRADESH, UTTARAKHAND)

INGREDIENTS

Hill lemon (galgal): 1 kg
Green chillies: 500 gm
Mustard oil: 150 ml
Red chilli powder: 1 tbsp
Turmeric powder: 1 tbsp
Asafoetida powder: ¼ tsp
Salt: 1 tbsp (or to taste)
Carom seeds: 1 tbsp
Fenugreek seeds: ½ tbsp
Jaggery, powdered: 100 gm

1. Heat water in a large pan over a high flame. Once it reaches a rolling boil, add the hill lemons and boil for 4–5 minutes. Drain the water and pat the lemons dry using a kitchen towel.
2. Cut the lemons into 1-inch pieces and remove the seeds. Wash the green chillies, discard the stems and chop them into small pieces.
3. Heat mustard oil in a pan over a high flame until it's smoking hot. Turn off the heat and allow the oil to cool slightly. Add turmeric, red chilli powder, asafoetida, carom seeds, fenugreek seeds and salt. Stir to combine.
4. Add the lemons and green chillies to the spiced oil. Mix everything thoroughly. Transfer the mixture to an airtight glass container and place it in sunlight for 2–3 days to cure. Stir occasionally for even flavouring.

VEGETABLE PICKLES

BIHARI ELEPHANT FOOT YAM PICKLE (OAL/SURAN KA CHOKHA)

INGREDIENTS

Elephant foot yam, cleaned, chopped: 250 gm
Turmeric powder: 1 tbsp
Green chilli-garlic paste: 1 tsp
Yellow mustard paste: 1 tbsp
Mustard oil: 150 ml
Nigella seeds: 1 tbsp
Carom seeds: 1 tbsp
Salt to taste

STEPS

1. In a pan, heat some water and add the yam. Let it boil before taking it off the flame.
2. After draining the yam, mash it thoroughly in a bowl. Now, add all the spices, including salt, chilli-garlic paste and yellow mustard paste to the mashed yam. Mix them together.
3. Pour the oil into this mixture and mix thoroughly.
4. Store the mixture in an airtight jar and store it in sunlight for 4–5 days. It will then be ready to consume.

North Indian Instant Pickle

Ingredients

Carrots, chopped: 500 gm
Cauliflower (flowers separated in medium size): 500 gm
Turnips, peeled and cut vertically: 500 gm
Jaggery, grated: 1 cup
Ginger, grated: 6 tbsp
Garlic, grated: 4 tbsp
Mustard oil: ¾ cup
Cumin seeds: ¾ cup
Cloves: 15
Black cardamoms: 4
1-inch cinnamon stick: 3
Red chilli powder: 1½ tbsp
Mustard powder: 1½ tbsp
Ginger garlic paste: 1 tbsp
Malt vinegar: 3 tbsp
Salt to taste

1. In a pan, dry roast cumin seeds, black cardamoms, cinnamon and cloves. Let the spices cool before grinding them together.
2. Meanwhile, mix the grated jaggery with vinegar. Mix the carrots, cauliflowers and turnips in a separate bowl.
3. In a pan, heat some oil. Add and cook ginger, garlic and the ginger garlic paste until it appears reddish. Next, add the jaggery and vinegar mixture to the pan. Cook them until the jaggery melts.
4. Next, add all the previously ground spices and salt into the pan. Mix the ingredients thoroughly.
5. To the pan, add the vegetables slowly. Do not add them all at once. Keep stirring the pot as you add in small batches.
6. Take the pickle off the flame. Store the pickle in an airtight jar once it cools down.

Instant Garlic Pickle (Lahsun ka Achar)

Ingredients

Garlic, whole, separated into cloves: 6
Mustard seeds: 2½ tbsp
Fenugreek seeds: 1½ tsp
Sesame oil
Tamarind paste
Turmeric powder: 1 tsp
Red chilli powder: 4 tbsp
Jaggery, grated: 1 tsp
Salt to taste

1. Dry roast some mustard and fenugreek seeds. Once cool, grind them.
2. Heat some sesame oil in a pan, add the garlic cloves and roast them mildly. Once the garlic cools, grind half of them to make a paste. Set aside the rest.
3. Take another pan and heat some more oil. Add some mustard seeds, curry leaves and the fresh garlic paste. Cook together.
4. Add salt, turmeric and red chilli powder. Stir to mix, and then add tamarind paste and cook.
5. Next, add the prepared ground spices, roasted garlic, jaggery and cook for 15–20 minutes on a low flame.
6. Cool the pickle and store it in an airtight jar. It is good to serve as is.

GOOSEBERRY PICKLE (AMLE KA ACHAR, BANARAS)

INGREDIENTS

For the Pickle Spice Blend:
Mustard seeds: 5 tsp
Fennel seeds: 2 tsp
Fenugreek seeds: 1½ tsp

For the Pickle:
Indian gooseberry (amla), large: 16
Raw mustard oil: ½ cup
Kashmiri chilli powder: 4 tsp
Mustard seeds: 2 tsp
Asafoetida: A pinch
Turmeric powder: 1 tsp
Salt: 2 tsp (or as per taste)

Steps

1. Wash the gooseberries thoroughly and dry them completely using a kitchen towel. Once dry, steam the gooseberries for 8–10 minutes until slightly soft. Let them cool completely. If using large gooseberries, separate into segments and remove the stones. For smaller berries, leave them whole.

2. Dry roast mustard seeds, fennel seeds and fenugreek seeds separately in a pan over a low flame until aromatic, being careful not to burn them. Let them cool and grind into a fine powder. Set aside.

3. Heat mustard oil in a pan until hot. Add mustard seeds and a pinch of asafoetida. Allow them to splutter briefly, then remove the pan to prevent burning.

4. Add the steamed gooseberries to the tempered oil and stir-fry for 1–2 minutes so they absorb the flavours. Add the chilli powder, turmeric powder, salt and the prepared spice blend. Mix everything well to ensure the berries are evenly coated.

5. Transfer the pickle to a clean, dry container. While it can be eaten immediately, its flavours deepen over time. Store in the refrigerator, where it will last for up to a month.

Winter Mixed Vegetables Pickle (Pachranga Achar, Amritsar)

Ingredients

Cauliflower: 400 gm
Turnips: 200 gm
Carrots: 400 gm
Green chillies: 800 gm
Lemons: 80 gm
Ginger: 30 gm
Garlic: 30 gm

Turmeric powder: 40 gm
Degi mirch: 50 gm
Salt: 150–200 gm (or to taste)
Raw mustard oil: 2 cups
Mustard seeds, dry-roasted and coarsely ground: 150 gm
Fennel seeds, dry-roasted and coarsely ground: 50 gm
Fenugreek seeds, dry-roasted and coarsely ground: 30 gm
Jamun vinegar (or white vinegar): ⅓ cup

Steps

1. Heat mustard oil until it smokes, then let it cool completely.
2. Wash and chop the vegetables as desired. In a large bowl, combine the chopped vegetables, spices, salt, cooled mustard oil and vinegar. Mix thoroughly.
3. Transfer the mixture to a clean, dry jar. Seal the jar tightly. For longer shelf life (up to a year), add vinegar. Place the jar in direct sunlight for 5–6 days, shaking it morning and evening.

Instant Radish Pickle (Mooli ka Achar)

Ingredients

Radishes, medium-sized, cut into thin sticks or slices: 3
Turmeric powder: 1 tsp
Fenugreek seeds: 1 tsp
Sesame powder: 2 tsp
Green chillies, chopped: 2
Lemon, juiced: 1
Red chillies, whole: 3
Salt: 1½ tsp (or to taste)
Mustard oil: 3–4 tbsp

1. Marinate the radish with salt and turmeric powder and let it rest for 15 minutes. Drain and squeeze out the excess water and let them rest again.
2. Add the lemon juice, green chillies and sesame powder to the radishes.
3. In a pan, heat some oil, and add red chillies and fenugreek seeds. Turn off the stove once the colour of the seeds changes.
4. Pour the oil and the tempered ingredients into the radish mixture. Mix well.
5. The pickle is ready to use. It is best eaten fresh but can be stored in the refrigerator for up to 1 week.

Lotus Root Pickle (Chuk-Nadur Khatey Kamal Kakdi, Kashmir)

Ingredients

Lotus roots, cut into 2-inch pieces: 500 gm
Salt to taste
Fennel powder: 1 tsp
Turmeric powder: ¼ tsp
Cumin powder: 1 tsp
Chilli powder: 1 tsp
Ginger powder: 1 tsp
Asafoetida: A pinch
Oil (or sesame oil): 3 tbsp
Water: 1½ cups
Lemon, juiced: 1

Steps

1. Wash and cut the lotus root into 2-inch vertical pieces. Heat 3 tbsp of oil in a pan, add a pinch of asafoetida and stir-fry the lotus root until slightly brown.

2. Add chilli powder, fennel powder, ginger powder, cumin powder, turmeric powder and salt to the pan. Stir well, ensuring the spices coat the lotus root evenly.
3. Add a small amount of water to deglaze the pan, then pour in 1½ cups of water. Cover the pan and let it cook for 20 minutes, or until the lotus root softens.
4. Remove the lid and add lemon juice, tamarind pulp or tartaric acid for a tangy flavour. Mix thoroughly.
5. Let the mixture boil for another 10–12 minutes. Turn off the stove and serve warm.

AXONE PICKLE (NAGALAND)

INGREDIENTS

Axone (Naga-style fermented soya bean): 6
Ginger, washed and cut: 640 gm
Oil: 10 tbsp
Chilli powder: 3 tbsp
Garlic cloves, chopped: 22
Salt to taste
Sichuan pepper powder, roasted: 1½ tbsp
Ghost peppers (bhut jolokias): 5
Sesame oil

STEPS

1. Start by sun-drying the axone for 6–7 hours.
2. Meanwhile, pound the ginger and squeeze out its juice. Let the ginger also sun-dry for a few hours.
3. Break the axone blocks into smaller pieces once its outermost layer has dried.
4. Heat oil in a pan and fry the ghost peppers in the oil. Once done, keep the ghost peppers aside and start roasting the

garlic in the same oil. When they turn golden brown, take it off the heat and let it rest.

5. Pound the cooled ghost peppers with salt until the texture is that of a coarse powder.

6. Stir-fry the axone for 10–15 minutes in oil. Once it is fried well enough, add in the ground ghost pepper powder, chilli powder and roasted garlic. Mix the ingredients well.

7. Add the Sichuan pepper powder and dried ginger next. Mix well.

8. Top it with some sesame oil and keep mixing.

9. The pickle is ready to use.

CHILLI PICKLES

RAJASTHANI GREEN CHILLI PICKLE

INGREDIENTS

Green chillies: 500 gm
Mustard seeds, ground: 3 tbsp
Turmeric powder: ½ tsp
Fennel seeds: 1 tsp
Salt: 2 tsp (or to taste)
Asafoetida: ½ tsp
Lemon juice: 2 tbsp
Oil: 3 tbsp

STEPS

1. Clean the chillies and make vertical slits without cutting them into pieces.

2. To make the stuffing for the chillies, combine turmeric, fennel seeds, mustard seeds and asafoetida. Add salt to

this mixture. Now, stuff the prepared mixture inside the slit chillies.

3. Heat oil in a pan. Once heated, allow the oil to cool down a little before pouring it into the stuffed chillies. Next, add lemon juice to the mix.

4. Deposit the mixture into an airtight container and let it rest. It will be ready for consumption in 2–3 days.

Bird's Eye Chilli Pickle
(Kon Jolokia Asar, Assam)

Ingredients

Bird's eye chillies, cleaned and stalks removed: 500 gm
Garlic cloves, peeled: 120 gm
Coriander seeds, whole: 1 tbsp
Cumin seeds: 2 tbsp
Fenugreek seeds: ½ tsp
Black mustard seeds: ½ tsp
White wine vinegar: 2 tbsp
Lemon juice: 1 tbsp
Salt to taste
Mustard oil: 450 ml

Steps

1. Wash and remove the stalks from the bird's eye chillies. Peel the garlic cloves. Sun-dry both the chillies and garlic for a day to remove excess moisture.

2. Dry roast the coriander seeds, cumin seeds, fenugreek seeds, and black mustard seeds in a pan on a low flame until they release a fragrant aroma.

3. Allow the spices to cool, then grind them into a coarse powder. Add vinegar and lemon juice to the spice mixture and mix well.

4. Mix the ground spice masala with the dried chillies and garlic, ensuring the masala coats them evenly. Let the mixture rest for some time to allow the flavours to infuse.

5. Heat mustard oil in a kadahi until it reaches its smoking point. Turn off the heat and allow the oil to cool completely.

6. Gently mix the chillies and garlic with the cooled mustard oil. Transfer the pickle to a clean, sterilized glass jar. Seal the jar and place it in sunlight for 4-5 days, shaking it gently each day to ensure even marination.

7. The bird's eye chilli pickle is now ready to enjoy! Store in a cool, dry place and always use a clean, dry spoon for serving.

Instant Chilli Pickle from Chamba Region (Chamba ki Chukh, Himachal Pradesh)

Ingredients

Dried red chillies: 4–5
Kashmiri red chillies: 3–4
Mustard oil: ½ cup
Garlic cloves: 6
Sugar/jaggery: To taste
Lemon juice: 1 tbsp
Salt to taste
Cumin powder, roasted: 1 tsp
Coriander powder, roasted: 1 tsp
Fennel powder: ½ tsp
Fenugreek powder: A pinch
Mustard powder: A pinch
Asafoetida: ½ tsp

1. To preserve the colour, soak the red chiles in warm water for 15 minutes before transferring them to a bowl of cold water.
2. Next, grind the chillies with garlic, water and a small amount of salt. Blend until a paste is formed. You can add some ginger to this paste if you so desire.
3. Heat oil in a pan, then add all the mentioned spices. Sauté for 30 seconds.
4. Now, add salt to the chilli paste you have made and simmer over a low flame. You may add some water, if necessary.
5. After this, mix in the sweetener of choice (sugar/jaggery). Simmer for 2–3 minutes.
6. Take the pan off the heat and mix in some lemon juice.

Manipuri Chilli Pickle
(Morok Pickle/U Morok Achar)

Ingredients

Ghost chillies, red and ripe: 3 kg
Yellow mustard seeds, coarsely ground: 2 tbsp
Fenugreek seeds, coarsely ground: ½ tsp
Turmeric powder: ½ tsp
Lemon, small, juiced: 1
Mustard oil: 1 cup or 200 ml
Rock salt/plain white salt: 1 tbsp

Steps

1. Heat mustard oil in a pan until it is smoking hot. Turn off the heat and allow it to cool completely.
2. Wash and thoroughly dry the chillies using a clean, dry cotton cloth. (To protect your hands, wear rubber gloves

or apply a thin layer of mustard oil.) Remove the stalks and cut the chillies into 4–5 equal-sized pieces. Set them aside in a glass bowl.

3. Using a clean, dry spoon, mix the cut chillies with dry spices and salt until the pieces are evenly coated.

4. Transfer the spice-coated chillies into a sterilized glass jar. Add the freshly squeezed lemon juice and the cooled mustard oil. Cover the jar tightly with a lid or secure it with a muslin cloth. Shake the jar vigorously to combine the ingredients.

5. Place the jar under direct sunlight for about a week to cure, shaking it gently once a day to ensure even mixing. Once ready, use a clean, dry spoon when serving to maintain freshness and prolong shelf life.

Local Berries and Chilli Pickle (Karonda Mirch ka Achar, Uttar Pradesh)

Ingredients

Karonda: 250 gm
Fennel seeds: 3½ tbsp
Mustard seeds: 2 tsp
Fenugreek seeds: 2 tsp
Red chilli powder: 2 tsp
Salt to taste
Green chillies, chopped: 100 gm
Nigella seeds: ¼ tsp
Asafoetida: ½ tsp
Mustard oil: 1¼ cup

Steps

1. Rinse the green chillies and karonda thoroughly. Allow them to air dry entirely.

2. Cut the bigger karondas in order to take out their seeds. Leave the smaller karondas as they are.

3. Heat up some mustard oil and then allow it to cool down a bit.

4. Meanwhile, separately dry roast the mustard, fenugreek and fennel seeds. Once cooled, crush into a coarse powder. Pour the heated mustard oil over the crushed spices.

5. Combine the karonda, salt, green chillies and spice-oil mixture in a bowl. Leave the bowl covered overnight.

6. Add the leftover mustard oil the following day and stir the mixture. Now, deposit the mixture in a dry glass jar, seal the jar and allow it to rest for 7 days.

MEAT PICKLES

INSTANT MEAT PICKLE (YARMU/YORKHUN, ARUNACHAL PRADESH)

(Contributed by someone from the Apatani tribe, who also shared that the same pickle is known by different names among different tribes, such as Lukmir and Yamter. The Apatani tribe that she belongs to uses the name Yarmu/Yorkhun. There are also personal variations in terms of ingredients used. For instance, some people like to add bamboo shoots.)

INGREDIENTS

Chicken (or any other meat of choice), boiled, shredded: 100 gm
Garlic, whole, chopped and sautéed in oil: 1
Dried red chillies: 3–4
Salt to taste
Oil for frying

1. Roast the dried chillies in a pan. After roasting, grind the chillies.
2. Meanwhile, boil and shred the chicken. After that, leave it to dry.
3. Once dry, heat the pan and fry the dried chicken till it becomes crispy.
4. Now add in the sautéed garlic, ground red chillies and salt as per taste.
5. You can serve it hot with any meal of choice, including rice and roti. You can store the rest in a jar to use thereafter.

Naga Instant Pork Pickle

Ingredients

Pork (no fat), boneless, washed properly and cut: 1 kg
Oil: 1 cup
Salt to taste
Ginger, minced
Garlic, minced
Ghost pepper: 3
Chilli powder (hotter than the usual): 2 tbsp
Sichuan pepper powder

Steps

1. Put the meat pieces in 2 cups of salted water and pre-cook for 20 mins. The meat should be tender and not overcooked.
2. Drain and allow the meat to cool down before cutting it into smaller pieces. After cutting, spread it out and let it dry.

3. Once the pork dries, heat oil in a pan, add ginger and garlic, and sauté well until the colour turns golden brown.
4. Add the pork, ghost peppers and lower the flame. Keep stirring to keep the mixture from burning.
5. Once the meat is cooked, cook on a high flame for some time to make it somewhat crispy and wait for the colour to turn golden brown.
6. Now, add chilli and Sichuan pepper powder, and take it off the flame. Once the pickle cools, place it in an airtight container.

KERALA-STYLE INSTANT BEEF PICKLE

INGREDIENTS

Beef, cleaned and cut: ½ kg
Ginger garlic paste: 1 tsp
Red chilli powder: ½ tsp
Turmeric powder: ½ tsp
Garlic cloves: 15
2-inch piece ginger, chopped
Green chillies, chopped: 5
Kashmiri red chilli powder: 2 tbsp
Garam masala: 1 tsp
Fenugreek powder: ¼ tsp
Black pepper powder: ¼ tsp
Mustard seeds: ½ tsp
Fenugreek seeds: ¼ tsp
Vinegar: 5 tbsp
Coconut oil: ½ cup
Curry leaves: 4
Salt to taste

1. In a pressure cooker, add the meat pieces and all the spices, along with ginger garlic paste, salt and a cup of water. Mix all ingredients and wait for 4 whistles before taking the cooker off the flame. The goal is to cook the beef well.
2. Take a pan and heat some oil in it to fry the cooked beef. Once brown, turn off the heat.
3. In a separate pan, heat oil again and add mustard seeds. Add fenugreek seeds when the mustard seeds start to splutter. Roast them in oil for a minute or two before adding green chilli, garlic, ginger and curry leaves, and sauté them.
4. Add garam masala, fenugreek powder and chilli powder. Stir in vinegar and bring it to a boil. Finally, add the cooked beef along with its oil and mix everything well. Turn off the flame and store the prepared pickle in a dry airtight jar.

ANDHRA-STYLE INSTANT MUTTON PICKLE

INGREDIENTS

Mutton, boneless: 1 kg
Oil: 1½ kg
Ginger garlic paste: 100 gm
Red chilli powder: 100 gm
Salt: 3 tbsp (or to taste)
Coriander powder: 3 tbsp
Turmeric powder: 3 tbsp
Garam masala powder (ground cumin seeds, coriander, clove, cinnamon, cardamom, black pepper, nutmeg): 1 tbsp
Lemons, juiced: 8

1. Clean the mutton and marinate with oil and turmeric powder for 30–40 minutes.
2. Now, cook the marinated mutton until all the water it releases evaporates.
3. Take another pan and heat some oil for the mutton to be deep fried. Once fried, let it cool.
4. In the same pan, add all the spices including the ginger garlic paste and salt. Add in the mutton and let all of it cook on a low flame.
5. Let the pickle cool down before adding lemon juice to it. Now, you can store the pickle in an airtight jar for your use.

FISH PICKLES

Bombay Duck Pickle (Bombil Pickle, Maharashtra and Goa)

Ingredients

Dried Bombay ducks: 100
Garlic, whole: 2
Red chilli powder
Ginger, chopped into chunks: 1
Turmeric powder: 1 tbsp
Vinegar: 2 cups
Garlic, chopped: ¼ cup
Ginger, chopped: 2 tbsp
Oil: 1 l
Curry leaves
Salt to taste

STEPS

1. First, clean the Bombay duck in vinegar, drain it and then fry it. Once fried, set it aside.
2. Meanwhile, make a paste from ginger, garlic, chillies and turmeric. Add salt.
3. Separately, fry the curry leaves and set them aside.
4. Now, use the same pan and oil to cook the paste you had made earlier. After cooking the paste for a couple of minutes, add the fish and cook on low heat for around 15 minutes.
5. Add the curry leaves set aside earlier, mix well and take the pan off the heat.
6. Let the pickle cool down before you store it in a dry airtight container.

PRAWN PICKLE (CHEMMEEN ACHAR)

INGREDIENTS

Chilli powder: 2 tsp
Turmeric powder: ¼ tsp
Fenugreek seeds: ½ tsp
Mustard seeds: 1 tsp
Asafoetida: A pinch
Garlic, diced: 5
Ginger, sliced: 5
Green chillies, slit vertically: 4–5
Vinegar: 4 tbsp
Oil: 3–4 tbsp
Curry leaves
Salt to taste

For the prawns:
Prawns: 350 gm
Chilli powder: 1 tsp
Turmeric powder: ¼ tsp
Salt

STEPS

1. Clean the prawns properly before marinating it (using chilli powder, turmeric powder and salt). Let it sit for 40 minutes.
2. Preheat the oven to 350 degrees Fahrenheit. Prepare the baking tray by spraying some oil on it before adding the prawns. Let the prawns bake for 20 minutes.
3. Now, heat some oil in a skillet and sauté the prawns. Set aside.
4. Add fenugreek seeds, mustard seeds and curry leaves to the skillet. Next, add and brown the chillies, ginger and garlic.
5. To the same skillet, add chilli and turmeric powder before adding the prawns again. Stir to mix. Now, take the skillet off the flame and add some vinegar.
6. Transfer the mixture to an airtight container and leave it undisturbed for 3 days before using it.

GOAN MACKEREL PICKLE (BANGDYANCHE LONCHE)

INGREDIENTS

Mackerels, large, cut into 3 to 4 pieces: 2
Turmeric powder: 2 tsp
Mustard seeds: ½ tsp
Fenugreek seeds: ¼ tsp
Asafoetida: 1 tsp
Red chilli powder: 3 tbsp

Tamarind, lemon-sized, made into a paste: 2
Garlic cloves, chopped into thin pieces: 20
Salt to taste
Oil: 2 tbsp

For the mackerels:
Turmeric powder: 1 tsp
Red chilli powder: 1 tsp
Salt: ½ tsp (or to taste)

STEPS

1. Clean and cut the mackerel. Marinate for about 30 minutes using 1 tsp each of turmeric powder, red chilli powder and salt.
2. Combine the tamarind paste, turmeric powder and red chilli powder in a bowl. Blend them with a spoon.
3. Heat oil in a pan and add mustard seeds, fenugreek and asafoetida to roast. Add garlic to the pan once the spices are roasted. Once the garlic is ready, take the pan off the heat to let it cool.
4. Now, grind the ingredients of the pan along with a little bit of oil to make a paste. Leave the rest of the oil in the pan.
5. Heat the remaining oil and add the freshly made paste to the pan. Now, add in the previously prepared mixture of tamarind paste, turmeric and chilli powder.
6. Finally, add the marinated fish to the pan. Add salt. You can now add a little water to the pan and let it simmer till the fish is cooked.
7. This pickle can be served as a condiment. However, it is not recommended to be stored for more than 2–3 days.

Jessica Khieya's Khasi Instant Fish Pickle
(Ktung Shira Pickle, Meghalaya)

Ingredients

Anchovies (small fish), dried: 300 gm
Onions, medium: 2 (1 finely chopped and 1 sliced)
Green chillies, chopped: 3–4
Garlic, minced: 1 tbsp
Tomatoes, chopped: 2
Salt to taste
Mustard oil for cooking: 4 tbsp

Steps

1. Rinse the dried fish under running water to remove excess salt and impurities. Soak the fish in warm water for about 10 minutes to soften. Drain and set aside.
2. Heat mustard oil in a pan over medium heat. Add the finely chopped onion and sauté until translucent.
3. Stir in the minced garlic and chopped green chillies. Cook for another minute. Add the chopped tomatoes and cook until they soften and blend with the mixture.
4. Incorporate the soaked and drained fish into the pan. Mix well to ensure the fish is coated with the aromatic mixture.
5. Season with salt to taste.
6. Cover the pan and let it simmer on a low flame for about 10–15 minutes, allowing the flavours to meld together.
7. If the mixture appears too dry, add a splash of water to maintain the moisture.
8. Once cooked, garnish with the sliced onion for added texture and flavour.
9. Serve hot with steamed rice or as a side dish.

BAMBOO SHOOT PICKLES

MESU PICKLE (HIMACHAL PRADESH, SIKKIM, WEST BENGAL)

INGREDIENTS

Bamboo shoot, fermented: 250 gm
Garlic cloves, chopped: 4–5
Chilli powder: 3 tbsp
Mustard oil: 1–2 tbsp
Salt to taste

STEPS

1. Mix the bamboo shoot, garlic, red chilli powder, and salt in a bowl.
2. Add oil to this mixture. Mix and put it in a dry container.
3. Once the mixture is in the container, pour more oil. Seal the container and let it rest for 2 days until it is ready to be used.

BAMBOO SHOOT PICKLE (BAANS KARIL KA ACHAR, CHHATTISGARH, JHARKHAND)

INGREDIENTS

Bamboo shoot: 500 gm
Green chillies: 250 gm
Turmeric powder: 1 tsp
Salt: 1½ tsp (or to taste)
Mustard seeds: 1 tbsp
Carom seeds: 1 tsp
Fenugreek seeds: 1 tbsp
Fennel seeds: 1 tbsp
Mustard oil: ½ cup

Steps

1. Prepare the bamboo shoot by peeling and slicing it. Boil it for 3–4 minutes and then, dry it properly.
2. Now, in a pan, add the mustard, fennel seeds and fenugreek seeds, and roast on a low flame. After it cools down, grind it coarsely.
3. Add the sliced bamboo shoot to a big bowl and add the ground spices, turmeric powder and salt. Mix well. Add in the green chillies and mix again.
4. Place the mixture into an airtight jar and keep it in the sun for 3–4 days before use.

Jessica Khieya's Khasi Instant Bamboo Shoot Pickle

Ingredients

Bamboo shoot: ½ kg
Mustard seeds, coarsely powdered: 1 tsp
Salt: 1 tsp (or to taste)
Asafoetida: ¼ tsp
Mustard oil: 2 tsp
Red chilli powder: 2 tsp

Steps

1. Start by slicing the bamboo shoots thinly and boiling them in water for about 10 minutes to remove any bitterness.
2. Drain and let them cool.
3. Heat oil in a pan on a low flame. Add red chilli powder (adjust to your spice preference) and roast for 30–60 seconds until fragrant.

4. Add the cooked and boiled bamboo shoots to the chilli oil. Stir well to ensure the bamboo absorbs the chilli evenly.

5. Toss in crushed mustard seeds and mix thoroughly. Roast the mixture for 5–7 minutes on a low flame, then add a pinch of asafoetida and roast for another 2–3 minutes.

6. Add water and salt to the pan. Cover with a lid and let it cook on a low flame for 5–7 minutes. Remove the lid and cook for another 5–7 minutes, allowing the bamboo shoots to absorb the water fully.

7. Once the water is absorbed, the pickle is ready to serve. For storage, transfer it to an airtight container and refrigerate. Consume within 2 weeks for the best flavour.

Rajashree Sharma's Assamese Bamboo Shoot Pickle

Ingredients

Bamboo shoot, grated and sun-dried for a day to dehydrate: 1 cup
Ghost pepper, chopped: 2
Salt to taste
Mustard oil: 2 tsp

Steps

1. In a clean, airtight glass jar, combine the sun-dried bamboo shoot, chopped ghost pepper, salt and mustard oil. Mix thoroughly to ensure everything is evenly coated.

2. Seal the jar tightly and place it in direct sunlight for at least one month to allow the flavours to develop fully before consuming.

STREET FOOD AND OTHERS

∾

Dahi Papdi Chaat Masala

Ingredients

For the Papdi:
Maida: 2 cups
Carom seeds: 1 tsp
Salt: 1 tsp (or to taste)
Ghee: 4–5 tbsp
Water as required

For the Green Chutney:
Coriander leaves: 1 cup
Fresh mint leaves: ½ cup
2-inch ginger, washed and sliced
Green chillies: 4
Cumin powder: 1 tsp
Dried mango powder: 1 tsp
Black salt: ½ tsp
Split Bengal gram, roasted: 1 tbsp
Salt: 1 tsp (or to taste)
Water as required

For the Sweet Tamarind Chutney:
Tamarind pulp: ½ cup
Seedless dates: 150 gm
Jaggery: 1 kg
Cumin powder: 1 tbsp
Kashmiri red chilli powder: 1 tbsp
Yellow chilli powder: 1 tbsp
Dried ginger powder: ½ tsp
Black salt: 1 tsp
Black pepper: ¼ tsp
Salt: 1 tsp (or to taste)
Water: 750 ml

For the Spice Mix:
Cumin seeds: 5 tbsp
Black pepper: 2 tbsp
Red chillies, whole: 6
Carom seeds: 1 tbsp
Salt: 1 tsp (or to taste)
Black salt: 1 tbsp
Chaat masala: 1 tsp

For the Assembly:
Curd: 4 cups
Powdered sugar: 2 tbsp
Black salt: 1 tbsp
Potatoes, boiled, cut in pieces: 4
Crispy fried papdi: 10
Spicy green chutney: As you prefer
Sweet tamarind chutney: As you prefer
Spice mix: As you prefer
Pomegranate seeds for garnish

For the Papdi:

1. In a mixing bowl, combine the refined flour, carom, salt and ghee. Mix well to incorporate the ghee into the flour.
2. Gradually add water and knead into a semi-stiff dough. Knead for at least 2–3 minutes.
3. Cover the dough with a damp cloth and let it rest for at least 30 minutes.
4. After resting, knead the dough once again. Divide the dough into small lemon-sized balls. Apply some oil and roll each ball into a 2-inch diameter circle. Prick the surface with a fork to prevent puffing.
5. Heat oil in a wok until moderately hot. Fry the papdi on a low flame until crisp and golden brown.
6. Remove the fried papdi and drain excess oil on absorbent paper.
7. Store the papdi in an airtight container.

For the Green Chutney:

1. Add all ingredients to a grinding jar.
2. Grind into a fine chutney. Store the chutney in the refrigerator.

For the Sweet Tamarind Chutney:

1. Soak tamarind and dates separately in hot water for 15–20 minutes. Squeeze the tamarind to extract the pulp.
2. Transfer the tamarind pulp and soaked dates to a mixer grinder and grind to a fine paste.
3. In a wok, strain the ground tamarind and dates paste through a sieve. Add jaggery, spices, salt and black pepper.
4. Cook on a medium flame until the jaggery melts, stirring occasionally. Skim off the scum that forms on the surface

and cook the chutney for 30 minutes until it reaches a thin, syrup-like consistency.

5. Allow the chutney to cool down. Store in a sterilized airtight jar and refrigerate.

For the Spice Mix:

1. In a pan over low heat, dry roast the cumin seeds until they darken in colour and become aromatic. Transfer to a plate to cool.
2. Dry roast the remaining whole spices until aromatic. Transfer to the same plate to cool.
3. Once cooled, grind the roasted spices along with the remaining ingredients to a fine powder.
4. Store the spice mix in an airtight container.

For the Assembly:

1. In a sieve, combine curd, powdered sugar and black salt. Strain while mixing well.
2. Dip the crispy papdi in the curd mixture. Top with boiled potatoes, sprinkle the special spice mix and add the chutneys.
3. Add some more curd and finish with pomegranate seeds. Adjust the toppings to your taste preferences.

Delhi Papdi Chaat Masala

Ingredients

Cumin seeds: 5 tbsp
Carom seeds: 1 tbsp
Dried mango powder: 5 tbsp
Dried mint leaves, ground: 3 tbsp
Ginger powder: 1 tbsp
Black salt: 1 tbsp
Salt: 1 tbsp (or to taste)
Yellow chilli powder: 1 tbsp
Red chilli powder: 1 tbsp

Steps

1. In a medium cast-iron or non-stick skillet, roast the cumin seeds and carom seeds over medium heat, stirring and shaking the pan until the spices darken slightly (for about 2 minutes). Transfer them to a bowl.
2. Allow the seeds to cool, then grind them into a fine powder using a spice or coffee grinder.
3. Return the ground mixture to the skillet and add the mango powder, tamarind powder, dried mint leaves, ginger powder, black salt, salt, yellow and red chilli powder.
4. Roast the combined mixture over medium heat for about 1 minute until thoroughly heated.
5. Let the blend cool completely before storing it in an airtight container.

Dahi Papdi Chaat Masala 2

Ingredients

Cumin seeds: 1 tbsp
Fennel seeds: 1 tsp
Black pepper: 1 tbsp
Green cardamom: 1
Black cardamom: 1
Mustard seeds: ¼ tsp
Coriander seeds: 1½ tsp
Salt: 1 tsp (or to taste)
Dried mango powder: 1½ tsp
Degi red chilli powder: ½ tsp

Steps

1. In a medium cast-iron or non-stick skillet, roast the cumin seeds, fennel seeds, black pepper, green cardamom, black cardamom seeds, mustard seeds, and coriander seeds over medium heat, stirring and shaking the pan until the spices darken slightly and release their aromas, for about 2 minutes. Transfer them to a bowl.

2. Allow the spices to cool completely, then grind them into a fine powder using a spice or coffee grinder.

3. Combine the ground spices with the dried mango powder, degi red chilli powder, and salt.

4. Mix well and return the blend to the skillet. Roast over medium heat for about 1 minute until the mixture is heated through.

5. Let the blend cool completely before storing it in an airtight container. Keep it in a cool, dark place.

Aloo Tikki Chaat Masala

Ingredients

Cumin seeds: 3 tbsp
Salt: 4 tsp (or to taste)
Fennel seeds: 1 tbsp
Black pepper: 3 tbsp
Asafoetida: 1 tsp
Coriander seeds: 3 tbsp
Clove: 1

Steps

1. In a medium cast-iron or non-stick skillet, dry roast the cumin seeds, fennel seeds, black pepper, coriander seeds and cloves over medium heat, stirring and shaking the pan until the spices are aromatic and a few shades darker. This should take about 2–3 minutes.
2. Remove from heat and let the spices cool completely.
3. Once cooled, grind the roasted spices along with the asafoetida and salt in a spice grinder or coffee grinder to make a fine powder.
4. Store the spice blend in an airtight container in a cool, dark place. This blend can be used for up to 1 month at room temperature or up to 1 year if refrigerated.

Easy Tikki

Ingredients

Red chilli powder: 3 tbsp
Coriander powder: 2 tbsp
Cumin powder: 2 tbsp
Black salt: 2 tbsp

Chaat masala: 2 tbsp
Salt: 2 tbsp (or to taste)

STEPS

1. Dry roast the coriander powder, red chilli powder and cumin powder separately in a medium cast-iron or non-stick skillet over medium heat for 1–2 minutes each (or until aromatic). Make sure to stir and shake the pan to prevent burning.
2. Remove the roasted spices from the heat and let them cool completely.
3. Once cooled, combine the roasted coriander powder, red chilli powder, cumin powder, black salt, chaat masala and salt in a bowl.
4. Mix well to ensure all the spices are evenly distributed. Store the spice blend in an airtight container in a cool, dark place.

KALA MASALA FOR PANI PURI

INGREDIENTS

Cumin seeds: ½ cup
Coriander seeds: ¼ cup
Black pepper: ⅛ cup
Red chillies, whole: 4
Carom seeds: 1 tsp
Mint leaves: ½ cup
Black salt: 1 tbsp
Salt: 1 tbsp (or to taste)
Citric acid: 1 tbsp
Dried mango powder: ¼ cup

1. In a medium cast-iron or non-stick skillet, dry roast the cumin seeds, coriander seeds, black pepper, red chillies and carom seeds over medium heat. Stir and shake the pan frequently until the spices become aromatic and a few shades darker (for about 2–3 minutes).
2. Add the dried mint leaves to the skillet and roast for an additional 1–2 minutes. Be careful not to burn the mint leaves.
3. Transfer the roasted spices and mint leaves to a bowl and let them cool completely.
4. Once cooled, grind the roasted spices and mint leaves to a fine powder using a mixer grinder.
5. In a mixing bowl, combine the ground spices with black salt, regular salt, citric acid and dried mango powder. Mix thoroughly to ensure all the ingredients are evenly distributed.
6. Store the kala masala for pani puri in an airtight container in a cool, dark place.

Royal Cafe-Style Lucknow Pani Batasha[1]

Ingredients

Khatai paste: 5 tbsp
Mint and chilli paste: 1½ tbsp
Salt: 1½ tbsp (or to taste)
Jaljeera powder: 1 tbsp
Cumin powder: ½ cup
Yellow chilli powder: ½ tbsp
Asafoetida: ¼ tsp
Cumin seeds, roasted: 2 tbsp

Fennel seeds (moti): 2 tbsp
Jaggery syrup (if you want sweet water): ⅛ cup
Fresh coriander, chopped: ¼ cup
Water: 1–1½ l

STEPS

1. In a large bowl, add 1 to 1½ l cold water.
2. Add all the ingredients to the water—khatai paste, mint and chilli paste, salt, jaljeera powder, cumin powder, yellow chilli powder, asafoetida, roasted cumin seeds, fennel seeds, jaggery syrup (if using) and fresh coriander.
3. Stir well to combine all the ingredients.
4. Serve the prepared pani with pani puri or pani batasha.

UP SPECIAL PANI PURI

INGREDIENTS

Dried mint powder: 2½ tbsp
Salt: 3 tsp (or to taste)
Sugar: ½ tsp
Cumin seeds, roasted: 1 tbsp
Dried mango powder: 3 tbsp
Black salt: 6 tsp

STEPS

1. Combine dried mint powder, salt, sugar, citric acid crystals, roasted cumin seeds, dried mango powder and black salt.
2. Grind the mixture into a fine powder using a spice grinder or blender.
3. Store the prepared masala in an airtight container for future use.

Old Agra Special Pani Puri

Ingredients

Mint leaves, chopped: ½ cup
Coriander leaves, chopped: 1 cup
1-inch ginger
Green chillies: 2–3
Tamarind: 1 tbsp
Jaggery powder: 4 tbsp
Cumin powder, roasted: 1 tsp
Chaat masala powder: 2 tsp
Water (for blending): ⅓ cup
Water (add as per the consistency you want): 1–1¼ cups
Boondi: 1–1½ tbsp
Black salt: 1 tsp
Salt: 1 tsp (or to taste)

Steps

1. In a blender, combine the chopped mint leaves, coriander leaves, ginger, green chillies, tamarind and jaggery powder.
2. Add ⅓ cup of water to the blender and blend the ingredients into a smooth paste.
3. Transfer the blended paste to a bowl. Add the roasted cumin powder, chaat masala powder and black salt or regular salt to taste. Mix well.
4. Pour 1 to 1¼ cups of water, adjusting the quantity to achieve your desired consistency. Stir to combine. Add 1–1½ tbsp of boondi to the pani.
5. Serve the pani with pani puri or pani batasha.

Chef Oindrila Bala's Bhaja
(For Bengali Phuchka/Pani Puri)

Ingredients

Cumin seeds: 5 tbsp
Coriander seeds: 2 tsp
Fennel seeds: 5 tbsp
Fenugreek seeds: ½ tsp
Red chillies, whole: 6
Mango powder: 2 tsp
Chaat masala: 2 tsp

Steps

1. In a medium cast-iron or non-stick skillet, roast the cumin seeds, coriander seeds, fennel seeds, fenugreek seeds and whole red chillies over medium heat. Stir and shake the pan continuously for about 2–3 minutes until the spices become aromatic and slightly darker. Be careful not to burn them.

2. Transfer the roasted spices to a plate and let them cool completely.

3. Once cooled, grind the roasted spices into a fine powder using a spice grinder or coffee grinder.

4. Add the mango powder and chaat masala to the spice blend. Mix thoroughly to combine all the ingredients.

5. Store the bhaja masala in an airtight container in a cool, dark place. It will stay fresh for about a month at room temperature or up to a year in the refrigerator.

Street-Style Jaljeera

Ingredients

Cumin seeds: 3 tbsp
Black pepper: 5
Asafoetida: 1 pinch
Salt: 1 tsp (or to taste)
Black salt: 1 tsp
Mint leaves: 20 gm
Lemon: 1
Ginger: 1 tsp
Green chillies: 2

Steps

1. Roast the cumin seeds and black pepper in a skillet over medium heat until they turn brown and start to release their aroma. Let the spices cool down completely.
2. In a blender jar, add the roasted spices and grind them into a fine powder.
3. Add the ginger, mint leaves and green chillies to the blender along with a little water. Blend the ingredients into a fine paste.
4. Take a large jar or bowl and add 1 l cold water. Add the prepared paste to the water and mix well. Squeeze in the lemon juice and add the asafoetida, salt and black salt. Mix everything thoroughly.
5. Strain the mixture to remove any solid particles. Store the strained water in the refrigerator to chill. Serve it chilled.

Jaljeera

Ingredients

Cumin seeds: 4 tbsp
Carom seeds: 2 tsp
Asafoetida, ground: 1 tsp
Dried mango powder: 4 tbsp
Dried mint leaves, crushed: 2 tbsp
Ginger powder: 1 tbsp
Black salt: 2 tsp
Red chilli powder: 1 tsp
Salt: 1 tbsp (or to taste)
Black pepper, crushed: 1 tsp

Steps

1. In a medium cast-iron or non-stick skillet, roast the cumin seeds and carom seeds over medium heat. Stir and shake the pan continuously for about 2 minutes until the spices are heated through and aromatic.
2. Once the roasted spices are cool, add the asafoetida and grind them to a fine powder using a mixer grinder.
3. Add the ground spice mixture to the pan along with the dried mango powder, ground mint leaves, ginger powder, black salt, red chilli powder, salt and freshly ground black pepper. Mix well and stir the mixture until it is heated through (for about 2 minutes).
4. Allow the spice blend to cool completely. Store it in an airtight container in a cool, dark place.
5. In a glass, add ice cubes, lemon juice and the prepared jaljeera powder. Pour a little soda into the glass and stir well. Top up the glass with more soda.

Bihari Aam Jhora

Ingredients

Raw mango, large: 2
Black salt: 1 tsp
Salt: 1 tsp (or to taste)
Sugar, powdered: 4 tsp
Cold water: 4 cups
Cumin powder, roasted: 1 tsp

Steps

1. Place the mangoes on an open flame to achieve a charred exterior and soft interior. Transfer the charred mangoes into a large bowl filled with cold water.
2. Pinch off a side of the mango skin and squeeze the juice into the water. Peel off the skin and scrape all the pulp into the water, including the pulp from the seed, using a stainless-steel spoon.
3. Add salt, sugar and roasted cumin powder to the mango pulp in water. Use an immersion blender to blend the mixture until smooth and homogenous. Adjust the consistency by adding more water if needed.
4. Refrigerate the mixture for a few hours to chill. Serve cold and enjoy!

Aam Panna

Ingredients

Sugar, powdered: 8 tbsp
Black salt: 1 tsp
Cumin powder, roasted: 2 tbsp
Dried mint leaves: 2 tbsp

Salt: 1 tsp (or to taste)
Black pepper powder: ⅛ tsp
Chilli powder: ⅛ tsp

STEPS

1. In a large bowl, combine sugar, black salt, roasted cumin powder, dried mint leaves, salt, black pepper powder and chilli powder.
2. Blend the mixture using an immersion blender or a regular blender until all ingredients are well incorporated.
3. To use this blend, dissolve the desired amount in cold water to prepare a refreshing drink. Follow your own recipe or steps for serving.

BIHARI SATTU JHORA

INGREDIENTS

Gram flour: 4 tbsp
Cold water: 3 cups
Onion, finely chopped: 1 tbsp
Ginger, finely chopped: ½ tsp
Green chilli, finely chopped: ½ tsp
Lemon juice: 1½ tbsp
Cumin powder, roasted: 1½ tsp
Black salt: ½ tsp
Salt: 1 tsp (or to taste)
Ice cubes
Fresh mint leaves (optional)

STEPS

1. In a mixing bowl, add 4 tbsp of gram flour and a little water. Mix it well to form a smooth paste without lumps.

Gradually add the remaining water to the paste, stirring continuously.

2. Add lemon juice, roasted cumin powder, finely chopped onions, finely chopped green chilli, finely chopped ginger, black salt and regular salt to the mixture. Stir well.

3. If using fresh mint leaves, tear a few and add them to the drink. Pour the sharbat into glasses. Add ice cubes if desired. Stir well before serving.

Kala Shikanji

Ingredients

Cumin seeds: 4 tbsp
Fennel seeds: 2 tbsp
Black pepper: 1 tsp
Green cardamom: 1 tbsp
Carom seeds: ½ tsp
Dried pomegranate seeds: 2 tbsp
Rock sugar (misri): ½ cup
Salt: 1 tsp (or to taste)
Black salt: 1 tsp
Dried mint: 2 tbsp
Dried ginger powder: 1 tsp

Steps

1. In a pan, dry roast cumin seeds, fennel seeds, black pepper, green cardamom and carom seeds on a low flame until they become fragrant and slightly darker in colour. Transfer them to a plate to cool down.

2. Once cooled, transfer the roasted spices to a grinding jar. Add dried pomegranate seeds, rock sugar, salt, black salt, dried mint and dried ginger powder to the jar.

3. Grind all the ingredients together to form a fine powder.

4. Store the prepared spice blend in an airtight container for future use.
5. Follow the steps mentioned above to prepare the beverage using this spice blend. Enjoy your refreshing drink.

Modi Nagar Famous Jain Shikanji

Ingredients

Crystal sugar: 100 gm
Cumin seeds: 4 tbsp
Green cardamom: 5
Black pepper: 1 tbsp
Black salt: 2 tbsp
Salt: 1 tbsp (or to taste)
Dried ginger: 1 tbsp
Dried mint powder: 1 tbsp

Steps

1. In a pan, dry roast all the whole spices (leaving half of the cumin seeds aside). Roast until they become fragrant and slightly darker in colour. Transfer them to a plate to cool down.
2. Combine the roasted cumin seeds with the unroasted cumin seeds, black pepper, black salt, salt, green cardamom, dried ginger, sugar and dried mint powder in a mixing bowl.
3. Grind all the ingredients together to form a fine powder. Store the prepared spice blend in an airtight container for future use.
4. Follow the steps mentioned above to prepare the beverage using this spice blend. Enjoy your refreshing drink.

Kerala-Style Rasam

Ingredients

Tomatoes, ripe: 3
Water: 3 cups
Garlic cloves, mashed: 5
Shallots, mashed: 5
Black pepper: 5
Tamarind pulp: 1 tbsp
Coriander leaves, chopped: ½ cup
Curry leaves: 2 sprigs
Green chillies, slit: 3
Black pepper powder: 1 tbsp
Coriander powder: 1 tsp
Rasam powder: 1½ tbsp
Asafoetida: ¼ tsp

For Tempering:
Ghee: 1 tbsp
Mustard seeds: 1 tsp
Dry red chillies: 3
Asafoetida: A pinch
Garlic, chopped: 3 cloves
Shallots, chopped: 3
Curry leaves: 1 sprig

Steps

1. Boil the tomatoes in 2 cups of water until soft. Remove the tomatoes, mash them well and strain the mixture. If any tomato pieces remain, blend them in a mixer and strain again. Add the tomato mixture back into the water used for boiling.

2. Add the remaining water to the tomato mixture. Add mashed garlic, mashed shallots, black pepper, tamarind pulp, chopped coriander leaves, curry leaves, slit green chillies, black pepper powder, coriander powder, instant rasam powder and asafoetida.

3. Close the pot with a lid and simmer the mixture until it boils. Boil for a couple of minutes, then switch off the flame.

4. Heat ghee in a pan. Add mustard seeds and allow them to splutter. Add asafoetida, dried red chillies, chopped garlic, chopped shallots and curry leaves. Fry the mixture until it becomes aromatic.

5. Add the prepared tempering to the cooked rasam. Let the rasam rest for about ten minutes to allow the flavours to meld.

6. Serve the rasam warm.

RASAM POWDER

INGREDIENTS

Dried red chilli, broken: 10
Coriander seeds: 4 tbsp
Dried curry leaves: 1 tbsp
Black pepper: 1½ tbsp
Dried yellow split pigeon peas: 1½ tbsp
Dried yellow split chickpeas: 1 tbsp
Cumin seeds: 2 tsp
Fenugreek seeds: 1 tsp
Black mustard seeds: 1 tsp
Turmeric powder: ¼ tsp
Asafoetida: ⅛ tsp

1. In a medium cast-iron or non-stick wok or skillet, roast all the ingredients together, stirring and shaking the skillet over medium heat until the spices become fragrant and turn golden (for about 3 minutes).
2. Let the roasted spices cool completely. Then grind them in a spice or coffee grinder to make a fine powder.
3. Store the spice blend in an airtight container in a cool, dark place. Follow the recipe as mentioned above.

MADURAI RASAM POWDER

INGREDIENTS

Coriander seeds: 3 tbsp
Red chilli, whole: 1½ tbsp
Pigeon pea: 2 tbsp
Black pepper: 1½ tbsp
Cumin seeds: 1 tbsp
Turmeric powder: 1 tsp

STEPS

1. Combine all the ingredients in a spice grinder or coffee grinder. Grind them into a coarse powder.
2. Store the prepared spice blend in an airtight container.
3. Once the spice powder is ready, you can either follow the rasam recipe mentioned above or use your own recipe for a flavourful variation.

MITHAI

INGREDIENTS

Saffron threads, dry-roasted and coarsely crushed: ½ tsp
Raw pistachios, shelled: 20–30
Almonds, coarsely broken: 15–20
Cashews, coarsely broken: 15–20
Green cardamom seeds, crushed: 1 tsp
1-inch cinnamon stick
Black cardamom seeds: ½ tsp

STEPS

1. In a small mixer grinder, pulse together pistachios, almonds and cashews in one or two batches until they form a coarse powder.
2. Combine the ground nuts with the green and black cardamom seeds and the crushed saffron threads.
3. Store the prepared masala in an airtight container.
4. This masala can be added to almost all desserts to enhance their flavour.

TAMIL NADU MASALA VADAI (LENTIL)

INGREDIENTS

Bengal gram: 2 cups
Onion, medium: 1
Green chillies, chopped: 5
Dill: 1 small bunch or ¼ cup
Ghee: 1 tsp
Garlic: 3 cloves
Salt: 1 tsp (or to taste)
Oil for frying: 2 cups

STEPS

1. Soak the Bengal gram in water for 1 hour. Finely chop the onion and green chillies. Clean and wash the dill and chop the leaves finely. Coarsely pound the garlic.
2. Clean and drain the soaked Bengal gram. Coarsely grind it in a mixer or food processor.
3. In a mixing bowl, combine the ground gram, chopped onion, chillies, dill, ghee, baking powder, garlic and salt. Mix thoroughly.
4. Shape the mixture into lime-sized balls and flatten them with your fingers. Heat the oil in a frying pan and deep-fry the vadai until they are golden brown and crispy.
5. Serve hot as a teatime snack.

Paruppu Vadai

Ingredients

Dried red chillies: 5
Cumin powder: 3 tsp
Fennel seeds: 4 tsp
Salt: 1 tsp (or to taste)

Steps

Use this spice blend and follow the steps in the vadai recipe mentioned above to create a differently flavoured vadai.

Jharkhandi Kachri Bada

Ingredients

Red chilli powder: 5 tbsp
Coriander powder: 5 tbsp
Cumin powder: 5 tbsp
Turmeric powder: 5 tbsp

Steps

1. Combine the red chilli powder, coriander powder, cumin powder, and turmeric powder thoroughly in a bowl to create an even spice blend.
2. Use this spice blend to follow the steps in the vadai recipe mentioned above.
3. Store the spice blend in an airtight container in a cool, dark place to maintain its freshness for up to 3–6 months.

Rohit Singh's Dal Vada

Ingredients

Cumin seeds, crushed: 3 tsp
Fennel seeds, crushed: 3 tsp
Black pepper, crushed: 2 tsp
Salt: 1½ tsp (or to taste)

Steps

1. Combine the crushed cumin seeds, crushed fennel seeds, crushed black pepper, and salt in a bowl until well mixed.
2. Use this spice blend to follow the steps in the vadai recipe mentioned above.

3. Store the spice blend in an airtight container in a cool, dark place for up to 3–6 months to maintain its flavour and aroma.

ALOO BONDA

INGREDIENTS

Potatoes, large, peeled and cooked in salted water: 6
Cooking oil: ¼ cup
Curry leaves, minced: A few
Mustard seeds, whole: ½ tsp
Onion, large, minced: 1
Ginger garlic paste, fresh: 2 tbsp
Turmeric powder: 1 tsp
Green coriander, washed and finely chopped: 1 medium-sized bunch
Green chillies, finely chopped: 3
Lime juice, fresh: 1 tsp
Salt: 1 tsp (or to taste)

For the Gram Flour Mixture:
Gram flour: 1½ cups
Salt: 1 tsp (or to taste)
Turmeric powder: ½ tsp
Chilli powder: ½ tsp
Baking powder: ½ tsp
Water
Oil for frying

STEPS

1. Place a saucepan over moderate heat and pour in the oil. Once the oil is hot, add curry leaves and mustard seeds to

the pan. When the seeds begin to sputter, lower the heat and stir in the onion.

2. Fry until the onions are transparent. Mix ginger garlic paste with a little lime juice and add to the pan. Fry the spices until they release their fragrant aroma.

3. Add chopped green coriander and chillies, together with the cooked potatoes. Fry the potato mixture. Add salt to taste and the remaining lime juice. The potatoes will become very soft; mash them while frying until well blended with the spices. Set aside.

4. Sift gram flour together with the next four ingredients. Pour in enough cold water to make a smooth paste. With your hands, shape the potato mixture into balls, each the size of a large walnut.

5. Place a heavy skillet over moderate heat and pour in one cup of oil. When the oil is hot, dip the potato balls into the gram flour mixture and coat evenly. Place in hot oil. Fry bondas until they are golden on all sides. Remove from heat and drain on absorbent paper.

6. Serve with green coriander chutney.

SAYALI'S BENGALI ALOO CHOP

INGREDIENTS

Potatoes, medium, boiled: 3
Green chillies, fresh, chopped: 2
Coriander, fresh, chopped: 2 tbsp
Red chilli flakes: 1 tsp
Garam masala: ½ tsp
Cumin seeds, roasted: ½ tsp
Salt: ½ tsp (or to taste)
Mustard oil: 1 tsp

Coriander, coarsely ground: ¼ tsp
Cornstarch: 2 tbsp

STEPS

1. Mash the boiled potatoes in a large bowl.
2. Add the chopped green chillies, coriander, red chilli flakes, garam masala, roasted cumin seeds, salt, mustard oil, coarse coriander powder and cornstarch to the mashed potatoes. Mix well.
3. All the other steps can be followed as above.

HALWAI-STYLE ALOO BONDA

INGREDIENTS

Potato, medium: 4
Oil: 2 tbsp
Black mustard seeds: 1 tsp
Asafoetida: ¼ tsp
Curry leaves: 12
Cumin seeds: ½ tsp
Fennel seeds: ½ tsp
Green chilli, small: 2
1½ inch ginger
Garlic: 6 cloves
Black pepper, crushed: 1 tsp
Turmeric powder: 1 tsp
Red chilli, whole: 2
Dried mango powder: 2 tsp
Green coriander, chopped: 2–3 tbsp
Salt: 1½ tsp (or to taste)
Black salt: ½ tsp (or to taste)

1. Boil the potatoes until tender, then peel and chop them into small cubes.
2. In a pan, heat oil over medium heat. Add mustard seeds and let them splutter. Toss in asafoetida, 10–12 curry leaves, cumin seeds and fennel seeds. Sauté for a few seconds until aromatic.
3. Reduce the flame and add small chopped green chillies, chopped ginger and chopped garlic. Sauté until the raw smell goes away. Add black pepper, turmeric powder and whole red chilli. Mix well.
4. Add the chopped potatoes to the pan and mix well to coat them with the spices. Sprinkle 2 tsp of dried mango powder and mix well. Add chopped green coriander. Add salt and black salt to taste. Mix well.
5. Fry these following the steps mentioned above.

Mumbai Vada

Ingredients

Potatoes, boiled, peeled and mashed: 3
Curry leaves: 8
Sunflower oil: 1 tbsp
Black mustard seeds: 1 tsp
Green chilli, finely chopped: 1
Garlic clove, finely chopped: 1
1-inch fresh ginger, peeled and finely chopped
Salt: 1 tsp (or to taste)
Turmeric powder: ¼ tsp

1. Heat the sunflower oil in a frying pan over medium heat. Add the mustard seeds. When they start to pop, add the curry leaves, chopped chilli, garlic, ginger, salt and turmeric.
2. Stir well and then add the mashed potatoes. Cook for about 2 minutes, mixing thoroughly to combine all the ingredients.
3. Remove the pan from the heat and let the mixture cool. Once cool, shape the mixture into 10 equal-sized balls.
4. Follow the frying method mentioned in the aloo bonda/chop recipe. Heat oil in a deep frying pan or wok. Fry the potato balls until they are golden brown and crispy on all sides. Remove them with a slotted spoon and drain on paper towels to remove excess oil.

MISAL

INGREDIENTS

For the Mixture:
Sunflower oil: 3 tbsp
Cumin seeds: 1 tsp
Mustard seeds: ½ tsp
Curry leaves: 10
Onion, finely chopped: 1
Green chilli, chopped: 1
Garlic cloves, finely chopped: 4
Ginger, peeled and chopped: ½ inch
Salt: 1½ tsp (or to taste)
Coriander powder: 1 tsp
Garam masala: 1 tsp
Cumin seeds, ground: 2 tsp

Tamarind paste: 1 tsp
Sugar, powdered: 1 tsp
Boiling water: 500 ml
Potato, peeled, boiled and diced: 1
Tomato, diced: 1
Sprouted moth (matki) beans: 1½ cup

For the Pav:
Salted butter: 4 tsp
Soft bread rolls (pav), small, split horizontally: 4

For Garnishing:
Lemon juice
Fresh coriander leaves, finely chopped: A handful
Onion, finely chopped: 1
Mixture (farsan): A handful

Steps

1. Heat the sunflower oil in a pan over medium heat. Add the cumin seeds and mustard seeds. Once they begin to pop, add the curry leaves, finely chopped onion and green chilli. Cook for 6–8 minutes until the onion turns golden brown.

2. Add the finely chopped garlic and ginger, and cook for an additional 2 minutes. Stir in the salt, coriander powder, garam masala, ground cumin seeds, tamarind paste and granulated sugar. Cook for 1 minute until well combined.

3. Pour in the boiling water, then add the diced potato, tomato and drained three-bean salad (or cooked mixed beans). Cover the pan and cook for 5 minutes until the sauce begins to thicken.

4. Heat the salted butter in a frying pan over medium heat. Lay the bread rolls in the pan with the cut sides facing

downwards. Cook for about 2 minutes until the cut sides are golden brown.

5. Place the vegetable mixture in a bowl. Squeeze a little lemon juice over it, then scatter with finely chopped coriander leaves, chopped onion and mixture mix.

6. Serve hot with the buttered pav.

KOLHAPURI MISAL

INGREDIENTS

Cumin seeds: 1 tsp
Fennel seeds: 1 tbsp
Coriander seeds: 2 tbsp
White sesame seeds: 2 tbsp
Cloves: 6
Green cardamom: 2
1-inch cinnamon stick
Dried coconut, roughly chopped: ¼
Poppy seeds: 1 tbsp
Dried red chillies: 8–10
Garlic cloves: 9
1-inch ginger

STEPS

1. Combine cumin seeds, fennel seeds, coriander seeds, white sesame seeds, cloves, green cardamom, a cinnamon stick, dried coconut, poppy seeds, dried red chillies, garlic cloves and ginger. Grind all the ingredients together to form a coarse spice blend.

2. Use this spice blend as directed in the original vegetable mixture recipe to create a different flavour profile. Follow all the cooking methods mentioned above for the vegetable mixture.

PUNE SPECIAL MISAL

INGREDIENTS

Onion, large, sliced: 1
Dried coconut, roughly chopped: ½ cup
Coriander seeds: ¼ cup
Garlic cloves, sliced: 10–12
Kashmiri dried red chillies: 4–5
Pandi dried red chillies: 10–12
Bedgi dried red chillies: 7–8
Black pepper: 10–12
Cloves: 10
Black cardamom: 2
Green cardamom: 12
Star anise: 3
Cumin seeds: 1 tsp
Fennel seeds: 1 tsp
White sesame seeds: 1 tbsp
1-inch cinnamon stick
Rock asafoetida: A small piece
Sea salt: 1 tsp
Poppy seeds: ½ tsp
Dried ginger powder: 1 tsp
Coconut oil: 1 tbsp

STEPS

1. Heat the oil in a non-stick pan. Add the roughly chopped dried coconut and sliced onion. Sauté until light brown. Add sliced garlic cloves and continue sautéing until golden brown. Transfer this mixture to a plate and allow it to cool.
2. In the same pan, dry roast the Kashmiri red chillies, pandi chillies and bedgi red chillies for about a minute. Transfer them to the same plate and let them cool.

3. Using the same pan, dry roast the black pepper, cloves, black cardamom, green cardamoms, star anise, cumin seeds, fennel seeds, white sesame seeds, cinnamon stick, coriander seeds and rock asafoetida until fragrant.

4. Add sea salt, poppy seeds and dried ginger powder to the roasted spices. Sauté for another minute and then set aside to cool.

5. Transfer the coconut–onion mixture to a blender and grind it coarsely. Transfer this mixture to a bowl. Grind the remaining roasted ingredients in the blender to a fine powder.

6. Add the ground spice mixture to the coarsely ground coconut–onion mixture. Mix well. Store the spice blend in an airtight container and use it as needed.

7. To prepare the dish using this blend, follow the cooking method described above to achieve a uniquely flavoured dish.

PUNE DABELI

INGREDIENTS

For Dabeli Masala:
Coriander seeds: ½ cup
Cumin seeds: 2 tbsp
Fennel seeds: 1 tbsp
Black cardamom: 4
Cloves: 2–3
Black pepper: 10–15
2-inch cinnamon stick
Dried Kashmiri chillies, broken in half: 2–3
Black salt: 2 tsp
Degi red chilli powder: 1½ tsp
Dried coconut, grated: ⅓ cup
Peanut oil: 2 tbsp
Jaggery powder: 2 tsp

For Chilli Garlic Chutney:
Dried Kashmiri red chillies: 15
Garlic cloves: 20
Peanut oil: 2 tsp
Sugar powder: 1 tsp
Bedgi red chilli powder: ½ tsp
Peanuts: ¼ cup
Salt: 1½ tsp (or to taste)

For Filling:
Boiled potatoes, grated: 3
Peanut oil: 2 tsp
Prepared dabeli masala: 2 tbsp

Other Ingredients for the Masala Peanut:
Roasted masala peanuts: ⅓ cup
Prepared dabeli masala: 2 tbsp
Onions, medium, roughly chopped: 2
Green chilli, chopped: 1
Coriander leaves, chopped: 1 tbsp
Lemon juice: 1 tsp
Tamarind chutney: As you prefer
Red garlic chutney: As you prefer
Sev: As you prefer
Pomegranate pearls for garnish
Butter: 1 tbsp
Laadi pav: 4

STEPS

For Dabeli Masala:

1. In a pan, add all the spices and dry roast on a low flame until the spices turn aromatic.

2. Transfer the spices to a bowl. In the same pan, dry roast the grated coconut until golden and transfer it to the bowl. Let it cool down. Grind the mixture into a fine powder.

3. Transfer the ground masala into a bowl, add peanut oil, sugar and mix well. Keep it aside for further use.

4. In a bowl, add Kashmiri red chillies, garlic cloves, salt, sugar, degi red chilli powder, peanut oil and peanuts. Transfer the mixture to a grinder, add a little water and grind into a smooth paste.

5. Transfer the chutney into a bowl and keep it aside for further use.

6. In a non-stick pan, heat peanut oil, and add the prepared dabeli masala. Mix well. Add grated potatoes and a little water and cook on a medium flame until the masala is well incorporated. Transfer the mixture to a plate and let it come to room temperature.

7. Sprinkle the masala peanuts, chopped onion mixture, sev and pomegranate on top.

8. Slit the pav in the centre and spread tamarind chutney on one side and red garlic chutney on the other side.

9. Stuff the prepared potato mixture into the pav. Roll the stuffed pav in sev.

10. In a non-stick pan, heat butter and toast the pav from both sides until slightly golden brown.

11. Garnish with coriander sprigs and pomegranate pearls. Serve hot.

Pune Dabeli 2

Ingredients

1-inch cinnamon sticks: 2
Black cardamom: 2
Cumin seeds: 2 tsp
Coriander seeds: 3 tbsp

Cloves: 8–10
Black pepper: 5–6
Kashmiri red chilli powder: 3 tbsp
Citric acid: ½ tsp
Sugar: 1 tbsp

STEPS

1. In a non-stick pan, dry roast the cinnamon stick, black cardamoms, cumin seeds, coriander seeds, cloves and black pepper until they turn golden brown. Transfer them to a plate and let them cool.
2. Once cooled, grind the roasted ingredients along with the chilli powder, citric acid and sugar into a fine powder.
3. Store the spice blend in an airtight container for later use.
4. To prepare the dabeli, follow the recipe steps mentioned above using this spice blend for a different flavour profile.

PUNE DABELI 3

INGREDIENTS

Coriander seeds: 1 tbsp
Black pepper: 1 tsp
Cumin seeds: 1 tbsp
Fennel seeds: 1 tbsp
Black cardamom: 1
Sesame seeds: 1 tbsp
1-inch cinnamon stick
Bay leaves: 2
Dried coconut: 2 tbsp
Red chilli powder: 1 tbsp
Black salt: 1½ tsp
Mango powder: 1 tsp
Cloves: 6

Star anise: 2
Sugar, powdered: 2 tbsp
Dried red chillies: 6
Turmeric powder: ¼ tsp

STEPS

1. In a non-stick pan, dry roast the coriander seeds, black pepper, cumin seeds, fennel seeds, black cardamom, sesame seeds, cinnamon stick, bay leaf, cloves, star anise and dried red chillies until they turn golden brown. Transfer them to a plate and let them cool.
2. Once cooled, grind the roasted ingredients along with the dried coconut, red chilli powder, black salt, mango powder, powdered sugar and turmeric powder into a fine powder.
3. Store the spice blend in an airtight container for later use.
4. To prepare a dabeli, follow the recipe steps mentioned above using this spice blend for a different flavour profile.

HOME-MADE DABELI

INGREDIENTS

Coriander seeds: 3 tbsp
Sesame seeds: 3 tbsp
Kashmiri chilli powder: 2 tbsp
Dried coconut: 2 tbsp
Fennel seeds: 2 tbsp
Cumin seeds: 2 tbsp
Cloves: 8
Dried red chillies: 6
1-inch cinnamon sticks: 2

1. In a non-stick pan, dry roast the coriander seeds, fennel seeds, cumin seeds, cloves, dried red chillies, cinnamon stick, coconut and sesame seeds until they turn golden brown and release their aroma. Transfer them to a plate and let them cool.
2. Once cooled, grind the roasted ingredients along with the Kashmiri chilli powder into a fine powder.
3. Store the spice blend in an airtight container for later use.
4. To prepare dabeli, follow the recipe steps mentioned above (using this spice blend for a different flavour profile).

Mangalorean Goli Baje

Ingredients

All-purpose flour: 1 cup
Curd: ½ cup
Rice flour: 1 tbsp
Cumin seeds: 1 tsp
Green chillies, finely chopped: 2
1-inch piece of ginger, finely chopped
Fresh coriander leaves, chopped: 1 tbsp
Curry leaves, chopped: 1 sprig
Baking soda: 1 tsp
Salt: 1½ tsp (or to taste)
Water, as needed
Oil for deep frying

Steps

1. In a mixing bowl, combine all-purpose flour, rice flour, cumin seeds, green chillies, ginger, fresh coriander leaves,

curry leaves and salt. Stir in the curd and mix well. Add a little water if needed to make a thick batter.

2. Let the batter rest for 30 minutes. This allows the flavours to meld and the batter to become slightly aerated.

3. Just before frying, add the baking soda to the batter and mix well.

4. In a deep frying pan, heat enough oil over medium heat. To check if the oil is ready, drop a small amount of batter into the oil. If it sizzles and rises to the top, the oil is ready.

5. Using your hands or a spoon, drop small portions of the batter into the hot oil. Fry the fritters in batches, making sure not to overcrowd the pan. Fry until golden brown and crispy, turning occasionally to ensure even cooking.

6. Use a slotted spoon to remove the fritters from the oil and drain on paper towels to remove excess oil. Serve hot with coconut chutney.

JHARKHAND PAV BHAJI

INGREDIENTS

For Bhaji (Vegetable Gravy):
Potatoes, medium: 4
Cauliflower, chopped: 1 cup
Carrot, chopped: 1 cup
Green peas: 1 cup
French beans, chopped: ⅓ cup
Water: 2½ cups

Other Ingredients:
Butter, salted or unsalted: 3 tbsp
Cumin seeds: 1 tsp
Onion, finely chopped: ½ cup
Ginger garlic paste: 2 tsp

Green chillies, chopped: 2
Tomatoes, chopped: 3
Kashmiri chilli powder: 1 tsp
Pav bhaji masala: 4 tbsp
Water: 2 cups, add as needed
Salt: 1½ tsp (or to taste)

For Pav Bhaji Masala:
Cumin seeds: ¼ cup
Fennel seeds: 2 tbsp
Coriander seeds: 2 tbsp
Mace: 4–5 blades
Cloves: 8
Black pepper: 1 tbsp
Black cardamom: 3
Star anise: 2
1-inch cinnamon sticks: 2
Dried red chillies: 6
Dried mango powder: 2 tbsp
Dried ginger powder: 1 tbsp
Black salt: 2 tsp
Turmeric powder: 1 tsp

Accompaniments:
Buns (pav): 12
Butter, for toasting pav: 4 tbsp
Lemon wedge: 1
Onion, finely chopped: 1
Coriander leaves, chopped: 4 tbsp

STEPS

1. Rinse, peel and chop all the veggies. Add all the chopped
    veggies to a pressure cooker with water. Pressure cook the

veggies for 5–6 whistles or about 10–12 minutes on a low to medium flame.

2. When the pressure settles down, open the cooker and check if the veggies are boiled well. Ensure they are cooked completely.

3. Heat a pan or kadahi and add butter. Once the butter melts, add cumin seeds and let them crackle. Toss in finely chopped onions and sauté on a low to medium flame till they turn translucent.

4. Add ginger garlic paste and sauté till the raw aroma goes away. Add chopped green chillies and finely chopped tomatoes and mix. Sauté till the tomatoes become soft and mushy and you see butter releasing from the sides (about 6–7 minutes).

5. Add Kashmiri red chilli powder and 4 tbsp pav bhaji masala. Mix well.

6. Add the cooked veggies along with the water. Mix and season with salt as per taste.

7. Use a potato masher to mash the veggies directly in the pan to your desired consistency.

8. Let the bhaji simmer for 8–10 minutes, stirring occasionally. Add more water if the bhaji looks dry.

9. Slice the pavs and lightly pan-fry them with butter until golden brown.

SERVING

1. Take the bhaji in a serving plate or bowl. Top it with one or two cubes of butter.

2. Place finely chopped onions, lemon wedges and chopped coriander leaves on the side. Alternatively, sprinkle onions, coriander leaves and lemon juice directly on the bhaji.

3. Serve the bhaji hot with the buttered pav.

Easy Pav Bhaji

Ingredients

Coriander seeds: 4 tbsp
Fennel seeds: 2 tbsp
1-inch cinnamon sticks: 2
Cumin seeds: 4 tsp
Turmeric powder: 2 tsp
Mango powder: 2 tsp
Black pepper: 1 tsp
Dried red chillies: 8
Green cardamom: 8
Cloves: 5
Mace, whole: 1

Steps

1. In a non-stick pan, dry roast coriander seeds, fennel seeds, cumin seeds, black pepper, dried red chillies, seeds from green cardamom pods, cloves, cinnamon stick and mace on a low flame until they turn aromatic. Stir continuously to avoid burning.
2. Transfer the roasted spices to a plate and let them cool completely. Once cooled, transfer the roasted spices to a grinder. Add turmeric powder and mango powder.
3. Store the ground spice blend in an airtight container.
4. To use this spice blend, follow the cooking steps mentioned above for a differently flavoured pav bhaji.

Delhi Pav Bhaji

Ingredients

Fennel seeds: 2 tbsp
Cumin seeds: 4 tbsp
Coriander seeds: 3 tbsp
Black cardamom: 1
Cloves: 20–25
Black pepper: ½ tsp
Kashmiri dried red chillies: 10–12
Bay leaves: 2
1-inch cinnamon sticks: 4
Salt: 1 tsp (or to taste)
Dried mango powder: 1½ tbsp
Black salt: ¼ tsp

Steps

1. In a dry pan, roast the fennel seeds, cumin seeds, coriander seeds, black cardamom, cloves, black pepper, dried Kashmiri red chillies, bay leaves and cinnamon sticks over medium heat until they turn golden brown and release a fragrant aroma. Stir continuously to avoid burning.
2. Once the spices have cooled, transfer them to a grinder. Add the salt, dried mango powder and black salt.
3. Store the ground pav bhaji masala in an airtight container.
4. To use this spice blend, follow the cooking steps mentioned in the pav bhaji recipe above for a flavourful pav bhaji.

Mahabaleshwar Pav Bhaji

Ingredients

Bay leaves: 6
1-inch cinnamon sticks: 2
Nutmeg, grated: ½ tsp
Star anise: 3
Green cardamom: 6
Black cardamom seeds: 2
Sankeshwari chillies: 5
Cloves: 10
Black pepper: ½ tbsp
Coriander seeds: 4 tbsp
Cumin seeds: 1 tbsp
Fennel seeds: 1 tbsp
Stone flower: 1 tbsp
Black salt: 1 tsp
Dried ginger powder: 1 tsp
Mango powder: ½ tsp
Asafoetida:

Steps

1. In a dry pan, roast the bay leaves, cinnamon, nutmeg, star anise, green cardamom, black cardamom seeds, cloves, black pepper, coriander seeds, cumin seeds, fennel seeds, Sankeshwari chilli and stone flower over medium heat until they turn golden brown and release a fragrant aroma. Stir continuously to avoid burning.
2. Once the spices have cooled, transfer them to a grinder. Add the black salt, dried ginger powder, mango powder, degi chilli powder and asafoetida.
3. Grind everything to a fine powder.

4. Store the ground spice blend in an airtight container. To use this spice blend, follow the cooking steps mentioned in the pav bhaji recipe above for a flavourful dish.

Bihar Pav Bhaji

Ingredients

Cumin seeds: 2 tbsp
Coriander seeds: 2 tbsp
Fennel seeds: 3 tbsp
Fenugreek leaves: 3 tbsp
Dried pomegranate seeds: 2 tbsp
Fenugreek seeds: 1 tsp
Cloves: 12
Black cardamom: 4
Carom seeds: ½ tsp
1-inch cinnamon sticks: 3
Star anise: 3
Black pepper: 1 tsp
Nutmeg, grated: ¼ tsp
Kashmiri red chillies: 15
Bay leaves: 6
Salt: 1 tsp (or to taste)
Turmeric powder: 1 tsp
Sugar: 1 tsp
Black salt: 1 tsp
Mango powder: 2 tsp
Asafoetida: ¼ tsp
Triphala powder: 2 tsp
Degi chilli powder: 2 tbsp
Dried ginger powder: 2 tsp
Citric acid: 2 tsp

Steps

1. In a dry pan, roast the cumin seeds, coriander seeds, fennel seeds, fenugreek seeds, cloves, black cardamom, carom seeds, cinnamon sticks, star anise, black pepper and Kashmiri red chillies over medium heat until they turn golden brown and release a fragrant aroma. Stir continuously to avoid burning.
2. Once the spices have cooled, transfer them to a grinder. Add the fenugreek leaves, dried pomegranate seeds, nutmeg, bay leaves, salt, turmeric, sugar, black salt, mango powder, asafoetida, triphala powder, degi chilli powder, dried ginger powder and citric acid.
3. Grind everything to a fine powder.
4. Store the ground spice blend in an airtight container.
5. To use this pav bhaji masala, follow the cooking steps mentioned in the pav bhaji recipe above for a flavourful dish.

HALEEM

Ingredients

Cracked wheat (dalia): 3 cups
Split black gram: 1 cup
Split chickpeas: 1 cup
Mutton, cut into small pieces and washed: 1 kg
Red chilli powder: 4 tbsp
Turmeric powder: 1 tsp
Ginger garlic paste: 2 tbsp
Garam masala: 4 tsp
Ghee: ½ cup
Onions, fried: 2 cups
Green chillies: 10
Black pepper: ½ tsp

Cumin powder: 5 tbsp
1-inch cinnamon sticks: 2
Coriander leaves: ½ cup
Onions, fried (for garnish): ½ cup
Lemon wedges (for garnish)
Fresh coriander (for garnish)
Cumin powder, roasted (for garnish)

STEPS

1. Soak cracked wheat and lentils for 2–3 hours, then drain and wash them.
2. In a pressure cooker, mix mutton with red chilli powder, turmeric powder, salt, ginger garlic paste and garam masala. Pressure cook for 5–6 whistles on a medium flame. Cool and shred the meat.
3. Heat ghee in a deep pot, add the remaining ginger garlic paste, green chillies and black pepper. Sauté until fragrant.
4. Add 8 cups of water along with cracked wheat and lentils. Boil until everything is fully cooked, then blend to a smooth paste using an immersion blender.
5. Add the shredded meat, remaining garam masala, cumin powder, cinnamon, green chillies, coriander and fried onions. Cook on a medium flame for 10 minutes.
6. Add 3 cups of water to adjust the consistency and simmer for about 30 minutes.
7. Serve hot, garnished with extra fried onions, lemon wedges, fresh coriander and roasted cumin powder.

RAZIYA DEHLVI'S HALEEM[2]

INGREDIENTS

Mutton, with fat: 1.8 kg
Wheat, soaked: 1.2 kg
White Kabuli chana, boiled: 250 gm

Milk: 1 l

Fresh cream: 250 ml

Ghee: 500 gm

Cardamom: 20

Cloves: 20

1-inch cinnamon sticks: 6

Saffron: ¼ tsp

Black pepper: 2 tbsp

Cumin seeds: 2 tbsp

Kewra water: 100 ml

Ginger paste: 125 gm

Red chilli powder: 100 gm

Salt: 80 gm (or to taste)

Curd: 250 gm

STEPS

1. Boil mutton until tender. Strain the mutton while keeping the broth aside. Mash the mutton and set aside.
2. In a large pot, heat 175 gm of ghee. Sauté cloves until fragrant. Add the ginger paste, mutton pieces and boiled white Kabuli chana. Add saffron and garam masala to the mixture. Cook until well-blended.
3. Cook the wheat in water until soft. Blend the wheat into a smooth paste. Mix the wheat paste with the prepared mutton broth.
4. In a large pot, mix the mutton broth, wheat paste and korma. Add milk and cook until well-blended. Stir continuously to avoid sticking.
5. In a separate pan, heat 175 gm of ghee. Sauté cardamom, cloves, cinnamon, black pepper and cumin seeds.
6. Add to the haleem mixture. Add cream, red chilli, salt and curd.
7. Cook until the desired consistency is achieved. Add kewra water and mix well.

8. Simmer for a few minutes to let the flavours blend. Garnish with the remaining garam masala.
9. Serve hot with naan or rice.

Note: This updated recipe is an inspired adaptation of the original version.

NUZHAT SHAIDA HALEEM

INGREDIENTS

Bay leaves: 6
Star anise: 3
Black pepper: 2 tsp
White sesame seeds: 2 tsp
Cumin seeds: 3 tbsp
Coriander seeds: 5 tbsp
Black cardamom: 6
Cloves: 1 tbsp
Dry ginger powder: 1 tbsp
Mace, whole: 1
Green cardamom: 12–15
Nutmeg, grated: ¼ tsp
1-inch cinnamon: 2
Kashmiri red chillies: 3 tbsp
Turmeric powder: 1 tsp
Rose petals, dried (optional): 3 tbsp
Salt: 1 tbsp (or to taste)

STEPS

1. Dry roast all the whole spices (bay leaves, star anise, black pepper, sesame seeds, cumin seeds, coriander seeds, black cardamom, cloves, mace, green cardamom and cinnamon sticks) in a pan until fragrant.

2. Allow the roasted spices to cool slightly, then grind them into a fine powder using a spice grinder.
3. Add the powdered spices (dried ginger powder, Kashmiri red chilli powder, turmeric powder, nutmeg and salt) to the ground whole spices, and grind again until everything is well mixed into a fine powder.
4. If using, add the rose petals, dried to the spice blend and either grind or mix them in thoroughly.
5. Once done, transfer the spice blend to an airtight container for storage.
6. Use the haleem recipe mentioned above. For 1 kg of mutton, use 10–12 tbsp of this spice blend. Follow the rest of the steps from the haleem recipe to prepare the dish. This spice blend will add a rich and aromatic flavour to your haleem.

HYDERABAD-STYLE HALEEM

INGREDIENTS

1-inch cinnamon sticks: 3
Black pepper: 10–11
Bay leaves: 3
Onion powder: 4 tbsp
Ginger powder: 2 tbsp
Garlic powder: 1½ tbsp
Red chilli powder: 1½ tbsp
Coriander powder: ½ tbsp
Turmeric powder: ½ tbsp
Salt: 1 tbsp (or to taste)
Garam masala powder: 1 tsp
Cardamom powder: ½ tsp

1. In a large mixing bowl, combine all the ingredients (whole and powdered). Mix the spices thoroughly. Grind them to a fine powder.
2. Transfer the spice mix into an airtight container to retain its freshness.
3. Use the prepared spice mix in your haleem recipe. For 1 kg of mutton, use 10–12 tbsp of this spice blend. Follow the cooking steps provided in the haleem recipe to create a flavourful dish. This spice mix will enhance the taste and add a rich, aromatic flavour to your haleem.

BENGALI HALEEM

INGREDIENTS

Dried red chillies: 6
Black pepper: 4 tbsp
Cloves: 15
Green cardamom: 15
1-inch cinnamon sticks: 2
Black cardamom: 2
Nutmeg, grated: ¼ tsp
Mace, whole: 1
Bay leaves: 4

STEPS

1. Dry roast the whole spices (cinnamon sticks, cloves, green cardamom, black cardamom, nutmeg, mace, bay leaves, dried red chillies and black pepper) until fragrant.
2. Allow the roasted spices to cool, then grind them into a fine powder using a spice grinder.

3. Use this spice blend in your haleem recipe. For 1 kg of mutton, use 8–10 tbsp of this spice mix. Follow the cooking steps provided in the haleem recipe to create a flavourful dish. This spice blend will add a rich and aromatic flavour to your haleem.

THE LAST PIT STOP

FINALLY, AS WE COME TO THE END OF THIS CRAZY SPICE trail, I want to take you, very briefly, on a quick and personal trip to some of my favourite spice bazaars from India.

Why, you ask?

The bazaars of South Asia have long served as the vibrant heart of its socio-economic and cultural landscape. These lively markets were more than mere trading hubs; they were the centres of social interaction, where peasants, townspeople, landholders and rulers converged. Offering an array of goods, services and news, the bazaars functioned as microcosms of the region's diverse environment, embodying the very essence of a society rich in culture, politics and tradition.

A term of Persian origin that gained currency in Indian and European languages, a 'bazaar' refers to a market or marketplace, generally a permanent market or street of shops.[1]

It has also been defined from classical to modern poets, philosophers, storytellers and other great thinkers. One of my favourites is in Persian by Amir Khusrau:[2]

man bi-dān nazram ki gar miram bi-sūyam bin-garī
bin kih chu'man chand kas murda-st dar bāzār-i 'ishq
I vow to die that you might look my way.
See how many have died like me in the bazaar of love.

Or the English poem by Sarojini Naidu 'In the Bazaars of Hyderabad':[3]

What do you sell O ye merchants?
Richly your wares are displayed.
Turbans of crimson and silver,
Tunics of purple brocade,
Mirrors with panels of amber,
Daggers with handles of jade.
What do you weigh, O ye vendors?
Saffron and lentil and rice.
What do you grind, O ye maidens?
Sandalwood, henna, and spice.
What do you call, O ye pedlars?
Chessmen and ivory dice.

In this poem, Naidu paints a colourful market of Hyderabad and takes you on a journey where you feel the market and immerse yourself; she wants you to explore the cultural diversity of traditional craftsmanship.

When I think of a bazaar or market, I think of a little Sadaf hopping on to his father's peacock-blue scooter with his brother every Sunday, heading to a lane where one could find everything—from spices to vegetables, meat and lots of stories. Our ritual was to go there, roam around and pick up the best produce. Then, my brother, Shabi, and I would sit at a street-side shop to enjoy either a spicy chaat or chole with puffy bhature.

A bazaar is also, therefore, where the story of spices really begins.

As an adult now, when I stand in the market, the spices, to me, seem like people—loud and colourful, each with a personality that could either bring a dish to life or completely ruin it. And just like people, the best blends are the ones that somehow make the chaos taste amazing.

According to Mohammad Gharipour's work, *The Bazaar in the Islamic City: Design, Culture, and History* (2012), the bazaars historically held importance as self-contained microcosms within cities, often acting as self-sufficient territories where people didn't need to leave for other wants. They commonly included religious places, schools, bathhouses, hospitals and even coffeehouses, making them central hubs of both commerce and social life.[4] The modern-day bazaars are somewhat similar, but they may not have all the amenities mentioned by Gharipour. However, you can surely see specialized sections or shops in one line selling a single product—some would be selling chillies only, followed by spice blends, and other whole spices or rare ayurveda and Unani spices too.

These bazaars played a crucial role not only in commerce but also as cultural and social centres, linking communities across different neighbourhoods. Food can be seen as a window into the kitchens of your neighbours—some might use hing, others kasuri methi, garam masala or mustard seeds. The unique spices and ingredients used by different communities help us understand and appreciate their diversity even more. And let's be honest—nothing quite tells you more about your neighbour than the aroma wafting from their kadahi—whether it's the bold punch of garlic, the fancy touch of saffron or a spice blend to complement a meat-based dish. Remember all those times you've gone to a neighbour asking, 'What are you making? It smells divine.' Truth be told, all their spices have come from these markets in the hood.

The famous chef and storyteller, the late Anthony Bourdain, emphasized the importance of visiting local markets as the first step upon arriving in a new city. He believed that even in the age of globalization, where corporate chains and food blogs have made many experiences feel familiar, markets still provide an authentic glimpse into a culture. 'You see what's for sale, you see what's in season, you see the fundamental colour palette of a cuisine,' he said, highlighting how markets reveal what a culture holds dear.[5]

I think many follow Bourdain's advice, and if I may, I would suggest the same. Go out, immerse yourself in the spice bazaar and see all that it has to offer. You'll witness the colours of the people through their ingredients, experiencing the flavours even before tasting them. The bazaar will humble you and allow you to live a little richer, even if just for a moment.

The local neighbourhood spice shop in Qazigund, Main market,
South Kashmir

A street vendor at Matia Mahal, near Jama Masjid, Shahjahanabad (Old Delhi)

Courtesy: Sadaf Hussain

A shopkeeper standing by his collection of dried spices, makhana and nuts in Rawatpara, Agra

Sacks of red chillies and grains at a local shop in Rawatpara, Agra

Customers interacting with a spice vendor in Yahiyaganj, Lucknow

A vibrant assortment of spices and dried herbs on display at a neighbourhood shop of Yahiyaganj in Lucknow

Entrance to a Posro (general store) at Mapusa Market, Goa, offering a variety of household items

Vendor at Spice Paradise, Jodhpur, offering a variety of grains and spices

ACKNOWLEDGEMENTS

NOTHING EVER HAPPENS BY ONE PERSON ALONE— not a great poem, a beautifully crafted story or even a giant degh of biryani. Everything takes a village. A poet or a storyteller needs people to praise and critique their work; a bawarchi needs suppliers, helpers and time to assemble all the components that bring an aromatic biryani to life. Writing a book, I've found, is much the same as making biryani, kabab or a perfect khasta kachori.

Working on this book, from day one, was a mammoth task—burning the midnight oil, spilling morning coffees, travelling around, unearthing spices, documents, stories and people. A book is never really finished, only abandoned in its best version. It always stays in beta. Many people helped me get to this beta version—from the first concept to pitching, editing and finally printing. It truly takes a village. And before that village comes running after me, wondering why I haven't mentioned them, I'd better acknowledge each and every one.

Shreya Punj and Tarini Uppal, former commissioning editors at Penguin Random House India, were there at the beginning, helping me get my pitch just right. Imagine them as the cauldron of the biryani—an essential that is sturdy and holds all the ingredients together. Without the right cauldron, nothing would come together as it should.

Archana Nathan, senior commissioning editor, then took this on and helped shape it with me. She guided me, helped narrow the focus, and even paid for my coffee and French fries while we sat through hour-long sessions that always began with me saying, 'Do you have ten minutes to chat?' Archana's seen it all—from the rough beginnings to the final pages. If I had to name her part in this biryani, I'd say she's the dum—that slow, patient magic that makes the biryani what it is.

Aparna Abhijit, the copy editor, was the rice and meat of this biryani—even though she's vegetarian! She made sure I wrote not too much, not too little, but just right, just like the balance you need between rice and meat. She kept me in check, each word weighed and used for the right reason. She also bore the brunt of my tantrums and ramblings, whether it was morning or evening, weekday or weekend. I wonder now which one of us really has no life.

Two invaluable people, Alfisha Sabri and Amogha Sharma, were the ghee and saffron of this biryani. They brought richness to the work—helping with research, translations and unearthing those fascinating stories and ingredients that added the flavour. Without them, the book would have lacked the subtle touches that make it palatable and memorable.

My family—Subuhi, Abbi and Shabi—were the spices of this book. For two years, they listened, provided feedback and waited patiently. Just as a biryani needs the perfect blend of spices to shine, they were the ones who brought depth and warmth to this journey. You know this already—you've seen the spice blend recipes in the book.

Shadab Khan, who designed the cover, has been the *pardah* of this biryani. Thanks to him, you picked up this book in the first place. They say, 'Don't judge a book by its cover,' but let's be real—people like Shadab exist so you do exactly that.

There are countless unsung heroes who helped me compile this book—friends and family who took me around town on my spice explorations. To Shreya Koul, Vidushi Sabharwal, Fatima Juned and Bhanu Pratap Singh, who generously shared photographs—you were the fancy cutlery that this biryani is served on, adding that final flourish.

To those who endorsed this book—each one of you is like the crispy fried onions sprinkled on top of a biryani, adding that irresistible layer of flavour that makes it complete. Your words and support have given this book a golden touch that drew people in.

And, of course, Pant Sahab, who graciously wrote the foreword—you are the yakhni, the aromatic broth that infuses every grain of rice with flavour and depth. Your insight and warmth set the stage for everything that follows, making this biryani all the richer.

I cannot thank all those who contributed to this book enough. Some volunteered, while others I coerced with puppy eyes and a twinkle that apparently worked. To those whose suggestions I couldn't incorporate—either because they didn't quite fit or were a little too brilliant and shifted the focus—think of your suggestions as the tej patta. You can add it if you want, but it doesn't make or break the dish. Just kidding—I'm genuinely thankful for all your generous input.

And finally, to you, dear reader. You are the raita to my biryani. As my ammijaan used to say, '*Biryani raita ke bina maze nahi deti.*' (Biryani isn't enjoyable without raita). You picked up this book, and for that, I'll always be grateful. I may not know you, but I'm thinking of you and thanking you, from the bottom of my heart.

Now that the acknowledgements are complete, I can finally sleep easy . . . or at least until someone reminds me of that one name I missed. But hey, just like biryani, it's the imperfections that make it memorable, right?

NOTES

Introduction

1   Stuart Farrimond, *The Science of Spice* (UK: Dorling Kindersley Ltd, 2018).

2   Marryam H. Reshii, *The Flavour of Spice: Journeys, Recipes, Stories* (UK: Hachette, 2017).

3   'Why Study at a French Culinary Institute?', Auguste Escoffier School of Culinary Arts, 16 May 2022, https://www.escoffier.edu/blog/value-of-culinary-education/why-study-at-a-french-culinary-institute/.

4   Marryam H. Reshii, *The Flavour of Spice: Journeys, Recipes, Stories*.

5   Chitra Divakaruni, *The Mistress of Spices* (New York: Anchor, 1998).

Essential Spices for Every Kitchen

1   Aparna Alluri, 'Asafoetida: The Smelly Spice India Loves but Never Grew', BBC News, 22 October 2020, https://www.bbc.com/news/world-asia-india-54617077.

2   Andrew Dalby, *Dangerous Tastes: The Story of Spices* (Berkeley and Los Angeles: University of California Press, 2000).

3   Ibid.

4   Ibid.

5   Heather Arndt Anderson, *Chillies: A Global History* (London: Reaktion Books, 2016).

6   John W. Parry, 'The Story of Spices', *Economic Botany* 9, no. 2 (April–June 1955): 190–207.

7   Rohitha Dasanayaka, 'Cinnamon: A Spice of an Indigenous Origin - Historical Study', ResearchGate, March 2019, https://www.researchgate.net/publication/331588549_Cinnamon_A_Spice_of_an_Indigenous_Origin-_Historical_Study.

8   James Hornel, 'Naval Activities in the Days Solomon and Rameses', *Antiquity* XXI, no. 81 (March 1947): 66–73.

9   Rohitha Dasanayaka, 'Cinnamon: A Spice of an Indigenous Origin - Historical Study'.

10 John W. Parry, 'The Story of Spices'.

11 Jack Turner, *Spice: The History of a Temptation* (New York: Knopf Doubleday Publishing Group, 2008).

12 James Hancock, 'The Early History of Clove, Nutmeg, & Mace', World History Encyclopedia, 13 October 2021, https://www.worldhistory.org/article/1849/the-early-history-of-clove-nutmeg--mace/.

13 Andrew Dalby, *Dangerous Tastes: The Story of Spices*.

14 F. N. Hepper, Pharaoh's Flowers: The Botanical Treasures of *Tutankhamun* (Kew: KWS Pub., 2009).

15 'Cilantro & Coriander (Coriandrum sativum)', University of Wisconsin-Madison Division of Extension, https://hort.extension.wisc.edu/articles/cilantro-coriander-coriandrum-sativum/, last accessed 11 November 2024.

16 Maryam H. Reshii, *The Flavour of Spice: Journeys, Recipes, Stories*.

17 Tonia Buxton, *The Secret of Spice: Recipes and Ideas to Help You Live Longer, Look Younger and Feel Your Very Best* (UK: Bonnier Books, 2019).

18 Susheela Raghavan, *Handbook of Spices, Seasonings, and Flavorings* (Boca Raton: CRC Press, 2006).

19 Ibid.

20 Ibid.

21 James Hancock, 'European Discovery & Conquest of the Spice Islands', World History Encyclopedia, 8 November 2021, https://www.worldhistory.org/article/1872/european-discovery--conquest-of-the-spice-islands/.

22 Robert N. Spengler, 'Origins of Mustard Cultivation.' *Genetic Resources and Crop Evolution* 62, no. 8 (2015): 1073–1083. https://doi.org/10.1007/s10722-015-0321-8.

23 'Mustard: History of the Yellow Seed', *Hektoen International: A Journal of Medical Humanities* (18 February 2020), https://hekint.org/2020/02/18/mustard-history-of-the-yellow-seed/.

24 'Mustard Seed', *Wisdom Library*, https://www.wisdomlib.org/concept/mustard-seed, last accessed 11 November 2024.

25 Jack Turner, *Spice: The History of a Temptation.*

26 'Long Pepper', Atlas Obscura, https://www.atlasobscura.com/foods/long-pepper, last accessed 11 November 2024.

27 Maryam H. Reshii, *The Flavour of Spice: Journeys, Recipes, Stories.*

28 'Star Anise', Encyclopaedia Britannica, https://www.britannica.com/plant/star-anise, last accessed 11 November 2024.

29 'Star Anise: A Timeless Spice with a Rich and Enchanting History', Spices Diary, https://spicesdiary.com/star-anise-a-timeless-spice-with-a-rich-and-enchanting-history/, last accessed 11 November 2024.

30 'Star Anise: The History of a Starry Spice', Spiceography, https://www.spiceography.com/star-anise/, last accessed 11 November 2024.

31 Y. Saideswara Rao and Mary Mathew, 'Tamarind', *Handbook of Herbs and Spices*, ed. Mary Mathew (UK: Woodhead Publishing Limited, 2012).

32 Manjit Kumar Ray, Dipak Kumar Santra, Piyush Kumar Mishra and Saurav Das, 'Indigenous Lakadong Turmeric of Meghalaya and Its Future Prospects', *Journal of Applied*

Biology & Biotechnology 11, no. 5 (September -October 2023): 133–42.

33 David E. Sopher, 'Indigenous Uses of Turmeric (Curcuma Domestica) in Asia and Oceania', *Anthropos* 59, no. 1/2 (1964): 93–127.

Biryani

1 Mirza Jafar Hussain, *Lucknow ka Dastarkhwan*, Rekhta books, https://www.rekhta.org/ebooks/lucknow-ka-dastarkhwan-mirza-jafar-husain-ebooks.
2 Ibid.
3 *Māddat al-hayāt: Risāla-i dar 'ilm-i tabbākhī* is a cookbook authored by Nurullah, a master chef at the Safavid court.
4 Salma Husain, *Nuskha-E-Shahjahani: Pulaos from the Royal Kitchen of Shah Jahan* (Delhi: Rupa Publications, 2007).
5 Nilanjan Hajra, *The History of Biryani*, https://www.sahapedia.org/the-history-of-biryani.
6 Salma Husain, *Food of the Mughals* [Lecture], hosted by S. Chatterji, Zoom, 27 October 2020.
7 Pratibha Karan, *Biryani* (Gurgaon: Penguin Random House India, 2017).

Chai

1 J.C. Marshman, 'Art. XII—Notes on the production of Tea in Assam, and in India generally', *Journal of the Royal Asiatic Society* 19 (1 January 1862): 315–20.
2 Mohona Kanjilal, *A Taste of Time* (Delhi: Speaking Tiger Books, 2021).
3 Philip Lutgendorf, 'Making Tea in India: Chai, Capitalism, Culture', *Thesis Eleven* 113 (2012): 11–31.

Chaat Masala

1 Chetna Makan, *Chai, Chaat & Chutney* (UK: Mitchell Beazley, 2017).

2 Ranveer Brar, 'Lucknowi Chaat Masala', Roundglass Living, https://roundglassliving.com/food/recipes/lucknowi-chaat-masala, last accessed 19 November 2024.

Chole and Rajma

1 K.T. Achaya, *A Historical Dictionary of Indian Food* (Delhi: Oxford, 2001).
2 M.C. Saxena and K.B. Singh, eds, *The Chickpea* (Wallingford, UK: CAB International, 1987).
3 Alan Davidson, *The Oxford Companion to Food* (UK: Oxford University Press, 2006).
4 Colleen Taylor Sen, *Feast And Fasts: A History Of Food In India* (Delhi: Speaking Tiger, 2016).
5 Vir Sanghvi, 'The history of food', 20 May 2022, www.virsanghvi.com, last accessed 13 May 2024, https://www.virsanghvi.com/Article-Details.aspx?key=1869.
6 Sohel Sarkar, 'Rajma chawal is more than everyone's comfort food', Whetstone, 8 February 2024, https://www.whetstonemagazine.com/south-asia-journal/rajma-chawal-is-more-than-everyones-comfort-food.

Curry

1 J.H. van Linschoten, *Discours of Voyages into ye Easte & West Indies* (London: John Windet for John Wolfe, 1598).
2 Hannah Glasse, *The Art of Cookery Made Plain and Easy*, published in 1747.
3 Colleen Taylor Sen, *Curry: A Global History* (England: Reaktion Books, 2009).
4 Madhur Jaffrey, *An Invitation to Indian Cooking* (New York: Knopf Doubleday Publishing Group, 1973).
5 Lizzie Collingham, *Curry: A Tale of Cooks and Conquerors* (New York: Oxford University Press, 2006).

6   Colonel Arthur Robert Kenney-Herbert (Wyvern), *Culinary Jottings for Madras* (Facsimile of 1885 ed.), (Sheffield: Prospect Books, 2008).

7   Colleen Taylor Sen, *Curry: A Global History*.

8   Mary Randolph, *The Virginia Housewife* (Washington: Davis and Force, 1824).

9   Eliza Leslie, *Directions for Cookery, in Its Various Branches* (Philadelphia: Carey & Hart, 1840).

10 Annabella P. Hill, *Mrs. Hill's New Cook-Book* (Massachusetts: Applewood Books, 2002).

11 Madhur Jaffrey, *An Invitation to Indian Cooking*.

12 Mirza Jafar Hussain, *The Classic Cuisine of Lucknow*, trans. Sufia Kidwai (Lucknow: Sanatkada Publications, 2016).

13 Salma Yusuf Husain, trans., *Nuskha-e-Shahjahani* (New Delhi: Rupa & Company, 2007).

14 Rana Safvi, *Shahjahanabad: The Living City of Old Delhi* (Delhi: HarperCollins India, 2021).

15 Neha Vermani (2023), 'Spread of Bounties: Culinary Manuals and Knowledge in Mughal South Asia', *Journal of the Royal Asiatic Society* 33(4), 1175–92.

16 Kunal Vijayakar, 'The Best Butter Chicken Recipe', Khaane Mein Kya Hai, 4 June 2024, https://www.youtube.com/watch?v=bpytnOf3ZXE&t=11s.

17 Isabella Mary Beeton, *Mrs Beeton's Book Of Household Management* (England: S.O. Beeton Publishing, 1861).

18 Rana Safvi, 'Kofta Curry', Rana Safvi: Heritage and History, https://ranasafvi.com/kofta-curry/.

Garam Masala

1   Margaret Shaida, The Legendary Cuisine of Persia (Massachusetts: Interlink Pub Group Inc., 2002).

2   Nancie McDermott, *The Curry Book: A Celebration of Memorable Flavors and Irresistible Recipes* (Houghton Mifflin, 1997).

3 Vikram Doctor, 'How garam masala symbolises India's culinary tradition', *Economic Times*, 4 August 2007, https://economictimes.indiatimes.com/how-garam-masala-symbolises-indias-culinary-tradition/articleshow/2254870.cms?from=mdr.

4 Susheela Raghavan, *Handbook of Spices, Seasonings, and Flavorings* (USA: CRC Press, 2007), p. 252.

5 Garima Arora, 'Garam masala: Why This Have-It-All Spice Must Be Added to your Tadkas, Curries and Sabzis', NDTV, 10 January 2020, https://www.ndtv.com/health/garam-masala-why-this-have-it-all-spice-must-be-added-to-your-tadkas-curries-and-sabzis-2162022.

6 Yamuna Devi, *Lord Krishna's Cuisine: The Art of Indian Vegetarian Cooking* (USA: Penguin USA, 1987).

7 Priyadarshini Chatterjee, 'Through Balance and Multiplicity, the Making of Garam Masala', Diaspora Co., January 2024, https://www.diasporaco.com/blogs/journal/through-balance-and-multiplicity-the-making-of-garam-masala.

8 Nancie McDermott, *The Curry Book: A Celebration of Memorable Flavors and Irresistible Recipes*.

9 J. Inder Singh Kalra, *Prashad-Cooking with Indian Masters (First)* (Mumbai: Allied Publishers Pvt. Limited, 1986).

Kabab

1 Charles James Wills, *Persia As It Is. Being Sketches of Modern Persian Life and Character* (London: S. Low, Marston, Searle & Rivington, 1886).

2 Naveen Joshi, ed., *Memorial Volume Amir Khusrau* (New Delhi: Publications Division, 1975).

3 Abul-Fazl 'Allami, *The Ain-i-Akbari*, trans. H. Blochmann (Delhi: Aadiesh Book Depot, 1965).

4 K.T. Achaya, *The Story of Our Food* (Hyderabad: Universities Press, 2003).

5   Guy Crosby, 'Why (and How, Exactly) Did Early Humans Start Cooking?', Literary Hub, 17 December 2019, https://lithub.com/why-and-how-exactly-did-early-humans-start-cooking/.

6   Pushpesh Pant, 'Mushrooming into delicious kababs', *Tribune*, September 2022, https://www.tribuneindia.com/news/features/mushrooming-into-delicious-kababs-435102.

7   Muḥammad ibn al-Ḥasan Ibn al-Karīm, *A Baghdad Cookery Book: The Book of Dishes* (Kitāb Al-ṭabīkh), trans. Charles Perry (United Kingdom: Prospects Books, 2005).

8   Lilia Zaouali, *Medieval cuisine of the Islamic world: A concise history with 174 recipes*, trans. M.B. DeBevoise (California: University of California Press, 2007).

9   Rana Safvi, 'A Nine Dish Salute to Mr. Johnson', Rana Safvi: Heritage and History, https://ranasafvi.com/a-nine-dish-salute-to-mr-johnson/.

10 Tarana Husain Khan, *Degh to Dastarkhwan: Qissas and Recipes from Rampur* (Gurgaon: Penguin Random House India, 2022).

11 Idara Hareem, ed., *Hareemi Dastarkhwan* (Lahore: Naseem Book Depot, 1949).

12 Raziya Mohammad Raheem Dehlvi, ed., *Shahi Dastarkhwan* (Delhi: Naya Kitab Ghar).

13 Pushpesh Pant, *Lazzatnama: Recipes of India* (New Delhi: Rupa Publications, 2024).

14 Razia Sultana Chaman Dehlavi, *Raziya Ka Shahi Dastarkhwan* (Delhi: Parvez Book Depo, 1981).

15 Jennifer Brennan, *Curries & Bugles: A Memoir & Cookbook of the British Raj* (Hong Kong: Periplus Editions (HK) Ltd, 2000).

16 Digvijaya Singh, *Cooking Delights of the Maharajas: Exotic Dishes from the Princely House of Sailana* (Mumbai: Vakils, Feffer & Simons Ltd, 1982).

17 Pushpesh Pant, *India: The Cookbook* (London: Phaidon Press, 2010).

18 Asma Khan, *Ammu: Indian Home Cooking to Nourish Your Soul* (United Kingdom: Ebury Press, 2022).

19 Digvijaya Singh, *Cooking Delights of the Maharajas: Exotic Dishes from the Princely House of Sailana*.

Local Spices of States

1 Marryam H. Reshii, *The Flavour of Spice*.

2 'Our Ethnic Cuisine', Nadar Sangam, 2 December 2023, https://nadarsangam.com/blog/article.php?post=our-ethnic-cuisine.

3 Colleen Taylor Sen, *Feasts and Fasts: A History of Food in India*, p. 18.

Nihari

1 Anoothi Vishal, 'The inheritance of flavours', *Forbes India*, 28 March 2020, https://www.forbesindia.com/article/forbes-lifes/the-inheritance-of-flavours/58517/1.

2 Madhulika Dash, '. . . . And the legend lived', *Deccan Herald*, 16 July 2019, https://www.deccanherald.com/lifestyle/and-the-legend-lived-747171.html.

3 Abdul Halim Sharar, *Guzishta Lucknow: Mashriqi Tamaddun Ka Aakhiri Namoona* (1958), https://www.rekhta.org/ebooks/guzishta-lucknow-mashriqi-tamaddun-ka-aakhiri-namoona-abdul-halim-sharar-ebooks-2, last accessed 29 October 2023.

4 Rana Safvi, 'A Nine Dish Salute to Mr. Johnson'.

5 Mirza Jafar Hussain, *Lucknow ka Dastarkhwan* (Lucknow: Urdu Academy, 1980).

Paratha

1   Preeti Kulkarni, 'Indian "Paratha" Among the Top Five Best Street Food in the World, Here Are the Top 50', *Travel + Leisure Asia*, 11 November 2022, https://www.travelandleisureasia.com/in/dining/indian-paratha-among-best-street-food-in-the-world/.

2   Bakhshish Singh Nijjar, *Punjab Under the Sultans*, Internet Archive, https://archive.org/details/punjabundersultans/page/n5/mode/2up, last accessed 6 November 2024.

3   G.K. Shrigondekar, *Manasollasa of Somesvara Vol. 1* (Baroda: Gaekwad's Orient Series 28, 1925); G.K. Shrigondekar, *Manasollasa of Somesvara Vol. 2* (Baroda: Gaekwad's Orient Series 84, 1930).

4   K.T. Achaya, *Indian Food: A Historical Companion* (New Delhi: Oxford University Press, 1998).

5   Sumit Paul, 'How Kolkata got its paratha', *The Hindu*, 15 November 2014, https://www.thehindu.com/opinion/open-page/open-page-how-kolkata-got-its-parantha/article6603360.ece.

Pickle

1   Pooja Pillai, 'Decoding the Indian culinary art of the Achaar', *Indian Express*, 24 November 2019, https://indianexpress.com/article/express-sunday-eye/can-everything-that-grows-under-the-sun-be-pickled-in-india-it-might-indeed-be-the-case-6132089/.

2   Jan Davison, *Pickles: A Global History* (London: Reaktion Books, 2018).

3   Madhur Jaffrey, *An Invitation to Indian Cooking*.

4   K.T. Achaya, *Indian Food: A Historical Companion*; Nemichandra, *Leelavathi Prabhandam* (ಲೀಲಾವತಿ ಪರಬಂಧಂ), Narasimhacharya S.G. and M.A. Ramanuja

Iyengar (eds) (Mandayam Digital Library, 1170), https://mdl.mandayamsabha.in/index.php?/book-details/181, last accessed 4 November 2024.

5   Jan Davison, *Pickles: A Global History*.

6   John Heywood, *A Dialogue Conteinyng the Nomber in Effect of All the Prouerbes in the Englishe Tongue* (London: Thomas Berthelet, 1561).

7   Sarah Diamond, 'Snack on This at Your Weekend Barbecue: The Etymology of "Pickle"', *New York Times*, https://www.nytimes.com/2024/07/14/insider/etymology-of-pickle.html.

8   Shalini Dhyani, 'Meet Sohphie: The wild delight of Meghalaya', *Down to Earth*, 12 July 2019, https://www.downtoearth.org.in/food/meet-sohphie-the-wild-delight-of-meghalaya-65596.

Street Food And Others

1   Chaat King India, 'Recipe: How to Make Golgappa Pani at Home', YouTube, 21 March 2021, https://www.youtube.com/watch?v=NJWfHq0Q5QA.

2   R.S. Chaman Dehlavi, *Raziya Ka Shahi Dastarkhwan* (Delhi: Parvez Book Depo, 1981).

The Last Pit Stop

1   Henry Yule and A.C. Burnell, *Hobson-Jobson: A Glossary of Colloquial Anglo-Indian Words and Phrases* (1903; reprint, New Delhi: Munshiram Manoharlal, 1968), pp. 75–76.

2   Paul Losenky, *In the Bazaar of Love: The Selected Poetry of Amir Khusrau* (Gurgaon: Penguin India, 2013).

3   Sarojini Naidu, 'In the Bazaars of Hyderabad', Allpoetry, https://allpoetry.com/In-The-Bazaars-of-Hyderabad, last accessed 6 November 2024.

4   Mohammad Gharipour, ed., *The Bazaar in the Islamic City: Design, Culture, and History* (Cairo: American University in Cairo Press, 2012).

5   Josh Eells, 'Anthony Bourdain's World Domination', *Men's Journal*, 25 June 2019, https://www.mensjournal.com/entertainment/anthony-bourdains-world-domination-20150914.

Scan QR code to access the
Penguin Random House India website